Automated Information Retrieval
Theory and Methods

Library and Information Science

Consulting Editor: *Harold Borko*
Graduate School of Library and Information Science
University of California, Los Angeles

The list of books continues at the end of the volume.

Automated
Information Retrieval
Theory and Methods

Valery I. Frants
Department of Computer and Information Science
Fordham University
Bronx, New York, USA

Jacob Shapiro
Department of Statistics and Computer Information Systems
Baruch College, City University of New York (CUNY)
New York, New York, USA

Vladimir G. Voiskunskii
National Library of Russia
St. Petersburg, Russia

Academic Press

San Diego   London   Boston   New York   Sydney   Tokyo   Toronto

This book is printed on acid-free paper.

Academic Press
a division of Harcourt Brace & Company
525 B Street, Suite 1900, San Diego, California 92101-4495, USA
http://www.apnet.com

Academic Press Limited
24-28 Oval Road, London NW1 7DX, UK
http://www.hbuk.co.uk/ap/

Library of Congress Cataloging-in-Publication Data

Frants, V.
    Automated information retrieval : theory and methods / by
V. Frants, J. Shapiro, V. Voiskunskii.
        p.   cm. -- (Library and information science)
    Includes index.
    ISBN 0-12-266170-2 (alk. paper).
    1. Database management.   2. Information storage and retrieval
systems.   I. Shapiro, J.   II. Voiskunskii, V.   III. Title.
IV. Series: Library and information science (New York, N.Y.)
QA76.9.D3F7165   1997
025.04--DC21   97-25849
                                                                CIP

PRINTED IN THE UNITED STATES OF AMERICA
97   98   99   00   01   02   BB   9   8   7   6   5   4   3   2   1

Contents

3

Information Crisis

4

Concept of an Information Retrieval System

5

Information Retrieval Language

6

Automatic Indexing of Documents

7

Automatic Indexing of Search Requests

8

Storage and Access to Information

9

Control and Feedback in IR Systems

10

Evaluation of Search Results

11

Evaluation of Macroevaluated Objects

12

Some Directions in the Development of IR Systems

Preface

Satisfying information need (IN) is one of the eternal human problems. However, it is also an eternally new problem because the conditions of life, its content, and humans themselves are constantly changing. Throughout history and its various stages of development, human beings have developed various methods and forms for satisfying IN. In this century, characterized by an unprecedented growth of information, efforts to develop methods for the satisfaction of IN received systematic attention. This eventually led to the creation of information science, all areas of which focus directly or indirectly on satisfying IN.

One of the more important new forms of satisfying IN is the information retrieval (IR) system. These systems were first studied almost half a century ago, and since that time a great number of ideas have been introduced, and extensive experience has been gained as the result of using many real functioning IR systems. These successes, both theoretical and practical, provide the foundation for the theory of IR systems presented in this book. At the same time, because the theory of constructing IR systems is only one area of information science, and this theory relies significantly on a number of fundamental results in information science, this factor will also be taken into consideration in its description.

This book could be viewed as consisting of six parts. The first part (which includes Chapter 1) examines the general principles of constructing any system, particularly an IR system. The second part (Chapters 2 and 3) provides a detailed analysis of basic (key) concepts such as IN, information, information crisis, and the notion of information retrieval. The third part (Chapters 4 and 5) examines the goal, function, and structure of an IR system and information retrieval language (IRL) used in an IR system. The fourth part (Chapters 6, 7, 8, and 9) describes the construction of an IR system, that is, the methods, algorithms, and approaches to the realization of every structural element of the system. The fifth part of the book (Chapters 10 and 11) deals with different approaches to evaluating the results of information retrieval, the IR system itself, and separate components of an IR system. The sixth part (Chapter 12) describes some new directions in the development of IR systems. The basic content and, in some cases, the orientation of the chapters can be summarized as follows.

Chapter 1 is intended primarily for those who are unfamiliar with the theoretical basis of systems analysis and design. The principles introduced in this chapter, which constitute the essence of the systems approach, are used in many of the subsequent chapters, and understanding these principles is often critical for understanding the text.

Chapter 2 provides an overview of the nature and properties of IN, that is, the need that an IR system must satisfy. It should be emphasized that in constructing an IR system, the knowledge of IN properties is very important because the quality of IN satisfaction depends on how fully and precisely the system takes these properties into account. It is for this reason that during the construction of every structural element of the system (the realization of every process in an IR system), the prime focus should be on taking into account the relevant properties of IN.

Some features of a search phenomenon, which do not depend on what is being searched, form the basis for creating any search system. These general features are described in Chapter 3. In the same chapter, a search for information is analyzed using these general features.

Chapter 4 gives a more precise description of the notion of the IR system and begins with a description of how to create IR systems. Following basic ideas of the systems approach (see Chapter 1), the goal of an IR system and its function are analyzed, and its structure is determined.

Chapter 5 examines the languages used for information retrieval. In addition to providing an analysis of theoretical questions, the chapter focuses particular attention on some practical approaches to creating such languages. The chapter describes a number of more popular criteria of similarity.

Chapter 6 begins the description of the construction of IR systems that is continued through Chapter 9. This chapter describes automatic methods for the indexing of documents. It also provides an example of a possible algorithm that is currently used in a functioning system.

Chapter 7 explores various approaches to automating the indexing of search requests. A large portion of this chapter contains a detailed analysis of existing problems, and at the end an algorithm for constructing query formulations in Boolean form is described in detail.

In describing Chapter 8, it is important to mention an approach used in this book. This chapter addresses questions dealing with storage and access to information. Because the methods for storage and access used in constructing IR systems are well known in computer science (within the context of courses on data structures and file organization, for example), we targeted the presentation to those readers who are not familiar with the material typically taught in these courses. For this reason, we avoided overloading the text with technical details.

Chapter 9 deals with the questions of realization in an IR system of a mechanism that allows the system to adapt to the user's IN. Furthermore, we solve another problem within the framework of adaptation—optimal search for an individual user. The chapter also describes a number of algorithms for solving these problems.

To understand the material on evaluating IR systems (described in Chapters 10 and 11), the reader must have some mathematical background. Further simplification of the described ideas and approaches without loss of coherence does not seem possible.

Chapter 12 considers different attempts for the further development of IR systems that use ideas borrowed from research on artificial intelligence. This chapter also presents one of the more promising new directions for perfecting IR systems based on a more complete accounting of the properties of IN.

Generally, in this book we attempted to write all chapters so that they would follow the same structure. Each chapter was to contain a definition of every object, phenomenon, and process; its general properties; and its role and place in information retrieval. Theoretical questions on the creation of IR systems are dealt with comprehensively and in detail in practically all 12 chapters of the book. Limitations can be found only in the presentation of methods used to construct an IR system, especially in Chapters 7 and 9. This may be explained by the high number of existing publications that deal with realizing different processes in an IR system in relation to all publications in the field of IR systems. Nearly a third of the publications in information science deal with information retrieval. Therefore, we found it impossible to include all approaches and methods for all components of an IR system, and hence we had to choose which methods would be included in the book. Because the purpose of the book (reflected by its title) is to describe the development of automated information retrieval systems, we did not include any manual methods and approaches to constructing different components of an IR system. In other words, we selected only the material that helped us demonstrate the importance and the possibility of a full automatization of any existing process in the system.

We should also point out some additional considerations in selecting the methods included in Chapters 7 and 9. In these chapters we examine algorithms used in the systems with Boolean searches. We did this for the following reasons. First, almost all functioning IR systems today use the Boolean search method. Because one of our objectives is to bring readers closer to the curent practice of using IR systems and to orient them toward the future development of the systems, not only is it expedient to discuss Boolean-oriented algorithms, but it is pragmatically justified.

Second, we are not aware of any books that discuss fully automatic methods for indexing search requests and feedback in functioning systems (that is, systems that conduct Boolean searches). This book intends to fill this void and thereby benefit those who already work with IR systems.

In addition, please note that the automated methods of the processes mentioned that are oriented toward other approaches (for example, the vector-space approach) are thoroughly addressed in existing literature (see, for example, Salton and McGill, *Introduction to Modern Information Retrieval,* which is fully cited at the end of Chapter 3). Therefore, we decided not to repeat this material in this book.

Because we did not attempt to write our book as an encyclopedia of the subject area, we excluded some technical and applied questions regarding IR systems (questions that would address such applications as reusable software and information filtering, among others). We tried to focus on theoretical questions regarding the creation of IR systems, which are independent of specific methods to be used in practically realized IR systems.

The text should be useful for computer science as well as information science and library science students. It is probably most appropriate for seniors and graduate students. Also, professional readers with academic or practical interest in the information retrieval field will, we hope, find it interesting and useful.

The authors express their gratitude to Professor Harold Borko of the University of California, Los Angeles, and to Professor Donald Kraft of Louisiana State University, whose involvement was one of the important factors in bringing this book to its published form. Many thanks to Michael Belkin, president of MCC International, for all of the friendly support he provided while the book was being written. Similarly, we are grateful to all those at Academic Press who participated in the book's publication. Finally, a big thanks to our families. They provided the coffee (in the case of two authors and tea with lemon for the third author) as well as encouragement and occasional inspiration during the long hours that were spent writing the book.

Valery I. Frants
Jacob Shapiro
Vladimir G. Voiskunskii

1

The System and the Systems Approach

1.1
Introduction

This book is about the satisfaction of one of the most important human needs—the need for information or, more precisely, the fulfillment of this need by information that is found with the help of an *information retrieval (IR) system*. For this reason, this text gives special attention to the creation of such a system and the automatization of all its processes associated with information retrieval. Because the creation of systems presupposes the use of a number of ideas and methods comprising the essence of the *systems approach*, we begin our discussion with a description of the basic assumptions of the systems approach, which will be used extensively in various sections of the book.

1.2
The Notion of "System"

In recent decades, the concept of a "system" has become very popular. There is no area of human activity, whether science, technology, or everyday practice, where it has not appeared. However, the systems approach and systems research are not principally new methods that have arisen only in recent years. The systems approach is a natural and, according to some philosophers, the only scientific method of solving both theoretical and practical problems, and it has been used over the course of centuries. Yet only in the last half of this century have the problems of the systems approach been addressed directly, and this examination has become a separate field of science.

Human knowledge about the surrounding world begins with the concrete individual objects and phenomena that we encounter everywhere. These objects and phenomena at first glance appear to exist by themselves, independent of each other, and the whole world seems to be an accumulation of different objects. But as time passes, our observations and experiences build up, our knowledge about objects and phenomena grow deeper, and each of us discovers that in the world, everything is interconnected. We discover fundamental connections and relations between objects, phenomena, and processes.

The interdependence of objects and phenomena in the world is not of a single form. The division between objects associated with one form of connection and objects associated with another form of connection is clearly delineated. Even the connections are determined by the difference in the characteristics of the objects. Thus the concept arises of a collection of a specific set, which is defined as a *species* or *type*. This concept already is not an abstract notion of "many" in which qualitative content has been dissolved nor of an "individual" devoid of internal parts; it is, in fact, something special, appearing simultaneously as "many" and as "individual." In *Categories* Aristotle noted that a type, and even more so a species, is that which reduces a set to one essence (Aristotle, 1979). Aristotle's contemporaries also understood that the concepts "species" and "type" contain something reflecting an objectively existing common element, that is, an interrelated set. Consequently, the common element contained in an interrelated set can be considered something unified, and this unified thing began to be expressed by the concept of a "whole."

According to Aristotle, the whole is that for which none of its parts is lacking, in the composition of which it is referred to as the "whole" from nature, as well as that which includes its objects in such a way that they create something unified (Aristotle, 1956).

Although a whole is broader in content than the concepts "species" and "type," it still reflects a specific class of an interrelated set. It distinguishes a set whose characteristic is a certain completeness or finality. In addition to the set as a whole, a "nonwhole" set also exists.

The ancient philosophers were not destined to develop a concept that would reflect any delimited interrelated set. Much later the notion became the concept of a "system." The ancient philosophers, in particular Epicurus, used this earlier concept to designate a specific sum of knowledge (Epicurus, 1963). In the following centuries, philosophers and naturalists, while continuing to use the concept "system" chiefly to designate a sum of knowledge, at the same time used it to define material aggregates. Thus, for example, Holbach viewed the objective world as a system of systems. In this connection he identifies the concepts "system" and "whole" (Holbach, 1963).

One of the first definitions of the concept "system" is given by Condillac in his treatise on systems. "Every system," he writes, "is none other than a configuration of various parts of some art or science in a certain order, in which all parts mutually support each other and in which the latter parts are enveloped by the first" (Condillac, 1958). Already this definition emphasizes the presence of connections, order, and interdependence in a system.

With the development of natural science, the idea about the unity of the laws of functioning as applied to various systems increasingly got hold of the minds of scientists. The avalanche of investigations of systems, which has been growing since the 1950s, is pursuing basically one goal—to find and substantiate common regularities of the operation of technical, biological, linguistic, economic, and other systems.

Intensive investigation of systems in various branches of science inevitably posed scientists with the problem of defining the system as a concept. What, properly, does the concept "system" reflect, what reality? L. von Bertalanffy, the founder of so-called *general systems theory,* defines a system as a complex of elements in interaction (von Bertalanffy, 1969). This idea is essentially developed also by one of the leading theoreticians of the systems approach, Russell Ackoff. He assumes that a system is a set of interacting elements, where each element is connected directly or indirectly with every other element, and any two subsets of this set cannot be independent (Ackoff, 1962). Not satisfied with this concept of a system, researchers in different sciences define it by taking into consideration the specifics of the subject of investigation. However, at present no single generally accepted concept of "system" exists. In this exposition of the material, we will confine ourselves to the following widely accepted definition: *A system is a complex of interconnected elements intended for fulfillment of a whole function.*[1] In this connection we will consider a system as consisting of those and only those elements that permit it to fulfill its whole function.

The common item in any of the definitions is that any system consists of elements. In this connection, an element within the limits of validity of a specific given property of the system is thought to be further indivisible. But indivisibility of an element is relative. The element itself can constitute a system and in turn also consist of elements. In other words, an element as such in an absolute sense does not exist outside a system.

Strictly speaking, a connected whole is formed by the elements integrated into our surrounding world, which is the only thing that can strictly be considered a system. However, to solve many theoretical and practical problems it is fruitful to consider as a system less grandiose unions of elements, such as a clock mechanism or a growing tree. A criterion for separating the collection of elements in a system is the degree of connectivity of those elements within the system and of the system with the outside world. The more united elements within the system, and the more isolated this collection of elements from the outside world, the more basis to consider the collection as a system.

It should be emphasized that it is not always the case that a delimited collection of interconnected elements forms a system, that is, could be considered as a system. *To be a system is not the property of an object.* In various problems and

---

[1] See details about the function of a system in Chapter 4.

at various levels of analysis, the same object can be investigated as a system or as a nonsystem. Thus, for example, an airplane can be studied as a system in the process of describing its whole function, phenomena of the dynamics of various internal and external interconnections. However, to solve other problems, this same airplane can be studied as a body characterized by a specific resistance to the air current flowing around it or as a structure having specific rigidity. Analogously, the description of a sequence of events of some historical process differs greatly from the analysis of structure in the same process; although in both cases we are dealing with the same object, only in the second case does the investigator operate with them as with a system, investigating those of its characteristics and components that stabilize and preserve the object while also determining the type and direction of its changes. Consequently, the object as such, independent of the problems of its investigation and the use of specific cognitive means, cannot obtain the system character (or nonsystem character). The possibility of a nonsystem investigation of complex objects helps to explain why it took so long to adopt the systems approach.

Thus, the term "system" characterizes not so much a specific class of objects as an approach to the investigation of these objects, an approach based on the study of properties and features of an object from the *systems point of view*. In this plan, the relationship of the designation of an object (its "name") to its "system" status carries special interest. The point is that the term "system" often enters into the designation of an object. A clear example of this is the *information retrieval system*. The presence of the word "system" in the designation does not make this object a system. We can consider this a system, that is, use the ideas and methods of the systems approach in the process of the object's creation or development or the analysis of its operation. However, if the systems approach is not used in the investigation, which is often the case, then an information retrieval system is not a system. This apparent paradox results from the designation of the object, which can also take a completely different "name."

1.3
The Main Characteristics of the Systems Approach

The origin of the systems approach in its modern form can probably be attributed to Norbert Wiener, professor of mathematics at MIT, who near the end of the 1940s published his well-known book *Cybernetics or Control and Communication in the Animal and the Machine* (Wiener, 1961). Wiener bases the idea of cybernetics on the unification of control processes and information processing in complex systems of any nature. At practically the same time, von Bertalanffy developed a program to construct a general systems theory, specifying the formulation of general principles and laws of the behavior of systems, independent of their form and the nature of their constituent elements and the relations among them.

One of the basic ideas that the systems approach has introduced into our worldview is a new perspective on the components from which the world surrounding us is constructed. The classical representation of the world, consisting of matter and energy, had to give way to a representation of the world consisting of three components: energy, matter, and particularly information. Without information, organized systems are impossible, and living organisms observed in nature and systems created by humans are organized systems. More than that, these systems are not only organized, but also preserve their organization over time, not dissipating it, as should have resulted based on the second law of thermodynamics. Continuous retrieval from the external world of the flow of information about phenomena occurring in it, and about processes taking place in the systems themselves, explains the fact of the preservation of organization.

The systems approach considers not isolated systems, but some collection of them, into which, generally speaking, the whole universe enters. It is distinguished by the relativity of the point of view in the sense that the same collection of elements in one case can be considered a system, and in another case for the solution of other problems it can be considered a *subsystem* of some larger system into which it enters. Thus, for example, an electric drill by itself can be considered a system, but it is possible to consider also the man who is performing work with the help of the drill as a system. In turn, both the drill and the man can be considered subsystems of a system such as a construction company. In nonorganic systems, planets, for example, the atmosphere, lithosphere, or nucleus can be considered a subsystem. As a subsystem of a living organism, one might consider its organs, circulatory system, lymphatic system, nervous system, and so forth.

The properties and features of any object cannot be correctly evaluated and studied without considering the manifold connections and interactions regularly formed between individual objects and the environment surrounding them. Consideration of the effect of the environment is characteristic in the systems approach during the process of investigating phenomena taking place within systems. However, no matter how detailed or rigorously we study the behavior of a system, we can never succeed in studying all the infinite set of factors directly or indirectly influencing its behavior. Therefore it is inevitable to assume the existence of some random factors that result from the action of these nonstudied processes, phenomena, and connections.

A *concrete system* consists of concrete objects (for example, machines, natural resources, models); its connections with the surrounding environment are expressed in the form of specific physical–chemical quantities (forces, flows of energy or matter, etc.).

Abstracting from concrete characteristics of individual systems and isolating the common (for some set of systems) regularities describing the change of their state under various influences, we arrive at the concept of an *abstract system*. This system is distinguished by the fact that its components are described not in terms of designations of objects, but in terms of some abstract collection of elements characterized (taken singly or as a whole) by specific properties that are common for a wide class of objects. In this scheme, Ackoff's definition of an abstract system is of interest: "An abstract system is a system all of whose elements are concepts" (Ackoff, 1962).

Connections of an abstract system with the environment are also defined in the form of quantitative characteristics independent of the qualitative nature of the concrete connections. The transition from consideration of concrete systems to consideration of an abstract system carries the same character as the transition from the study of operations on concrete numbers in arithmetic to the study of operations on abstract numbers in algebra.

Figure 1.1 shows schematically a system in the form of the part of space in which all its elements are concentrated and it also shows how the system is connected to the surrounding environment. The arrows indicate the directions in which the actions are transmitted. X designates actions of the system on the environment, and Y designates the actions of the environment on the system under consideration. These connections can convey actions concentrated at specific points of the system, for example, in the form of a force applied to an element of the system; they can have distributed character as well, acting on the surface or on each point of the whole system or some part of it. As distributed actions one can consider the actions of temperature or pressure on the surface of a system, the actions of gravitational or magnetic fields, and so forth.

In the systems approach, the concept "system" is closely associated with several other concepts: "information," "motion," "structure," "control,"

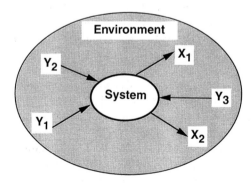

Figure 1.1
A system and its environment; Y refers to input actions, X refers to output actions.

"model," and "function," to name a few. This extension of the original conceptual basis gives the systems approach a certain advantage over a nonsystems investigation, because it permits construction of a more multifaceted representation of the nature of a system as well as of the methods for its study. We will now illustrate some of these concepts in more detail.

1.4 ———————————————————————————————————

Motion

In mechanics the term "motion" is used narrowly to denote the change in position of some object in space over the course of time. In the systems approach, motion has a more general meaning, that is, any change in an object over time. For example, a change in body temperature and a change in a bank account balance can be called motions.

Because the regularities of motion of the most varied objects have much in common, it is useful to consider the laws of motion not of concrete systems (of which there are many) but of abstract systems. In the systems approach, one of the most important concepts connected with motion is the concept of the "state of a system." Ackoff gives the following definition: "The state of a system at some moment of time is the set of values of the essential properties which the system has at that moment."

The number of properties of any system is undoubtedly large. For each concrete investigation, only some of them are significant. Consequently, the significance of specific properties can change with a change in the purpose of the investigation. Thus the state of any system can be characterized with specific precision by the collection of values of the essential properties. This collection of values permits one to compare the state of the same system at various moments in time in order to detect its motion. For example, in some cases we may be interested in only two possible states (such as inclusive or exclusive, or yes or no). In other cases we may be interested in a large number of possible states (such as the velocity or temperature of the system).

Various forms for describing the state of a system exist. It is possible, for example, to list values of all properties $X_1, X_2, \ldots X_n$, determining the state of the system at a specific moment of time and to list their values for fixed moments. However, we consider a more convenient method of representation of states and the motion of systems to be the method based on the concept of the state space.

We will designate by n the number of properties determining the state of the system under consideration. For $n = 1$, $n = 2$, and $n = 3$, the state of the system can be illustrated graphically in space with the number of dimensions equal to n. If $n > 3$, then we lose the possibility of graphic representation of the

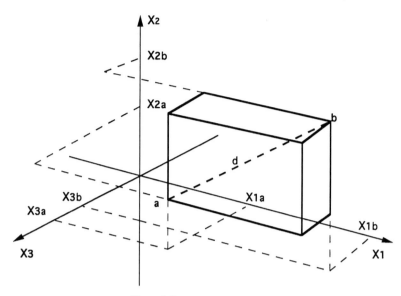

Figure 1.2
Distance between points in space.

state of the system. Nevertheless, very important inferences about properties of systems can be made from arguments using the representation of the state of a system in the form of points in a corresponding space even in cases when $n > 3$.

Although the concept of an n-dimensional space is abstract, its properties in many respects are derived from properties familiar to us from one-, two-, and three-dimensional spaces. In particular, one of the basic geometrical concepts—the distance between two points—can be introduced in four-dimensional space in the same way it is done in three-dimensional space. The distance d between points a and b in three-dimensional space is just the length of a diagonal of a parallelepiped (see Figure 1.2) whose vertices include a and b and whose edges are parallel to the coordinate axes.

It is known that the length d of the diagonal of a right parallelepiped with edges

$$X_1 = X_{1b} - X_{1a}, \qquad X_2 = X_{2b} - X_{2a}, \qquad X_3 = X_{3b} - X_{3a}$$

is found by the expression

$$d = \sqrt{X_1^2 + X_2^2 + X_3^2} \, . \tag{1}$$

Analogously, for an n-dimensional space, the distance between point a with co-ordinates $(X_{1a}, X_{2a}, \ldots, X_{na})$ and point b with coordinates $(X_{1b}, X_{2b}, \ldots, X_{nb})$ can be defined as the quantity

$$d = \sqrt{X_1^2 + X_2^2 + \ldots X_n^2} \, , \tag{2}$$

where $X_1 = X_{1b} - X_{1a}$, $X_2 = X_{2b} - X_{2a}$, . . . , $X_n = X_{nb} - X_{na}$. The quantities X_1, . . . X_n are represented by the edges of an n-dimensional right parallelepiped analogous to the three-dimensional parallelepiped illustrated in Figure 1.2.

The space in which each state of the system is represented by a specific point is called the *state space of the system*. The number of dimensions of the state space equals the number of independent properties (which often are called "parameters") that determine the state of the system. Each state of the system is characterized by a set of specific values of variables X_1, X_2, . . . , X_n, which identify a point in the state space. This point is called the representative point (it "represents" the given state of the system), and variables X_1, X_2, . . . , X_n are called coordinates of the system.

In real systems, not all of the coordinates can be changed in unbounded limits (i.e., $-\infty < X < \infty$). Most coordinates can take only values lying in a bounded interval, that is, those satisfying the condition

$$a_i \leq X_i \leq b_i,$$

where a_i and b_i are boundaries of the interval of possible values of coordinate X_i. The region of the state space in which a representative point can be found is called the *region of admissible states*. In the following, when speaking about a state space, we will have in mind only its admissible region.

However, even within the limits of the region of admissible states, it is not always true that any point represents a possible state of the system. Only a *continuous state space* has this property, corresponding to a system whose coordinates can take any values (within the admissible limits). Some systems, however, are *discrete,* in which coordinates can take only a finite number of fixed values. The state space of such systems is discrete as well. In this case, a representative point can occupy only a finite number S of positions

$$S = s_1 \cdot s_2 \cdot . . . \cdot s_n,$$

where s_i is the number of discrete states of the ith coordinate.

1.5

Input and Output Quantities

The motion of a system—the change of its state—can take place under the influence of external actions or as a result of processes occurring within the system itself.

An infinite set of various external actions, strictly speaking, exerts influence on each system, but not all of these actions are essential. Thus, it is obvious that the force of attraction of the moon does not exert an essential influence on the motion of an automobile with respect to the earth, although in principle such an influence does occur. From the set of all external actions, we choose only those which, under the conditions of the problem under consideration, essentially influence the state of the system. These external actions will be called *input quantities* (or input actions), and elements of the system to which the input actions are applied will be called the *inputs* of the system.

On the motion of an airplane, for example, an essential influence is exerted by such factors as force and direction of the wind, density of the atmosphere, position of the rudders, and pulling forces of the engines. All these factors are considered input actions on an airplane.

It is often useful to consider as the *output quantities of the system* not the coordinates X determining its state, but some other quantities Z uniquely determined by the coordinates of this system. In this connection, each of output quantities Z_i is associated with coordinates of the system by its functional dependence:

$$Z_i = \phi_i(X) \qquad \text{(if there are } k \text{ outputs, then } i = 1, 2, \ldots, k).$$

The system in this case can be represented in the form of the part of S that transforms input actions Y to coordinates X and the set of functional transformations ϕ that transform coordinates of the system to the output quantities. Figure 1.3 illustrates the transformation of input quantities to output quantities.

The necessity of considering output quantities that are different from the collection of coordinates determining the state of the system arises when the problem consists not of changing the system into a given state, but of achieving a goal functionally associated with the state of a system. Note that this goal is achieved by consciously influencing the system's state, that is, by *controlling* the system. The problem of controlling the process of manufacturing a synthetic fiber, for example, stems from obtaining a fiber of the required strength Z_1 and resilience Z_2. These quantities are associated with the functional dependence with these coordinates of the process: temperature of the material (X_1), content of the admixture $(X_2, X_3, \ldots)$ in basic raw materials, and so on. It is clear that in similar cases one must distinguish output quantities from coordinates characterizing the state of the system.

To solve control problems, it is important to distinguish two types of input quantities: control actions and perturbing actions. Control actions include those quantities whose values can be managed to control a system and that can be

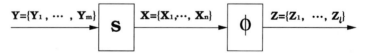

Figure 1.3
Diagram of transformation of input quantities to output, where Y represents input quantities, X represents system coordinates, Z represents output quantities, S represents transformer of input quantities to system coordinates, and ϕ represents transformer of coordinates to output quantities.

changed to realize the motion preferred in comparison with other possible motions of the system. In the given example of an airplane, control actions are created by the steering surfaces and pulling forces of engines, which are dealt with according to the pilot's judgment.

Perturbing actions, the remaining essential actions on the system, are, for example, the effects of the wind and atmospheric density on the motion of the airplane.

The action of a system on the surrounding environment is characterized by the values of its output quantities. The collection of output quantities and their changes determine the behavior of the system; in fact, they permit an external observer to evaluate the correspondence of the system's motion with the goals of control. In the airplane example, output quantities are the course and velocity of its motion, because values of these quantities are determined by the direction and speed of translation of its mass. The goal of control in this case consists of delivering the load to a given place at a given time. Input actions on the organism of an animal are, in particular, actions perceived by its sense organs, and output quantities are motions of its organs.

A change of input quantities, as a rule, causes a change of output quantities. However, changes of output quantities do not always follow immediately; they can sometimes lag but they can never anticipate changes of input quantities, for the former are consequences of the latter, the reason for the system's motion.

Note that perturbing actions affecting the motion of the system not only can have an external source, but can arise within the system as well, such as from changes to properties of its elements after lengthy operation or as a result of a breakdown of the normal operation of the system's elements.

Sometimes it is convenient to consider a system separated into its subsystems, interacting with each other. In this case, some output quantities of one subsystem can simultaneously be input quantities for another subsystem, as shown in Figure 1.4.

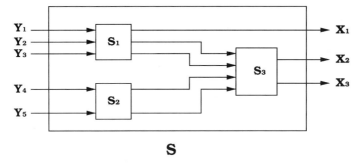

Figure 1.4
Example of the interaction of subsystems within a system.

The motion of the system can be considered a goal of the transformations of its states. It is possible to assume that the transition of a system from state a_1 at time t_1 to state a_2 at time t_2 results from a transition of a_1, t_1 to a_2, t_2. The change of output quantities of any system under the influence of changes of input actions can also be considered as their transition.

1.6

Modeling

The existence of similar characteristics for various objects has been used as a basis for the scientific approach to the study of the nature of the most varied phenomena. Essentially, in all sciences, in explicit or implicit form, the concept of a model has been introduced, reflecting similar characteristics of the studied phenomena and objects. But nowhere is the conception of modeling carried through as precisely and sequentially as in the systems approach, where it appears in the most general form and is the fundamental concept determining the methodology used to study the behavior of a system.

Modeling as a method of scientific investigation arose from the necessity to solve problems that for some reason could not be solved directly. Direct investigation of systems is made difficult or impossible when the nature of the system is not easily understood, when the system does not yet exist and the best alternative for its creation needs to be chosen, when the investigation of the system requires much time or effort or is economically unfeasible, and so forth.

For a long time people have used modeling as a means to knowledge. When encountering some unknown, humans first tried to compare this unknown with something they already knew. Comparing an unknown with a known elicits a transfer of knowledge from the second to the first; in other words, the known emerges as a model of the unknown.

The concept of a model is based on the presence of some similarity between two objects. The similarity can be external to the system, or it can belong to the internal structure of objects that are completely dissimilar externally, or it can belong to specific properties of the behavior of objects that do not have anything in common either in form or in structure. The concept of similarity applies to a very wide class of objects, including objects of living and nonliving nature, artificial objects created by people, drawings, symbols, and so on.

If a similarity can be established between two objects, at least in one specific sense, then the relation between these objects can be defined for both the objects and their models. This means that one of these objects can be considered the original and the second considered its model. Consequently, *it is characteristic that all scientific models are representatives of an object of investigation with the model's similarity to the object defined in such a way as to allow one to obtain new knowledge about this object.* As for the specifics of this representative, the character and completeness of the similarity or the correspondence of the model and the original, goals, designations, capabilities of the model, and so forth, can be different.

We will use ~ to denote the similarity of the original and the model such that if an object A is a model of object B, then this relationship can be written in the form $A \sim B$. In this connection, depending on the goals of the investigations, we will also have $B \sim A$, since similarity of objects is always mutual; that is, ~ is a commutative operation. Original-model relations can take place not only between two objects, but also between any number of objects. Thus, for example, for a collection of objects A, B, C, D, where any two objects are similar, B can be considered either a model of objects A, C, and D or the original for models A, C, and D.

External similarity is a similarity of form—for example, objects such as a ship and its illustration (in the form of a three-dimensional model or a set of blueprints of the ship) or a bronze casting and its plaster model. Similarity of structure can be found in a system of instruction and its structural diagram, a city water system, or a city electric power system.

For investigation of a system, the most important similarity between systems resulting in original-model relations is a similarity in their behavior, permitting one to model their motion. At the basis of behavior modeling lies the fact that identical behavior can be observed—for specific conditions—for systems that differ in form, in structure, and in the physical nature of the processes taking place within them.

In the systems approach for posing and solving modeling problems, the concept of a *black box* turned out to be fruitful. *A black box is a system in which only input and output quantities are known to the investigator but the internal structure is unknown.* In this connection, several important conclusions about the behavior of a system can be made by observing only the reaction (behavior) of output quantities after a change in the input quantities. This approach in particular allows one to study systems whose structures either are unknown or are too complicated for analyzing their behavior from the properties of their constituent parts and the connections between these properties.

Let the behavior of a system be determined by its input actions $Y_1, Y_2, \ldots,$ Y_m and output actions $X_1, X_2, \ldots, X_n$ (see Figure 1.5). By observing the behav-

Figure 1.5
Black box.

ior of this system for a sufficiently long time and, if required, by exerting actions on its inputs, one can achieve a level of knowledge about the properties of the system such that it is possible to predict the motion of its output coordinates for any given change in inputs.

However, no matter in what detail we study the behavior of a black box, we cannot deduce basic inferences about its internal structure: different systems can have the same behavior.

Systems characterized by identical sets of input and output quantities and identical reactions to external actions are called *isomorphic*. Isomorphic systems are obviously indistinguishable from each other from the perspective of an observer to whom only their input and output coordinates are accessible. An example of an isomorphism is the indistinguishability of gas and thermoelectric thermometers from the viewpoint of an experimenter, no matter what experiment he or she conducts on them before resorting to opening the black box.

The study of systems by the black box method cannot lead to a unique deduction about their internal structure, for the behavior of a given system (considered as a black box) does not differ from the behavior of all systems isomorphic to it. In this connection one should consider that for any concrete system, it is possible to select an infinite set of concrete systems isomorphic to it. However, the black box concept is widely used in science, although not always in a clear manner. In essence, a black box is any object under observation for which all of the conclusions about its properties are based on an investigation of its external properties, without resorting to an investigation of its structure and the properties of the elements of the object. The black box method is especially important for investigation of the behavior of a system, and because behavior is almost always of interest in the analysis of systems, the black box method is one of the basic instruments in the investigation of systems.

For any set of isomorphic systems, there exists an original–model relation in the sense that any system in this set can be considered as the original or as a model of the rest. *However, the isomorphism conditions are not the necessary conditions for correspondence of a model to the original.*

Among the coordinates of a system that determine its state, some can be more essential or less essential in relation to the problem being solved by the investigator. If we exclude inessential coordinates from consideration, then instead of the original system X with dimension of state space n, we obtain a simpler system Y with dimension of state space $n' < n$. Then each given state of X will have a corresponding state of system Y (because assigning values to inessential coordinates does not keep us from determining the state of Y with respect to the essential coordinates of system X). But to each specific state of system Y, there will not exist a unique value of the state of system X, this is because in assigning a state of system Y, we do not fix the values of inessential coordinates.

System Y obtained from original system X by means of its simplification (at the expense of lowering the number of coordinates considered or more coarse estimates of their values) is called a *homomorphic* or simplified model of system *X*. Relations between the original *X* and its homomorphic model *Y* are unequal, for *X* cannot be considered as a homomorphic model of *Y*.

In the plan of what has been mentioned, mathematical models are of interest. *A mathematical model of a system is a description in some formal language that permits us to deduce inferences about some characteristics of behavior of this system with the help of formal procedures on its description.* Because a mathematical description cannot be comprehensive and ideally precise, mathematical models do not describe real systems but instead describe their simplified (homomorphic) models. In this connection, types of mathematical models are completely different; they can be characteristics of systems given by functional dependencies or graphs, equations describing the motion of systems, tables or graphs of transformations of systems from particular states to other states, and so on. One should remember that *a model is always a simplification of the original and is usually some distortion of it.*

1.7
Control

In the systems approach, questions associated with control are rather important and are even separated into an independent scientific specialty that Wiener named *cybernetics.* Cybernetics, as the science of control, studies not all systems in general but only *controlled systems,* which frequently are called *cybernetic systems.* On the other hand, the region of applications of cybernetics extends to the most varied systems—technical, biological, and social among them—in which control is carried out. More than that, in practice we deal with controlled systems as a rule. In other words, the class of cybernetic systems is dominating.

One of the characteristic features of a controlled system is the ability to change its motion, to make a transition to different states under the influence of various controlling actions. Thus, an automobile can occupy different positions in space and can move in different directions and with different speeds depending on how it is controlled.

As noted earlier, the desired behavior of a controlled system is achieved with the help of controlling actions, under whose influence the system acquires a better (in a specific sense) state than it would have acquired in the absence of the controlling actions.

To clarify our sense of the word "better" as used here, imagine an artificially controlled system created by humans and used for our purposes. The behavior of the system is evaluated by its creator, and the word "better" means better in relation to the goals of the subject-creator of the system. On the other hand, biologically controlled systems were created in the evolutionary process of living nature, and for them it is impossible to point to a subject having definite goals that can be achieved only if control is carried out. However, even for biological systems, the concept "better behavior" has meaning, which is that the character of an organism's behavior in the environment surrounding it has an essential influence on its survival and reproduction. Therefore, evaluation of the organism's behavior as a controlled system is determined by its interrelations with its environment; "better" behavior, therefore, is that which increases the chance of the given organism to survive and produce offspring.

We mentioned earlier that some external actions on a system, specifically those that can manage its control, are called controlling actions. An action on a system's behavior can be brought about through an action on its coordinates, as well as through a change in the parameters (transition to another state) of the controlled system—*the object of control.* Thus, for example, one can gain control of the rotational speed of a turbine by changing the water pressure h, which is an action on the coordinate representing the rotational moment of the turbine. If the pressure is unknown, the same effect is achieved by changing the incline angle α of the blades on which the water is falling. A change in the angle α results in a change in parameters that determine the characteristics of the turbine—its internal properties. The possibilities of control are greater, and control can be carried out more effectively, the wider the range of values that the controlling actions can take in the control process. However, in real systems the range for which each controlling action can change is limited. In the given example of controlling a turbine, both pressure h and angle α can change only within the specific limits

$$h' \leq h \leq h'', \qquad \alpha' \leq \alpha \leq \alpha''.$$

Because control of any object can be carried out with the help of certain controlling actions, each of which is bounded by some limiting values, in *the space of controlling actions* $Y_1, Y_2, \ldots, Y_m$, we can distinguish a region Q satisfying the conditions

$$Y_i' \leq Y_i \leq Y_i'' \ (i = 1, 2, \ldots, m),$$

within which lies points that represent all possible collections of controlling actions (see Figure 1.6). This region usually is called the *region of possible actions.* Often controlling actions can take only a finite number of fixed values (or may be limited to a finite number). Then the region of possible controlling actions will contain a finite number of possible collections of controlling actions, which are called *the set of possible actions.*

The temperature of a refrigerator, for example, can be maintained near an assigned value by means of injecting and ejecting a refrigerant substance. The set of possible actions of this system consists of two controlling actions: "on" and "off."

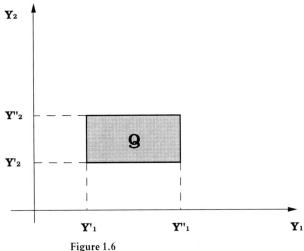

Figure 1.6
Region of possible controlling actions.

In order to control a system, it is necessary to change controlling actions on this system by a specific method. Such a change to the controlling actions can be carried out with the help of *control signals* that maintain communication about the required values of the controlling actions. The collection of elements of the system that operate the control signals is called the *control structure*. If the desired behavior, the conditions for system operation, and its properties are known beforehand, then information about the sequence of controlling actions can be introduced into the controlling structure early on, in the form of *a control program*. Such a control is called a *programmed control*. In other cases, when all data necessary for the creation of a programmed control are unknown beforehand, forming of the controlling actions can be organized into a controlling structure on the basis of information about the conditions arising in the process of system operation. Data about the state of the controlled system, about its desired state, about possible actions, and about characteristics of the controlled system can serve as this information. Processing this information in the control structure by means of specific rules forms a basis for the controlling actions. The collection of rules, by which information appearing in the control structure is processed in the control signal, is called a *control algorithm*.

Note that control is usually needed not only for normal system operation, but also to guarantee that it is developing in the desired direction: for development of an organism from an embryo, for development of a business venture, for development of an economy, and so forth. Control of development arises from the formation of a plan to develop the system and from the realization of this plan.

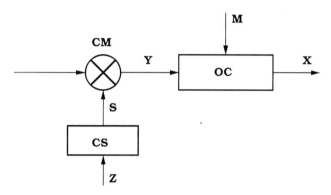

Figure 1.7
The interaction of a control structure with the object of control.

Within the framework of the systems approach, various (in general, similar) definitions of the concept "control" exist. We will use the following: *Control is the action on a system chosen from a set of possible actions, directing the operation or development of a given system.* Figure 1.7 depicts a generalized diagram of a control system.

The object of control and its associated control structure form a *control system*. In order for control signals (S) developed by the control structure (CS) on the basis of information processing (Z) to change the controlling actions (Y), mechanisms are necessary that change the controlling actions in correspondence with the control signals—*control mechanisms* (CM). Input (M) in the diagram represents disturbances influencing the essential output quantities of the system (X). Note that even a human being can play the role of control mechanism, for example, a helmsman turning the rudder of a ship in correspondence with received commands. In this case the helmsman is an element of the control system.

In control systems, four basic types of control problems are considered: program control, stabilization, monitoring, and adaptation.

The problem of *program control* arises when assigned values of control quantities X_0 change in time in a previously known manner. For example, during the control of a ballistic rocket its result at a given trajectory must emerge from a previously known program $X_0(t)$ that measures the change of its position in space and its speed. To control the position of a telescope so as to compensate for the rotation of the earth, the telescope also must be moved by a specific program.

Problems of *stabilization* arise from problems associated with maintaining some of the system's output quantities—*controlled quantities* X near some given constant values X_0, in spite of the action of disturbances M affecting the value X. Thus, to sustain the normal lifetime of a warm-blooded animal, such quantities as body temperature, blood composition, and blood pressure must be stabilized, in spite of changes in the external environment. In power supply systems, voltage and frequency of the current in a network must be stabilized independently of changes in energy use.

When a change in given values of controlled quantities is previously unknown, the problem of *monitoring* arises, that is, how to maintain more precisely the correspondence between the current state of the system $X(t)$ and the value $X_0(t)$. The necessity for monitoring arises, for example, in control of the production of goods during conditions of unforeseen changes in demand; as another example, a radar antenna must turn in order to follow the unforeseen motions of a maneuvering airplane.

A more complicated control problem is *adaptation*. It arises when the control problem cannot be defined as a problem of providing correspondence between the state of a system and its assigned state (fixed or changing), because information about the given state could not have been introduced into the control system earlier nor obtained in the process of its operation. *The process of a change of the properties of a system that permit it to achieve the best or at least optimal operation in changing conditions is called adaptation.*

The property of adaptation distinctly appears in the mechanism of homeostasis, in that a living organism has the ability to maintain its essential coordinates within admissible (physiological) limits during significant changes to conditions in which the organism lives. Adaptability of the mechanism of homeostasis is illustrated by the reaction of warm-blooded animals to a change in the temperature of the environment. During relatively low environmental temperatures, the thermal regulation in the organism is carried out at the expense of a change in blood flow to the surface layer, providing optimal conditions for the organism to exchange heat with the environment. For sufficiently high environmental temperatures, the mechanisms of diaphoresis and respiration provide an intensive release of heat excesses during the process of thermal regulation. Thus, the organism adapts to changing conditions by adapting and changing its behavior and by striving to provide homeostasis (in the given example, the organism strives to maintain body temperature within admissible limits).

Technically or economically controlled systems may be made more adaptable to changing conditions through the use of various modes of choice in the regime of operation or the algorithm for forming the controlling actions, in correspondence with the changing conditions of the system's operation. These changing conditions can consist of changes to the external environment or of changes to properties and characteristics of separate parts of the controlled system. The choice of the most favorable or admissible state of the system is often carried out by means of a *search*.

When choice of the "most favorable" or "best" is required during adaptation, the problem of *optimization* arises. It is well known that the concept "optimal" always means "the best of the available, of the possible." In other words, where no choice exists, the concept of optimality is not used. It is clear that "optimal" does not mean "good"; it just means that other possible choices are even worse.

It was noted earlier that the problem of any control is to actively exert influence on the object with the purpose of improving its behavior. But in order to compare various forms of behavior in controlled systems, and to identify the best of them, it is necessary to propose some standard appropriate for this purpose, a quantity characterizing the effectiveness of the control—an *effectiveness criterion* J.

Depending on the purpose of the system and its operating conditions, various quantities can serve as effectiveness criteria. Thus, for a system designed to control the motion of a train, the effectiveness criterion can be the time T of its motion from its departure station to its destination station; for an irrigation control system, it might be the increase ρ from realization of the yield taken from irrigated lands. Each control alternative has a corresponding specific value of effectiveness criterion J, and the problem of *optimal control* is to find and realize the control alternative for which the corresponding criterion takes the most favorable value. In the illustrated examples, the problem is finding a program for changing the traction of the locomotive for which the duration of the trip is minimal or finding an irrigation program for which maximal yield would be obtained from the realization of harvest. In this connection, it is necessary to take into account that controlling actions can change only within specific bounded limits; they must not go outside the limits of the region of possible (admissible) actions. In addition, other limitations can be placed on a system, for example, a limitation on the complexity of the control algorithm.

Thus, *by optimal control we mean a collection of controlling actions that provides the most favorable value of the effectiveness criterion (criteria).*

In many systems, in particular in information system, problems associated with the optimization of processes often arise, such as the problem of making a system progress from some initial state X_i to an assigned state X_0 with the help of a controlling action Y. In a state space, points a_i and a_0 correspond to states X_i and X_0, and transition of the system from a_i to a_0 is a trajectory connecting these points. Using controlling actions Y, it is possible to select many alternatives of control that will satisfy the requirement of a transition of the system from state a_i to a_0. Each of these control alternatives has a corresponding trajectory connecting a_i with a_0. However, in relation to the effectiveness criterion J, these trajectories are nonequivalent, for each of them corresponds to a specific value of J equal to $J_1, J_2, \ldots$. The problem of finding an optimal control may in this case be treated as the problem of choosing from a set of possible trajectories connecting a_i with a_0 that for which the effectiveness criterion would have the most favorable value.

Any control is carried out on the basis of information. However, properties of control systems essentially depend on the kind of sources of information that are used in the control structure for the formation of control signals. Systems exist in which the information Z obtained by the control structure does not include data on the state X of the controlled object. Then a program of a sequence of changes of control actions $Y_0(t)$ or data on perturbing actions $M(t)$ can enter into Z. In the latter case, to obtain a control signal S the controlling structure must contain data on what the value Y must be for each value M, which must be known in order to achieve the goal of control.

Much more common are systems in which information on values of controlling quantities is used for the formation of controlling actions. It is these systems that are the basic objects of consideration in cybernetics. In fact, these systems are called systems with feedback.

The originality and importance of the cybernetic approach to control are seen in the application of a general principle of control—the principle of feedback. *Feedback in a more general form is the mechanism of calculating the difference between the goal of a system's operation and its result.* Wiener characterized feedback as "the property allowing [one] to regulate future behavior by the previous fulfillment of directives" (Wiener, 1961). A generalized diagram of a system with feedback is depicted in Figure 1.8.

Feedback usually consists of a feedback line (FL) as well as a feedback mechanism, which is realized in the control structure. As seen in Figure 1.8, the input-control action Y on the object of control (OC), because of feedback through the control structure (CS), depends on its output quantity X. In other words, there is a flow of information from output to input.

Feedback is one of the most important concepts of the systems approach. It helps to explain many phenomena taking place in controlled systems of various natures. Feedback can be detected by investigating the processes taking place in living organisms, economic structures, and technical systems, to name a few.

Feedback that increases the effect of input actions on an output quantity is called *positive,* and feedback decreasing this effect is called *negative.* Negative feedback enables equilibrium to be restored to a system when it has been broken down by an external action, and positive feedback causes a still greater deviation

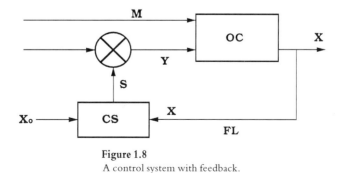

Figure 1.8
A control system with feedback.

than that caused by an external action in the absence of feedback. An example of a process with positive feedback is any chain reaction, and an example of negative feedback is any mechanism of homeostasis. Negative feedback has in fact proved to be a valuable principle to which controlled systems owe their progress. The stabilizing action of negative feedback is an important element of both monitoring and adaptation.

During systems analysis, processes with negative feedback may be somewhat hidden from direct observation. However, consideration of these processes is extremely important for understanding the nature of these systems. Thus, stabilization in an economic system is illustrated by the following example showing the action of negative feedback. The higher the price for pork, the greater the number of farmers who will raise pigs; but the more pork produced, the lower the price for it. However, the lower the price for pork, the fewer the number of farmers who will want to produce it; but the fewer producers, the less pork is produced and the higher the price for it. An analogous example is the establishment of balance in ecology. The more hares (food), the more wolves (consumers). But the more wolves, the fewer hares. The fewer hares, the fewer wolves, and so on. Usually when a different use of automatized controlled systems is being created, basic attention is focused on the creation of efficient feedback, because the quality of system operation on the whole depends on the quality of the feedback.

1.8
System Design

One of the most important results of the systems approach is the development of unique methodological principles for the creation of systems of the various classes. This advance was mostly due to the work of Rosenblueth, Wiener, and Bigelow (1943) and, in particular, the later work of Wiener. In these works the authors point out the causality in the creation of systems, their goal. Essentially the goal always appears in the form of some standard to which one must strive. Thus, the goal can be considered a theoretical model carrying subjective character. Any goals in the final analysis result from human needs and thus their achievement is always considered a fulfillment of a need. For this reason, the first step in system's creation includes the investigation of concrete need and, based on this investigation, the formulation of the system's goal. This step is called the *goal definition stage.*

Usually realization of a goal does not cause great difficulties, because as a rule it is preceded by a detailed analysis of the nature and peculiarities of some specific human need. However, a rather natural idea of looking at the goal of a system proved to be revolutionary, because it led researchers to view systems as functional essences. It became obvious that it is conceptually more useful to move from functionally representable wholes to structurally representable parts, and not vice versa. Before the appearance of the above-named works, systems creators typically constructed their understanding of a whole by unifying the results of the analysis of separate parts, while today the understanding of different parts is obtained by decomposing a representation of the whole. This orientation of investigations came to be called *the systems point of view*.

Within the framework of the systems point of view, determining the whole function of the system becomes especially important. This is the *function determination stage*. We say the "whole function of the system," because it is necessary to formulate the function of the system as a whole and not of its separate parts.

The concept of "function" in the systems approach is understood as the purpose of the system, its obligation. The function can be represented as some law that governs how the system behaves in order to fulfill its purpose or as a set of rules to achieve the goal that dictate how the elements of the system interact. In other words, function is the description of a requirement for the system's output that explicitly or implicitly indicates the quality of the output characteristics. Thus, in determining the function we in essence assign an "obligation" to the system with the subsequent stages of the system's creation geared toward the realization of the function. Because the quality of system operation is determined by the level to which it achieves the goal of its creation, it becomes obvious that in determining the function it is necessary to orient oneself to this goal while, whenever possible, taking into account more completely the available characteristics and needs.

Thus, it was noted earlier that before the revolution in viewpoints, scientists strived to understand the functioning of a whole based on an analysis of the structure of parts and structural connections between parts. At present, scientists increasingly are trying to penetrate the structure of parts of the system, relying on an understanding of the functioning of the entire system as a whole. For exactly this reason, at the third stage of a system's creation, starting with the formulation of the system's function, the system's structure is determined. This is the *structure creation stage*.

The concept of "structure" came from the Latin *structura,* which means formation, arrangement, and order. When applied to the systems approach, structure refers to the formation of a system, that is, a collection of elements included in the system and their interactions. By definition, a system is a complex of interacting elements intended for the fulfillment of a whole function. It is obvious, then, that the complex itself and the interconnections (i.e., the structure) depend on a specific function. In other words, different functions predetermine different structures. In fact, the requirement to fulfill the function determines the presence of a specific element in the system and stipulates the order of their interactions. Note that by defining the structure, one is also defining the boundaries of the system. Therefore the assertion that a specific element is part of a system has meaning only when its presence is justified by requirements resulting from the definition of the function. Thus, it is possible that with one definition of the function, some element will be a part of the system; however, with a different definition, the same element is not included in the system.

Determination of a structure (i.e., the choice of necessary elements and the connections between them) assumes a transition to the next stage of creating the system, that is, to the *design stage,* during which each element of the system is developed. For example, in systems where the elements are processes, and all the processes are automatized with the help of a computer, one design stage is the development of an algorithm for each process. In technical systems, this stage can be the development of a concrete engine or a concrete transmission, for example. Obviously it is not always necessary to re-create all elements of a system. In some cases system creators can use previously prepared elements or subsystems. Suppose, for instance, that one had created a managerial system for a company. After determination of the structure of the system, for which one of the elements is a manager, the design stage becomes the selection of concrete candidates for managerial positions.

Designing each element of the system is followed by the *implementation stage.* In the examples presented earlier, this stage involves writing and debugging of the programs of the implementation algorithms, manufacturing and installing a developed motor, and hiring a selected candidate for a given position.

The final phase is the *evaluation stage,* during which the system's effectiveness is evaluated. This stage occurs when the goal for creating the system has been achieved. Quite often during this investigation significant difficulties arise. For example, it may be unclear as to how to evaluate the education system. Various evaluation criteria exist, depending on the goals and problems of the investigators. In addition, there are different methods of measurements, which may variously evaluate the subjective character of many estimates—often leading to diametrically opposed results. Therefore in many cases the investigation of a system's effectiveness becomes an independent scientific problem.

Thus, we sum up the stages of system creation.

1. *The goal definition stage.* The present need is studied and, on the basis of properties internally inherent to it, a goal for creating the system is formulated.
2. *The function determination stage.* The whole function of the system is determined and directed toward the achievement of the chosen goal.
3. *The structure creation stage.* The system's structure is created, enabling it to fulfill the previously determined function.
4. *The design stage.* A design is developed (methods, algorithms, etc.) to realize the created structure.
5. *The implementation stage.* Practical implementation of the investigations conducted at the design stage is carried out.
6. *The evaluation stage.* The effectiveness of the created system is studied.

Note that within the framework of the systems approach, the direction of systems analysis is developing. More than that, within the framework of systems analysis there exists extensive literature discussing the creation of computer-based information systems. Many practical recommendations on the creation of systems are available for each of the stages indicated, although the implementation stage is covered in the greatest detail.

1.9

Conclusion

In the present chapter, we tried to show that the systems approach is one of the main tools for constructing complex objects of any nature. Viewing these objects as systems allows us to understand their function, structure, and character of interaction among different system elements. This understanding allows us to substantially simplify (and speed up) the practical realization of these systems, to reduce the cost of their development, and to avoid many mistakes. Another important advantage of the systems approach is the existence of standard methods for developing, analyzing, and controlling systems. As will be seen later, such controls as adaptation and optimization will play a significant role in the development and use of systems.

Because one of the important goals of this book is to analyze the method used to create information retrieval systems, almost all stages of systems creation will be considered in detail. We say "almost all stages" because in a book we can consider completely only the first four stages and can partially consider the sixth (even without implementation, we can discuss the method of investigation used to determine the effectiveness of information retrieval systems).

"Systems Everywhere" is the title of the first section of the introduction to Bertalanffy's book *General System Theory,* and in fact this is true. Our whole world is a system of systems. Therefore, in the present chapter we have tried to illuminate the basic ideas and methods characteristic to the modern systems approach.

References

Ackoff, R. L. (1962). *Scientific method: Optimizing applied research decisions.* New York: John Wiley & Sons.

Aristotle. (1979). *Categoriae.* Oxford, New York: Clarendon Press.

Aristotle. (1956). *Metaphysics.* London: Dent, New York: Dutton.

von Bertalanffy, L. (1969). *General system theory, foundations, development, applications.* New York: Braziller.

Condillac, E. B. (1958). *Treatise on advantages and drawbacks of systems.* Moscow: Progress.

Epicurus. (1963). *Letters, doctrines, and parallel passage from Lucretius.* Chicago: Northwestern University Press.

Holbach, P. A. (1963). Selected works. Moscow: Progress.

Rosenblueth, A., Wiener, N., & Bigelow, J. (1943). Behavior, purpose & teleology. *Philosophy of Science, 10,* 18–24.

Wiener, N. (1961). *Cybernetics or control and communication in the animal and the machine.* New York-London: The MIT Press and John Wiley & Sons.

Bibliographic Remarks ———————————————

For a more detailed look at different aspects of the systems approach described in the chapter, the reader is referred to the following publications.

Ackoff, R. L., & Emery F. E. (1972). *On purposeful systems.* Chicago and New York: Aldine, Atterton.

von Bertalanffy, L. (1969). *General system theory, foundations, development, applications.* New York: Braziller.

Wiener, N. (1961). *Cybernetics or control and communication in the animal and the machine.* New York-London: The MIT Press and John Wiley & Sons.

2

Vital Activities and Needs

2.1

Introduction

Every living thing strives to survive. Humans are not an exception to this rule. All of our actions and our conscious behaviors determine a historically developed and constantly self-renewing strive for self-preservation, for improving the conditions of our existence. It is customary to assume that prolongation of life—survival—is the goal of a person's activity, one's life's work. This work itself is determined by needs—that is, our reaction to our own needs. These needs constantly prompt us about what is concretely necessary for us to do to ensure successful survival. Thus, throughout the course of human history, our constant concern has been the satisfaction of our own needs.

The need for information is among the most important of life's needs. It is information that permits one to successfully adapt to the external conditions of existence—the environmental conditions. The intellect, whose food is information, permits humankind to realize this adaptation by making the environmental conditions not only part of the intellect's personal "I" but also part of the social "we." The latter flows from the social nature of people—one of the most important factors for human survival. To us, society is not only a part of the environment to which we must adapt. Much of what is vitally important to people is provided only with the help of society. For example, to satisfy an information need (IN) we use information obtained by others, with the help of means and materials created by others. This is why the strive to survive is often transformed into a strive to preserve society, to protect it.

The development of society, its progress, and its economic well-being depend in many respects on the intellectual productivity of the creative layer of society. This productivity can be intensified by increasing the quality of the information service for each producing intellect. In other words, if we want to receive from each intellect according to his or her ability, we must provide information according to his or her needs. For the high-quality satisfaction of an information need, it is necessary to know and take into account the properties of this extremely important inherent human characteristic (the IN), and in creating any form of information service, it is crucial to take into account the properties of the IN. The quality of these forms—for example, the quality of an information retrieval (IR) system—will be determined by how completely and effectively these forms account for the properties and characteristics of the IN during their service to the user. Hence, is important to understand the nature of a person's IN, as well as its properties and characteristics. This chapter deals with these issues.

2.2

The Individual as a Functioning System

To explain the role of an IN in a person's life, it is beneficial to consider the person first. A person is a complex biological system whose vital activity is carried out by its organically innate functioning algorithms for each of the processes of its subsystems. Moreover, the work of these algorithms in the complex is itself an algorithm of the vital activity satisfying the whole function of the entire system—the function of life.

A healthy system is biologically balanced and is in a comfort state. The mechanisms of homeostasis as parts of the vital activity algorithm are responsible for preserving this balance and for maintaining the system in the comfort state, that is, in that state under which the system most easily survives and fulfills its function.

Obviously life is not a prerogative of people. We are only an element of a system such as the biosphere. This concept designates all life on our planet. Who would think that systems such as a virus and a man could have anything in common? However, they are united by one property—they are living. They have algorithms of life: metabolism, reproduction, growth, motion, adaptability, mutability. The last two properties provide survivability of the individual and of the species. In living systems these algorithms are developed in such a way as to guarantee preservation of the species.

All life has a cell structure, and it is possible to trace some rising expediency of life from the simplest to the most complex, from the elementary (lower) level to a more complex (higher) level, and to trace the subordination of simple to complex, of lower to higher. Thus, the cell is subordinate to the organism, the organism to the species, and the species to the biosphere, subordinate in the sense that their life and death are justified as long as they are directed to the survival of a higher level. In a certain sense, cells play the same role for the organism as the organism plays for the species, and the species for the biosphere. Algorithms of living creatures are divided into three types, depending on the goals they satisfy: those for oneself, those for the family, and those for the species. They do not always act harmoniously—in various periods of life this or

Algorithms of living creatures.
What exactly does it mean?

that one prevails. In addition, each element of the system in turn has its algorithms, which in principle can be classified by the same criteria: for a given part (for example, a cell), for a higher system (an organ), or for a still higher system (the organism). The inherent algorithms can be suppressed in the interests of the higher system. This situation exists, for example, in an organism where cell algorithms have different character, part of them working "for themselves," others for the organism. An organism's regulating systems, for example, suppress the excessive multiplication of cells for which every living system strives.

The memory that preserves the algorithms of a species of organisms is *deoxyribonucleic acid (DNA)*. Its molecules are located in the chromosomes of the nucleus of each biological cell. DNA reproduces itself precisely during cell division, which over a number of generations of cells and organisms guarantees the transfer of hereditary traits and specific forms of metabolism. The hereditary traits themselves are encoded in specific parts of the DNA molecules called *genes*. Each gene is responsible for the formation of some elementary trait. A unique property of genes is their combination of high stability (nonchangeability over a number of generations) with the capacity for inheritable changes, or *mutations,* which are sources of the genetic diversity of organisms and the basis for natural selection.

To understand the survival of a species, it is useful to consider one-celled creatures, such as microorganisms. Their structure consists of molecules of complex organic compounds, and their external function is represented by algorithms of multiplication and chemical actions on the surrounding environment. The possibility that a concrete system (organism) will survive is very limited, because both the perception of information about the external environment and the possibility of processing it in the system itself lie within rather narrow limits. For example, a microorganism does not know that it is located in a small reservoir that will soon dry up and thus entail its death. It also is not in any condition (it does not have the mechanism) to make a decision about moving over a still-existing isthmus to a reservoir that is not drying out. However, survival of the species is not in danger; it is maintained by a huge rate of reproduction (the loss of microorganisms in the dry reservoir is compensated in a nondry one very quickly) and by the very active changeability, mutations, whose results are realized through wide natural selection. It is important to mention here that molecules of DNA in one-celled organisms are less stable than they are in higher forms and they can change comparatively easily, which enables mutations and thus the survival of the species. K. Grobstein (1974) illustrated this point. A population of bacteria was placed near a hot spring. In the center of this spring the temperature was $80°C$, and within a radius of about three meters the temperature gradually lowered to room temperature. The majority of bacteria can exist only at temperatures below $30°C$. If some mutant organisms, which are less sensitive to elevated temperatures, are contained in the population, they can reproduce in the zone maintaining a temperature of $30°C$. In the population colonizing this region, mutant forms will usually arise that are still more resistant at elevated temperatures. Thus the zone will be colonized, which corresponds to a temperature of about $40°C$ up to a zone with a temperature of $80°C$. In fact, thermophile bacteria can be observed in hot springs, existing in conditions that would seem incompatible with life. Moreover, these bacteria cannot even exist in conditions lower than $30°C$. They would need to mutate again.

These examples of a species' mechanisms for survival can be considered as models that are, to varying degrees, characteristic for all forms of life in general and for humans in particular. The human organism contains no fewer than 100 types of different cells that are joined into tissue and organs to form one whole. It is known that cell repair takes place in almost all tissues of an organism, although at different rates. Thus, the lifetime of mucous membrane cells in the small intestines is a day, of skin cells the lifetime is from 5 to 35 days, and of liver cells it is 180 days. The total number of cells to have been a constituent part of an organism during the course of its life is an astronomical number, about 10^{18}. Each day approximately 10^{12} cells divide, and among every million dividing cells is one mutationally changed cell that does not resemble its related cellular environment. Considering that if in the course of a life 20,000 cell generations are replaced, the collection of mutationally changed cells will equal nearly 20 billion. Obviously, it does not mean that human mutation is mandatory and easy. Immune protection is the force that destroys mutated cells. However, several factors, such as specific changes in the external environment, can influence this protection, and a species can adapt to new conditions of existence. We say "species" and in this connection recall that an "organism" of a species consists of living individuals. Thus, we proceed with our consideration of a person as a functioning, balanced system.

To preserve the balance, that is, the normal course of all processes, the system needs matter and energy. For example, both are needed for cell repair. Clearly, the system's habitat is the source of its necessary resources. It is also obvious that this environment is not some nourishing broth, and replenishing these resources requires some effort. In other words, to obtain what is necessary from the outside, the system must in some manner contact its environment, and frequently these contacts require a significant expenditure of energy. It is also clear that these contacts must be purposeful and coordinated, not random, haphazard, and undirected. For this reason the system has a subsystem, called a *nervous system,* whose function is to control and direct the system, including the system's interaction with the external environment. We will discuss in some detail how this is carried out.

The diversity of the external world and the change in our internal states are detected by a system (an organism) with the help of a very large number of *receptors,* special biological monitors that react by an electrical impulse (signal) to specific changes either in the external environment or in the internal states of the system. Note that the receptors in a human being number into the billions.

Receptors in a system are divided into two groups: the first is the *exteroceptors,* which translate stimuli perceptible from the outside (from the habitat), and the second is the *interoceptors,* which perform the same function within the organism by scanning all of the organism's subsystems. The arising signals (nervous stimulations) are transmitted to the central nervous system, which consists of the spinal cord and brain. Different parts of the brain are responsible for different functions, and different receptors transmit signals to different parts of the brain. Incoming signals from interoceptors communicate about deficiencies of matter and energy, and those from the exteroceptors communicate about the situation in the habitat.

Signals from the interoceptors entering into specific parts of the brain cause stimuli in these parts, that is, they perturb specific *neurons* of the brain (brain cells). A characteristic property of neurons is that the electric potentials (signals) developed by them during stimulation are not distinguished by magnitude; the signal equals either zero or its maximal value. This means that neurons "work" with the help of binary input—they are either perturbed or not, either 1 or 0. Perturbed groups of neurons produce a pattern in the brain (that is, they *concretize* a problem, such as the organism's need for matter). Thus, the place where the pattern arises and its form correspond to a specific problem of the system and indicate exactly what the system needs.

The development of the pattern activates brain activity—that is, the *psyche* begins to work—allowing the system to feel and to comprehend. The purpose of mental activity is the elimination of a problem arising in the system. Therefore, mental activity is directed to the search for an algorithm for the system's behavior, behavior contributing to the achievement of the goal. The first step of mental activity is addressing a region of the brain such as the memory. The memory stores knowledge (i.e., patterns) of those problems that arose earlier, and the system's behavior algorithms correspond to these problems for specific conditions of the external environment. The latter is extremely important, because the problem is eliminated in the process of interacting with the environment and depends on the behavior of the system in a concrete environment. Thus, the signals about the external environment, perceivable by other parts of the brain from the exteroceptors, are absolutely necessary.

In those cases when both the problem and the state of the habitat are known to the system, that is, when analogues of interoceptor and exteroceptor patterns are in memory, and when the systems' memory contains a prepared behavior algorithm (also a pattern), the brain communicates signal to specific subsystems (organs), and this begins the process of a system's conscious behavior (activity). Here a mental process is carried out in a somewhat different form. After the beginning of the activity in this process, control of each stage of activity is carried out (constant feedback that considers changes of the external environment as well as the intermediate results of the activity, which can lead to correction of the behavior algorithm) until the problem is eliminated.

When no prepared behavior algorithm is in memory, the system tries to create one with the help of intellectual activity (one of the varieties of mental activity). This condition signifies that either the organism needs something principally new, that is, a similar pattern has never before arisen in the system's brain, or the situation in the habitat is an unusual one for which the system has no behavior experience. The second case is more significant. What is new in the current state of the habitat cannot be used by behavior algorithms available in memory. This occurs because the new situations are not foreseen by the algorithms, and an uncertainty arises in the system; that is, the system does not know how to behave in the new situation. Moreover, the system's attention is focused on this "essentially new" thing, and the system enters into a stable mental state, such as an interest in investigating the new thing, which in essence is one of the manifestations of the information need. *Information for the system is everything that decreases uncertainty during the development of a behavior algorithm.* An arising need initiates the algorithms and methods of investigating the new thing that are available in the system's memory. In this way, the system begins to act in the direction of investigating the new, in the direction of increasing knowledge. The accumulation of knowledge, that is, the system's ability to foresee the effect of the new, is carried over from one new thing to another until the algorithm necessary to achieve the goal is finally formed.

The preceding process is one of the main processes to provide for the system's functioning. However, the system's survival depends not only on the timely and full supply of matter and energy. Obviously, the habitat was not created expressly for people, and in addition to what we need, it provides that which we do not need at all. More than that, it provides that which immediately threatens the system's life—it provides danger in the form of birds of prey, poisonous animals and plants, and natural calamities, for example. Acquired dangers also exists, such as crime or intense traffic. For this reason the system constantly needs information about the habitat. It wants to know what can be expected from the environment; in other words, we talk about the historically formed constant need for information about the state of the external environment.

The existence of this need is well illustrated by an experiment carried out by biologists. A "rat zone" was created for a particular group of rats, based on conditions under which the needs of living rats that are known to biologists were completely satisfied. In each case by setting up the dimensions and the structure of the living space and a means for feeding, the experimenters investigated specific characteristics in natural conditions. In one corner of the space in which the rats lived, a track was made that led to a completely empty chamber by means of a narrow and winding corridor. Neither the corridor nor the chamber were lit. Moreover, the corridor was equipped with a number of effects to frighten the rats. In spite of the availability of all necessities, particular individuals showed an interest in inspecting the track but, as a rule, upon encountering the frightening effects, they gave up. Only a few—in spite of clear indications of fear, such as squeaking and defecating or stopping and backing up—got to the chamber, inspected it, and returned. After this, they showed no more interest in this track.

It is clear that curiosity—the information need—is not developed to the same degree in each rat, not all proved to be prepared to take a risk for the sake of satisfying the information need, but as the unknown territory became known, what to expect from it became familiar.

In the process of satisfying this organic need, the organism accumulates knowledge about surmounting various dangers, and in a number of cases the system lays out standard behavior algorithms worked out as a result of frequent application. For example, when crossing the street we usually look both ways, and when we are certain that no danger exists, we begin our motion. We do this automatically, as if unconsciously, but having turned our head we attentively look to see whether an automobile is on the street. Note that a primordial set of knowledge produced by a species is built into the system genetically. This was corroborated by the following experiment. The shadow of a vulture was shown to incubated chicks hatching out of eggs, and the chicks ran around in panic. However, the shadow of a dove did not cause any panic because they "knew" that a dove's shadow did not carry information about danger.

Thus, even a brief consideration of the basic mechanisms of survival shows rather clearly how insufficiencies of matter and energy on the one hand, and the desire to survive in the habitat on the other, are transformed into an information need. In fact, the strive to survive is permeated with the need for information, a constant hunt for it. It was mentioned previously that after the interoceptors send signals to the brain (an unconscious information process), conscious information activity immediately begins. In fact, any purposeful actions, any conscious behavior or activity, are possible only as reactions to needs and only on the basis of available information. The more information the system has, the more chances it has to survive.

Note that *something* is information for a system only when the system takes it as information, as a *something* that eliminates uncertainty from the behavior algorithm. The system itself imparts to this *something* the property "to be information." Because the satisfaction of an information need itself comes from and has meaning only within the framework of a concrete information need for a concrete system, it is possible to speak about the subjective character of the perception of the product, which depends on the total set of patterns in the system's memory and on the concrete needs of the system. Obviously, information for a given system can be something that will never be information for other systems, and that which is information for other systems may never be information for a given system.

Because we mentioned the notion of information (later we will devote a separate section to it), we should point out the duality of this notion as encountered in practice. This duality could be illustrated by the following example.

Consider the well-known notion of "food." Any object that the system views as a source of matter and energy (which could be consumed to support life) is considered by the system as food. It is not important if the system actually uses this object as food or not. In other words, there are objects in nature that could be perceived by a human being as food. On the other hand, the real food is only the objects that the human being actually consumes. Hence, when using the term "edible" objects (for a system), one usually means a potential food. The object becomes actual food only when it is eaten by the subject. For example, a rabbit could be considered potential food, but it becomes actual food for a wolf only after the wolf eats the rabbit.

The situation with information is analogous. From the accepted notion of information, any set of symbols that the system could use to extract information should be considered as an object carrying *potential information*. Remember that from the point of view of semiotics, the symbol is a representation that carries information for a system about an object, phenomenon, relationship, and so on. Given a set of symbols different systems could extract different actual information. In other words, a particular system can extract from potential information only that which it considers useful to remove uncertainty from a behavior algorithm; that is, it extracts *actual information*. Now that it is clear that actual information only exists as a specific need for a particular system, we can speak of its subjective character.

Because we are interested in satisfying the information need (with, as we now know, actual information), we now proceed with the discussion of the psychological state that is called information need.

2.3

The Information Need

The previous section showed that a physiological need, in the most general sense of the term, is the subject's need or requirement for something that will only be satisfied by some form of activity (such as lying down to rest or scratching an itch) or through some product (such as potable water or warm clothing). But whatever physiological need is satisfied, this is done only with the help of a behavior algorithm created on the basis of information. In other words, a mental state such as an information need precedes any activity and is an indispensable partner in satisfying any physiological need.

It is obvious that the subject of the need is an individual, which in the future will be called "the user." The user experiences a need as anxiety, stress, excitement, discomfort, or some other similar emotion. Of course, each of the named mental states has its nuances, but they all can be referred to as members of one class—the state of displeasure. Satisfaction of a need (process) yields a sense of relaxation, relief, or enjoyment. This class of mental sensations exem-

plify the state of pleasure. A similar polarization of mental states was noted comparatively long ago. By the middle of the 19th century, the German psychologist
Fechner (1996) had already proposed a theory of pleasure and displeasure. He
noted that insofar as conscious stimulation always relates to pleasure and displeasure, both pleasure and displeasure can be represented as having a psycho-
physical relation to stability conditions. This direction was further developed at
the beginning of the 20th century in the theory of psychoanalysis created by the
Austrian psychologist Freud (1961). He formulated the pleasure principles, the
principles lying at the base of the subject's mental activity. However, the nature
of these mental states were not investigated at the time. Authors considered pleasure and displeasure to result from not just something, but something given, a
starting point, the origin of vital activity. They assumed the presence of the soul
(a particular nonmaterial substance independent of the body) of which pleasure
and displeasure are characteristic (a property of the soul). Freud, who was dissatisfied with this explanation (perhaps due to lack of information), wrote:

> We would have been filled with gratitude for a philosophical or psychological theory
> that would have been able to explain to us the significance of how imperative the
> feelings of pleasure and displeasure are for us. Unfortunately, nothing is being sug-
> gested which is acceptable to us. This region is the darkest and most inaccessible
> region of mental life. (Freud, 1961)

It should be pointed out that long before information science came into
existence as a separate field to deal explicitly or implicitly with the satisfaction
of the IN, psychologists studied the IN, although not too intensively and without much success. With the development of the field of information science,
interest in the study of the IN increased considerably. For example, the yearbook of the International Federation of Documentation (1973) pointed out that
144 works on IN study were published by 1967. Nevertheless, despite the fair
number of studies, no essential results have been obtained, as was mentioned in
the yearbook's preface:

> IN studies have obviously not lived up to the expectations, because they only helped
> to discover what has already been known through the practice of publishing scien-
> tific and technical literature, as well as from the experience gained from library/
> bibliographic work.

Some authors (Jahoda, 1966) even denied the value of IN study, whereas others
(O'Connor, 1967, 1968) believed that it was impossible to determine what IN
should mean. Moreover, since the mid-1970s, to a certain extent as a result of
such beliefs, the number of publications that featured IN study has decreased
dramatically. Nevertheless, the situation has proved to be not so gloomy. Several
authors (see, for example, Allen, 1991; Bates, 1989; Belkin, 1987; Belkin &
Croft, 1987; Fidel & Soergel, 1983; Lancaster, 1968; and Ingerwersen, 1994)
introduced some interesting ideas that led to a better understanding of such a
phenomenon as IN. This chapter is based on the approach developed by Voiskunskii & Frants (1974) and Frants & Brush (1988).

It is obvious that an IN is directed to some object or phenomenon of the world surrounding us. However, the thematic boundaries of this mental state are not always clearly defined. In fact, in satisfying an IN we always strive for clarity. But clarity ensues only when we can make a decision using obtained information (that is, we must either decrease the uncertainty in the behavior algorithm or achieve final goal). In other words, with the achievement of clarity, the process of satisfying a concrete IN is concluded. However, in many cases we cannot know beforehand exactly what information leads to the achievement of clarity. We want information, we want it very much (displeasure), but unfortunately we do not always know exactly what we want. This occurs because we imagine only the final product, the results of our physiological desire, and do not imagine exactly what information can lead to this result (pleasure). Only by obtaining information and juxtaposing it with available knowledge (with those patterns stored in memory) do we either elevate our knowledge to a level of clarity or make certain that the obtained information is insufficient, leading us to continue the process of collecting it (the process of satisfying an IN). Also, under the influence of the obtained information, the thematic boundaries of the IN itself can be changed. Thus, for imprecise thematic boundaries, the feedback mechanism distinctly appears in the process of satisfying the IN.

The model previously described is not just theoretical. Figure 2.1 illustrates the availability to the user of types of IN with or without precise boundaries. The "perception" of an IN is possible in those cases when the user *expresses* it. The expression of an IN is understood to be a process that results in a record of information about the IN that is obtained in some language. A *record in a*

Part (a)

1. How many periodicals did the New York public library receive during the last month?
2. What is the melting temperature of lead under standard conditions?
3. What was the most expensive annual tuition at a private university of the United States in 1994?
4. What was the closing gold quotation at the New York Stock Exchange last Wednesday?

Part (b)

1. How are statistical methods applied in interpreting experimental results?
2. How can malignant tumors be treated?
3. How can information needs be satisfied?
4. Can translation be automated?

Figure 2.1
Examples of queries representing various types of IN.

natural language, obtained as a result of a user's attempt to express his or her IN, will be called a *query* or a *search request.*

A first glance at the lists in Figure 2.1 already indicates that *different groups of queries*—(a) and (b)—possess different characteristics. In fact, the IN expressed in the first four examples is different from the IN expressed in the next four examples. If an IN of the first type (the first four examples) has thematic boundaries that are completely determined, and if as the result it can be expressed exactly, then the second type of IN (the second four examples) has boundaries that are not precisely determined, and it cannot be expressed exactly. In fact, if any group of users asking the fourth query in part (a) is given an answer (the required gold rate is named or a document given in which this rate is indicated), then each member of this group (under the condition that the query still interests them until the answer is obtained) will find the obtained data interesting, and it is not at all important how they react to the obtained information. In part (b), users asking the same query and obtaining an identical answer (for example a document or documents) can give, as is well known, completely different evaluations of obtained data.

Another difference in the types of IN under consideration is that if only one answer is necessary and sufficient to satisfy an IN of the first type (for example, any of the available documents containing the required information), then to satisfy an IN of the second type, most often all available documents of interest to the user prove to be insufficient. A consequence of this property is that upon obtaining the appropriate document, both the query and the need of the first type disappear. It goes without saying that this occurs when an IN of the first type is represented by only one query. Otherwise, the query disappears, and the IN of the first type diminishes as much as it was represented by this query. In the second case, the obtained information (for example, some set of documents of interest to the user) generally changes an IN of the this type and develops it, and the query remains for an extended period of time.

The next distinction (property) emphasizes the fact that much less intellectual power is required to perceive the information that answers an IN of the first type than is needed to perceive the answers of the second type. In fact, it is not difficult to evaluate the answer to the question of how many periodicals were received by the New York Public Library (second query, first type of IN). However, to investigate the operation of a new algorithm for translating a text from one natural language to another (fourth query, second type of IN) is quite difficult.

Another important distinction is the fact that formulation of queries for an IN of the first type does not present the user with a particular difficulty, whereas in the second case, as a rule, it is far from simple.

Following the accepted terminology (see Frants & Brush, 1988) we will call an IN of the first type a *concrete information need* (CIN) and an IN of the second type a *problem oriented information need* (POIN). It is not difficult to imag-

CIN	POIN
1. The thematic boundaries are clearly defined.	1. The thematic boundaries are not defined.
2. The request is put into exact words, that is, it corresponds exactly to the CIN thematical limits.	2. As a rule, the request does not conform to the POIN.
3. To satisfy a CIN only one good document is needed.	3. As a rule, the POIN cannot be satisfied, even with all good documents existing in the system.
4. As soon as the good document is found, the CIN disappears.	4. As soon as good documents are delivered, the thematical limits of POIN may change and the POIN itself remains for a long time.

Figure 2.2
Comparative characteristics of CIN and POIN.

ine that other types of IN distinct from these exist (i.e., types having properties that neither the CIN nor the POIN have).

The characteristics given in Figure 2.2 (contrasted point by point) describe the differences between the two types of IN.

The relationship between a query and a need is particularly interesting, especially in the case of a POIN where this psychological state, as noted earlier, does not have precise thematic boundaries. Lancaster (1979), one of the most authoritative experts in this area, studied this relationship. He noted that the lack of precise thematic boundaries not only hampers the formulation of a query, but also may lead to situations in which the formulated query does not coincide with the thematic boundaries of the POIN. Either the query does not intersect with POIN, or it coincides with POIN only partially, or it is entirely included in the POIN (it is a part of it), or it exceeds the thematical boundaries of the POIN by including it entirely. Thus, the same query asked by different users can reflect (represent) a different POIN. Figure 2.3 illustrates the indicated relationships.

It is not unusual for a user who is trying to express his or her POIN more precisely to formulate not one but several queries. Strictly speaking, this is pos-

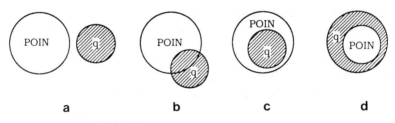

a   b   c   d

Figure 2.3
Possible relationships between need and query.

sible when two different users have absolutely the same POIN, but this does not mean that they will ask the same query or collection of queries.

When discussing the relationship between a query and a need, one should especially emphasize that the query does not always uniquely indicate the type of IN that is expressed by this query. This occurs when the same query can represent different types of IN. For example, the second query of the IN of first type (CIN) at one time was a query representing a POIN (until melting temperature of lead was determined). However, even today it can represent a POIN if for some reason the user is interested in the melting temperature with a precision up to 27 places, for example. The same can be noted in consideration of queries representing POIN. For example, if an exhaustive answer can be given to the query (to the second query of POIN)—for example a pill is indicated that has no negative side effects and cures 100% of those affected—then this query will represent a CIN. In other words, the presence of different type of IN depends on the way the user views the information required and the user's obtaining of the information, a transformation of one type of IN to another can occur.

It is also of some interest to consider the relationship between an IN and information. For example, different types of IN require their own most "suitable" information. It is also possible to classify different types of information connected with specific type of IN. In fact, for that humankind has strived for standardization and unification, even today we deal with different types of documents. Moreover, a tendency toward replacing existing types by any one universal type is not evident. This can be explained by the fact that one type of information is most conveniently represented in the form of a scientific article, another in the form of a table, a third in the form of a dictionary, a fourth in the form of a graphic, and so on. Thus, the availability of different types of information leads to different types of documents. However, information is only a product of the satisfaction of an IN. This means that for different types of IN, different types (forms) of documents are required. In fact, to satisfy a POIN, scientific articles, books, and other documents are used. To satisfy a CIN, reference books, tables, dictionaries, encyclopedias, and other sources are used. As with different types of IN, types of information have a definite set of properties specific to each type. Thus, it is impossible to represent the material included in this chapter graphically or in the form of a dictionary, for example.

Some argue that there are differences in the IN for, say, physicists, chemists, mathematicians, biologists, and so on. But in reality, these differences are no greater than the differences in the IN of two mathematicians asking queries from different areas of mathematics. In other words, these are the typical differences in the thematic boundaries of an IN. An information need (mental state) of mathematicians, chemists, and biologists is identical in nature, types, and properties.

In some cases, investigators speak about a collective need for information in a particular field, business, or other specific area, and it is often believed that such IN has its own characteristics. Here one should note that only a user can be the bearer of an IN, and a collective need can be considered only as the sum IN of a collection of users.

Thus, in concluding our discussion of IN, we should emphasize the importance of its further study, because the methods and forms of its satisfaction must take into account, as much as possible, the nature of its origination as well as its characteristic properties. In discussing IN, we have also made more precise the "product" of its satisfaction—that is, information. We have also made more precise the sense in which the concept of information will be used later in this chapter. However, in view of the importance of this concept, we shall present several additional explanations concerning it.

2.4

Information

The role of information in the life of an individual human being, as well as for society as a whole, is simply enormous. In our analysis of vital activity, we showed that information is one of the main resources for man's survival. It would seem then that there should be, if not complete, at least significant clarity about the notion of information. However, in reality this is not so. It is a fact that in recent decades, both in popular and in specialized literature, a great deal has been written about information. But the descriptions were often so contradictory that the combined efforts have succeeded in thoroughly confusing the reader. It cannot be said that we suffer from insufficient commentary and definitions of this concept. On the contrary, rarely has any concept had such a number of explanations. However, in science the following law often holds: the more points of view there are on a problem, the more unsuccessful one may be at understanding the situation.

We see our task not in formulating yet another, this time "correct" definition encompassing all sides of so multifaceted an object as information, but just the opposite. We want to show that, depending on the goals and the problems lying before investigators in various areas of knowledge, the use of the term "information" becomes so multidefined and contradictory that a single definition would be impossible to develop. In this present discussion we will narrow the application and utilization of the concept of information to the framework of information science, and we will describe its most significant characteristics and properties for a given area. Of course, this will not add clarity to the use of this concept in other areas.

In analyzing the concept of information, it is difficult to find any major description with which all investigators would agree. For example, some investigators consider information a material phenomenon, others an ideal one; some suggest that information can be only comprehended (that it is semantic, i.e., it has meaning, sense), others are sure that information cannot carry any meaning; some consider information as existing objectively, whereas for others it is subjective, some consider information to be a form of relationship between the user and the signal or signals, implying, consequently, that information does not exist without a user, others assert that information existed before the appearance of man and that it can exist by itself. In spite of the presence of diametrically opposed views, one should recognize that all are right. But are they right within the framework of the axiomatics, the initial concepts, the points of view, the goals and the problems, the areas of use for which they have chosen? This lack of a clear definition causes well-known difficulties, because today the term "information," used without any reservations or explanations, is in some cases the source of misunderstandings or an incorrect understanding of what has been said.

The term "information" comes from the Latin word *information,* and it traditionally denotes explanation, notification, or communication about some event or activity. This concept was closely connected with meaning and entailed its use. In the mid-20th century, mathematicians began to apply new meaning to the term "information" that differed from what this term meant in everyday life.

It should be said that mathematicians quite often resort to such crafty devices. In this way they are fundamentally distinguished, for example, from chemists. A chemist, after developing a new compound or preparation, immediately contrives a simple and clear name for it: for example, "metoxychlorodiethylaminomethylbutylaminoacridine" or "4-oxy-3-metoxy-benzaldehyde." For a chemist, 30 to 40 letters are usually sufficient for this.

The mathematician does not trouble himself by thinking up new terms. He takes a commonly known word and uses it at his whim. You probably would never guess that a field is what we call a ring, whose set of nonzero elements form a group with respect to the law induced by the multiplication defined on this ring. If after reconciling ourselves to this definition of a field, we want to know what the mathematicians mean by a ring in this connection, we will find that a ring is a set with the algebraic structure defined by two internal laws, the first of which is the law of a commutative group on this set, and the second law is associative and is doubly distributive with respect to the first.

Thus, the term "information" appeared with new meanings almost simultaneously in the work of Wiener (1961) and in the work of Shannon, a mathematician who worked at Bell Laboratory (Shannon & Weaver, 1959). Both works were originally published in 1948. Developing ideas of the general character of control in objects of any nature, Wiener extended the use of the term "information" by transferring it from humans only to animals in general and then machines in particular. The latter seemed especially important because it permitted an explanation, by the same mechanisms, of both the goal-oriented behavior of people and the goal-oriented behavior of machines. In other words, the new concept of information now included any controlling signals in any machines, and "information" was said to mean those signals received by a system (whether the system was alive or not, without distinction), which changed the state of the system in a definite way. In terms of the concept "information," now doubts were arising about its connection with meaning. However, the new ideas turned out to be so important and fruitful that exactly this understanding of the term became widespread and customary for specialists in many fields.

Using the term "information" in his work, Shannon departed significantly from its commonly accepted interpretation. He now did not take meaning into consideration at all, and he was not interested in whether the information would ever be used. What interested him was precisely the transmission of information in communication channels, with the least possible loss and distortion. This position is completely understandable, because during the transmission of information, the question about its content does not even arise. Shannon's article (coauthored with Weaver) was titled "A Mathematical Theory of Communication," and one of the main problems solved in this work was the removal of the effects of noise during the transmission of communications.

In this work, Shannon proposed a probabilistic method of measuring the amount of information in a communication (information, not meaning!). The expression that he proposed for calculating the maximal capacity of a communication channel is one of the most important contributions to the theory of communication. It establishes the greatest amount of binary units (bits or "yes-no" solutions) that can be transmitted along a channel for a unit of time with probability of error as small as desired. This maximal speed of the transmission of information can be approached without limit by improving the coding method, but it cannot be surpassed.

The problems Shannon solved were significantly narrower than those solved by Wiener and became one of the parts of cybernetics (i.e., the direction of scientific investigations resulting from the work of Wiener). However, it is Shannon's work that served as the foundation for modern means of communication—*those means which are used to transmit information to the users.*

The probability-statistical theory of information (as Shannon's theory is often called) was only the first and most important among other mathematical approaches to the measurement of information. In the combinatorial approach, for example, the amount of information is defined as a function of the number of elements of a finite set in their combinatorial relations. Representatives of the topological approach introduce spatial structures, in particular graphs, as the basis of definitions of the amount of information. In the algorithmic approach, the measure of the amount of information contained—for example, in object A with respect to object B—is taken as the minimal "length" of a program on the basis of which object A can be unambiguously transformed into object B.

At practically the same time, biologists also introduced their contribution to the departure from the accepted meaning of the term "information." They began to refer to inherited traits as information. In this case, information was transmitted by an especially material object (that is, by the DNA molecule) without any technical lines of communication, certainly not in the brain. In every case, having received a molecule of DNA, the object did not realize that it had received information, in whatever sense of the word.

The wide and diverse use of the term "information" is of interest to philosophers. An extensive literature dedicated to this concept has appeared. In attempting to recognize and generalize its varied uses, philosophers proposed new interpretations that only widened the circle of meanings for this term. For example, representatives of neothomism asserted the transcendental nature of information. In neopositivism and existentialism, information is considered a subjective phenomenon, among other things. The subject area of the concept of information is intensively discussed (is it a property of all material objects, of only of those that are living and self-governing, or only of conscious beings, etc.). The idea of diversity, proposed by Ashby (1964), proved to be rather widespread among philosophers. Investigating properties of information, he noticed that information cannot be transmitted in a larger amount than the amount of diversity permits. He formulated the idea of necessary *diversity,* the essence of which is that the receiving system increases its internal diversity as the diversity of the external influences decreases. This approach did not so much bring clarity to the understanding of information, as returned it somewhat to its original meaning and most of all pointed out its role in the survival of a system.

Thus, the varied uses of the term "information" have served as a basis for its transformation from a term rarely used or understood—and not attracting attention to itself over the course of many centuries—to a term extremely current, debatable, and surprisingly widespread. It may be useful (and interesting) to mention several definitions given for information, including the definitions by Wiener and Shannon. "Information is the designation of the content obtained from the external world in the process of our adaptation to it and the adaptation of our senses to it," wrote Wiener (1954).

"In general, information . . . can be defined as that which remains invariant under any reversible recording or transfer of communication," noted Shannon (1951). Brillouin wrote, "Information is a raw material and consists of a simple collection of data, whereas knowledge assumes some reflection or reasoning organizing the data by means of their comparison and classification" (1964). In discussing information in Shannon's terms, he noted, "We define information as the result of a choice; we do not consider information as the basis for a prediction, as a result of which it can be used to make another choice. We completely ignore the human value of information" (Brillouin, 1963). Further, "We attach to the word 'information' a precise but in fact limited meaning. We connect information with negentropy, and consequently, with improbability. . . . In this definition in reality there is nothing of life (the human element), and we will never confuse our information with science or knowledge" (Brillouin, 1963).

In Webster's dictionary, "Information is something received or obtained through informing: as, knowledge communicated by others or obtained from investigation, study, or instruction" (*Webster's 3rd International,* 1961). A remark of Wiener is of interest: "Information is information, not matter or energy" (Weiner, 1961).

It would seem that the presented definitions are sufficient to illustrate the complexities associated with a single and "right" understanding of information. Nevertheless, in spite of the obvious difference in the approaches, the traditional meaning of "information" has not been lost and is becoming increasingly timely. In terms of this, one should note that the assignment of multiple meanings to the term has long caused dissatisfaction among some investigators. For example, one of the most authoritative experts in the area of information exchange, Cherry, in analyzing Shannon's direction, noted: "In some sense one has to regret that mathematical concepts . . . in general have been called 'information'" (Cherry, 1966). Some philosophers also mention this. However, in reality it is too late now to introduce changes into different uses of this term and they have to be somehow reconciled. Thus, we go on to a refinement of the concept, which we shall be using in further exposition.

It is obvious that the term "information" in information science is used in its traditional meaning. In our analysis of vital activity, we considered information as the product of satisfying an IN, with *the information as the product existing only as long as the IN exists.* We especially emphasized the meaning of information for the development of behavior algorithms, and in connection with this we indicated that information for a system is everything that decreases uncertainty during the formation of the system's behavior algorithm. In other words, *information is a form of relationship of the user to the signals,* signals in the broad sense. This can be a word, the noise of an approaching train, a scent or a mosquito bite, a pain in the back, or cold wind.

Of course different users can relate differently to a cold wind or to the same word. However, when this relation affects a decision process or the formation of a behavior algorithm, it is possible to assert that the system extracts information contained in the signal and transforms it into actual information. In fact, in this sense one should understand the subjective character of information which we discussed earlier. Hence, on the one hand the actual information can satisfy the information hunger of the user (the user's IN), and on the other hand, without the user this information does not exist. That is the reason why in analyzing information processes one always assumes the existence of a user. In some cases this is not explicit and the user is not some concrete person but rather an abstraction, such as when information is created by a person. Any author has in mind some reader, even when writing an intimate diary (in which case the designated reader often *is* the author). It is often said that some book (or other document) contains information. However, in essence, it implies that this book either has or will have a reader sometime (a user of the information generated by the book). In other words, if someone is absolutely sure that a certain book is not needed by anyone and no one ever under any circumstances will use it, then that person will not claim that this book contains information. In some cases, speaking about the presence of information outside the user, one refers to the experts who select the documents (for this, instead of "document" we often say "information") for input into a system. But first, in *selecting* they are now users; second, they are selecting in fact for the users of the system, that is, again for its (the information's) users.

In terms of what has been said, some well-known questions are of interest. For example, is actual information always something new or can it be old? Essentially the answer is already contained in the concept of actual information itself, in its definitions given earlier. It is obvious that in those cases when something decreases uncertainty in the behavior algorithm, this is already actual information and this is always something new. Another question: Is actual information something true or can it be false? Again, if we base our response on its behavior, then, first, it is already actual information, and, second, it is always true. We do not make conscious and free decisions being aware that they are mistaken. Only the result of actions can show us the falsity of some of our premises.

There is an opinion that in the process of contact, saying something to an interlocutor, we send him information. Thus it objectively exists and is outside the user. We send the interlocutor a communication in which our knowledge, that is, the information available to us, is encoded (for example, by vocal means). This does not mean that it exists without a user. We are its users and carriers. We are the subjects using it. And it is not at all obligatory that any other user perceives it. However, if another does perceive it, then the perceived information can be distinguished subjectively from the sent information. In this case, the process of expressing the information available to us is our activity and this process is an intermediate step of satisfying some of our needs.

There is an ongoing controversy about the presence of particular specific properties in information. We will touch on only some aspects of this discussion. Consider the following example: Suppose that a teacher explains the Pythagorean theorem to one hundred students. The question arises: Did the amount of information increase as the result of his presentation? *Yes,* if we think about each of the hundred students, knowledge increased for each of them. *No,* if we think about the amount of original information that people had already accumulated, its amount did not change. For this reason, in the first case we talk about *acquired* actual information, and in the second case we talk about *accumulated* potential information. In other words, as in many cases described earlier, everything depends on the point of view and the tasks of the investigator. This example illustrates the relatively frequent consideration of potential information as a commodity. It is not difficult to see that the teacher sells his or her wares (information) for pay.

Thus, in the example we mentioned that in some sense the amount of information increased, and in some sense its amount did not change; the question of whether it decreased (for example, for the teacher) does not even arise. This seems obvious, even though teachers sell their wares by giving the information that they have to others. Nevertheless, this position is confusing to some because in their opinion it creates a strange situation: no matter how much information from our memory that we transfer to others, its amount does not decrease. Here again it is appropriate to recall Wiener's remark: "Information is information, not matter or energy" (Wiener, 1961). Apparently some investigators in this situation are somewhat bothered by our usual "material" notions of wares. However, all agree that the teacher does not transmit either matter or energy to the students.

Perhaps it is useful and instructive to compare the need for food with the need for information. It is obvious that food exists as long as an entity using it exists (i.e., the organism eating it). Actual information should also be interpreted in exactly the same way. It exists as long as a user of it exists. If, for example, no one will ever eat rabbits, then rabbits will not be actual food because actual implies the existence of a user of this food. This approach is also valid in relation to information. If no one ever "eats" information, that is, if certain signals are never in any way taken into the consideration, then these signals are not the source of actual information. The user makes signals informative as he or she sees fit.

It should be noted that up to now both information and signals have been considered in broad terms. However, it is necessary to narrow somewhat any further discussion of these concepts, at least down to those forms that are present in any information activity within the framework of information science. In other words, we will focus our attention on the satisfaction of IN with the help of documents or, as they are sometimes called, documentary information. For this reason, we now turn to the discussion of such objects as documents, objects containing potential information.

2.5

Document

It is difficult to say when humanity felt the necessity of preserving information outside of memory. However, it is possible to say with confidence that this occurred in the period between the creation of language and the creation of writing. The phenomenon of writing itself was early society's answer to an arising necessity. With the appearance of writing, the *document* also appeared, which we shall define as a *material carrier with information fixed on it*. Within the framework of our conceptions about information, which were described earlier, we will make more precise the sense in which information is fixed on a document. For this we will consider from whose point of view something that is fixed is considered information, and then how it is fixed.

First note that the information described in a document represents information that has some importance for the author and hence is actual information that the author *expresses* with the help of some means of fixing it in the document. In analyzing the nature of the origin of IN, as well as the role of information in the process of vital activity, it was shown that IN itself as well as the realization of information, are mental states that in many cases are difficult to express exactly. Therefore, by *expression* in this context we mean a recording of information realized in some language by the author of the document. How well the fixed (documentary) information corresponds to what the author of this document wanted to express depends on the author's ability to express his or her mental state on the one hand, and on the author's fixing technique and skills on the other hand.

From the time of their appearance, written documents satisfied an important function for society—the transmission of information in time and space. Apparently *pictograms,* which were representations of the general content of communication in the form of pictures or a sequence of pictures, were used as the first attempts to fix information. Pictograms have been known as far back as the neolithic period. Cave walls, rock faces, and stones have been used as information carriers. Strictly speaking, pictograms are not a means of fixing any definite spoken language, that is, they are not writing in the proper sense. Nevertheless, with their help, the creation of the first documents became possible, although documents such as rock faces or cave walls were at times extremely inconvenient to use (for example, when moving from a residence it was impossible to take them along). Practically, the creation of written documents began with the invention of phonetic writing, in which each sound was denoted by a special symbol. This invention proved so successful that such symbols have been successfully used up to now. Essentially for the last millennia (writing has been known from the end of the fourth to the beginning of the third millennium B.C. (in Egypt and Mesopotamia) only the carriers and the technical means of fixing information have been perfected and changed. Note also that with the development of both, the concept of a document has been enriched to now include new forms; and not all documents are now written, (consider photographs, phonetic recording, etc.). However, we will focus on written documents, and in the following discussion when speaking of a document we will mean a written document.

The creator of a document expresses in it "something" that is information from the creator's point of view (this "something" corresponds to the creator's IN). Recall that during our earlier discussion of the need for information itself, it was shown that various types of IN exist, and that for each type of IN, information is required corresponding to the given type. Thus, it is valid to speak about various types of information, types that are generated by existing types of IN and suitable for satisfying exactly these types of IN. To illustrate this point it was mentioned that one type of information is most conveniently represented as a research monograph, another as a table, a third as a dictionary, a fourth as a graph, and so forth. That is how historically different types of documents came about. Because different types of IN are satisfied by different types of information, different types of documents are used to satisfy these types of IN. For example, to satisfy a POIN, research papers, books, and so on are used, whereas to satisfy a CIN, reference books, tables, dictionaries, and encyclopedias would be preferable.

It is obvious that all existing types of documents originated in different times, and over the course of the past several centuries (especially in the present century) they have undergone significant evolution. Books, for example, already have existed for several millennia, patent specifications for half a millennium, the scientific journal for a little more than 300 years, the journal article in its present form for just less than 150 years, and the citation index for about 40 years. Today no acceptable universal classification of documents exists. Apparently this has occurred because types of IN, as well as types of information satisfying them, are not used as a basis for classifying documents.

We will conclude our discussion of the document with its meaning for the user. In fact, it is the user who really needs the document (to try to satisfy an arising IN). Of course, the extraction of information from a document on the whole has an individual character. In other words, different users can extract different information from the same document. This depends on several factors, first of which is the tasks facing the user (whose solution requires collecting the missing information) as well as on the level of the user's knowledge and the user's ability to perceive information. The same document can be of interest to one and boring to another, or useful to one and useless to another, depending on whether or not the user obtained needed information with the help of this document.

Today documentary information serves as a basic means of satisfying IN. Therefore, in further discussions of new approaches and methods of satisfying IN, we will direct our attention to existing types of documents. Although researchers are still studying the notion of a "document" (see, for example, Schamber, 1996), the explanation given in this chapter is sufficient for understanding the rest of the chapters in this book.

2.6

Conclusion

A study of the nature of information need (IN) and its properties is one of the central problems addressed in information science. This is not surprising when one considers that any known information activity and even whole industries exist because of IN and were created to satisfy it.

Information is essential to human beings and precedes our simple actions as well as more complex actions directed toward establishing better conditions for survival in the future. For example, a person who wants to drink has to know (have information about) where drinking water is and how to drink it. This information will determine the person's behavior. If this ☞ information is not available, then the person will need to obtain it. In other words, the person's behavior will be determined by the available information about the methods of obtaining the necessary (to have a drink) information. If such information does not exist, then the person chooses his or her actions randomly, realizing that this approach is not reliable.

The fact that IN represents a person's psychological state is important for understanding the problems related to its satisfaction. The difference in properties of different psychological states in connection with the need for information determines different types of IN. In this chapter we identified only two types of IN: CIN and POIN. To satisfy different types of IN, it is necessary to develop different systems while taking their properties into account.

In discussing the notion of information, we mentioned that it exists only because IN exists. Everything that is used to satisfy the user's IN (or some part of IN) is therefore information for this user. The notion of IN described in this chapter is crucial for understanding the proposed solutions for creating IR systems and is the basis for the mechanisms of interaction between the user and the system.

References

Allen, B. L. (1991). Cognitive research in information science: Implications for design. *Annual Review of Information Science and Technology, 26.*

Ashby, W. R. (1964). *An introduction to cybernetics.* London: Chapman & Hall and University Paperbacks.

Bates, M. J. (1989). The design of browsing and berrypicking techniques for the online search interface. *Online Review, 13,* 407–424.

Belkin, N. J. (1987). Discourse analysis of human information interaction for specification of human-computer information interaction. *Canadian Journal of Information Science, 12,* 31–42.

Belkin, N. J., & Croft, W. B. (1987). Retrieval techniques. In M. Williams (ed.), *Annual review of information science and technology.* New York: Elsevier, 109–145.

Brillouin, L. (1963). *Science and information theory* (2nd ed.). New York: Academic Press.

Brillouin, L. (1964). *Scientific uncertainty and information.* New York: Academic Press.

Cherry, C. (1966). *On human communications* (2nd ed.). Cambridge, MA: MIT Press.

Fechner, G. T. (1966). *Elements of psychophysics.* New York: Holt, Rinehart and Winston.

Fidel, R., & Soergel, D. (1983). Factors affecting online bibliographic retrieval: A conceptual framework for research. *Journal of the American Society for Information Science, 34,* 163–180.

Frants, V. I., & Brush, C. B. (1988). The need for information and some aspects of information retrieval systems construction. *Journal of the American Society for Information Science, 39,* 86–91.

Freud, S. (1961). *Beyond the pleasure principle.* New York: Liveright.

Grobstein, C. (1974). *The strategy of life* (2nd ed.). San Francisco: W. H. Freeman.

Ingwersen, P. Polirepresentation of information needs and semantic entities: elements of a cognitive theory for information retrieval. Proceedings of the Seventeenth Annual International ACM SIGIR Conference on Research and Development Information Retrieval, Dublin, Ireland, 1994.

International Federation of Documentation (FID 478). (1973). VINITI, Moscow.

Jahoda, G. (1966). *Information needs of science and technology*. Background review. In Proceedings of the 1965 Congress FID, Washington, DC, October 7–16, 1965, vol. 2. Washington, DC: Spartan Books.

Lancaster, F. W. (1968). *Information retrieval systems: characteristics, testing, evaluation*. New York: John Wiley & Sons.

Lancaster, F. W. (1979). *Information retrieval systems: Characteristics, testing, evaluation*. New York: John Wiley & Sons.

O'Connor, J. (1967). Relevance disagreements and nuclear request forms. *American Documentation, 18*(3), 165–177.

O'Connor, J. (1968). Some questions concerning "information needs." *American Documentation, 19*(2), 200–203.

Schamber, L. (1996). What is a document? Rethinking the concept in uneasy times. *Journal of the American Society for Information Science, 47*(9).

Shannon, C. E. (1951). The redundancy of English, In Cybernetics, Transactions of the Conference, New York.

Shannon, C. E., & Weaver, W. (1959). *The mathematical theory of communication*. Urbana, IL: The University of Illinois Press.

Voiskunskii, V. G., & Frants, V. I. (1974). Correction of query formulations in documentary information retrieval systems. *Nauchno-Tekhnicheskaya Informatsiya (NTI)*, ser. 2, no. 2, 1–12.

Webster's third international dictionary of the English language, Unabridged. vol. 1, (1961). Springfield, MA: Merriam.

Wiener, N. (1954). *The human use of human beings, cybernetic and society*. Boston: Houghton, Mifflin.

Wiener, N. (1961). *Cybernetics or control and communication in the animal and the machine*. New York-London: The MIT Press and John Wiley & Sons.

Bibliographic Remarks ─────────────────────────────

Additional material about information need can be found in the following publications.

Frants, V. I., & Brush, C. B. (1988). The need for information and some aspects of information retrieval systems construction. *Journal of the American Society for Information Science, 39*, 86–91.

Frants, V. I., Shapiro, J., & Voiskunskii, V. G. (1996). Development of IR systems: New direction. *Information Processing and Management, 32* (3), 162–175.

Kochen, M. (1975). Organizing knowledge for coping with need. Paper presented at the Third International Study Conference on Classification Research, Bombay, India, January 1975.

Lancaster, F. W. (1979). *Information retrieval systems: Characteristics, testing, evaluation*. New York: John Wiley & Sons.

For more details about the notion of information and its properties the reader is referred to the following publications.

Cherry, C. (1966). *On human communication*. (2nd ed.). Cambridge, MA: MIT Press.

Wiener, N. (1961). *Cybernetics or control and communication in the animal and the machine*. New York-London: The MIT Press and John Wiley & Sons.

3

Information Crisis

3.1

Introduction

Satisfying an information need (IN) is one of the eternal human problems. However, it is also an eternally new problem, because the conditions of life, its content, and human beings themselves are constantly changing. At each stage, arrayed in long-familiar attire, this problem includes something new and unique, organically corresponding to its own time.

Historically, two methods of satisfying an IN have developed. The first method is to try to obtain the necessary information from the mass of information that is available to human beings, and the second is to extract from nature the necessary information oneself. In these terms, the testimony of Emilio Segre, a Nobel laureate in physics, about his joint work with Enrico Fermi, another prominent physicist and Nobel laureate, is of interest (Segre, 1973). He recalled that Fermi often preferred to derive the formulas of interest to him, instead of looking for them in the specialized literature. Fermi repeatedly made wagers with his friends that he could do this faster than they could find this or that formula in the literature, and he usually won such wagers.

The path by which the user extracts information to satisfy an IN belongs to the sphere of human activity called science. When following the other path, seeking answers from masses of available information, we are dealing with information already obtained (as a rule, with the help of science), and processes such as gathering, storing, retrieving, and distributing this information, as well as several auxiliary processes that furnish these basic processes, pertain to so-called information activity.

Information activity is closely associated with science, because information sources circulating within the framework of this activity are, as a rule, the product of science. In other words, the more successfully scientific activity is carried out, the more information circulates within the framework of information activity. However, in a certain sense, the two methods of satisfying the IN are in contradiction. For the first approach, there is always too much information, and in the history of the development of forms and methods to satisfy IN with available information, various critical situations have arisen (which were overcome, for example, by the invention of writing, paper, printing, etc.). As for the second approach, there is always too little information. However, in both cases society is ready to invest more and more resources for science (to stimulate the development of new information) as well as for information activity (to stimulate its efficient utilization).

The idea of too little information has constantly served as a basis for the development of science, and since the beginning of the 20th century it has resulted in exponential growth of scientific activity, including capital investment in science and the number of scientists. This in turn inevitably resulted in the phenomenon that is often called the information explosion (the exponential growth of information during a particular segment of time). In the following we will be interested in satisfying an IN with the help of information activity, which means the historical development of this activity will be of particular interest. We will also consider some of the previous information crises, the conditions that spawned them, and the methods for overcoming them. This historical background can prove to be useful for understanding the modern information crisis, which will also be considered.

3.2

Information Activity and Information Crises

Chapter 2 showed that information is always necessary for human survival. However, how far back can we trace the history of information activity? It is difficult to answer this question, but apparently the first result of this activity was the creation of language. *Language was created in connection with the growth of IN, on the one hand, and with accumulation of information (experience) on the other. It had to provide an instrument (means) with which it was possible to satisfy an IN more successfully and to contact one's contemporaries.*

Try to imagine the beginning of information activity, that is, the process of creation of language. Many millennia have passed since the time when our distant ancestor, fearfully looking around, raised himself on his rear extremities, and awkwardly swinging, learned to move on them alone. This was a significant event because the forward extremities turned into hands and our ancestor's horizon was significantly widened. Rather quickly he discovered that he could communicate his desires to those like him. The first people probably used their hands for these purposes. Whoever was strongest was listened to more attentively and understood. Undoubtedly this method was being developed when someone first had the sense to grab a stick. With its help, our ancestor much more successfully made his simple views on life understood by his kinsmen.

Gradually this extremely indelicate, but mainly inconvenient method to transfer information began to be seen as not the only option possible. It turned out that it was possible to express one's desires and intentions by an approving growl, threatening scream, or one-syllabled cry. Gradually these sounds were put together, and the animal-like scream was transformed into the resemblance of speech. Cave people began to invent the first words.

Clearly, the words and their meanings were developed jointly by many people over a long period of time. The vocabulary accumulated very slowly (many linguists believe that the formation of language takes hundreds of thousands of years). However, even with the small number of words that our ancestors had mastered, they could exchange a lot of information. For example, it has been determined that in the biblical Ten Commandments, people used only about 300 words. For the American Declaration of Independence, 1500 words were used. And a report on the establishment of new prices for coal in the United States, published at the end of the 1960s, contains 26,811 words.

It is believed that language finally developed approximately 25,000 years ago. With the existence of language, it became significantly easier to satisfy an IN. In other words, a person's chances for survival significantly improved. Due to the constant accumulation of information, the problem of storage arose. People were used as the first "warehouse" of information. Such warehouses were the oldest person of the tribe, the chief sorcerer, the high priest, and so forth. Possession of information was one of the important privileges and functions of these people. However, a "document" in the form of a mortal had an essential deficiency—upon this warehouse's death information often disappeared. A much more reliable document was necessary as more and more information was accumulated over time, and the need for it only increased. Thus, writing began to be developed, which emerged about six thousand years ago.

With the creation of writing, humankind was faced with a new problem—developing an efficient information carrier. Rock faces or cave walls did not prove to be very convenient. Perhaps the first artificially created carriers were clay tablets, which are known to have been used from the fourth millennium B.C. (Sumerian tablets). Since that time, information activity was much more explicit. It was necessary to know how to produce these tablets, to prepare an instrument for applying the text, to know how to preserve them (to protect them from rain, cracking, splitting, and crumbling) and to know how to use them.

How might a society overcome the crisis caused both by the growth in the amount of information accumulated by humankind and by the ever-increasing demand for it. The concrete information crisis was that the available form of information storage (a human being) became an obstacle in satisfying an IN because it could not cope with the assigned task. It was impossible to improve this form; therefore, it was necessary to replace it. Thus the creation of the written document proved to be not only the method for overcoming the information crisis but also a qualitatively new stage in the satisfaction of IN. Thus, it is not difficult to see that the information crisis manifested itself as a crisis of form, in this case the form of information storage. It should be emphasized that this crisis was overcome over the course of millennia. However, at that time any step on the road to progress took a long time. Even the stone age itself lasted eight thousand centuries.

After the appearance of the written document, humankind concentrated most of its information activity on improving this form. The following directions were pursued:

1. The creation of more convenient and durable material for the carrier of information.
2. The creation of instruments for applying text to the carrier.
3. The creation of pigments used for applying text.
4. The creation of methods of storage and use of documents.

We would like to point out that for the last millennium after its creation, writing itself did not undergo serious changes nor did it cause an information crisis. From time to time critical situations have arisen in each of the four directions listed. In the first direction, rock faces as the most ancient carriers of information were replaced by clay tablets, which, by the way, were not totally clay (the Sumerians added river silt to clay for strength and durability). Tablets were replaced by papyrus, then parchment appeared, and finally this was replaced by paper. Other, not so widespread, carriers of information also existed—bark strips, bone fragments, shells, and silk fabric, among others. However, the existence of various carriers did not always imply a solution to the problem connected with the existence of an information crisis. In several cases these were only alternatives in the search for material that would enable early society to overcome the crisis.

It is of interest to consider how the information crisis was connected with the material that was then being used to carry information. For example, in the 2nd century B.C., in the city of Pergamum, parchment began to be produced from cowhide. Rather quickly it became the basic material for carrying information in Europe. However, by the 12th century the need for information became so great (i.e., the number of users of accumulated information proved to be as large as the number of writers, including copyists who produced manuscript books) that the need for a new carrier became clear. By simply extrapolating the development of the available information situation into near future, people recognized that cattle would be insufficient for the production of parchment. In fact, for one average-size church book, almost a whole herd of cattle was needed. At the beginning of the 13th century, paper appeared in Europe. The low price of this material was remarkable in comparison with parchment.

It is known that paper first appeared in China in the 2nd century A.D., where it replaced silk. Chinese masters collected the bark of the mulberry tree, separated fibers from the inner side of the bark, and then carefully compressed these fibers, finally forming white sheets. This was the ancestor, although a distant one, of modern paper. Paper was brought to Europe, already free of defects, by peoples of Central Asia, Arabs, and Byzantines. Its road was slow but unstoppable. Through Samarkand, paper reached Echmiadzin and Baghdad, then Cairo and Constantinople, and then Europe. Its appearance in Europe apparently served as one of the factors that helped to launch the beginning of the Renaissance.

Thus, the information crisis under consideration was a crisis of a specific type of material, a type that, at a specific point in time, could not in principle satisfy the growing information needs of society. Overcoming the crisis with the help of the transition from parchment to paper proved to be extremely successful, as proven by the fact that this carrier is being used successfully even today.

In the second of the indicated directions of information activity, means of writing on a specific carrier were created and developed. For example, on clay tablets, texts were applied by sharpened sticks; for writing on silk, brushes were used; on papyrus people wrote with reed pens. The number of readers was constantly growing, so to satisfy a reader's inquiry (IN), people began not only to write original texts, but also to copy what was already written. Thus, in the course of millennia not only authors were writing—the profession of copyists was born. Consequently, the development of methods and instruments of applying text to a carrier went in two directions—one that best served the authors of documents and another for the reproduction of what was written.

In spite of the fact that the method of writing for authors with the help of a writing instrument has been preserved up to our day (although alternative methods also appeared, for example, typewriters), crisis situations have arisen in each of the directions mentioned. The most well-known crisis affected the second direction. It arose precisely with the existence of a method of reproduction that would help the process of copying. In fact, if one computes by decades the growth of the number of manuscript books produced in the course of the first half of the 15th century, and then extrapolates this growth to the end of the 15th century, it would turn out that by the end of this century there would not be enough people in Europe to copy the books. However, the rate of growth in the number of copies of books not only did not decrease, but, on the contrary, it increased as in 1448 Gutenberg invented printing. In other words, the information crisis of the 15th century was a crisis of the traditional method of hand-copying of books, a method with a multicentury history. The new method allowed the crisis to be overcome.

Important crises also affected the first direction. For example, with the appearance of paper, there also appeared an instrument for writing, such as the goosequill. For hundreds of years the whole world wrote with goosequills. At the beginning of the 19th century, Russia alone sold to England 20 to 30 million goosequills annually (quite a number considering that one goose gave from 10 to 20 quills suitable for writing). In order to produce a pen from a goosequill, it was necessary to clean it from coating, to dry it by a specific means, to increase its durability with the help of special compounds, and then to dry it again. Of course, some losses accompanied this technological process. By the middle of the 19th century, the number of people who could read and write was in the millions, and extrapolation of the almost exponential growth of literacy into the near future showed that a significant fraction of adults of the population would be occupied either with raising geese or with production of quill pens.

In 1780 the Englishman Harrison invented the steel pen. Of course, at the beginning it cost more than several geese, but after 70 to 80 years it practically displaced quill pens. Thus, a crisis situation produced by a type of instrument that was no longer able to provide the growing information needs of society was overcome. (As a reminder of how times have changed, the first version of this book—the manuscript—was obtained with the help of the laser printer!)

The examples of different information crises described in this chapter lead to the following conclusion: *Historically, information crises have arisen when available means, methods, or forms used in information activity could not manage the existing flow of information for satisfaction of the IN*. Therefore it is valid to talk about a crisis of means, a crisis of methods, or a crisis of forms at a particular time period.

It is clear that any means, methods, or forms, including those used in information activity, are finite. The life span of some is millennia, of others centuries, and still others prove to be one-day butterflies. It is obvious that these means, methods, and forms do not die off immediately or in one day, and sometimes for specific conditions and tasks they are preserved for a long time. For example, in spite of modern publishing technology, even today the Torah is copied only by hand; or in spite of the invention of paper, even today we see modern "graffiti" on rock faces. Of course, each of the means, methods, and forms was an element of progress in the history of humankind, which by dying away gave place to more modern counterparts that would correspond to users of their time. Thus, historically from method to method, from form to form, information activity developed. From this point of view, we will consider the modern information situation.

3.3

The Modern Information Crisis

In the first half of the 20th century, unprecedented growth of scientific activity took place. We will discuss only some indicators characterizing this growth. For example, according to UNESCO data (1973), in 1800 there were 1000 scientists in the whole world; in 1850 they already numbered 10,000; in 1900 there were 100,000; in 1950 there were 1 million; and by 1970 their number reached 3.2 million people. When the number of people occupied with scientific investigations reached 2 million people (approximately in 1960), it was estimated that more than 90% of investigators working in all epochs of human history were our contemporaries (Auger, 1963).

Because the unique responsibility of the scientist is obtaining new information, and the form of accounting is publishing this information, then it is not difficult to imagine how the flow of information circulating within the framework of information actively has increased. In 1910 approximately 13,000 journal articles and books on chemistry and chemical technology were published in the world, and 1900 books on physics were published, in 1975 these numbers were respectively 413,000 (an increase of almost 32 times) and 85,000 (an increase of almost 45 times) (Michailov, Cherny, & Gilarevski, 1976). The number of periodical scientific publications also grew continuously. In 1900 fewer than 10,000 titles of scientific-technical journals were issued, by 1980 their number exceeded 50,000. It is estimated that more than 4 million such articles are published in the world annually.

Some of the first people to perceive the negative effects of the great growth in the amount of available information turned out to be exactly those who produced this information—scientific workers. Robert Oppenheimer (one of the leading American physicists, who directed the development of the first atomic bomb) pessimistically noted that "we need new knowledge like a hole in the head" (Price, 1961). And this is how French physicist (Nobel laureate) Louis de Broglie characterizes the state of the investigator faced with the ever-increasing flow of information: "The scientific worker often feels buried under the mass of articles and monographs being issued in all corners of the globe. . . . Sinking in a never ending stream of publications, he is always risking overlooking what is the main thing" (De Broglie, 1962). "It is not ruled out that many interesting results get lost in a heap of insignificant accounts not subjected to reading," warned Norbert Wiener (1954). It is not difficult to compile a list of similar sayings, but one should not think that they are peculiar to just the 20th century.

In practically all epochs, scientists have not ceased to complain about the abundance of information. This can be confirmed by the following examples. In the library of Assyrian king Ashurbanipal (during the middle of the 7th century B.C.), there were more than 30,000 cuneiform tablets on all branches of knowledge of that time (Johnson, 1965). Historians say that by 47 B.C. the holdings of the famous Alexandrian library contained about 700,000 scrolls. Describing the unusually rapid growth of holdings at the Alexandrian library, the prominent Swiss Hellenist Andre Bonnard wrote:

> The library grew not only due to the purchase of classical works, but also due to the exceptional fruitfulness of authors of that time. One philologist, named Didymus, put together three thousand five hundred scrolls of commentary. If even then an over-extensive work usually consisted of several scrolls, then nevertheless a similar abundance seems rather formidable. The names of more than one thousand one hun-

dred Hellenistic writers are known to us, including the names of scientists and philosophers. Simply a flood! A literary catastrophe! Such an amount of literature!
(Bonnard, 1962)

Note that these expressions and exclamations of Bonnard about a book
flood belong not to the middle of the 20th century, but to the 2nd and 1st
centuries B.C. The citations, presented here indicate that already, 2000 years, ago
more manuscripts were written than one was in a position to read in an entire
lifetime. It is necessary also to consider that in those distant times, books were
accessible to only a small number of philosophers, scientists, writers, and poets.
This means that even in ancient times the ratio of the number of books to the
number of people in the literate population was quite large.

It is also interesting to mention what Bonnard called exceptional fruitful-
ness. Our contemporaries clearly hold an edge. The record holder here is probably entomologist Theodore Cockerell: in 67 years he wrote 3904 (!) articles; in
his best years 2 articles per week appeared in print.

A contemporary of Shakespeare, suggesting to him the subject of *Twelfth
Night,* writer B. Rich wrote in 1613: "One of the illnesses of our century is
the quantity of books. They have so multiplied in the world." (Price, 1966).
G. Leibnitz at the end of the 17th century noted:

With each year the number of books issued grows again, and in this connection as a
consequence of the propensity of people to novelty, bad books often force out good
ones, so that much useful information is lost and vanishes in the dense thicket of
innumerable books. (Gere, 1981)

Nobel laureate, English physicist Rayleigh wrote in 1874:

People of science must often experience a panic attack, when they contemplate the
flow of new knowledge which each year brings. . . . It seems that any new, however
significant, addition by this time to the already existing information makes this bur-
den almost unbearable. (Novikov & Egorov, 1974)

It should be said that since then the volume of scientific information has grown
hundredfold.

Thus, it is not difficult to see that there has always been "too much information." However, this has not always produced an information crisis. It was
because the forms available for information activity either were able to cope
with the existing information situation or were capable of further development
and attainment of a level capable of coping with the needs of the time. Why
then does an information crisis exist today?

First, when we say "too much information," this is an emotional rather
than a quantitative evaluation. We will try to clarify for whom or for what it is
"too much information." Does this produce a problem and, if so, what kind?
To answer these questions, consider and analyze the situation from the point of
view of an expert on methods and forms used in information activity. That way
it is possible to establish which questions lead to a dead end. To do this, these

questions can be formulated as follows: "Is it possible that there are not enough carriers of information?" No, no problems exist with the production of paper today. "Then is it possible that there exist difficulties with the publication of what is written?" Again no. Modern technology can cope with the available information flow without difficulty. "Might there exist principal difficulties with the storage of information (for example, insufficient space)?" Not so. "Is it impossible to gather information?" Again no.

It is not difficult to continue the list of questions to which negative answers can be given with certainty. However, this is unnecessary because in this case it is simpler to analyze the situation not from the point of view of experts, but from the point of view of users, which by the way, we all are. We will put the questions before the user in the following manner: "What principal information problem are you faced with today? How would you describe the main problem in dealing with information?" The answer will be unambiguous. The most acute problem is the *problem of access to information,* and one of the most important parts of this problem is the *problem of information retrieval.* This is exactly the nature of the *modern information crisis;* traditional methods and forms of information retrieval proved to be clearly unsuitable for the existing (and ever-increasing) volumes of information, as well as the rapidly growing IN of society.

It was mentioned earlier that the first people affected by the information crisis were the scientific workers themselves. Difficulty in satisfying their own IN practically forced them to search for new ways, new forms, and new methods to bring forth satisfaction and, as a consequence of this, by the middle of the 20th century a new scientific direction was established—*information science.* It should be especially stressed that we are speaking of a new direction of scientific investigations, not about a new subject of investigation. If historically various information crises have been overcome with the help of inventions, and not with the help of systematic investigations, today it is investigations that permit information activity to be refined. Practically every third publication in the area of information science is dedicated to information retrieval (Jarvelin & Vakkari, 1993).

Almost simultaneously with the rise of information science, there appeared a principally new form of satisfying IN aimed at overcoming the crisis situation connected with information retrieval. This form was the information retrieval system (IR system). In fact, it would not be an exaggeration to say that today the majority of scientific investigations in information science are devoted to the study of IR systems, and one of the main directions of study focuses on improving the quality of information service to users with the help of IR systems. Of course, this does not mean that information science is the science of creating IR systems. However, our present ability to overcome the information crisis is closely tied to the construction of effective IR systems. We say our "present" ability because in the future information crises may not be connected with information retrieval and consequently a majority of future scientific investigations may be concentrated in a different area. At this point we would like to speculate about the next information crisis.

A manifestation of a future information crisis could appear in any known forms existing in the framework of information activity, although with different probabilities. It is clear that a crisis situation will arise again as the result of, on the one hand, increasing need for information and, on the other hand, growth in the volume of information that we will not be able to process with the existing forms used to satisfy IN.

Let us ask the following question: "What will happen when we successfully overcome the present information crisis, that is, when we succeed in creating highly effective IR systems?" Then IR systems will find all the required information. Clearly, this is good. However, the increasing flood of information may lead to a situation in which an IR system, for a specific search request, will return an amount of relevant information that the user will not be able to absorb. In such a case, it is possible to talk about a crisis situation based on the physical ability of a human being to absorb a very limited amount of information. Because, clearly, the users cannot be replaced or altered, one of the possible solutions might be to create advanced expert systems capable of analytically and logically processing information, performing automatic reasoning, and so on. In other words, it is necessary to develop systems capable of helping (simplifying) the absorption of information; for example, they might, at least partially, free the user from his or her work with information or condense existing relevant information to a size acceptable to the user. Even today there are attempts to create and use expert systems in information retrieval. There is some literature on the use of automatic reasoning in IR systems and other methods developed within the framework of artificial intelligence.

The previous discussion does not necessarily mean that the next information crisis will be connected with the absorption of information. This is only an assumption, and moreover it is possible to argue against it by pointing to the natural process of the differentiation of science and of specialization: with the growth of information the users' expertise is becoming more and more narrow and hence removing from their IN bigger and bigger parts of the existing flow of information. Maybe this tendency will prevent the described scenario.

In any case let us return to the existing information crisis and mention once again that today substantial efforts in information science are devoted to solving problems connected with the search for information. However, information science has to deal with any problems related to information activity. Thus, *information science is the science of satisfaction of an IN with available information, and the subject of investigation of this science is itself an IN, as also are the means, methods, and forms of its satisfaction.* Such understanding follows from the previous discussions of IN, its nature and characteristics (see Chapter 2), because in the final analysis any information activity and any information processes are directed (and intended) precisely for satisfaction of an IN. That was the origin of information activity thousands and thousands of years ago, though the activity is constantly changing, and information retrieval is one (and currently an extremely important one) of the constituent parts of this activity.

It should be especially stressed that people have no need for search; we have a need for information. However, when we consider that we have "a lot" of information, then the problem of search usually arises. Obviously, the search, or retrieval, is one of the ancient methods used humankind to find an object by which or with the help of which it is possible to satisfy some of our existing needs. In the next section we will consider information retrieval in more detail.

3.4
Search for Information

Searching is one of the most common of human activities. In general, the phenomenon of searching is intuitively clear. Still, in spite of this it is useful to consider some of the most essential properties of this phenomenon. We are used to idioms with different meanings, such as "the search for mineral resources," "the search for defects," or "the search for improved design." Obviously in these examples, some actually existing objects or phenomena are sought. Of course, an actually existing object or phenomenon under specific conditions can be recognized and thus can be found. On the other hand, the "search for happiness," or the "search for a place in life" are well known. In these cases the objects of the search are not clearly defined, it is complicating to recognize them, and, consequently, not only is the search conducted with difficulty, but it is also difficult to determine from the result whether the search is successful.

Of course, those general properties are intuitively clear, and they permit us to combine in our consciousness various everyday, scientific, and technical situations in the concept of "search." First, it is clear that in all the situations mentioned, something or someone is found. Consequently, a search presupposes the existence of a "goal." The name of some goal is the defining addition to the word "search" in the examples described here.

Further, it is necessary to note that we do not speak about a search if within the framework of an arising need we have complete information about the required goal, and a previously known path leads to it. A search assumes motion toward a goal in the presence of a set of paths; it is a *process* unfolding in time; it is, as a rule, a repeating sequence of actions. Any reasonable search is carried out in correspondence with some plan that is a rule for choice of subsequent actions, a search *algorithm*.

Obviously the required elements of any retrieval process are recognition and choice. This means that any retrieval algorithm must include some criteria in correspondence with which recognition of the desired objects or phenomena is carried out. In fact, the choice of criteria for a search is based on the choice of a language in which the search is carried out. *Any search can be carried out only with the help of a language,* natural or artificial (for example, the language of mathematics, the language of signals, the language of form, or of color). The set of objects among which the search is carried out must be represented in the language of the search. The need for which the search is carried out also must be formulated in this language, then comparison must be carried out (by a person or a mechanism specially created for this purpose) of the set of objects with the formulated needs. Of course, the rules for comparison are determined by the language in which the objects of the search and the need are given. If as a result of the comparison some objects correspond to the chosen criterion, then these objects are considered to be found. The following example illustrates a search process.

In searching for specific edible roots, our distant ancestor determined their location, for example, by the form or color of the stem or of the leaves. Of course, our ancestor must have known the language of forms and the colors of plants. By comparing a plant (represented by an object of specific form and color) with the theoretical image of the desired plant (represented in the same language), our ancestor determined the degree of their similarity and made a choice. On the other hand, suppose that during a search for food, our ancestor tried to determine the location of an animal by its characteristic cry (quacking). In other words, the first hunter was also familiar with a specific language of sounds. However, it is obvious that the hunter did not try to formulate this need in the search for roots in the language of sounds and in the search for animals in the language of colors and forms. Our ancestors clearly understood which language was needed for which search.

Schematically any search can be represented in the form of Figure 3.1 (adapted from Salton & McGill, 1983). It is obvious that this scheme is useful in

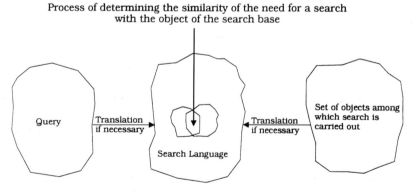

Process of determining the similarity of the need for a search with the object of the search base

Query | Translation if necessary | Search Language | Translation if necessary | Set of objects among which search is carried out

Figure 3.1

Block-diagram of the search process. Source: Adapted from G. Salton and M. J. McGill, *Introduction to Modern Information Retrieval* (New York: McGraw Hill, 1983), p. 11.

the search for edible roots, in the search for new planets in the universe, and in the search for a wife or a husband. It is useful also in the searches that interest us, particularly for *information retrieval.*

Note that the addition of the word "information" to the word "retrieval" relates to the goal of the search. In fact, because the product of satisfying an IN is information, *the goal of information retrieval is to find the information required to satisfy the IN.*

In our analysis of the concept "document," we noted that within the framework of the problems considered in the present book, in any discussions concerning information retrieval (except for those specially stipulated) we mean information contained in documents.

The notion of information retrieval has been known for a long time. Many scrolls in the Alexandrian library had titles, that is, a special element of text intended for search. By the title of a book or article, the reader can judge in the majority of cases whether this book or article will interest him or her and whether it is worth getting acquainted with in more detail. In the same library in about 250 B.C., Callimachus put together a catalog of the library's holdings— a volume of 120 scrolls. Nevertheless, in spite of ancient historical roots, even today the concept of information retrieval often causes discussion. As a rule, the discussions concentrate around the following questions: "What does it mean 'to seek information'?" "What in fact are we seeking?" In order to answer these questions we will begin considering information retrieval from the general notion of searching (see Figure 3.1).

First we recall that in our discussion the physical objects involved in information retrieval are written documents. Further, since retrieval can be carried out only in some language (natural or artificial), then the language in which the documents are written, or some other language, can be used as the search language. It is obvious that in the latter case a translation of the content of the documents into the same language in which the search is carried out is necessary. In information science, *information retrieval language* (IRL) is a language in which information during the search process is expressed and which is the basis for selection criteria. Of course, for a search process the need for information must be formulated in the same language. In this connection, assuming that any information retrieval is carried out only because the user has an information need, the need for retrieval is the result of the user recognizing the existing IN. Moreover, users who carry out the search on their own do not have to express (for example, to pronounce aloud) this recognition for outside observers. Obviously, the actual process of information retrieval involves comparing objects of the search with the need for them.

We will consider the case in which the user chooses the necessary information, that is, the case when the user carries out the comparison without outside help. How and what does the user compare in the search that is being carried out? The user reads a document, somehow interprets its content, and evaluates (compares) this content with respect to the uncertainty which is the basis of the existing IN. When the result of the interpretation has personal meaning (coincides with the existing need), the user considers that the information is found. It is not difficult to note that in this process information is in fact sought. However, this process is more complicated when the search is not carried out directly by the user but with the help of intermediaries, which can be people or mechanisms.

In this case the answers to the questions asked earlier are not so obvious. A statement by Lancaster, one of the most well-known researchers in information science, is significant. In his book *Information Retrieval Systems* (1979) he wrote, "Information retrieval is the process of searching some collection of documents." Further along he stated:

> Information retrieval is not a particularly satisfactory term to describe the type of activity to which it is usually applied. An information retrieval system does not retrieve information. Indeed, information is something quite intangible; it is not possible to see, hear, or feel it. We are 'informed' on a subject if our state of knowledge on it is somehow changed. Giving a requester a document on lasers, does not inform him on the subject of lasers. Information transfer can only take place if the user reads the document and understands it. Information, then, is something that changes a person's state of knowledge on a subject.

The complexity in the concept of the nature of information retrieval was noted also by other investigators, such well-known experts as Van Rijsbergen (1979) and Meadow (1993), and their views are similar to Lancaster's position (1979). Next we will consider the retrieval process in more detail.

We will begin with a case in which, during retrieval, the intermediary is a person. Thus, obtaining a search request from the carrier of an IN, the intermediately compares her interpretation of this request with her interpretation of the content of the collection of documents. Then, using some semantic criteria, the intermediary selects texts (communications) that are significant from her point of view, and these are considered as found. It is important to note that the procedures of comparison and choice constitute the retrieval process.

Then what is the intermediary searching? The answer would seem simple. The intermediary is searching for documents. However, we recall that a document is information fixed on some material of the carrier. Can we say that the intermediary is searching only for information fixed on the carrier or is she searching for a material of the carrier? What does the intermediary compare and what does she choose? It seems more appropriate to speak of searching for information.

In the analysis of the concept "information," it was pointed out that information is subjective. Therefore, in this case the chosen texts are not necessarily informative for the user herself. However, a retrieval is carried out only as long as it is assumed that the information chosen by the intermediary will be information for the user; that is, it will be actual information. Thus we completely agree with Lancaster, noting that as a result of information retrieval (by the intermediary), the user receives selected documents. In fact, because information "is something quite intangible," any transfer of it is possible only with the help of a carrier. In this connection, it is possible to change the carrier without changing the information, and as a rule, many would consider that we are dealing with the same document. But if without changing the carrier, the information is changed, then in the overwhelming majority of cases the document will be considered to be new.

The information character of information retrieval carried out without the participation of a person is even less obvious. For such a search, concrete material objects are compared, which can be various electrical signals, their combinations, and so on. However, one must recall that these signals are information translated into the language of signals (which in this case is also the IRL) and contained in the documents of the retrieval set as well as in the request received from the carrier of the IN. Of course, it is difficult to talk about the quality of a translation, but in a certain sense it is possible to talk about recording information, because we do not assume that during the translation into the language of signals, for example, information contained in the document is completely lost. Moreover, in this case, information retrieval is carried out exactly because preservation of the information properties of the text is assumed during translation. Still, we cannot speak with certainty about what information is being sought. Here the comparison itself and the criterion of choice are formal and have a "mechanical" character, not "intelligent" as in the preceding case. We say not "intelligent," but how can we then speak about information. If it is not information that is being sought, then what? This question frightens us more than any consequences of accepting the view that this is a search for information.

Thus, in considering information retrieval it can be noted that the complexities with its understanding are connected first of all with the nature of the concept "information" itself, and the lack of a single view on this phenomenon by various authors also causes a different interpretation of several information processes. One of them is information retrieval.

It should be pointed out that information retrieval and the perception of information by the user are not equivalent. For example, a person can perceive information communicated to him or her by some person (society) not necessarily in the process of information retrieval. However, in retrieval performed by the user we can say that these processes coincide. In any case it is not easy to distinguish them. In fact, when "something" from what is perceived (read) in the process of information retrieval acquires meaning for the user (decreases uncertainty in the behavior algorithm), then, on the one hand, the information was found by the user, whereas, on the other hand, the user perceived the information. Here it is useful to note the correct statement made by Lancaster: "Information transfer can only take place if the user reads the document and understands it." Then it is clear why it is necessary for the user to read the documents. This leads to the following fact regarding information retrieval: the retrieval performed by the intermediary always precedes the user's analysis of the documents but does not exclude it entirely. The basic advantage of any retrieval by the intermediary is that it reduces the size of the collection for user's analysis. Therefore, it is expedient to consider an IR system as the most modern form of reducing the size of the search collection to some level acceptable to the user for his or her analysis. Considering the sizes of existing collections of documents, the development of effective IR systems becomes extremely important.

3.5
Conclusion

The continuous development of information activities throughout human history encountered many crisis situations. In other words, at different stages of this development the forms existing at that time could not cope with the flow of existing information and had to give way to new forms capable of successfully functioning under new conditions. The essence of the current information crisis is well understood by researchers, which is why the development of automated IR systems became a necessity. This new form (the IR system) is designed to overcome the current information crisis by successfully satisfying IN under new conditions. Therefore, in the subsequent chapters we will consider the creation of such systems in great detail.

It should be pointed out that this object, called an IR system and intended for the realization of the automatic search for information, will be considered as a system (using an approach discussed in Chapter 1). This is done because the system's approach substantially simplifies the development of IR systems and allows us to concentrate on the quality of information service to the user. Therefore, the discussion that follows can be viewed as consisting of two parts. In the first part, we analyze the goal, function, and structure of an IR system (described in the next chapter), that is, its theoretical basis; in the second part (described in a number of subsequent chapters), we analyze the construction or concrete realization of each element of the system, that is, its practical realization. Of course, special attention is paid to the automatization of all processes in the IR system.

References

Auger, P. (1963). *Tendency in research*. UNESCO, Paris.
Bonnard, A. (1962). *Greek civilization*. Moscow: Progress.
DeBroglie, L. (1962). *Track of the science*. Moscow: Progress.
Gere, W. (1981). *Liebnitz and his time* (Vol. 2). Moscow: Progress.

Jarvelin, K., & Vakkari, P. (1993). The evolution of library and information science 1965–1985: A content analysis of journal articles. *Information Processing and Management, 29* (1).

Johnson, E. D. (1965). *A history of libraries in the western world*. New York: The Scarecrow Press.

Lancaster, F. W. (1979). *Information retrieval systems: Characteristics, testing, evaluation*. New York: John Wiley & Sons.

Meadow, C. T. (1993). Text retrieval systems. San Diego: Academic Press.

Michailov, A. I., Cherny, A. I., & Gilarevski, R. S. (1976). *Scientific communication and information*. Moscow: Nauka.

Novikov, E. A., & Egorov, V. C. (1974). *Information and scientist*. Leningrad: Nauka.

Price, D. J. (1961). *Science since Babylon*. New Haven: Yale University Press.

Price, D. J. (1966). *Small science, large science*. Moscow: Progress.

van Rijsbergen, C. J. (1979). *Information retrieval* (2nd ed.). London: Butterworths.

Salton, G., & McGill, M. J. (1983). *Introduction to modern information retrieval*. New York: McGraw Hill.

Segre, E., Enrico Fermi—Physicist (1973). Moscow, MIR.

UNESCO, Statistical Yearbook. (1973). Paris.

Wiener, N. (1954). *The human use of human beings; cybernetic and society*. Boston: Houghton, Mifflin.

Bibliographic Remarks ————————————————————

We recommend the following additional readings.

Johnson, E. D. (1965). A history of libraries in the western world. New York: The Scarecrow Press.

Price, D. J. (1961). Science since Babylon. New Haven: Yale University Press.

4

Concept of an Information Retrieval System

Introduction

Chapter 3 showed that the current information crisis is caused by the problems associated with the search for information. As the text explained, these problems are not solvable within the framework of traditional library forms of retrieval (and this is the essence of the present crisis). The development of information science was society's reaction to the crisis occurring within the sphere of informational activity.

Practically at once with the rise of information science appeared a principally new form of information retrieval, the information retrieval system (IR system). Today, hopes for a successful solution to many of the existing problems associated with satisfying information need (IN) are connected with IR systems. Within the framework of information science, an extensive literature dedicated to various aspects of creating and using the IR system has appeared. Suffice it to say that in the opinion of many investigators, today about 30% of all scientific publications in information science are directly related to IR systems (Jarvelin & Vakkari, 1993). However, in spite of the fact that "IR system" has become a common and widely used term, a rigorous, unambiguous, and widely accepted concept of it does not exist, and in various publications this concept acquires different shades of content as it correspondingly changes its scope. Such a situation in some cases not only prevents mutual understanding among the developers of IR systems but also leads to some dubious solutions in their design. Therefore in this chapter we will introduce the concept of an IR system that will be used consistently in subsequent chapters.

4.2

IR System as Object

Do a camel and an ocean liner have anything common? The question seems to be a joke for which there is an original and witty answer. However, if we place both of these objects into a certain class of transportation means, then their similarity not only does not seem strange, but it seems trivial and ordinary. A horse, a camel, an automobile, and an airplane all are clear and obvious examples of objects from this "transportation means" class. Moreover, we are certain that almost any reader can without difficulty continue this list.

Each object in the class "transportation means" has its own "name" (for example, "camel," "automobile"). If we tell someone that we used a transportation means and do not specify the name of this means, then it is not obvious to the listener which object of the class "transportation means" we used. In other words, the concept "transportation means" is collective and characterizes a whole set of objects.

This discussion of "transportation means" is important and useful for understanding some characteristics associated with the definition of the concept "IR system." The problem in understanding the meaning of the term "IR system" is based on the disagreement among different investigators: some suggest that this term denotes an object, whereas others suggest that it is intrinsic only to a class of objects, not to some concrete object.

Keep in mind the fact that the term "IR system" arose about 40 years ago, and the term was used to designate an object in which the process of seeking information through comparison and selection was carried forth without the direct participation of a person but instead was, as a rule, realized on a computer. Nevertheless some investigators rather quickly began to use the term "IR system" to designate a *class* of objects. Their position was formulated as follows: "Any system that is designed to facilitate literature searching activity may legitimately be called an information retrieval system. The subject catalog of a library is one type. So is a printed subject index" (Lancaster, 1979). In some cases the list of examples of an IR system is supplemented by such objects as a thesaurus, a telephone book, and the universal decimal classification. It is clear that under this approach an IR system appears in the role of "transportation means," that is, in the capacity of some class represented by objects created to facilitate the process of information retrieval.

Such an approach is completely legitimate, for example, in discussing the goal of different means used within the framework of informational activity. However, we note that the listed objects, for example, the traditional (manual) subject catalog in a library or a printed subject index, in themselves are not in a position to carry out a search, that is, to conduct a comparison and selection of information. They are only auxiliary means that a person might use in the process of performing comparison and selection. As a rule, these means are used when the user is attempting to retrieve the information on his or her own. In other words, *this form of the term "IR system" does not require that the system retrieve the information on its own.* In addition, it seems that objects included in the class of such IR systems and having the IR system's commonly accepted (and as a rule useful) name—such as a thesaurus—are called systems on the basis that they are related to information retrieval. Recall that an object is not a system just because it contains a collection of properties inherent in making it a system. An object can be considered a system when the investigation of its properties and characteristics is performed from the systems point of view. However, we have not seen articles using the systems approach, say, during the analysis or creation of a printed subject index.

In some situations it is assumed that an object is made into a system by having the word "system" added to its name, or because someone has already analyzed the given object from the systems point of view. For example, this explanation of the concept of an IR system is sometimes used: "an information retrieval system is an information system, which is a system . . ." (Salton & McGill (1983). This type of statement does not correspond to the concept "system" that is accepted in the systems approach (see Chapter 1).

Thus, in the present book *when we use the term "IR system" we mean an object,* and only that object, *that is in a position to carry out a retrieval of information without the participation of a human being* and only with the help of a computer. This is exactly the object—in this new form—that will help society to overcome the information crisis described in the previous chapter. This form is not a continuation and development of the previous forms used for carrying out information retrieval. An ocean liner is not a more developed camel. For this reason, the developers of IR systems were (and are) faced with many new problems within the framework of informational activity (older forms) that were not considered earlier.

In the following exposition *we will consider an IR system as a system,* that is, in the analysis of IR systems we will use principles of the systems approach. Because the development of any system begins with an exact definition of the purpose of its creation, we begin our consideration with the definition of this purpose for an IR system. After this, starting with the formulated goal, we determine the function of the system, a function that provides, as a minimum, the acceptable fulfillment of the indicated goal. Then we will consider the structure of an IR system capable of realizing the function that we formulated. The enumerated steps not only precede construction of each structural element of the system (several following chapters will be dedicated to this) but also help us to understand the object, which we call an IR system.

4.3

The Purpose of Creating an IR System

In analyzing the vital activity of a human being, we noted that one's actions are a reaction to arising (in the process of this activity) needs and are directed toward their satisfaction. Moreover, *any conscious behavior can be considered goal-oriented* (Ackoff & Emery, 1972), where, again, it is directed to satisfying existing needs. Occasionally this is not obvious, since a specific action may represent only a link in a chain of actions directed toward satisfaction of some need. However, it is important to understand that both the origination and the direction of any activity are inseparably connected with some need. Such a direction toward a need (both of actions and behavior) itself suggests some general purpose of an activity—a purpose connected with the satisfaction of an existing need. Therefore any *goal can be defined as an ideal, mental anticipation of the results of an activity,* which is, in the final analysis, directed toward satisfaction of a need.

It is obvious that we are interested not in just any need but in the need for information. Thus, an IR system is created with the goal of satisfying an IN. However, such a definition of goal seems too general and clearly does not express the specifics of an IR system. In fact, satisfaction of an IN is the goal of informational activity in general, and in a specific sense, of any other existing form within the framework of this activity. Of all forms existing in informational activity, we are considering only those that are connected with information retrieval and, more precisely, only those that are in a position to carry out retrieval without the participation of a person (automatically); therefore we will reformulate the given definition in the following manner: *IR systems are created with the goal of automatic information retrieval for satisfaction of an IN.* It is not difficult to note that the given definition agrees with the representation of an object (IR system), which was considered earlier. This is a workable definition, however, we will narrow it further and define more accurately exactly what kind of IN we will satisfy.

Thus, IR systems are aimed at the satisfaction of IN and if we want to create *something for satisfaction of some need,* then this something must take into account the properties and characteristics inherent to this satisfiable need. In Chapter 2, in consideration of the IN, we showed that the IN is not homogeneous and that it consists of various types that differ by exactly those inherent properties. Therefore, in creating an IR system, we must clearly describe for which type of IN it is intended. Moreover, we must know also the properties characterizing this type, that is, we must be able to describe for which properties of which type of IN it is intended. Thus, *for satisfaction of different types of IN the creation of different types of IR systems is necessary,* and the types of these systems are determined by the types of IN for which they are intended (Frants & Brush). We will consider this proposition in more detail.

Two examples of the different types of IN were introduced previously. POIN (problem-oriented information need) and CIN (concrete information need). Now we will consider which IR systems can be used to satisfy these types of IN (i.e., we will determine the requirements for the systems satisfying the mentioned types of IN). We first describe basic properties of the indicated types of IN, because the IR systems must take into account precisely these properties. The more completely the properties of a concrete type of IN are taken into account, the higher quality its satisfaction will be.

Recall that the properties of the types of IN under consideration were described and analyzed in the Chapter 2. POIN is characterized by the following set of properties (we will call them attributes):

1. The thematical limits of POIN are not well defined.
2. The request, as a rule, does not represent the POIN exactly.
3. POIN, as a rule, cannot be satisfied even with every pertinent[1] document existing in the system.
4. The thematical limits of POIN may change over time, and the POIN itself lasts for a long time.

For an IN of the CIN type, the following attributes were identified:

1. The thematical limits of CIN are defined exactly.
2. The request is expressed exactly, that is, it strictly corresponds to the thematical limits of the CIN.
3. For satisfaction of a CIN, as a rule, one pertinent document is sufficient.
4. After the pertinent document is found, the CIN "disappears."

We will begin our consideration of the differences in IR systems satisfying these types of IN by examining attributes 3 and 4. From these attributes for POIN, it follows that with the appearance of new information in the IR system, it is necessary to continue servicing the user, that is, to specify a cycle of reporting for each user. (It is not important what the intervals between cycles are.) Therefore, in an IR system intended for satisfaction of a POIN, the necessity arises for storage (for subsequent searches) of information about the POIN (for example, requests or their translations into the retrieval language) of each user. Such cyclic service is usually called *selective dissemination of information* (*SDI*). From these attributes (3 and 4) for a CIN, it follows that it is not necessary to have several cycles of reporting to the user when an IR system is intended for satisfaction of the CIN. Consequently, in such a system it is not necessary to store the information about the CIN and to organize SDI. From attribute 3 it also follows that IR systems intended for satisfaction of a CIN may provide the users with only one document for each given request. However, in an IR system created for satisfaction of a POIN, it is necessary to give users all documents found.

Perhaps more essential differences between systems follow from consideration of attributes 2 and 4. Taking into account only these attributes signifies that in systems designed to satisfy POIN, we need some mechanism that will permit the decrease of discrepancy between the POIN and its representation in

---

[1] A document is called pertinent if from the point of view of the user it satisfies (partially or completely) his or her information need. For more details on pertinence, see Chapter 5.

the system, whereas in an IR system satisfying a CIN, such a mechanism is not necessary. We will establish in more detail why attributes 2 and 4 require the existence of a special mechanism (for the case of POIN).

From the analysis of attribute 2, as indicated in the Chapter 2, various relations between a request and a need are known. This means that, as a rule, information about a POIN introduced into the system does not exactly represent it, since the request is simply some information about the POIN, somehow (possibly successfully) reflecting the POIN. Because IR systems are created with the purpose of satisfying an IN, and in this case the POIN, it is possible to make the following plausible assumption: an information retrieval for satisfaction of a POIN will be more successful as it is more precisely represented in the system.

This is only one of the reasons indicating the necessity of the previously mentioned mechanism for taking into account discrepancies in IR systems satisfying POIN. Even when the request ideally reflects the POIN and there is no discrepancy between them, after one iteration in providing the user with results from the search, the need can change somewhat (attribute 4), for example, under the influence of information obtained in the previous iteration. This change could be small enough so that the user does not feel it necessary to reformulate the request. It is obvious that in this case again the necessity arises for a mechanism to decrease the indicated discrepancy, and attribute 4 of POIN creates the need to decrease the discrepancy by a permanent process of iterative character.

The presence or absence of the previously mentioned mechanism in essence means the presence or absence of feedback in the system (which will be considered later in the analysis of the structure of a system), and the above description briefly explains its required use in systems intended for satisfaction of POIN. In systems satisfying CIN, there is no reason to use feedback; consequently, feedback, as a rule, is not used in such systems.

Thus, we have considered some aspects of the influence of types of IN on the construction of IR systems. These aspects indicate the cardinal differences in systems and also the importance of taking into account the properties of distinct types of IN for the construction of effective IR systems created for the satisfaction of different types of IN. We wrote "created for the satisfaction of different types of IN." This statement reflects reality, because in practice, the types of IR systems created for the *satisfaction of CIN* are usually called *factographic*. On the other hand, the types of IR systems created for the *satisfaction of POIN* are called *documentary.* Theoretically it is possible to create a system satisfying all types of IN. It is clear that such systems first must take into consideration the properties (occasionally contradictory) of those types of IN for which they are created and second, must have a mechanism capable of recognizing which type of IN is represented by the request entered into the system.

In this book we will consider only the type of systems intended for satisfaction of POIN: documentary IR systems. Now, after this refinement, we again can reformulate the goal of the creation of IR systems, specifically documentary systems. Thus, *documentary IR systems are created with the goal of automatic information retrieval for the satisfaction of a POIN.*

Now we can proceed with the formulation of the function of the system, in particular of a documentary IR system.

4.4

Function of a Documentary IR System

To determine the function of a documentary IR system, we are interested in the function of the entire system as a whole—not the functions of its separate parts. We recall that this function is usually called the *whole* or *external* function of the system (Ackoff & Emery, 1992). It is convenient to consider the whole function as a description of requirements to the system's output directed toward satisfaction of the goal according to which motion is carried out in the system as well as by how elements of the system interact.

Generally speaking, formulation of the function is necessary during the creation of any new system. In those cases when we are creating another copy of a known system and we are satisfied with the function of this system, a new function need not be determined. For example, if we want to create a new model of automobile, we do not need to redefine the function of an automobile. In this case we will propose only a new solution, which will allow us to better fulfill a known function. Sometimes the known function of a system may not satisfy the developers because it does not fully satisfy the goal of the system. In other words, even if the function of the system is fully realized, the quality of achievement, determined by how completely the function fulfills its goal, may not satisfy the developers. For this reason, it is possible to formulate another function leading to a better satisfaction of the goal.

We will consider some requirements for the formulation of the function. Because the function is formulated starting from the purpose of the system's creation, and it is assumed that the system realizing this function enables the achievement of the mentioned goal, then in this way, directly or indirectly, the function must include some conditions providing for achievement of the goal. It would seem that the simplest solution is to begin with the requirement of ideal achievement of the goal, as this would satisfy all those who need this system. However, the function of a system is not simply the formulation for the accompanying documentation. The process of creating a system following the function definition is the process of realizing the function. Starting from this, first note that it is often impossible to formulate the "ideal" with respect to the achievement of a specific goal satisfying a given need. For example, even in the satisfaction of our own need for food (about which it seems we should know all, completing this process daily, and more than once), we cannot with absolute certainty say what quantity, what products, in what combination, and at what interval we will need food at each concrete moment for the maximal positive effect with respect to our personal health and, consequently, for maximal lengthening of life (survival). Second, there are often no necessary resources (products) for an ideal satisfaction of a need. For example, if for the satisfaction of an IN using a collection of documents in an existing IR system, the required document is not present or the necessary information has not yet been extracted from nature with the help of science, then the necessary resource is unavailable and the IN cannot be ideally satisfied. Finally, we are often not in a position (i.e., the level of knowledge, ability, technology, etc., is insufficient) to create a system that will ideally achieve the goal. All these points are important, because it is meaningless to formulate the function of a system that will be impossible to create. For this reason, during the creation of a system, the function appears in the role of a technical specification with an indication of a specific quality, achievement of which is required for fulfillment of the function. Moreover, the system that is assumed successful is only that system which fulfills the formulated function (saying that it "successfully functions"), where the stability of fulfillment of the function becomes one of the main indicators of the quality of the system's operation.

The quality of achievement of the goal determined by the function must be acceptable to the system's user. But what does the acceptable quality of satisfaction of a POIN mean from the point of view of the carrier of POIN (the user)? In fact, exactly this quality (at minimum) must be included into the goal function of the documentary IR system. It is extremely difficult (if at all possible) to give a complete set of parameters and their exact values indicating "acceptable quality." So, how do we define "acceptable quality"? As an answer to this question, the following approach, for example, can be used.

It is clear that any user during his or her life has constantly satisfied a POIN and is familiar with different methods and ways to satisfy POIN. The IR system that will be used to replace other methods must be somewhat better than the alternative methods available to the user. Of course, the creators of a system understand those difficulties and the quality with which the user is dealing, if only because they themselves are users. In fact, for this reason, during the formulation of a function, we take into account some parameters of goal achievement (parameters that we think are essential for the user), and we assume it at least exceeds those indicators of these parameters that are inherent to alternative (accessible to the user) methods.

The preceding approach describes the minimally acceptable level for developing an IR system. This approach is especially expedient for creation of a principally new system, because formulation of a function "at minimum" often facilitates (simplifies) realization of the system. However, this is only one possible approach. It is also possible to develop an IR system starting from the ideal (maximal) by relaxing the requirements and "removing oneself" from the ideal just so far as to be able to physically realize the system. In our case, when we speak about relaxation we mean relaxation in the requirements in the quality of different properties of POIN. This approach requires constant analysis of the possibility of realizing the formulated function; otherwise (i.e., in the case when its realization does not appear possible), one must reformulate the function by further removing it from the desired ideal.

A rather well-known example of a function "at minimum" formulated for a documentary IR system is the following: "the function of any IR system (even if this is only the librarian in a village library) consists in determination of the location of information and extraction of it from the place of storage" (Meadow, 1973). We will analyze this function, as it is of definite interest. First, we will turn our attention to the remark included in parentheses, "the function of any IR system (even if this is only a librarian)." It is not difficult to note that in this definition an IR system is a class of objects carrying out a search, and an object such as a librarian is called an IR system only because a search is carried out by him or her. It is clear as well that in this connection the librarian is not considered a system (i.e., none of the investigators who call the librarian an IR system created the librarian with the use of the systems approach). However, if we omit the remark concerning the librarian, the function is completely admissible for the object called a documentary IR system.

What is required from a system realizing this function? Obviously the system must determine the location of information (the system's storage) and extract it from the place of storage. And that is all. If the system performs this, then the function is being fulfilled. In other words, whatever information the system extracts, it is fulfilling its function. This in fact is the minimum quality, if by this we mean the correspondence of the information found to the user's POIN. Moreover, this minimum can be significantly worse than the usual level achieved by the user, such as when all extracted information is not actual information for the user (it is obvious that even then the system fulfills the formulated function). However, and this is important, in the formulated function, what is taken into account is not the correspondence of the found information to the POIN, but another parameter extremely important in light of the modern information crisis. This is the parameter taking into account the possibility of determining the location of information and extracting it from any storage accessible to the system. Thus, a system satisfying the formulated function must "find" and "extract" information from some collection(s) of documents. Of course, when this collection consists of a thousand documents (not to mention hundreds of thousands and even millions), then a system fulfilling the formulated function would clearly outperform a person, because traditional methods assuming the participation of a person in a search would be practically useless. That is why we speak about a crisis of forms, and in fact an IR system satisfying the function just described permits us to deal successfully with the crisis.

Note that for realization of such a function on a computer, the retrieval scheme illustrated in Figure 3.1 was completely suitable. In fact, that is the general structure of practically all systems that appeared during the first decade in the development of IR systems.

Thus, the initial stage when a function was realized "at minimum" was compensated by the possibility of carrying out the process of retrieval directly on a computer. However, in due time the creators of IR systems began to stress the correspondence between the found (extracted) information and the POIN. The highest priority was given to the parameters characterizing satisfaction of the user's POIN. Now the attention of investigators was concentrated in the direction of creating a structure that would permit improvement of the values of these parameters, including all those elements of the IR system that were sufficient for realization of the indicated function. Clearly this gave positive results. However, some of the properties of POIN were not considered. For example, a feedback mechanism (which takes into account attributes 2 and 4 of POIN) was lacking. It is interesting to note that authors who first attempted (in the 1960s) to realize the user's feedback pointed out that feedback "may prove useful" or "may improve results of a search," but until the 1970s no one said that it was necessary.

Hence, a new function that took into account important properties of POIN was being formulated, a function that would "at maximum" lead to the better satisfaction of POIN. But what does a "maximum" applied to information retrieval mean? What is the best for which we can really aim and which can we really achieve? If by this we mean being absolutely successful in all respects, then executing an absolutely successful information retrieval is obviously not possible, because not all the parameters characterizing the search are known, and it is also unknown whether we have the best values and whether it is possible in general to obtain simultaneously the best values of all these parameters. Thus, ideal information retrieval is not possible. Therefore we will take a step down from the ideal, and instead of ideal retrieval we will consider an *optimal retrieval*—the secret goal of any retrieval (and apparently of the majority of known processes in general) toward which all developers are striving. An optimal retrieval is the maximum that will not raise objections of any user.

We recall that by definition the concept "optimal" assumes the best of what is possible within the framework of the considered system. To find this "best" we need to choose among the "available" (possible) alternatives. In speaking about the optimal retrieval of information, we assume that for an IR system, the best possible state—among the set of its possible states—is the one in which the result of a search will be best from the point of view of the user. But is it really possible to create an IR system realizing optimal retrieval? To answer this question, we will consider what in fact is necessary for creating such a system. It is first necessary to have a choice of various methods or algorithms for at least one of the processes participating in information retrieval (see Figure 3.1) and influencing the results of the search. This is not a problem because due to the explosion of information science today we in fact have a set of methods and algorithms for all processes participating in retrieval. But the existence of these methods is still insufficient for creating an "optimal" IR system. It is also necessary to know how to choose the best of the available methods or set of methods. This problem was solved at the beginning of the 1980s when a simple criterion was developed for evaluating different methods in a search process. Hence, it is possible to create IR systems that realize optimal search. We can formulate the function of a documentary IR system as follows: *the function of a documentary information retrieval system is to fulfill an optimal, from the user's point of view, retrieval of information to satisfy this user's POIN with any information about the user's POIN given to the system* (Voiskunskii & Frants, 1974; Frants, 1986).

It should be pointed out that the requirement about "any information" about the user's POIN is a consideration of attribute 2 of POIN (Chapter 2); in other words, this means that regardless of how well the request is stated, the user must obtain optimal output from the system. Attribute 4 is also taken into consideration because the optimization will require a feedback process and the change in the user's POIN will be accounted for. The function also provides for the highest quality output because only the best output (out of all possible outputs of a system) is given to each user. In Chapter 9 we will consider in detail how this is carried out in the description of the mechanism realizing the optimization.

Having defined the function of a documentary IR system, we can consider its structure. In the following section we will determine what kind of system structure enables realization of the formulated function. In this connection, we will use the term "information" as it is accepted in the systems approach.

4.5

Structure of a Documentary IR System

In considering the general rules for creating systems, it was suggested that to define the structure of a system we in essence provide a set of elements necessary to fulfill the formulated function and establish an interconnection between them. From the definition of the concept "system" it follows that only those elements that are essential to fulfilling the given function must enter into this set. But how do we choose those elements that are needed for realization of the function? First, we note that all of the known functions of an IR system contain the requirement of realizing the process of information retrieval. Moreover, as indicated previously, a function formulated "at minimum" contains only this requirement. Therefore, at the beginning it is expedient to consider the structure of a system fulfilling a "minimal" function, that is, a system carrying out the retrieval.

A general scheme of any retrieval was considered in detail in Chapter 3

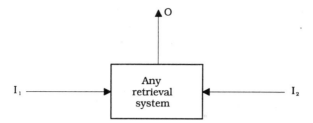

Figure 4.1
System for the retrieval of objects.

and is graphically represented in Figure 3.1. One should especially emphasize that, independent of what we are in reality seeking, in any retrieval system there must be two inputs from the external environment; in fact, the system must admit objects of retrieval (input 1) and the requirements for retrieval (input 2). The output of such a system consist of the objects found (chosen) in the process of retrieval. For example, in a retrieval system realized for selecting eggs of specific size on a bird farm, one input consists of the eggs collected at the farm (objects of retrieval) and the second input includes instructions on their size (retrieval requirements). The output in this system will be some set of selected eggs whose size corresponds to the given instructions. Thus, it is convenient to represent any retrieval system graphically in the following form (see Figure 4.1).

On the other hand, it is not difficult to see that this representation of a retrieval system on the whole is identical to the block diagram of the general process of retrieval given in Figure 3.1, and in essence it is itself a "black box," with two inputs and one output. Because in this book we are interested specifically in information retrieval, further discussions of this "black box" will exemplify only IR systems. Such a system is represented in Figure 4.2 in somewhat more standard (for a "black box") form.

We will consider Figure 4.2 in somewhat more detail. In analyzing the process of information retrieval (Chapter 3), we showed that the object of retrieval in an IR system is information contained in a document. Consequently, documents appear as input 1 of this system. We also stated that the requirement for such a retrieval is formulated by a user and represents information about the IN of the user as he or she determined it to be. Thus, as a rule, search requests

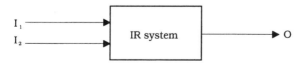

Figure 4.2
IR system in the form of a "black box."

of the user appear as input 2 of the IR system. We wrote "as a rule" because in some cases in an IR system, instead of search requests, by which we usually mean the expression by users of their IN in a natural language (see Chapter 2), other forms of retrieval requirements are used. For example, users have to formulate (for input into the system) the retrieval requirement in retrieval language, that is, the expression of an existing IN in an information retrieval language (IRL) different from natural language. The output in an IR system is the set of documents found during the search, which is usually called the *output*.

When we say that a system fulfills its function (or that it functions), we mean that the system (i.e., the complex of interacting elements) carries out a process, as a result of which the goal of creation of the system is achieved with the quality stipulated in the function. In order to see the process of functioning of an IR system, and thus the complex of interacting elements composing it, it is necessary to peek into the so-called black box illustrated in Figure 4.2. Naturally in the process of the functioning of the black box, the transformation of inputs 1 and 2 into the output takes place.

Documents and search requests enter the system through inputs 1 and 2, respectively. Documents entering at input 1 are translated (if this is necessary) into the language of the IR system, that is, into the IRL used for the retrieval. This operation is called *indexing of documents*. The result of the translation of the document into the IRL, which will be used for comparison and selection, is called a *document profile*. Search requests entering at input 2 are also translated into the IRL, and this process is called indexing, that is, *indexing of search requests*. The result obtained in this translation (in the retrieval language) is called *query formulation*. It is clear that the processes of indexing (of documents and search requests) precede the processes of retrieval (i.e., comparison of query formulations with the available document profiles, selection of the document profiles according to some criteria, and the formulation of the output). Thus, processes of indexing and the process of retrieval are integral parts of the functioning of the IR system as represented in Figure 4.2. Moreover, these processes are completely sufficient for realization of a function "at minimum." Therefore we "open" the black box and represent the structure of this system in Figure 4.3.

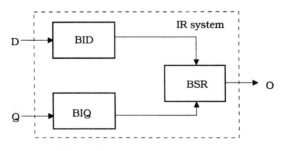

Figure 4.3
Enlarged block diagram of an IR system.

The illustrated structure contains three elements forming the system. The element BID (block of indexing of documents) is used to translate documents from the natural language into the IRL. The element BIQ (block of indexing of search requests) is used to translate search requests into IRL. The results of indexing (translations) enter the element BSR (block of storage and retrieval) in which a search for information is performed. The arrows indicate flows of information circulating in the system (interactions between elements).

One should note that in some cases this structure can be simplified. Although it seems that the diagram is already as simple as possible, it can be simplified even more, such as when any text of a document in a system is considered a document profile. It might seem that this takes place only when a natural language is used as the IRL (which is not feasible for IR systems today and which will be considered in more detail in Chapter 5). However, in practice, within the framework of the IRL of such systems, any text is considered the final set of words from the dictionary of the IRL, where, as a rule, the order of words in the text and punctuation marks are not taken into account. We call such systems *free text searching*. Simplification is also possible when the user sends a query formulation into the system instead of sending a search request. It is clear that in the first case there is no need for the indexing of documents, and in the second case there is no need for the indexing of search requests.

The structure illustrated in Figure 4.3 is realized in many actual systems and is well known in the scientific literature. However, as indicated previously, in the function of this system there are no explicit requirements for the quality of information retrieval. Clearly this does not mean that the creators of systems realizing this function do not care about the quality of satisfaction of the IN.

After the appearance of the first IR systems, the euphoria caused by the ability to use the computer in the process of information retrieval disappeared rather quickly. From the beginning there was a general tendency to improve the quality of the service to users. This led to the introduction of various parameters by which quality was evaluated, and improvement of these parameters became one of the most important concerns of investigators. Much work has been done in recent decades aimed at improving IRL, developing better methods of indexing documents and search requests, and finding more efficient methods of storage and information retrieval. This work provided positive results, and in due time we may expect further improvement in these various aspects. However, the general structure of an IR system as illustrated in Figure 4.3, in principle, is not able to give high-quality results in satisfying POIN, because it is unable to take into account the extremely important properties of POIN. In other words, it is not sufficient to create the high-quality elements of a system. It is necessary for the system's structure itself (i.e., the set of interrelated elements) to correspond to requirements of providing quality service to users. It is clear then that a function that takes into account the quality of satisfaction of POIN must be realized. Such a function was formulated earlier. The requirement contained in it for carrying out an optimal retrieval is the requirement of taking into account the quality of service to the user, and it points to the necessary existence within the structure of the system of an element fulfilling this requirement. Moreover, because optimization is one of the tasks of control, it is necessary to consider a documentary IR system as a controllable system (Frants & Shapiro, 1991). We recall that in a controllable system an indispensable condition of any optimization is the existence of feedback. Consequently, the requirement of carrying out optimal information retrieval assumes the necessary existence of the element of feedback in the structure of a documentary IR system. The necessity of the existence of feedback in the system also follows from another important factor implied from the definition of the function of a documentary IR system. This factor is the following condition: it is not the information need in general that must be optimally satisfied, but specifically the POIN of the user. In other words, in the realization of the function of a documentary IR system it is necessary to consider the properties of POIN.

In analyzing the influence of types of IN on the types of IR systems, it was pointed out that consideration of attributes 2 and 4 of POIN assumes existence in an IR system of a mechanism that decreases the discrepancy between the user's existing POIN and its representation in the system. It was mentioned that feedback must be used for realization of this mechanism. However, we did not dwell on why feedback is necessary in this case. Therefore we will discuss this in detail.

We will consider a case in which users' search requests enter the system. This is not only the most frequently encountered but also the most expedient situation, which will be considered in detail in Chapter 7. We recall that attribute 2 of POIN tells us that, as a rule, the system receives information that does not reflect POIN precisely; that is, the information contained in a search request does not correspond to POIN exactly. However, now, after our consideration of BIQ in Figure 4.3, we can say that there is also another source that causes the system to use imprecise information about POIN in its retrieval process. The issue is that inside the system the user's search request is translated from a natural language into an IRL (if the IRL is distinct from the natural language). Today in documentary IR systems, different methods of indexing search requests are used (or, as it is often said, different methods of constructing query formulations), but all of the methods are far from the ideal. Given the same search request each of the methods may (and most often does) result in a different query formulation, which will represent the actual POIN of the user differently in the system. Because retrieval of information is carried out on the basis of the constructed query formulation in the system, the output, generally speaking, corresponds to some hypothetical POIN represented by the query formulation and not to the actual POIN of the user (Frants & Shapiro, 1993).

We will illustrate what we have just said with the help of Venn diagrams. In Figure 4.4(a), region A represents the actual POIN of a user. (By actual we mean in fact a POIN that must be satisfied as a result of a search.) In Figure 4.4(b), a

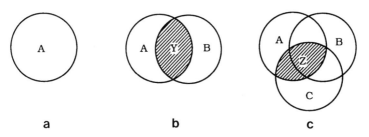

Figure 4.4
Example of the discrepancy between actual POIN and its representation in the user's search request and IR system.

new region B represents the expressed POIN given in the user's search request. In other words, by formulating a search request, the user "shows" the system the need that in some way corresponds to A; that is, the user thinks that he expresses A, although he actually expresses B. Area Y (the intersection of A and B) shows which part of the actual POIN was given to the system. In Figure 4.4(c), a new region C is introduced, which represents the satisfied POIN, that is, the POIN that will be satisfied by the system's output. Area Z (the intersection of A and C) shows which part of the actual POIN was satisfied.

But the system's goal is to satisfy the actual POIN (represented by A). Hence, after the output satisfying region C is obtained, it is necessary to have some mechanism to determine the existence and the level of discrepancy between A and C. Afterward, this mechanism will generate controlling signals to change the system's state so that the system's next output will correspond more closely to the actual POIN. But the mechanism minimizing the difference between the action's goal and its result is feedback in its general form (see the definition for feedback in Chapter 1). Hence, to generate controlling signals we need to use the feedback mechanism. Thus, the necessity of control with the help of feedback follows also from the requirement to closely match regions A and C.

The character of control in this case is different from optimization, which is a special case of adaptation. But what kind of control is it? We will consider this question in more detail.

It is known that in control systems, four basic types of control problems are addressed: stabilization, program control, monitoring, and adaptation. Hence, in discussing control systems the following terminology is used: "systems of stabilization," "systems of program control," "servo systems," and "adaptive systems." The most complicated type of control is adaptation, and that is exactly the type of control that is characteristic for a documentary IR system. Why should an IR system be considered an adaptive system?

Adaptation is the process of change in the system that allows it to obtain the best or at least acceptable level in the system's operation under changing conditions. Attribute 4 of POIN indicates that the system is functioning when region A (the actual POIN) is constantly changing and, as we mentioned earlier, the system must satisfy this changing POIN. Unfortunately, the dynamics of changing the actual POIN is not known; hence, it is impossible to obtain an analytic expression (say, a function) of POIN change in time (otherwise it would be possible to use program control). In other words, the documentary IR system is trying to satisfy actual POIN without precise knowledge about the POIN (attribute 2) and with unpredictable changes occurring in its boundaries (attribute 4). Furthermore, we also cannot assign to the system some theoretically best state for which search would be optimal at a given moment of time (in this case it would be possible to use a servo system), because information about the given state cannot be introduced earlier into the system (there is no information for this), nor obtained in the process of its operation during formation of the output (there is no information for this). This is exactly the type of situation where the problem of adaptation arises. One should especially emphasize that we are speaking about control in a system and adaptive attributes of the system. In other words, we are speaking about the adaptation of the system to the user (to the user's actual POIN) and not about adaptation of the user to the system.

Thus, the properties of POIN and the requirement of giving the user optimal output assume that a mechanism of adaptation exists in the system; that is, it means that a documentary IR system is an adaptive system. The mechanism of adaptation in an IR system in essence solves two problems. First, by choosing the best state of the system, the mechanism provides the best output for the user, even when the quality of the request is low. (It is clear that in this case the best answer may not satisfy the user.) Second, the system adapts to a changing POIN even when the system is in the best state for a given user. In other words, if the first problem is with optimization, and this problem assumes that only one choice of the state (best) of the system will be sufficient for further service of an individual user, then the second task is the problem of carrying out iterative retrievals and correction of the discrepancy before each iteration. The second problem must be solved after the first and it must be solved more than once. We especially emphasize that, in addition to the discrepancy, the second problem takes into account the iteration requirement following from attributes 3 and 4 of POIN. In fact, attribute 3 implies that even when we give the user all pertinent documents available in the system, as a rule the POIN will not be completely satisfied, and in some cases it may grow. Therefore, a consideration of attribute 3 indicates the usefulness of SDI, which is the form of iteration when the collection of documents changes; and a consideration of attribute 2 indicates the usefulness of the iterative searches for a constant collection of documents. Attribute 4 of POIN points to its change over time and again signifies the necessity for iterations. In the following, when we talk of "adaptation" we will have the second problem in mind.

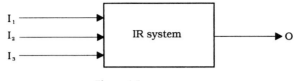

Figure 4.5
Documentary IR system.

Now that we already know that a documentary IR system must include a mechanism of feedback, we will consider the structure of this system. In Figure 4.5, a documentary IR system is represented in the form of a black box.

Notice that in this system there are already not two, but three inputs. Inputs 1 and 2 are already known to us, because they were considered in our earlier discussion (see Figure 4.2); and input 3 is used to enter information for the mechanism of feedback. This information is the reaction of the user to the output obtained from the system. (Incidentally, we note that in adaptive systems, information for control originates, as a rule, from the object to which the system is adapting.) On the basis of information obtained by the system through the feedback line, the following occurs:

1. The system is transformed into the best state (optimization).
2. The system is adapting to the imprecise representation of the user's POIN.

Since a documentary IR system is a control system, and any control system consists of an object of control and a mechanism of control, in Figure 4.6 the documentary IR system is represented as a control system.

The mechanism of control is the mechanism of feedback, consisting in turn of a mechanism that optimizes retrieval and adaptation to POIN. If the

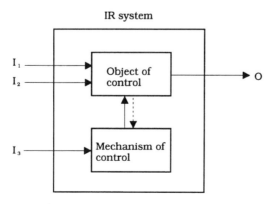

Figure 4.6
Documentary IR system as a control system.

Mechanism of control

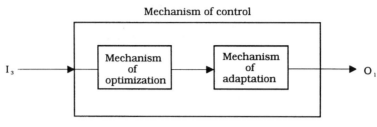

Figure 4.7
Block diagram of the control structure.

output given to the user was the union of outputs obtained during different states of the system, then the user's initial reaction to the output provided by the system initiates the mechanism of optimization. Only after this mechanism transforms the system into the best state does the mechanism of adaptation begin to operate. When the output is formulated by only one state of the system, the reaction of the user to this output does not include a mechanism of optimization; it is immediately transferred to the mechanism of adaptation. Thus, reaction to the output originates in the mechanism of adaptation through the mechanism of optimization. An enlarged block diagram of the control structure is given in Figure 4.7.

It is clear that information about which states formulated the output originates in the control structure, not from the user; but it is communicated within the system from the object of control (see the dotted line in Figure 4.6). However, what is the object of control; that is, what is it necessary to control?

First, we note that control in any system influences the output of the system. In our case, the result is the output of a documentary IR system. Thus, the object of control must contain all those elements that affect the formulation of the output, because controlling actions on any of its elements can cause it to change. Earlier we showed that for formulation of the output, it is necessary to carry out information retrieval, and that the system represented in Figure 4.2 is able to fulfill this retrieval completely. Thus, what Figure 4.2 represents as a retrieval system is only a subsystem of a documentary IR system and is its object of control. This is why inputs 1 and 2 belong to the object of control, and input 3 belongs to the mechanism of control. Because the structure of a subsystem, the object of control, is represented in Figure 4.3, the structure of a documentary IR system is shown in more detail in Figure 4.8.

It is possible to control (i.e., to change in an oriented way) the output of a system, by acting either on each of the elements of the object of control or on any combination of these elements. Because this depends on the construction of the system chosen by its creators, the controlling actions in Figure 4.8 are shown by dotted lines.

Thus, we have defined the structure of a documentary IR system, taking

[handwritten marginal note, left margin:] Control of process! not object (Q.&D) input

[handwritten note, bottom:]
1. Feedback control on query formulation.
2. Feedback control on retrieving process.
3. Feedback control on doc indexing ???

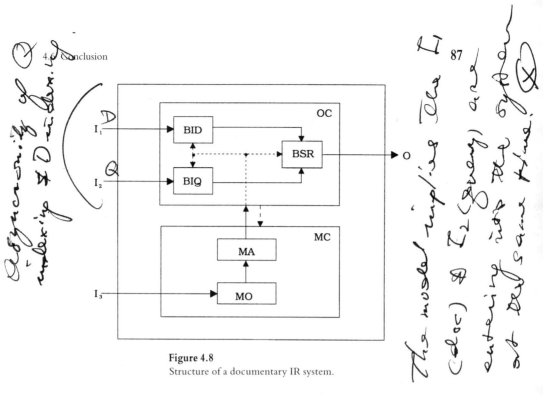

Figure 4.8
Structure of a documentary IR system.

into account the requirements of its predefined function, that is, accounting for the properties of POIN and optimal service to the user. In all of the discussions that follow, we will deal exclusively with documentary IR systems, and for simplicity we will drop the word "documentary" from its name.

4.6

Conclusion

In this chapter we discussed the notion of an IR system, which is necessary for all steps in its development. Detailed analysis of the goal of an IR system allows us to formulate its function, which assumes optimal service for each individual user in the framework of a given system. In formulating the function of an IR system, we took into account, as much as possible, the properties of IN. This is important because the quality of any IR system depends on how fully these properties are taken into account. Moreover, discovering new properties of IN (in our case, properties of POIN) and then finding ways to use them in developing IR systems are only some of the more promising directions toward the improvement of IR systems.

On the basis of formulated function, which plays a role of certain "specification," and also using general properties of any search process, we considered the structure of an IR system. The structure described in this chapter is aimed toward the formulated (in this book) function and developing this structure is a necessary step before constructing individual elements of the system. Because every element of the system represents some process, the construction of an element requires finding some method of realizing this process. It should be pointed out that in constructing an IR system it is necessary not only to have its structure but also to have an information retrieval language. This issue is discussed in Chapter 5.

References

Ackoff, R. L., & Emery F. E. (1972). *On purposeful systems*. Chicago and New York: Aldine, Atterton.

Frants, V. I. (1986). *Soviet automated information retrieval*. Washington, DC: Delphic Associates.

Frants, V. I., & Brush, C. B. (1988). The need for information and some aspects of information retrieval systems construction. *Journal of the American Society for Information Science, 39*, 86–91.

Frants, V. I., & Shapiro, J. (1991). Control and feedback in a documentary information retrieval system. *Jasis, 42*(9), 623–634.

Frants, V. I., Shapiro, J., & Kamenoff, N. I. (1993). One approach to clarification of users and automatic clustering of documents. *Information Processing and Management, 29*(2).

Jarvelin, K., & Vakkari, P. (1993). The evolution of library and information science 1965–1985: A content analysis of journal articles. *Information Processing and Management, 29*(1).

Lancaster, F. W. (1979). *Information retrieval systems: Characteristics, testing, evaluation*. New York: John Wiley & Sons.

Meadow, C. T. (1973). Analysis of information systems (2nd ed.). New York: John Wiley & Sons.

Salton, G., & McGill, M. J. (1983). *Introduction to modern information retrieval*. New York: McGraw Hill.

Voiskunskii, V. G., & Frants, V. I. (1974). Function and development of documentary information retrieval systems. *Automated Systems and Computers*, (5).

Bibliographic Remarks

The following references contain discussions dealing with the theoretical aspects of goal, function, and structure of IR systems.

Ackoff, R. L., & Emery F. E. (1972). *On purposeful systems*. Chicago and New York: Aldine, Atterton.

Frants, V. I. (1986). *Soviet automated information retrieval*. Washington, DC: Delphic Associates.

Frants, V. I., & Shapiro, J. (1991). Control and feedback in a documentary information retrieval system. *Jasis, 42*(9), 623–634.

Lancaster, F. W. (1979). *Information retrieval systems: Characteristics, testing, evaluation*. New York: John Wiley & Sons.

Salton, G., & McGill, M. J. (1983). *Introduction to modern information retrieval*. New York: McGraw Hill.

5

Information Retrieval Language

Introduction

It is only natural that the necessity of creating an IR system has led researchers to the study of the information retrieval phenomenon itself, its nature and its characteristics. This is why in Chapter 3 we reviewed the general characteristics of any retrieval process, including information retrieval. We also noted in that chapter that any retrieval is possible only through the use of a language (natural or artificial), and languages used in the retrieval of information are called information retrieval languages (IRL). Thus, in creating any new form of information retrieval, it is necessary not only to select an IRL but to clearly understand that the form itself (its constructive embodiment) depends a great deal on the chosen IRL. For this reason, in Chapter 5 we review IRLs that are usually used in a new form of information retrieval, specifically the IR system. However, before discussing IRLs used in the IR system, we will try to answer several general questions that are not so much of a constructive nature but of the ideological one.

The first question can be formulated as follows: Is it necessary to create a special IRL if there are natural languages successfully being used by people? In other words, why not use a natural language as the IRL in creating an IR system. To answer that question let's briefly review the evolution of the retrieval methods and languages used in retrieval in order to clarify some notions related to natural language and its use in retrieval.

5.2

Languages and Methods of Information Retrieval

In fact, everything started with the retrieval of information using a natural language. During the dawn of the formation of the first storages for manuscripts (or the first libraries), ancient users of information found needed texts by reading every document in the collection themselves and, in that manner, found (if they found it) the document they needed. But reading manuscript after manuscript, even in those times when the amount of information (documents) was immeasurably smaller, was tiring and took a long time. That is why, even then, the first means (methods) appeared aimed at making the retrieval easier for the users. Undoubtedly, one of the first means (and possibly the first) was the creation of catalogs, which at first constituted a simple list of all the documents in a collection. The use of catalogs during a search frees users from the need to read the documents themselves; instead the required documents were retrieved using an existing list and again a natural language.

Humankind has accumulated at least four thousand years of experience in preparing catalogs. The insignificant amount of evidence accessible to study the catalogs of the ancient world provides us with only the most general idea of the ways of cataloging of that time. The most ancient of the preserved catalogs, a list of documents, was discovered on a Sumerian clay plate (approximately 2000 B.C.). More than 60 titles of compositions were written on both sides of this small plate, which was only a little larger than a matchbox in size. Since at that time compositions did not have headings, the first lines of the text were recorded. Of course, the first lines of the text did not always provide enough information for the user to determine whether he needed the document or not. However, the idea in this type of approach was extremely important, because it allowed one to review not the text itself, but its representative.

The next development in this direction was the use of headings. For example, headings were contained in the texts found on plates from the library of the Assyrian czar Ashurbanikal in Ninevia (7th century B.C.). In fact, the introduction of headings in manuscripts was in essence an attempt to lessen the amount of time needed to review the documents by way of a brief formulation (i.e., a compression) of the main subject of a written work. Retrieval by the use of headings, of course, also made use of a natural language. Although this was a faster method of retrieval compared to that which used the full texts of the manuscripts, it was not a convenient one, for in this case the reader anticipated a direct review of all documents comprising the library collection. This is exactly why headings began to be used predominantly as a description of documents in the catalogs. The first known indications of such use of headings belong to the catalog of the Alexandria library (3rd century B.C.). In that same catalog, the name of the author who had written the document was an element of the document's description.

As subsequent methods of retrieval were developed, the desire to review only a portion of the catalog, instead of the entire catalog, arose. One of the earlier methods of implementing this approach was to arrange descriptions of the documents in the catalog alphabetically, according to the names of the documents' authors. It should be noted that retrieval by the author's name anticipates that the user knows the "address" of the document, an assumption that was very often far from reality. This is why such catalogs did not always (not for all users) reduce the size of the reviewed collection. However, as in the case of text "compression," collection "compression" was one of the most important directions for perfecting the methods of retrieval. The subsequent development of catalogs, which are even now one of the main forms of information retrieval in libraries, continued in these directions. Today, more than 30 different types of catalogs are being used in informational activity.

Within the framework of the described approaches, other (not catalog) forms facilitating the retrieval of information were being developed. For example, for the purpose of compressing the text, the use of headings led to the use of abstracts (which again found application in some types of catalogs) and then to the creation of special publications for the purpose of retrieval, specifically journals of abstracts. Obviously, even in such journals the retrieval was performed using a natural language.

Since ancient times, principally different methods of using a natural language in retrieval have also been known. Thus, thousands of years ago religious schools had people who were trained to know some parts of Talmud (Jewish religious law) by heart. Their obligations included (and this was their job) answering any question with regard to the contents of a book with a quote, which they did successfully throughout their lifetimes. Perhaps, these were the first people to professionally engage in the retrieval of information. Moreover, this was possibly the first method by which the retrieval was conducted—that is, not by the user directly, but by an intermediary.

Thus we have provided examples of information retrieval performed by humans. In each of the mentioned cases, the use of natural language for retrieval seems to be clear. But why is it clear? Why do we believe that people performed comparison and selection using a natural language? To answer this question, let's clarify our understanding of the language we will use within the framework of this book.

Because the societal nature of humans anticipates survival precisely within the framework of society and with the help of society, it becomes necessary for humans, in order to exist, to have tools or means through which to exchange information with society. The language of humans, which is usually understood to be a *system of symbols and rules* (explicit or implicit) designed for the purpose of exchanging information among people, is such a means. Through the help of a language, people can influence society for the purpose of obtaining a reaction that is in the person's interest. Also, through the help of a language, people can perceive the influence of society on them. In this manner, we can assert that every *natural language was created in the course of many centuries of societal practice as a means for an individual to communicate with society.* Moreover, it has become customary to consider these languages created by people as natural.

In determining a language, we wrote a "system of symbols and rules." We consciously call a language a system because this allows us to consider it as a whole. In this case, the symbols appear as the elements of this system, and their interrelations (rules) are determined by both a syntax and semantics of a specific language. We should specifically emphasize that what we have in mind are language symbols. A language symbol has become accepted to mean any language unit (word, phrase, or sentence) that serves to define objects and manifestations of reality and their relationships. It is important to note that a symbol is two-sided because the term "symbol" includes both its physical appearance and the significance of its meaning, or simply its meaning.

For a fuller understanding of the phenomenon of language, it is useful to consider its structural components. It is possible to consider any natural language as consisting of the following four elements: the lexical, grammatical, phonetic, and semantic components. The lexical component of a language consists of all the words in this language. Although this set of words changes with time (some words cease to exist and new words appear), for a certain segment of time this set is well defined. The grammatical component includes the rules for the formation and use both of the forms of words and of sentences, as well as changes in words and their combinations in a sentence. The phonetic component is basically represented by speech, that is, rules of pronunciation (accent, intonation, etc.) for both individual words and any of their combinations allowed within the framework of the grammatical component.

These three components are sufficiently well defined and exist in a language not by themselves, but as a means through which one can transmit a certain thought. However, these means alone are not enough to successfully encode meaning in communication. Even if used properly, one may not obtain phrases with any meaning. Let's consider, for example, the following text: "Fun heater of New York was blue with banana neighing. Medicine was bending. Sorting violins of zero were making silent noise with bald poking." In this example, although both the lexical and the grammatical components of the language were taken into account, the text is absent of meaning. Not only are the sentences of the text without meaning, but so are the combinations of words within those sentences. In a sense, this is an extreme example. Texts that at first glance appear entirely understandable also may be meaningless. The following two examples are taken from Voiskunskii (1990). Mur, a famous linguist, illustrates this type of meaningless with the following phrase: "It's raining, but I don't think so." The second illustration is originally from Ionesko's *Bald Singer,* one of the best representatives of the absurd theater.

> Mrs. Smith: You know, they have two children, a boy and a girl. What are their names?
>
> Mr. Smith: Bobby and Bobby, like their parents. Uncle Bobby Watson, the senior Bobby Watson, is rich and likes Bobby, he can surely provide for Bobby's education.
>
> Mrs. Smith: That would be natural, and aunt Bobby Watson, the old Bobby Watson, could, in turn, raise Bobby Watson, the daughter of Bobby Watson. Then, the mother of Bobby Watson can get married again. Does she have anyone in mind?

Mr. Smith: What do you mean, cousin Bobby Watson?

Mrs. Smith: Who? Bobby Watson?

Mr. Smith: Which Bobby Watson are you talking about?

Mrs. Smith: About Bobby Watson, the son of old Bobby Watson the friend of the uncle of late Bobby Watson.

Mr. Smith: No. That's not the one. That's a different one. This Bobby Watson is the son of the old Bobby Watson, the aunt of the late Bobby Watson.

Mrs. Smith: Are you talking about Bobby Watson the traveling salesman?

Mr. Smith: All Bobby Watsons are traveling salesmen.

It is not hard to see that something is wrong with meaning when it comes to these examples. The semantic component, then, exists specifically for the purpose of giving text meaning. However, it is somewhat difficult to *see* this component. In a certain way, the semantic component signifies the use of the other components of a language; it allows one to express or perceive the meaning present in communication, meaning that is born out of mental activity. In other words, the semantic component also consists of some rules of language that involve rules of coding and the recognition of meaning. Often these rules are not clearly formulated but rather are based on feeling and training. Note that in many cases, even when other components of the language are used incorrectly, the meaning of the communication is not affected. For example, everybody understands the meaning of the following phrase (even with the incorrect grammar): "I not understand English."

Actually, a language is not something isolated from thought. It is not a material product of nature or of the world around us. It is also not a relationship (physical) between material objects. It is something that is created by biological species as a result of the work of the intellect, and it is created in a way that makes it convenient for the intellect to use it.

All natural languages are similar in structure (Chomsky, 1972). For example, they all include lexical, syntactical, semantic, and phonetic components. This is explained by the fact that human intellects are similar in nature. In addition, the purpose of all languages is the exchange of information. In other words, humans were historically in need of language (a tool) for the purpose of exchanging information with those similar to them because doing so facilitated their more successful adaption to the actual physical world. Descartes had noted that our language is a language to be used for describing the interaction of physical bodies and not for contemplating, and that the laws of contemplating are different from physical laws (Chomsky, 1972). That is the reason why a system of terms for describing contemplation does not exist. Chomsky, one of the most authoritative linguists of our time, expressed this thought as follows: "There exists a significant gap, a gaping abyss to be more exact, dividing on one side the system of terms which we are able to use with sufficient degree of clarity, and, on the other side, the nature of human intellect" (Chomsky, 1972). It is commonly acknowledged that it is extremely difficult to formulate clear rules related to semantic component. Nonetheless, by exchanging communications, we always "feel" which of them have meaning (i.e., the semantic component is present) and which do not (the semantic component is violated).

Because meaning is the prerogative of the human intellect, the use of the semantic component of a natural language may be performed only by people. Thus, speaking of "natural language," we mean, first of all, a system that has as one of its most important and *indispensable* properties: the presence of something that is perceived by humans as meaning. Moreover, all existing language components are present only to the extent to which they facilitate the transmission and perception of meaning. For this reason, when any manipulations are being performed or will be performed with the use of language components but not with its semantic component (in other words meaning will not be considered), we can say only that *the elements of a natural language, not the natural language itself,* are involved in a process.

In the previous examples of retrieval using a natural language, the content of the text is compared to the requirements of retrieval, and the person performing the retrieval first takes into account the meaning and selects only those documents that contain the required meaning. *It is exactly that type of retrieval (retrieval by meaning and selection by meaning) that is considered a retrieval using a natural language.* This is the viewpoint that we will use from now on.

The understanding of the natural language we have described is based more on the generally accepted intuitive perceptions than on formal definitions. First of all, we were led to this understanding by an analysis of a large number of definitions present in various dictionaries, encyclopedias, textbooks, and term definitions that are reasonable (in the sense that the authors use the generally accepted notions) but still not quite formal. Actually, they suggest that we consider as natural any language that a child first begins to master. However, there have been cases in which a child in an Esperanto family first began to speak Esperanto. Often a language that is capable of further development is considered the natural language. However, it is possible to name a number of artificial languages (Esperanto, for example) that developed with time. Other definitions known to us have their own inconsistencies.

A significant reason for using the previously mentioned "reasonable" approaches for the purpose of understanding the substance of a natural language included our own attempts to provide a strict definition of the natural, as well as the artificial, language. In doing so, we analyzed the language from different viewpoints. For example, we attempted to trace the origins of a language. Thus, in various religious books, myths, and legends of most peoples, the language is assumed to have a divine origin. Consider the Bible story of the Tower of Babylon and the involvement of such gods as Mercury of the Romans, Tot of the Egyptians, Nabu of the Babylonians, Tsen Tze of the Chinese, Brahma of the Hindu, and a great many others. As a result, out of all our attempts to provide a definition, the strictest one turned out to be the following: a natural language is any language having a divine origin. As a counterpart to that definition, it has been proposed that any language created by man be considered an artificial language. Since scientists are never too serious (none of our colleagues took this definition seriously), we have rejected the use of this definition also.

Thus, in summarizing we emphasize that a retrieval using a natural language is a comparison and selection on the basis of the semantic component of a natural language (with the use of the meaning) and that this retrieval is performed only by humans. Thus, in answering the questions posed earlier, it may be asserted that with the help of each of reviewed methods of retrieval, the retrieval itself was performed using a natural language. Then why should the artificial IRL be created? The fact is that the crisis in information retrieval occurred precisely because practically all utilized methods of retrieval through the middle of the 20th century anticipated that the retrieval would be performed by humans. But the increase in the amount of information in a search process was too overwhelming for a manual processing, which forced a move away from a search "by meaning," that is, from a retrieval using a natural language. This required the use of artificial languages whose semantic component is not intended for typical intellectual activity. In connection with this fact, we will discuss in some detail why a search performed by humans hinders the satisfaction of the human's IN.

The ideas of the compression of texts and collections (used in search processes for thousands of years), which always assumed a manual review of the "compressed," in some sense reached a dead end. With an explosion in the amount of information available in this century, even compressed collections are too large to be reviewed manually. Also for the first time, the researches noticed that the speed with which a person reviews collections of documents is limited by the person's physical characteristics, and this speed has not changed over time. This observation led to the idea of speeding up the search by replacing humans with some device capable of performing searches at qualitatively different speeds. As the result, today computers play the role of such a device. In other words, for the first time in the history of information retrieval through IR systems the idea of speeding up the process of reviewing the information collected was considered. This replacement of a human by a device (a computer) resulted in many new problems related to the organization of searches in artificial languages.

Artificial languages for the purpose of retrieval appeared a long time ago. Thus, as the idea of compressing collections of information, developed, that is, the desire to review only a portion of the collection and the wish to make retrieval subject-based (theme-based), the ideas of classification were introduced. Library classifications with their own specially created specific languages appeared. Apparently, these languages (which are often called classification languages) became the first IRL that differed from the natural ones. Very little data on the classifications utilized in ancient libraries exist today. However, these classifications were developed in a rather detailed way in ancient times. This

level of development can be judged by the extent of the libraries and the high
level of classification of sciences of that time, as well as by some indirect evidence
contained in the literary memorials of ancient times.

It should be noted that the development of the library-bibliography classifications was in many ways moving in parallel to the development of science.
At different times, various researchers have significantly influenced this development. For example, the works of K. Gesner, a Swiss librarian (1548),
F. Bacon, an English philosopher (near the end of the 16th century), G. Leibnitz
(the 17th century), and others may be noted. The fastest progress in the development of library classifications was made at the end of the 19th century and in
the first half of the 20th century. These classifications have influenced both the
arrangement of documents in a collection and the catalogs that reflect this arrangement. But the catalogs using these classifications constituted only auxiliary
(albeit important) means of retrieval that, while playing an important role in
improving information retrieval, still involved using the natural language for
which retrieval was performed by humans. As we indicated in Chapter 3, the
current information crisis has presented problems that the traditional classification methods could not solve. This is exactly why we will not discuss in great
detail the classification languages that are typically used in the traditional library
methods but will move, instead, to the consideration of languages used in the
IR system.

5.3

IRL for the IR System

In Chapter 4, we noted that the retrieval of information in the IR system,
that is, direct operations of comparison and selection of information, is performed using a computer without the participation of people. It is understood
that the absence of humans during a retrieval means the impossibility of using a
natural language for the retrieval. Thus, the *creation of an artificial language for the
IR system is a necessity*—at least until such time as when an artificial intellect that
is able to master the semantic component of a natural language is created. With
this in mind, note that the creation of such an intellect does not look very promising today. But what should an artificial IRL be like? The following exposition
is an attempt to answer this question.

Based on the fact that during the process of retrieving information, the
IRL must represent the objects of the retrieval, as well as the search requests (see
Chapter 2), we will begin by defining *what* should be understood by such representation in an artificial IRL, that is, what must be represented and how it may
be represented. Apparently, for the purpose of performing a quick retrieval, IRL
must, to the fullest extent, take into account the specifics of the objects to be
retrieved and the requests for the retrieval. (From this point, when we say IRL

we will mean only artificial IRL intended for use in the IR system.) It is clear that the objects of a retrieval in the IR system are the documents in the collection. Let's recall that a *document* refers to a material carrier with attached information. Specifically, the IR system deals with documents whose material carriers contain a text entered with the help of the written component of a natural language. (It should be noted that out of more than 3000 natural languages currently used by people, fewer than 10% have written components.) Obviously then, in order to perform a retrieval, the IRL must represent not the material carriers but only the information that is attached to them. This representation must be "something" that would allow the required information to be found, and this "something" has to be different for different types of information.

But what differentiates one type of information from another? First is the difference in how each reflects the fragments of reality. Based on the fact that the information in written documents is encoded in the form of text communications using a natural language, after the reading of the texts, these differences are perceived by humans as different meanings of those communications. Because only the meanings of communications present an interest for the users, it is precisely the meanings that must be found in a retrieval. Thus, in submitting the documents to the IRL, we are, in a sense, attempting to somehow present (encode in the IRL) the meaning of the communications attached to these documents. It should also be remembered that the representation of meaning in the IRL must be convenient for a retrieval performed on a computer and not for some other goals. For example, if the available representation seems sufficient for a high-quality search, we should not be concerned with how the quality of the meaning will be perceived by the person reading such representation.

We noted earlier that the IR system for the IRL must represent not only the documents, but also search requests. It is apparent that in formulating search requests humans also encode some meaning in the communication (request) and basically rely on the fact that the documents containing communications with similar meaning will be found in a search process. In this case, the meaning contained in the request must somehow be represented in the IRL.

Thus, we have shown that the meaning of the documents from the collection of documents, as well as the meaning of requests entered into the system by a user, must be represented in the IRL. These representations are then compared using some formal criterion and the necessary information is selected. We would like to point out that in this process, the computer is not operating with meanings but with the representations of meanings. Of course, they are not the same. After all, it does not surprise us, for example, that an elevator button represents a floor, a social security number represents each person legally residing in the United States, and so forth. Now, after understanding *what* must be represented in the IRL, let's consider *how* it may be done.

Many linguists believe that artificial languages are created and exist only on the basis of natural languages. The existing practice supports this opinion. In some sense all artificial languages are created and used for the needs of humans. Not one of the known artificial languages has a component that did not exist in a natural language. However, because retrieval in the IR system is performed using a computer, it is not hard to note that in the appropriate machine operations of such retrieval, the phonetic component of the IRL is not used. Subsequently, a need for its creation does not exist. The remaining components seem to be necessary. Within the framework of the existing perceptions of retrieval, any language must have vocabulary and some type (even the simplest kind) of grammar, both of which are auxiliary means for giving meaning to a communication with the help of the semantic component of a given language. The giving of meaning (the use of the semantic component) in different languages often has different goals. In some languages, these meanings are used for human communication, in others for directing (for example, the language of stoplights regulating traffic), still in others for retrieval. That is why, in addition to the rules for representation of the meanings of documents and requests, the rules of selection and output of the objects must be formulated on the basis of the semantic component of the IRL, despite the fact that the object to be retrieved in the IR system is a meaning required by the user. These rules (as opposed to the rules for the expression of meaning in a communication using a natural language) may be formulated strictly and, subsequently, they may be implemented with the help of a computer (in other words, they are implemented within the IR system). Thus, we will once again note that *the main property of an artificial IRL is that its semantic component allows one to formalize the rules of selection and the output of information.* Actually, some formal rules of selection could be based on the semantic component of a natural language. However, if these rules are used during the search process, then the search is performed not in a natural language but in artificial language. Now we can consider a number of general ideas which form the foundation for the creation of the IRL and begin our consideration of the lexical component of the IRL.

It seems there are few requirements for the lexical component of the IRL. It may be asserted that through the help of words, the IRL must provide the representation of that information, which is being searched for by the users; that is, the meanings of available words must allow the retrieval of information needed by the users. It also appears important for the IRL vocabulary to cover the area that is represented by the document of the collection. In creating the vocabulary of a specific language (in creating the alphabet and forming the words of the IRL), it is possible to indicate a number of features that seem quite desirable (but not absolutely necessary). Some examples are as follows:

1. The selection of an alphabet is determined mainly by considerations of practical convenience. It would be desirable for it to consist of a minimum necessary number of standard symbols used by a computer.
2. It is desirable for the lexical component of the IRL to be convenient for use by a computer. For example, for the purpose of organizing the

Where does this come from? 99

storage and retrieval of information in a computer, it is convenient to use words of equal length.

In speaking about the grammatical component (syntax) of the IRL, we emphasize that all grammatical rules must be strictly formulated (formalized). This is necessary for the retrieval with a computer. A number of other considerations are possibly not as crucial. To some degree, all of them are dictated by two factors: (1) the requirements of automatic retrieval (by a computer) and (2) the quality of retrieval performed by a computer. For example, the use of a more developed grammar leads to an increase in the complexity of software for the IR system. Programs become more complex and bulky, they take up more memory, and the length of the retrieval time increases. However, if this increase in complexity greatly improves the results of the search, that is, noticeably improves the quality of information services from the viewpoint of the users, for example, then within the framework of a specific IR system such increase in complexity may be considered useful.

syntax

All of the components we have reviewed were created (and exist) so that a language could fulfill its intended purpose. Because in our case the intended purpose of the IRL is the retrieval of information, its semantical component should allow us to formulate the rules of selection and output of information. It is apparent that these must be formal rules and that they must ensure the acceptable quality of retrieval.

In the development of a specific IRL, one should take into account that with the passage of time, languages in general and IRLs in particular change. This primarily applies to the vocabulary of a language. Hence, the IRL being created must possess the ability to be modified as the language of documents and requests changes.

We have provided some of the most important requirements for the IRL. However, all these requirements have significance only within the framework of the general approach to the organization of retrieval without the participation of humans. They acquire a constructive quality only within the framework of a specific idea of performing such retrieval. Therefore, we will subsequently spend some time on the idea of the automatic retrieval of meaning-based information (through the help of a computer); that is, we will attempt to answer the question, "How can *this* be done without the participation of humans?"

The idea of automatic retrieval is based on the work of American mathematicians Mooers (1948) and especially Taube, Gull, and Waschel (1952). We will begin with our review with the work of Taube et al. By 1952 Taube et al. developed the system Uniterm, which utilized formal rules for the retrieval of documents. In creating the system, Taube assumed that *the meaning of the request, just like the meaning of the document, may, with accuracy sufficient for purposes of retrieval, be transmitted by a set of certain words encountered in its text.* In other words, he believed that for purposes of retrieval, the contents of documents and requests will be transmitted to a sufficient extent by their vocabulary, that is, *only* by the lexical component of the natural language. Moreover, he believed that not all words of a document or a request were necessarily important in transmitting meaning. Of course, this did not mean that all words could not be considered important. This only meant that not all *had* to be considered important. Taube presumed that those words that were important in the opinion of the IR system creators for the transmittal of the meanings of texts must be included in the vocabulary of the IRL system. He suggested that such words be called *uniterms*. The name is a portmanteau created from combing the words "unit" and "term," and it is intended to emphasize the system's use of single terms. A little later, other terms, specifically *keywords* or *descriptors,* began to be used instead. The majority of researchers uses these later terms.

Now let us discuss why the words of the texts in natural language must comprise the lexical component of the IRL. It would seem that in cases in which the meaning of the texts is transmitted by all words of such texts written in natural language, that is, when all the words of a natural language are meaningful words, the need to create an artificial IRL does not exist. However, this is not so. In reality, Taube's suggestion means that for purposes of retrieval, one may ignore both the grammatical and the semantical components of the texts in natural language when transmitting the meaning. Obviously, the use of the lexical component of a natural language does not mean the use of the natural language itself. The same lexical components may exist in the natural as well as the artificial languages. Their principal differences are their different grammatical and semantical rules. It is precisely these rules for the artificial IRL that comprise the basis of Taube's idea. "If we presume," he reported, "that the meaning of a communication is transmitted only by a set of words contained in that communication, then the documents which contain a set of words contained in some request also contain the meaning possessed by the request" (Taube et al.). This leads to the following rules for a grammatical component and the rules for selection and output based on the semantical component. We start with grammatical rules.

1. The contents of each document in the IRL must be represented by a set of keywords (uniterms), not in any particular order, encountered in the text of this document.
2. The contents of each request in the IRL must be represented by a set of keywords (uniterms), not in any particular order, encountered in the formulation of this request.

The rules of comparison and selection are formulated in the following way:

1. The set of keywords of a request must be compared with the set of keywords of each document.
2. When the set of keywords from a document contains all the keywords from a set of a request, the document is considered found.

The IRL proposed by Taube was an important step on the way to creating the modern IR systems, because the implementation of these simple and formal rules on the computer did not pose difficulty. It should be noted that even now this approach forms the basis of the overwhelming majority of the IRLs in use.

During the initial stages of the creation of IR systems (the early 1950s), no practical attempt was made to use the entire lexical component of a natural language as the lexical component of the IRL. This approach was only considered theoretically. This was, first of all, explained by the fact that the speed and memory of the first generation of computers were literally in the infant stages. In addition, technical methods, other than typing, for entering information into a computer were practically nonexistent. Partly because of that, the indexing of texts was often looked at not only—not even primarily—in terms of transferring texts into an IRL. It was generally accepted that the indexing process must significantly reduce the volume of the entered text, and a number of researchers considered this property to be the main intent of indexing. This belief led to a substantial effort on the part of IRL developers to select a small number of lexical units that would be able to represent as great a portion of the meaning of the text being indexed as possible.

But what is a part of the meaning? This question was addressed by C. Mooers who viewed meaning as something single, homogeneous, and consisting of a certain set of independent elements. In September of 1948, C. Mooers patented an automatic document retrieval system which he called a system of "zato-coding" (Mooers, 1951). In 1950, he introduced the term "descriptor" to define the lexical units of an IRL utilized in his retrieval system. The author described the essence of the method of text indexing, which was utilized in the IR system he created in the following manner:

> The subject of each document is characterized or described by means of a certain set of descriptors borrowed from the formal vocabulary of relevant terms. As a rough approximation of what I mean, I recall the subject heading list." . . . Each document is characterized by a certain set of descriptors from the descriptor dictionary. Each descriptor from this set is applicable or, in a certain sense, correct with respect to the information content of the information element (element of meaning). In this case descriptors function independently from each other. The fact that this set consists of several descriptors can imply that they form some interrelated composition in the source document. This also can imply that they correspond to different independent ideas spread throughout the document. (Mooers, 1951)

According to Mooers, a descriptor is a word or a word combination designating a certain concept with more or less broad meaning. The meaning of the descriptor is not necessarily required to coincide with the meaning normally corresponding to the word or word combination used as a descriptor. Each descriptor is supplied with an explanation mark disclosing its specific meaning in the given IRL. Normally, descriptors have broader meaning than corresponding words and word combinations. Next we give an example of building an alphabetically ordered list of descriptors with explanations (descriptors are underlined and supplied with 3-digit numbers) and synonymous words and phrases that are not descriptors (are not underlined and do not have numbers).

Static   135
In combination with the descriptor "stability" it corresponds to the study of the static stability.
Statistical mechanics
See descriptor "thermodynamics"
Statistics
See descriptor "probability"
Stability   136
In aviation technology this descriptor, combined with the descriptors "static," "dynamic," "roll," and "longitudinal," corresponds to the loss of aircraft stability. It also corresponds to the loss of stability due to buckling and to other types of construction instability. When studying stability and controllability, it is used together with the descriptor "derivatives."

Such an approach allowed Mooers not only to form a list of several hundred descriptors, but also to obtain encouraging results in the search performance. His ideas were adopted by IR system developers almost immediately, primarily due to the evident simplicity of the very approach to the choice of IRL lexical units. With all of the technical imperfections of computing hardware of the 1950s, this approach was feasible (it could be implemented on computers); in combination with ideas of Taube, it allowed the construction of sufficiently economical and useful IR systems.

Another one of Mooers' contributions was his innovative terminology, which definitely had a positive influence on the development of information science. He was ingenious in introducing new terms. Besides the term "descriptor," he also introduced the terms "information retrieval," "information retrieval system," "information retrieval language," "descriptor dictionary," "search image," and other terms widely used in the field of information retrieval.

Thus we have considered the origin of the fundamental ideas that encouraged the creation of IRL. Today most of the IRL languages are of the type developed by Mooers and Taube, and such languages are frequently called *descriptor IRLs*. Obviously, all the ideas just considered represent only the first steps toward the creation of descriptor languages. The retrieval quality provided by the first languages was far from satisfactory for their users. Almost immediately the researchers started intensive efforts on improving the descriptor languages and this work included all three components of IRL. Next we briefly characterize several approaches in the descriptor IRL development and in some cases illustrate the development by examples.

5.4 _____

Some Tendencies of IRL Development

The attempts to enhance different IRL components have been aimed at improving retrieval results provided by IR systems. As we mentioned earlier, the information retrieval is the search for something with a meaning to the user and this meaning is encoded in the text of the document. Therefore, developers of IR systems want to represent this meaning in IRL as precisely as possible. In other words, if the meaning is represented incompletely or is misrepresented, the retrieval result may be unsatisfactory. Thus, the main direction in IRL development is the search for ways, methods, and rules favoring a more complete representation of the meanings of documents and search requests. The more advanced IRLs allow us to formulate more refined (and sophisticated) formal rules, taking into consideration the more refined features of the natural language that express the desired meaning. In this case, we can consider IRL as a simplified model of natural language.

In making grammatical and semantical components of IRL more complicated, we are hoping that this IRL will better represent the meaning encoded by natural language. However, the gap between the quality of its expression in the natural language and that in IRL will remain unbridgeable. In other words, as long as IRL is different from the natural language, the quality of the meaning representation in it will be inferior to that of the natural language. When would we be able to say that the development of language (IRL) in the mentioned direction gets to the point where the representation of meaning in this language is close to the representation of meaning in the natural language? Probably when the semantic component of the natural language is understood well enough that we can rigorously formalize all the rules so that they are as effective as the informal rules existing in the natural language. Will these rules ever be formulated? Concerning this subject, there are many more pessimistic forecasts than optimistic ones. Many pessimists are the people who have already tried to work in this direction. Optimists are normally represented by people who have never tried to do anything themselves, but believe that this will be done by someone else. We would like to note that if an IRL featuring not only all of the advantages of natural language but also some additional positive characteristics—such as the full set of formal rules representing the semantic component—is created, humanity will probably find it more convenient to abandon natural languages altogether and will use only IRL.

We start our discussion of IRL development with some ideas concerning the lexical component of the language. Initially the major concern of most IR system developers was the way to form descriptors for IRL. The very term "descriptor" soon acquired its contemporary meaning. In essence, *any word formed for an IRL was called a descriptor.* Moreover, *IRLs using descriptors were referred to as descriptor languages*. Obviously, specially formed words (descriptors) needed to be "memorized," that is, to be fixed in dictionaries specially prepared for this purpose in concrete IR systems. The latter circumstance was especially important because a certain word could be a descriptor in one system (and entered into the dictionary) and might not be a descriptor in another system. Such dictionaries were later called *descriptor dictionaries,* and the systems for which they were used were called *descriptor systems* or *controlled vocabulary systems*. The terminology presented here has been widely adopted, although many specialists do not use it. In some books devoted to IR systems, one would not find the word "descriptor" at all. Their authors use such words as "term" or "keyword." However, we note again that the terminology we use has been widely adopted and therefore can be regarded as universally accepted.

Already at the initial stages of IR systems creation, it became evident that (for the purposes of computer implementation) it was more convenient to use a certain compact code of standard length as a descriptor, rather than a word or a word combination of the natural language. A part of the alphabet, decimal numbers, or combinations of characters and digits were frequently used as descriptors. Even Mooers' technical implementation of IRL (on special cards) included descriptors represented by randomly chosen codes, each consisting of four groups of digits. The choice of the way to represent (to write) descriptors is not a great problem for developers. It is easily resolved in each concrete case. Eventually, their major concern is what "block of meaning" should an IRL word represent; that is, what meaning should be assigned to a descriptor? According to Taube's approach (discussed earlier), one can assume that the meaning of the text is contained in the words of this text, while the meaning of each idea in the text (a "block of meaning") is represented by a certain nonempty set of these words. Therefore developers decided not to supply each descriptor with an explanatory article but to use some set of words that would give the descriptor a certain collective meaning. In other words, the meaning of the descriptor equals the union of meanings of words from the word group attributed to the descriptor. Such a word group is frequently called the *conditional equivalence class*.

To illustrate, here are several fragments of the information science descriptor dictionary developed at Fordham University. This dictionary was created for educational purposes by students studying information retrieval systems in the Department of Computer and Information Science:

B073
  Librarianship
  Library system
  State library system
  Scientific library
  Science library
  Research library

Technical library
Science and technical library
C052
   Note
   Letter
   Memorandum
   Report
   Paper
   Article
K006
   Automatic information retrieval
   Bibliographic retrieval system
   Document retrieval system
   Information retrieval system
   Text retrieval system

Three descriptors appear in the preceding example, namely B073, C052, and K006. Obviously, these descriptors constitute a letter-and-digit code that is four symbols in length. Each descriptor has its conditional equivalence class, which should include at least one word of the natural language. Normally, *words and word combinations included in the conditional equivalence class are called keywords.* Note that the conditional equivalence class of the B073 descriptor contains eight keywords, which are words and word combinations of the natural language. Keywords of the C052 descriptor are represented only by words, and those of the K006 descriptor are represented only by word combinations. The meaning of the B073 descriptor consists of the meanings of all eight words making up the conditional equivalence class of this descriptor. Meanings of other descriptors are given in the similar way.

As a rule, descriptor dictionaries are created for collections of documents on the same topic. For instance, for the mathematical document collection, a mathematical descriptor dictionary is compiled, whereas the collection of medical documents requires a descriptor dictionary on medicine. Normally, depending on the subject, descriptor dictionaries contain about 1000 descriptors each. Probably, this can be explained by the fact that the 1000 most frequently used words of the natural language make up 80% of all texts.

The developers of descriptor dictionaries had to resolve many problems, some of which we list here:

1. Who should be engaged in the creation of the IRL for IR systems?
2. How many descriptors should the dictionary contain?
3. What meaning should be attributed to each concrete descriptor?
4. What are the criteria for including a specific word of the natural language in a certain conditional equivalence class?
5. Can this process be automated?

Regarding the first question, some investigators hold that IRL should be created by linguists, whereas others suggest that the best quality will be provided by experts in the areas for which IR systems are created. For instance, a geological descriptor dictionary should be compiled by geologists, whereas a dictionary on computer science is the business of experts in this area. Some investigators reason that IRL should be created by the developers of IR systems, that is, by experts in the field of information science. One would admit that there are a lot of arguments in favor of all these points of view, which is probably why, in practice, IRLs are created by experts from all the professions mentioned, and in many cases they are created by groups that include experts from all three categories.

Somewhat more difficult questions arise when resolving the other problems mentioned. In essence, they all question *how* to create IRL? Traditionally, experts have created descriptor dictionaries "manually" (or, as one would say, "on an intellectual level") using their own vision of the problem, knowledge, and comprehension. This led (since the late 1950s) to the appearance of a considerable bulk of publications describing some well-intentioned advice and wishes, usually called methodological recommendations. They were based either on the personal experience of authors or on speculative concepts that seemed reasonable to them (see, for example Broadhurst, 1962; Francisco, 1956; and "The Uniterm System," 1955). Although some of these recommendations were rather useful, they failed to play even a third-rate role in the creation of IRL. This can be illustrated by the following example. Many recommendations have been offered on how to translate from one natural language to another. However, when one does not know a language, no recommendations will help. On the other hand, brilliant knowledge of two languages makes translation possible without any recommendations.

The situation with descriptor dictionaries is quite similar. Developers need to know very well what a descriptor language is. But that is not enough. "Manual" creation of IRL is based on the developer's personal decision to form each descriptor. Therefore, a developer's success essentially depends on his or her knowledge of the subject matter of the document collection and on the knowledge of all features and fine points concerning the further use of the dictionary in a concrete IR system. This by no means implies that no methodologies are needed. They are needed. For instance, most of the methodologies for creating descriptor dictionaries recommend the use of concise dictionaries, encyclopedias, terminological manuals, thesauruses of natural language, and so on. Although this advice is obviously useful, the success of the personal creation of the dictionary nevertheless depends on the skills of its developer. That is why we will not concentrate on either manual methods or manual methodologies. Because manual methods were labor intensive, qualitatively unstable, and personality dependent, developers searched for ways to compile dictionaries automatically. Therefore, in the following section we shall confine ourselves to

the consideration of methods used for the automatic selection of terms for
descriptor IRLs.

5.5

Automatic Methods of Descriptor Dictionary Compilation

Actually, descriptor dictionaries were compiled manually not because the
developers considered manual methods superior to automatic methods. There
were just no ideas at the time to explain how to automate the process. Nevertheless, the majority of investigators did understand the advantages of automation. G. Salton, one of the most distinguished creators of IR systems, indicated that

> in normal conditions the creation of a dictionary for a given subject area requires
> advanced skills, persistence and intensive will. . . . Since the volume of the problem
> is large, frequently the whole committee is organized to resolve arguable points and,
> eventually, to create a dictionary. Such a dictionary created by a committee may not
> satisfy anyone despite great efforts to create it.
>   Obviously, if one follows this scheme of compiling dictionaries, any profit
> resulting from the automated retrieval will be immediately lost due to the com-
> plexity of the dictionary creation. That is why this situation has encouraged many
> attempts either to create dictionaries completely automatically or, at least, to use
> methods more effective than the work of a committee. Any sufficiently universal
> method of dictionary creation not only saves time and reduces costs, but also pro-
> vides essentially more freedom in choosing types of retrieval procedures to imple-
> ment. (Salton, 1968)

Virtually all ideas of the automatic choice of words for descriptor dictionaries follow from certain statistical characteristics of texts composed in various
natural languages. An intensive study of the statistical laws of languages started
almost simultaneously with the creation of computers. Even in the early 1950s,
linguists paid great attention to the possibilities provided by computers. For instance, for various characters in an alphabet, frequencies of use were calculated
using large text collections. These frequencies were calculated for different al-
phabets and languages. Frequencies of the joint appearance of characters in
words (for two characters, three characters, and so forth) were also calculated.
As an example, in Figure 5.1 we present part of the character frequency table for
texts in Russian.

Frequency characteristics of characters have found numerous applications
in information encoding and transfer. However, for problems of information
retrieval, the calculation of word (rather than character) occurrence frequencies
turned out to be even more important. A fragment of the word list with the
relative word frequencies is given in Figure 5.2 as an example. Such lists were

Letter	Frequency	Letter	Frequency	Letter	Frequency
O	0,09	M	0,026	й	0,010
E	0,072	D	0,025	X	0.009
A	0,062	П	0,023	Ж	0,007
И	0,062	Y	0,021	Ю	0,006
T	0,053	Я	0,018	Ш	0.006
H	0,053	Ы	0,016	Ц	0,004
C	0,045	3	0,016	Щ	0,003
P	0,040	Ь,Ъ	0,014	Э	0,003
B	0,038	Б	0,014	Ф	0.002
Λ	0,035	Г	0,013		
K	0,028	Ч	0,012		

Figure 5.1
Character occurrence frequencies in texts written in Russian.

Term	Frequency
the	0,069,971
of	0,036,411
and	0,028,852
to	0,026,149
a	0,023,237
in	0,021,341
that	0,010,595
is	0,010,099
was	0,009,816
he	0,009,543

Figure 5.2
Relative word occurrence frequencies in texts written in English (the total number of words is 1,000,000). Source: Adapted from H. N. Kucera & W. N. Francis, *Computational Analysis of Present-Day American English* (Providence, RI: Brown University Press, 1968).

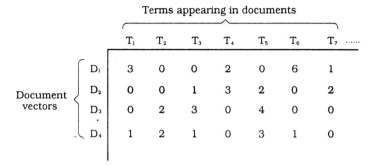

Figure 5.3
Term-document matrix.

constructed for many languages. Figure 5.2 is compiled from the selected texts with the number of words totaling one million (Kucera & Francis, 1968).

As we will show later, several ideas for the automatic compilation of descriptor dictionaries include the use of such word lists. Nevertheless, first approaches did not make use of them. Next we describe one of the first methods, which is rather representative for the mid-1960s. This approach suggests using the terms contained in a set of documents retrieved from a collection of documents considered typical for a given subject area. Then frequencies of word occurrences in the chosen documents are calculated. Each document is identified by its words with high occurrence frequencies. Then a term-document matrix is constructed. An example of such a matrix is presented in Figure 5.3.

The matrix element lying on the intersection of the i-th row and j-th column represents the weight of the j-th term in the i-th document. Given this matrix, one can use well-known methods of statistical processing to calculate coefficients of similarity between terms on the basis of the joint occurrence characteristics of words in the chosen documents. The similarity coefficient is calculated for each pair of terms depending on the frequency of their joint occurrence in the collection of documents. According to Figure 5.3, terms T_1 and T_6 are attributed to both documents D_1 and D_4, though with different weights. At the same time they do not appear in documents D_2 and D_3. This method assumes that these two terms may belong to the same conditional equivalence class of the created descriptor dictionary (Salton & McGill, 1993).

It should be noted that the idea of this method is rather schematic. For instance, nothing is said about the calculation of term weights and why documents should be identified by words with high occurrence frequency (note that, according to Figure 5.2, the most frequently used words are "the," "of," and "and"). Furthermore, the approach discussed is based on a not-so-obvious assumption that the joint occurrence of words in documents is an evidence in favor of term similarity or close interrelation. This seems to be the reason why we were not able to find references to the practical use of this idea. However, we have presented it here because it is virtually the only known idea concerning conditional equivalence classes containing more than one word.

The other ideas considered the word occurrence frequency and turned out to be useful both for the creation of descriptor dictionaries of the "uniterm" type (with conditional equivalence classes containing one word each) and for the automatic selection of terms for Mooers-type dictionaries. In the latter case, selected words are grouped into conditional equivalence classes manually.

We will now describe one of the most well-known methods. First, the relative word occurrence frequencies are calculated for the collection of documents (or for its sufficiently representative part). Then the words are selected with relative occurrence frequencies exceeding their relative occurrence in texts of the given language by $n\%$ (some predetermined value). Obviously, to perform such a selection one needs to input into the computer both the collection of documents in which the word occurrence frequency is calculated and the dictionary of the relative word occurrence frequencies (a fragment of which is given in Figure 5.2). When one wants to select m words for the dictionary, it is not difficult to find the value of $n\%$. For instance, assume we want our dictionary to contain 1000 words, that is, we want to select about 1000 words that are most typical for the collection of documents entered into the computer. Then let the first approximation of $n\%$ be, say, 30%. If we obtain considerably more than 1000 words then we can increase n and repeat the selection. Otherwise n should be reduced and the selection should also be repeated. These procedures can be repeated until the quantity of selected words satisfies the developer. Obviously, link-words and general-use words would not be selected in this case. For example, in the document collection devoted to computing hardware, the occurrence frequency of such a commonly used word as "the" will not increase by, say, 30%, whereas the occurrence frequency of special words used in this subject area will definitely increase. As practice shows, such an increase sometimes exceeds 100%.

The graphical illustration of the method just described is given in Figure 5.4. Line A in this figure represents the average occurrence frequency of words in the language. Points mark the frequencies of the words used in the collection of documents. The line h represents the given value of the excess over the average word occurrence frequency. This value is chosen to fit the minimal required quantitative composition of the dictionary. All words (points) reaching or exceeding the h level are included in the dictionary being created.

Another powerful method to select the most important (representative) terms from the collection of documents is the weighting method. According to this method, a term is considered as important for the given collection of docu-

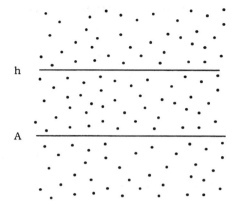

Figure 5.4
The graphic representation of the method used to select words whose relative occurrence frequencies exceed their average values by h%.

ments if it appears in the collection with maximum frequency *and* appears in common texts rather seldom. Thus weights are calculated as follows:

$$w = \frac{f_i Q}{q F_i},$$

where

f_i = occurrence frequency of the i-th word in the collection of documents;

q = number of words in the collection of documents;

F_i = occurrence frequency of the i-th word in texts in the language in which the documents are written; and

Q = number of words in the texts that are used for the computation of the occurrence frequency of each word in the language.

Obviously, to select the most weighted words and include them in the dictionary, one should input both the collection of documents (or a sufficiently representative part) and the dictionary of relative word occurrence frequencies into the computer.

Let us look at the following example. Assume we have entered into the computer 500 abstracts of articles about various aspects of information science. Also assume that the average length of an abstract is 100 words. Suppose that the frequency dictionary containing 1,000,000 words (its fragment is presented in Figure 5.2) is also stored in the computer. Now assume that a certain term has appeared 120 times in the collection of documents, whereas its occurrence frequency (from a sample of 1,000,000 words) in the given language is 150. Substituting these values into the preceding formula, we obtain the following:

$$w = \frac{120 \times 1000000}{50000 \times 150} = 16.$$

If we want our dictionary to contain the 1000 most important terms, we can easily arrange this after calculating all word weights of the collection of documents. Note that this method prevents us from selecting link words and commonly used words because these do not acquire high weights.

We have now considered the main approaches to the automatic construction of descriptor dictionaries. This problem seemed to be one of the most important problems in developing IRL. However, recent works in the area show the aspiration of developers to consider all words in the collection of documents as descriptors. This tendency becomes especially evident when dealing with new IR systems. In other words, in this case there is no need to create special descriptor dictionaries. This new angle to the approach taken by Taube has become practically feasible (and useful) due to the explosive development of computer technologies rather than to theoretical discoveries in the field of information science. The speed of modern computers and the size of internal memory have caused the revision of several theoretical principles that until recently had been regarded as unshakable. Also, the descriptor dictionary is not the only example of the influence of computer technology on IR system development. This fact will be quite apparent in the subsequent chapters.

Remember that the use of dictionaries similar to those applied to the natural language does not imply the use of the natural language itself, because the retrieval in the system does not utilize either grammatical or semantic components of the natural language. In addition, in some cases so called *nonimportant words* (link-verbs, commonly used words, etc.) are rejected from the collection of documents. Dictionaries of nonimportant words (and not the descriptor dictionaries) are compiled for this purpose. Obviously, to select nonimportant words, one can use the automatic methods for the selection of terms described earlier (with minor modifications). For instance, after weights of all terms in documents are calculated, one can select those with minimal weights, that is, those that are least representative for a given collection of documents.

Later in the book, when discussing the process of automatically indexing documents, we will consider the construction of document profiles both for systems using only descriptor dictionaries and for those utilizing dictionaries of nonimportant words (these dictionaries are also sometimes called dictionaries of stop-words).

Now, having considered the lexical component of IRL, we can proceed with the description of its grammatical and semantic components.

5.6 _____

Semantic and Grammatical Components of IRL

It should be noted that, excluding cases when developers work with a free text search (see, for example, Lancaster, 1979), the compilation of descriptor dictionaries is virtually the only significant activity performed when creating IRL for a concrete system. Indeed, as a rule, system developers do not create semantical or grammatical components of IRL. The reasons are similar to those given by people who develop new models of cars without introducing principally new internal-combustion engines; in developing new models, such experts base their work on well-known principles accepted through many years of practice. In essence, the same process occurs during the creation of IR systems. The majority of investigators base their work on IRL principles formulated decades ago. This means that they consider semantic and grammatical components of IRL as something given. However, what is given are not universal rules but different alternatives for developers (although very few). Moreover, these alternatives are based on the ideas of Mooers and Taube. It seems that we can refer here to a family of descriptor languages because they have different grammatical or semantical components. Thus, as one can see from the analysis of existing systems, given a choice of a descriptor dictionary, developers choose rules for grammatical and semantical components of IRL that they think will provide for the highest quality information retrieval. Obviously, no universal opinion exists concerning the quality of existing rules. However, those rules chosen (and used) by the majority of developers might be considered as most appropriate. But what rules do developers actually use and what are the most popular among them? To answer this question, we will discuss the various existing rules; that is, we will describe the main existing rules for the IRL components under consideration.

The semantical and grammatical components of IRL are used to represent both the objects of retrieval and the requirements for them. In other words, grammar and semantics are necessary for writing (composing) phrases (texts) in IR language. During retrieval, these phrases should represent documents and search requests. Obviously, these phrases do not represent physical properties of documents and search requests, but instead these phrases represent their content and meaning. Another obvious fact is that phrases representing meanings in IRL are intended not for reading, but for finding information in IR systems. Therefore both grammatical and semantical rules are introduced in a form that allows them to be used directly during information retrieval. In essence, it is the selection criterion that determines the usage of specific grammatical rules in writing phrases in IRL. However, as was pointed out earlier, to introduce a selection criterion itself one needs the semantical component of IRL. Indeed, to find required document meanings one needs to represent them in an appropriate way to have a possibility of recognizing these meanings and selecting them according to the search request. It is the semantical IRL component that serves as such an "appropriate" representation of meanings, both of documents and search requests.

It should be emphasized that the "appropriateness" of this representation is only in how effective it is in a selection process. For instance, if we manage to represent the document meaning in IRL in a way that makes a human being understand it in the proper way, and if, at the same time, the selection criterion fails to account for most of the characteristic features of this representation (for example, due to the absence of corresponding formal components representing the meaning) and therefore fails to find the document required by the user, then we cannot consider the meaning as appropriately represented.

Following Taube, many investigators believe that it is quite sufficient to represent the meaning of source texts by unordered sets of descriptors with meanings coinciding with the notions from the represented text. However, other experts reason that phrases in the form of unordered sets of descriptors do not permit high-quality information retrieval. That is why they propose more elaborate rules to represent meanings based on more advanced semantical components. Regarding these rules, it is clear that the purpose of introducing more elaborate semantical components is not to obtain better representations for the reader's benefit but to formulate new selection rules for better retrieval. In most cases, having proposed certain modifications in the semantical component of IRL, investigators also propose a selection criterion that takes these modifications into account. As mentioned earlier, the simplest method of the meaning representation (unordered set of descriptors) as well as the way to use it for retrieval was based on the ideas of Taube. Let us consider the causes of the developers' dissatisfaction with the representation of documents and search requests in this way.

The fact that an unordered set of descriptors and a natural-language text represented by this set are not equivalent in meaning is obvious. It is also obvious that the unordered set of descriptors is not just a simplified representation of the natural-language text. First of all, it constitutes a certain schematic (artificial) representation of the text. Such a representation is convenient just for formal operations of information retrieval. Indeed, given such a set of descriptors, one can hardly understand the contents of the text represented by this set. In addition, given a set of descriptors, it is possible to compose a large number of natural-language texts that are quite different in meaning. In other words, any unordered set of descriptors is actually a representation of a certain set of different (possible) meanings. Let us consider the following example where a search request from the user interested in the automatic indexing of search requests for automatic document retrieval was given to the experimental adaptive IR system created at Fordham University. In the framework of the descriptor dictionary of this system, the request contains the following descriptors: "document," "search request," "indexing," "retrieval," and "automation." The latter descriptor represents the terms "algorithmization" and "automatic" contained in one conditional equivalence class. Obviously, all documents, dealing with the automatic indexing of documents for the purposes of retrieval based on search requests will be found. Besides, the system will retrieve all documents dealing with indexing (not only automatic indexing). Thus, if one selects all documents containing a given set of descriptors, these documents may have different meanings and hence we can select a certain subset of different meanings from the set of meanings represented by the given set of descriptors.

However, because we look for the single meaning from the possible set of meanings (namely, the meaning in which the user is interested), the retrieval of any other meanings contained in document texts is considered to be a retrieval error (although this follows from the semantic component of IRL). Furthermore, documents with other meanings (from the set of selected documents) are commonly called *noise* or noise documents, and system developers try to reduce noise in the output by introducing additional rules in the semantic component of IRL. Indeed, it seems intuitively clear that as more language features inherent to natural languages are accounted for in the indexing of documents and search requests, fewer different (possible) meanings will exist for a given representation. It is clear that the fuller incorporation of the semantic component of the natural language into IRL not only provides for a closer representation of the unique meaning contained in the source document, but it also brings IRL closer to a natural language. However, the distance between the most advanced, modern IRL and natural languages is tremendous, and the tendency to minimize this distance is more theoretical with very few practical results.

Thus one of the main directions in changing the semantic component of IRL can be explained by the aspiration to reduce the noise in the output. However, many investigators still do not think the semantic component should be changed. First, they say, the number of possible meanings represented by an unordered set of descriptors is not so large because systems are usually created for a certain subject area and this restricts the number of possible meanings. Second, the introduction of additional rules for the semantic component of IRL does not eliminate noise. It can only reduce it; that is, the problem of noise is not resolved. Besides, it is not so clear whether the retrieval results are enhanced, although the complexity of retrieval and the increase in cost are evident. Third, the potential of Taube systems is far from being exhausted. The growing interest in the free text search lends great support to this point of view. Another strong argument is the fact that the majority of contemporary IR systems use unordered sets of descriptors, at least for the representation of documents. However, the attempts to use more complex semantic components of IRL should have more than just theoretical interest. These attempts may be considered as one of the directions toward "intellectualizing" information retrieval. This direction essentially depends on successes achieved in such areas as linguistics and artificial intelligence (AI). That is why it seems useful to present here several well-known ideas in the development of the semantical components of IRL. But first let us see what resources have been considered by the developers using the representation of texts in the form of an unordered set of descriptors, which represents an indirect approach to the development of the semantical component (it was often done unconsciously). In addition to allowing us to present ideas used in many existing systems, it will also open the possibility of evaluating the effects of changing the semantical components of IRL in an explicit (conscious) form.

The main efforts in developing Taube's approach have been concentrated on the selection criterion. Recall that the following approach was proposed initially: a document is considered selected when the set of descriptors representing a given search request is contained in the set of descriptors representing this document. Obviously, the representation of document and request contents in the form of unordered sets of descriptors is quite sufficient for such a selection criterion.

Despite the usefulness of the underlying idea of the method—it allowed information retrieval to be formalized—retrieval results obtained with this criterion were frequently inadequate. One of the main problems was that the number of descriptors representing search requests varied over wide range. To illustrate the negative consequences of such a variation, consider the following two real search requests submitted to an IR system with a collection of documents in the area of information science (the IR system was developed in VINITI, Moscow, in the early 1970s):

1. Study of the information need (IN).
2. Automatic methods for correcting query formulations in a descriptor documentary IR system using the selection criterion in the Boolean form.

Considering the descriptor dictionary of this system and the fact that each of these requests will be represented as a set of descriptors with conditional equivalence classes containing words from the requests, the query formulations will be as follows. The first query formulation will be represented by the set containing one descriptor, "information need." The second one will be represented by the set of nine descriptors, namely: "automation," "method," "correction" (this word belongs to the same conditional equivalence class that contains the term "feedback"), "query formulation," "descriptor," "document," "IR system," "selection criterion," and "Boolean logic." If the system uses the selection criterion mentioned here, the retrieval based on the single descriptor, "information need" (first query), will, as a rule, provide a large number of documents. Among these will be a considerable number of noise documents, because all documents using the term "information need" in discussing some other ideas (not only those concerning the study of such a need) will be retrieved.

When considering the second search request, one finds the opposite situation. If we try to find documents with representations containing all nine of the descriptors listed, we will most likely find very few documents; that is, a number of documents important for the user will not be found. Moreover, in many systems the average number of descriptors in sets representing the contents of the documents (in document profiles) does not exceed twelve (this average is typically based on the system's design). This implies that the retrieval to the second query may give no results at all. In other words, there may be a document with the profile containing eight descriptors all coinciding with those out of the nine descriptors listed, but the document will not be selected.

Developers of IR systems very early noticed all of the negative factors resulting from the use of the previously mentioned selection criterion. This stimulated an intensive search for solutions capable of improving retrieval results. Eventually, these efforts concentrated on the following directions:

1. Modification of the selection criterion.
2. Modification of the rules for constructing query formulations.
3. Modification of the explicit ("realized") semantical component of IRL.
4. Various combinations of items 1, 2, and 3.

Actually, these directions correspond to ways of improving IR systems in general, and not only systems based on Taube's approach to the meaning representation. However, because we are considering these particular systems we will be interested in the first two directions (separately and jointly).

As we have noted, the efforts of many investigators were aimed at finding more effective search criteria. In this area the first idea was to use a partial (and not the complete) match of the descriptor set representing the request with that representing the document. At least, this appeared to be a remedy for many of the negative situations just illustrated (with a query with nine descriptors). Various approaches were proposed. For instance, in the IR system developed by the IBM Corporation the following selection criterion was used (at the end of the 1950s and the beginning of the 1960s) (Tritschler, 1962). The degree to which the document profile with the query formulation coincide (i.e., the degree to which the descriptor set representing the document matched that representing the request) is denoted by G. This value was measured in percent. The total number of descriptors in the document profile was denoted by d, and i was the number of document profile descriptors coinciding with those of the query formulation. The formula for G read as follows:

$$G = \frac{i}{d} 100\%.$$

Experts at IBM reasoned that appropriate values of G for different systems varied within 15% with a lower limit no less than 25%. For example, in a system where the degree of the coincidence $G \geq 30\%$ is assumed sufficient and the size of the document profile is twelve descriptors, any document with the document profile containing at least four (any) descriptors coinciding with those from the set representing the request (from the query formulation) is considered as fitting the selection criterion. If we now return to the second request of the preceding example (with query formulations containing nine descriptors), we will see that the use of such (less stringent) selection criterion (the document profile is not required to contain all nine descriptors—any four will suffice) reduces the number of documents that are present in the system but are not found (specialists would say that "losses are reduced") and, as a rule, improves the retrieval results.

Thus, the introduction of the partial match criterion reduces losses. But what about noise? How can one reduce it? Noise reduction is what the second direction mainly seeks to achieve. Indeed, if one constructs the descriptor set representing a search request of only those descriptors with conditional equivalence classes including words of the query, one would frequently encounter situations similar to that produced by the first request in the example (where the query formulation contains only one descriptor). This means that the criterion developed by IBM (again assume $G \geq 30\%$) will yield only those documents with document profiles containing three or fewer descriptors. It is clear that the system may contain no such documents and hence no documents will be selected. Yes, noise is reduced (in some cases down to zero), but one can easily imagine the user's reaction. Therefore, experts (responsible for constructing query formulations in the IR systems) proposed in some cases to include in the query formulations descriptors that were not directly derived from the search request but were somehow related to the request. This will increase the size of the query formulation above some reasonable threshold. Such an approach will reduce noise; for example, the query formulation corresponding to the first request will be augmented by other descriptors that are required to be present in the document profile and hence the set of selected documents will be smaller. This approach was combined with the partial match criterion allowed, in many cases, for the attainment of an acceptable retrieval quality. It was done because the query formulation already contains more than one descriptor, and the value $G \geq 30\%$ in such a query formulation means the use of more representative—that is, more representative than one consisting of three or fewer descriptors—document profiles (which is more realistic in functioning IR systems). The search in the collection with more realistic document profiles assumes the use of at least two descriptors in the query formulation, which are used together during search. The analysis of the following IBM criterion better explains several features of information retrieval.

One can easily see that for $G \geq 30\%$, any document with a profile containing twenty-seven descriptors can be found only with a query formulation containing at least nine descriptors all coinciding with those in the twenty-seven descriptors of the document profile. Obviously, such query formulations are not so common, and hence the search will result in many losses. In other words, this feature of the criterion means that the more aspects are discussed in the document, the less the probability of finding it. Mainly this concerns large manuscripts, textbooks, and so on. Also the requirement to match the large number of descriptors in the case of multiaspect documents implies that the value of an aspect detailed in a book represented by thirty descriptors is considerably less than the value of the same aspect in a short report represented by six descriptors. Thus, given the search request, the probability of yielding the report and "loosing" the book is rather high. More detailed analysis of this criterion shows that, for instance, the set of three descriptors representing a certain request generates seven subsets, which will be used in the retrieval process. During such a retrieval, one subset (only one) containing three descriptors will be used to search among documents represented by sets containing seven, eight, nine, and ten descriptors, subsets (three) containing two descriptors (among sets containing four, five, and six descriptors), and those (also three subsets) containing one descriptor (among sets containing three and fewer descriptors).

To a certain extent, this analysis characterizes the main directions in the efforts to create IR systems. The consideration of early attempts to improve retrieval results shows that developers concentrated mainly on descriptor sets representing search requests. Virtually all modifications have been proposed for these particular sets leaving aside sets representing documents. This partly comes from the fact the number of search requests is much smaller than the number of documents, so it is more convenient to change hundreds of requests than thousands of documents. However, another important factor is the understanding that each request is unique and, as a rule, does not exactly describe (reflect) the IN it presents to the system, while documents are written for a variety of users, and hence it is not efficient to adapt them for a single user.

One of the most important ideas contributing to the creation of successfully functioning IR systems was to represent a query formulation not in the form of a single unordered set of descriptors but in the form of a set of such sets. This idea was based on the understanding of several features and properties of natural languages and the representation of the same meaning by different words. As an example, consider two real search requests given to the IR system on information science: (1) "Algorithmization of the construction of query formulations" and (2) "Automatic methods of search requests translation from natural language to IRL." One can easily see that these requests reflect similar IN but include not only different words but also a different number of words. Moreover, after translating them to IRL, one may obtain different descriptor sets and, as a consequence, different retrieval results. A similar effect on the search results may be due to another well-known factor—the possibility of expressing meaning by a different numbers of sentences.

Obviously, different natural-language formulations (texts) expressing the same meaning do not imply the use of different semantical components. In all cases, one such component exists—the semantical component of the natural language. The same is true for IRL: the search request representation in the form of several unordered sets of descriptors instead of a single set (as well as representing request by different descriptors within the set or by sets of different sizes) does not imply the use of some distinct semantical component of IRL (we mean, distinct from Taube's semantical component). Therefore, when discussing the ways to improve IR systems using this component, we first assume the request representation in the form of unordered sets of descriptors. We say "first" because this particular approach has been the most popular for creating IR systems and, more importantly, is used in the majority of contemporary functioning systems.

But why has this approach turned out to be so popular? Mainly because the selection criterion using this approach accounts for a possibility of different expressions of meaning in natural-language texts (as was discussed earlier). Indeed, when writing documents, their authors use different words to describe the same phenomenon. This means that in an IR system, different documents describing the same phenomenon may be represented by a different sets of descriptors. Hence, the use of several descriptor sets representing the request (rather than one set) increases the probability of finding the required documents, because now not a single descriptor set mandatory for all required documents is used; instead, a collection of sets is used, each of which might be sufficient for successful search. Such a criterion is normally called the *selection criterion in the Boolean form* or the *Boolean selection criterion*. Now we consider this criterion in more detail.

First, note that the use of the term, "Boolean expression," for an unordered set of descriptors is due to the fact that both the form of its representation in information retrieval and the operations in which this set is used could be implemented within the framework of Boolean algebra. In essence, the Boolean criterion is simple, and it looks natural and reasonable. It could be illustrated by the example most people are familiar with, the lottery game.

Assume that a person in New Jersey is interested in participating in the state's lottery. By buying a ticket, a player formulates his request for a "win" in the lottery. This request is represented by the set of, say, six numbers. According to the rules of the New Jersey lottery, these numbers should be from 1 to 49 and there should be no repetitions in the set. Using formal mathematical symbols we write

$$U = \{x : x \in N,\ 1 \le x \le 49\},$$

where U represents the set of numbers participating in the lottery and N represents the set of natural numbers. We also write

$$S = \{a,\ b,\ c,\ d,\ e,\ f\},$$

where a, b, c, d, e, and $f \in U$. S is the set of six numbers chosen by the player (hence, they are all distinct). $S \subset U$; that is, S is a subset of U. S will be called a query-set.

Note that the collection of possible subsets of U consisting of six elements includes about 20 million combinations. During a lottery, a single win-set is formed. This set, denoted by T, is formed from the set U and includes six different numbers. In other words, $T \subset U$. Obviously, finding T is a more rare event than finding a required document in an IR system (in addition, the collection is smaller and several documents are normally required). However, we are not interested in the probability of winning in the lottery, but in the selection (winning) criterion. The win-set will be selected from the collection if every number in the query-set appears in the win-set. In other words, all numbers, a, b, c, d, e, and f from S coincide with numbers from T, (i.e., $S = T$). To indicate that all numbers a, b, c, d, e, and f have to appear at the same time, the language of Boolean algebra could be used. Therefore, $a \wedge b \wedge c \wedge d \wedge e \wedge f$, where ($\wedge$) denotes the logical AND. To "win," one needs all elements (numbers) unified by AND to coincide with the numbers in the win-set.

One can obviously improve the win-retrieval results (increase the probability of winning) by buying several tickets instead of one. This means that the player will use

$$M = \{S_1, S_2, \ldots, S_n\},$$

where for all $1 \leq i \leq n$, $S_i \subset U$, $|S_i| = 6$, $S_i \neq S_j$ for $i \neq j$; and n equals the number of tickets bought.

In this case, the retrieval will be performed according to several unordered sets of six numbers. For instance, if a person buys five tickets, she has five different sets, namely S_1, S_2, S_3, S_4, and S_5. It is clear that the retrieval will be successful if S_1 or S_2 or S_3 or S_4 or S_5 coincides with the win set. In Boolean algebra, such a condition is written as follows:

$$S_1 \vee S_2 \vee S_3 \vee S_4 \vee S_5.$$

Here $\vee$ denotes the logical OR; that is, it prescribes the coincidence of any of five sets to be considered as a success. Now let us write this Boolean expression in more detail so that we represent each S_i in the form of the element set by means of the AND operator. This provides the following: $(a_1 \wedge b_1 \wedge c_1 \wedge d_1 \wedge e_1 \wedge f_1) \vee (a_2 \wedge b_2 \wedge c_2 \wedge d_2 \wedge e_2 \wedge f_2) \vee (a_3 \wedge b_3 \wedge c_3 \wedge d_3 \wedge e_3 \wedge f_3) \vee (a_4 \wedge b_4 \wedge c_4 \wedge d_4 \wedge e_4 \wedge f_4) \vee (a_5 \wedge b_5 \wedge c_5 \wedge d_5 \wedge e_5 \wedge f_5)$. This Boolean expression is in what is called the *disjunctive normal form*.

Thus the lottery game provides a clear illustration of the Boolean criterion used in the information retrieval process. The use of the Boolean criterion in IR systems is more flexible than that in the lottery game. For example, information retrieval does not require alternative sets to be of equal size. In other words, whereas in the lottery all sets are of equal size (six numbers), IR systems

Don't think so. Boolean logic can be better explained in the context of word/descriptor appearance!

allow for the variation of sizes over wide range, and a single-descriptor set is as valuable as descriptor sets of any other size. Consider the following example. Assume that from a given search request an IR system has generated two descriptor sets, S_1 and S_2, to perform the retrieval. Assume also that the set S_1 contains only one descriptor, a ($S_1 = \{a\}$), and the set S_2 contains three descriptors, b, c, and d ($S_2 = \{b, c, d\}$). Then, using the disjunctive normal form, the query formulation can be written as follows:

$$a \vee (b \wedge c \wedge d).$$

It is clear that both sets "have equal rights"; that is, a document matching any of them is formally considered as required by the user and is included in the selection. In essence, this corresponds to the feature of the natural language mentioned previously: each set from the query formulation accounts for a different lexical expression of the same meaning. It is worth stressing that alternative sets constructed are unique; that is, in one query formulation there should be no descriptor sets being subsets of other sets.

As mentioned earlier, the Boolean criterion is utilized in a majority of practically functioning IR systems. Therefore, in Chapter 7 we will consider in greater detail the methods of constructing query formulations for systems using this criterion.

Thus one can conclude that the main direction in the IR system development based on the approach to meaning representation offered by Taube includes the query representation in the form of unordered descriptor sets and the use of Boolean criterion. However, in parallel, investigators have been attempting to change the semantical component of IRL. The use of weights seems to be the most interesting approach in this direction. In this approach, the developers considered the quality of the meaning representation in the form of unordered descriptor sets insufficient. They have proposed to characterize descriptors by the extent of their importance in the text, that is, by their weights. The more important descriptor, the larger its weight. Thus two sets containing the same descriptors can represent the contents of the corresponding texts in different ways, and the search results can be different too. Similar to other directions in IR development, investigators have concentrated on the representation (here, with the aid of weights) of search requests. Obviously, such an addition to the meaning representation should be accounted for by the selection criterion. Next we discuss several, better-known criteria of this kind.

It seems that one of the first weighting criteria was developed by IBM almost simultaneously with the partial matching criterion previously described above (Ofer, 1964). When constructing the query formulation (building the set of descriptors representing the search request), the user evaluates each descriptor of the request and assigns to each descriptor a weight coefficient. A special standard scale of points is used for this purpose. This scale contains both positive and negative values of importance. Besides, the user can specify a certain mandatory numerical value measured in conditional units (points), which a document should reach to be selected. A document is considered as selected (found) if the sum of weight coefficients of the query formulation descriptors coinciding with document profile descriptors is no less than the user-specified value. Let us illustrate this criterion by the following example.

Assume that an IR system uses the 18-point weight scale with 9 positive and 9 negative points (this particular scale has been used by IBM). Assume now that the user has selected the descriptor set, $W = \{a, b, c, d, e, f\}$, for the query formulation and has assigned the following values to the descriptor weights: $a = 7$, $b = -4$, $c = 2$, $d = 9$, $e = 1$, and $f = 6$. Assume also that the user has specified the threshold value, $P = 16$, for documents to be selected. Then the document is considered as found if its document profile contains such descriptors of the query formulation that the sum of their weights is no less than 16 (Kraft, 1963).

It is worth noting that deeper analysis of this criterion shows its similarity with the Boolean selection criterion. Indeed, in the preceding example the document is selected if its document profile contains descriptors (a) and (d) and does not contain (b), or if it contains descriptors (a), (d), and (f) together with (b). Other adequate document profiles may include (a, c, e, f) without (b); (d, e, f), again without (b); and so forth. This can be written as $(a \wedge d \wedge \sim b) \vee (a \wedge d \wedge f \wedge b) \vee (a \wedge c \wedge e \wedge f \wedge \sim b) \vee (d \wedge e \wedge f \wedge \sim b) \ldots$ where $\sim$ denotes the Boolean logical NOT. This expression differs from previous Boolean expressions by the presence of this particular operator.

Such a similarity with the Boolean criterion has led some investigators to assert that all weighting criteria are just Boolean criteria represented in a distinct form. This is, however, not true. There are weighting criteria that cannot be used (represented) in the Boolean form, and the retrieval cannot be classified as Boolean. The most well-known criterion among these is that developed by Salton (1971) and used in the SMART system. We will now consider this criterion in more detail.

Although in the majority of approaches only search requests were indexed using weights, a number of methods included weighting of both requests and documents. As an example, consider the weighting criterion used in the IR system developed by the U.S. Department of Interior, Bureau of Reclamation (Hilf, 1963). In this system documents are represented by 15 to 25 descriptors each. Descriptors which represent the main contents of the document most adequately (in the opinion of the person who performs indexing) are marked by a star (no more than four descriptors will be included in this category). The user also marks no more than four descriptors, which are most informative in the search request. The developers of this system used the following selection criterion: either (1) at least one descriptor from the document profile coincides with at least one descriptor from the query formulation and at least one of these is marked with a star or (2) at least three descriptors from the document profile coincide with those from the query formulation (marking in this case is ignored).

Earlier we have mentioned the weighting criterion used in the SMART system (Salton, 1971). The authors of this system themselves have characterized this system as follows: "The SMART system is perhaps the best known of the experimental systems" (Salton & McGill, 1983). This seems to be true, at least according to the number of publications devoted to this system, which exceeds the number of publications on any other experimental or practically implemented system. The correspondence criterion used in this system has the distinction of being very original and also of being used exclusively in a computerized environment. In essence, each search request to the SMART system results in the sorting of documents; that is, the number of times the collection of documents is sorted is equal to the number of search requests. Documents sorted according to a concrete search request are placed in order of decreasing values (calculated using the weights) of the correlation between a search request and the documents in the collection. It is assumed that a document with the highest correlation value is the most appropriate for the corresponding search request and should be read first by the user. Let us look at its implementation in more detail.

All descriptors of the system dictionary form the space of terms. Document profiles are built in this space. Each descriptor has the corresponding coordinate in this space. Document profiles are represented by vectors in the term space. If a certain document deals with the i-th descriptor, then the i-th coordinate of its vector is nonzero; otherwise it is zero. Concrete values of nonzero coordinates are identified with their weights in the document profiles considered. Manual indexing implies that weights are specified by a human being and in this case the quality of indexing depends on the skills and experience of the person performing the indexing. However, various methods have been developed for the automatic weight specification. For example, the descriptor weight can be defined as equal to the appearance frequency of this descriptor in the document.

Query formulations are also built as vectors in the term space. The extent of proximity of a document profile (let us denote it as $\mathbf{A}$) to the query formulation (let us denote it as $\mathbf{B}$) is commonly defined as a cosine of the angle between the corresponding vectors:

$$r(\mathbf{A}, \mathbf{B}) = \frac{\mathbf{AB}}{|\mathbf{A}||\mathbf{B}|},$$

where $\mathbf{AB}$ is the scalar product; and $|\mathbf{A}|$ and $|\mathbf{B}|$ are lengths of vectors $\mathbf{A}$ and $\mathbf{B}$. The value $r(\mathbf{A}, \mathbf{B})$ is sometimes called the coefficient of the correlation between the query formulation and the document profile. Vectors $\mathbf{A}$ and $\mathbf{B}$ are considered close if their correlation coefficient is close to 1. Because all vector coordinates are non-negative, the minimum possible value of the correlation coefficient is zero. This value corresponds to a case when all terms in the query and the document are different. Vectors of both document profile and query formulation consist of the descriptors and the values of nonzero coordinates. Let

term ID./token

vectors **A** and **B** be represented as $\mathbf{A}[16(1), 27(3), 195(4), 327(1), 592(3)]$ and $\mathbf{B}[16(2), 82(3), 195(2), 327(2), 984(2)]$. Then their correlation coefficient is

$$r(\mathbf{A, B})$$

$$= \frac{1 \times 2 + 3 \times 0 + 0 \times 3 + 4 \times 2 + 1 \times 2 + 3 \times 0 + 0 \times 2}{\sqrt{1^2 + 3^2 + 4^2 + 1^2 + 3^2} \times \sqrt{2^2 + 3^2 + 2^2 + 2^2 + 2^2}}$$

$$= \frac{2 + 8 + 2}{\sqrt{36} \times \sqrt{25}} = \frac{12}{30} = 0.4.$$

Thus, the collection of documents is ordered (sorted) in the order of decreasing cosines of angles between query and document vectors. But what does the user obtain? Obviously, it is not practical to select all documents in the collection, even if it is sorted. Therefore, various approaches to the selection criterion have been proposed. For example, it has been suggested that the user should obtain all documents with correlation coefficients above a certain specified value. However, this approach has several shortcomings. First, in situations when all correlation coefficients are below the threshold, nothing will be selected. On the other hand, too many documents may be selected for a given request; that is, too many documents may have correlation coefficients above the specified threshold.

Another proposal has been to select exactly N (say, 10) best documents (with the highest correlation coefficients). In this case, however, specificity and "broadness" of search requests are not considered. Furthermore, this approach implies that all requests have the same number of corresponding documents in the system. The authors of the system consider it important in generating the output to take into account the user's determination of the number of documents in the output. Before the search is started, users are asked to specify the number of documents in the output. For example, when specifying the search request, one user would like to obtain 6 documents, another would like to have 17 documents, and some other user, say, 38 documents. Clearly, each will receive the exact number of documents requested regardless of the number of appropriate documents. In each case the documents obtained will have a higher correlation coefficient to the query than the documents that were not selected.

Note that with the development of more advanced methods for on-line services, this problem has lost its validity. For example, in the on-line search mode, the user can view as many documents as he or she wishes. To a certain extent, a problem still exists in the *selective dissemination information* activities, when a system sends information to its users according to their long-term search requests on a regular basis (for example, once a month). However, the number of such systems is getting smaller and smaller.

Another point is worth noting in connection with the SMART system. In the mid 1960s—by the time the main principles used in the SMART system had been developed—developers were rather pessimistic about the problem of sort-

Cognitive strain.

ing (or, as some scientists say, the problem of *ranging*) the whole collection of a document. The main problem was that the calculation of scalar products required considerably more computer operations than a simple comparison did. Hence, information retrieval in the SMART system took much more time than retrieval in Boolean systems (which additionally utilized special file organization allowing the reduction of the number of comparison operations). The increase in CPU time made the search more expensive. Therefore, the idea of splitting the retrieval collection into groups (subsets) of similar (in meaning) documents soon appeared. The creation of the scheme for dividing the collection of documents is usually called the *classification,* while distributing documents into groups (classes) according to this scheme is called the *clusterization.* With the aid of document classification, Salton reasoned, the retrieval can be made more efficient by using sorting only for certain parts (classes) of the collection. Although ignoring the larger part of the collection can cause large losses in the retrieval, the improvement in retrieval time has been considered a more essential factor. Therefore, since the late 1960s a considerable number of publications on classification and clusterization have appeared describing elaborate methods and algorithms mostly for the improvement of the SMART system. However, in this case, new developments in the field of computer science (and the sharp improvement in the internal performance and memory of computers) has been making this problem less and less important. Moreover, in the near future, with the appearance of computers with massive parallel processing, sorting collections containing tens of thousands of documents will not be a problem. This will significantly improve the efficiency of the SMART system.

Thus, generally speaking, changing the semantical component of IRL by assigning weights to lexical units of the language is of certain interest and, in our opinion, is rather promising. At least, one can hardly deny that the potential of this direction is far from being exhausted.

It would seem that changes in the semantical component of IRL should have included the introduction of certain grammatical rules of the natural language for the representation of texts. Such attempts have been made; however, we are not familiar with any of the functioning systems or interesting experimental systems where this approach is used, and therefore we will not consider it in this book.

Having considered the semantical component of IRL, let us discuss its grammar. As we have mentioned, IRL grammar (the grammatical component) is first of all intended for writing (fixing) meaning representations of documents and search requests on a certain physical medium. As seen from the previous consideration, the number of different meaning representations in IR systems is quite small. Therefore, the previous examples are sufficient illustrations of IRL grammar used to represent meanings of documents and queries. However, we have not accentuated the rules for writing meaning representations. We will provide a more detailed explanation of these rules next.

Let us start with Taube's search criterion. In this case, the meanings of documents and search requests is represented in the same form, that is, as sets of descriptors. For example, denoting the document profile as D and the query formulation as Q, we might have the following representation:

$$D = \{a, m, k, x, y, z\} \qquad Q = \{b, f, k, z\},$$

where $a, b, f,$ and so forth are descriptors from the dictionary used in the system. The same representation is also sufficient for a search criterion that takes partial matching into consideration.

When the meaning of the search request is represented by a set of descriptor sets (the Boolean criterion) and the meaning of the document is given by a single set, the expression of the document profile is the same as in the preceding example, whereas the query formulation is given (i.e., is written as) in the disjunctive normal form. In a special case when indexing provides only one set of descriptors, the expression of the query formulation coincides with that of the document profile. For example, the set $S = \{d, n, o, p, r\}$ with descriptors $d, n, o, p,$ and r can represent the contents of both a document and a query given to the system. However, the expression

$$a \vee b \vee c \vee (d \wedge u) \vee (m \wedge n) \vee (m \wedge k \wedge w)$$

can, in the framework of the approaches to meaning representation described above, only be a query formulation (Frants & Shapiro, 1991).

When the semantical component allows us to use descriptor weights, the descriptors of the query formulation—and sometimes those of the document profile—are supplied with weights assigned to them either with or without weight values. For example, the use of weights in the system developed at the U.S. Department of Interior (mentioned earlier) is confined to only marking weighted descriptors by a star. Thus, grammatical rules to represent both document profiles and query formulations in this system have the following form:

$$M = \{a, b^*, c, d, e^*, f^* \}.$$

Here M may represent either a document profile or a query formulation; $a, b, c, d, e,$ and f are descriptors; and (*) marks the descriptor's importance (in our example $b, e,$ and f are important descriptors).

When descriptors are characterized by different values of weights, one can write corresponding sets as follows:

$$N = \{a(3), b(1), c(-2)\},$$

where N may be the representation both of a document and a query; $a, b,$ and c are descriptors; and numbers in brackets give the importance of corresponding descriptors.

All of these examples, in our opinion, are quite exhaustive in describing the existing grammatical means (grammatical components) used to represent documents and queries in IRL.

The grammation concept of CRL still remains vague inspite of that.

5.7

Relevance, Pertinence, Recall, and Precision

In discussing information retrieval in IR systems and the formal criteria of the selection of documents, we talked about the output of this search process (i.e., the IR system selects documents required by the user). We have not called them pertinent, although this term was used in Chapter 4. The reason is that pertinent documents are normally understood as those corresponding to the user's information need (from the user's point of view). However, in IR systems, the user does not take part in the information retrieval. Hence, the documents selected by the system (according to formal rules) cannot be classified as pertinent documents. For this reason, in information science documents "needed by the user," with the "need" determined (on the basis of the search request given by the user) using some method by anyone other than the user, are called *relevant*.

Throughout its history (probably dating back 4000 years), information retrieval has always dealt with relevant documents (that is, long before "needed by the user" acquired the terminology "relevant"). However, as the understanding of the nature and properties of information needs has improved, the term "relevance" has acquired different meanings. The exact meaning of this term when used by authors in different articles was often not obvious. This term is used not only in the retrieval of the documents for the output but also for the evaluation of document quality as well as the quality of the IR system. In general, "relevance" is one of the most frequently used terms in scientific publications discussing IR systems. Therefore, we would like to consider it in more detail.

As a rule, when speaking about "relevance," authors imply one of the following three meanings (see, for example, Barry, 1994; Howard, 1994; Jones, 1994; and Park, 1994). The first meaning corresponds to the formal generation of the output in the system, that is, to the formal criterion for the selection of documents required by the user. The second refers to the expert's evaluation of the output formed in the system and hence to the evaluation of the entire system. The third meaning of the term coincides with that of "pertinence" as used by some authors; that is, they use "relevance" instead of "pertinence" meaning "pertinence."

Let us first consider the generation of the output. It is clear that essentially the formal criterion for the document selection constitutes the criterion to select relevant documents, that is, documents required by the user. Indeed, the goal of IR systems developers is to retrieve documents that are of interest to the user. Recall from Chapter 2 that the user is interested in documents that contain the required information. The extent of the user's interest in the document depends on the amount of information it contains that satisfies the user's IN. Thus a formal selection criterion using a specific system constitutes a concrete rule to determine the relevance of documents. Obviously, this rule can be successful to a different degree, but it is the developer's choice to have the computer perform the relevance evaluation. This is probably the very essence of the IR system creation, and it is the meaning of the assertion that IR systems find only relevant documents.

This particular meaning of the term "relevance" is greatly debated. But still some investigators suggest that documents found by the IR systems should not be called relevant. In other words, there is a desire to reduce the number of meanings of this term. For example, Lancaster proposes that instead of using the term "relevance" one should "simply refer to document representation 'matching a search strategy' and documents 'matching an intended strategy'" (Lancaster, 1979). However, more investigators propose to call selected documents *formally relevant* and, speaking about the situation under consideration, they use the term *formal relevance*. Thus, they separate this situation from that corresponding to the most frequently used meaning of the term "relevance." The latter is considered next.

The most frequently used meaning of the term—and probably the universally adopted one—is connected to the expert's evaluation of documents retrieved by the system. Actually, it is the expert who decides on the relevance of a retrieved document (its need by the user) or its irrelevance (it is not needed by the user) after reading it. Usually it is decided during the evaluation of the information retrieval efficiency. Of course, in order to decide the relevance of a document the expert should know what the user requires. As a rule, such knowledge is formed after the expert has read the user's search request. It is after reading the request that the expert acquires an understanding of the user's IN. This IN may differ from the IN the user has tried to express, as well as from the IN the user has managed to express. We illustrate this point in Figure 5.5.

In this figure we give a model of possible situations concerning the user's IN. In part (a), a certain *ideal* IN, *A*, is presented. Such an IN could appear when in the course of activities the user encounters an uncertainty in the behavior algorithm. In other words, if after facing the uncertainty the IN *A* has appeared and if the information satisfying *A* has been found, this behavior uncertainty would have been completely eliminated. Part (b), together with IN *A*, shows IN *B*, which has really appeared instead of ideal IN *A*. In this case, the *actual* IN, *B*, is more "narrow" than the ideal one (although it is possible to have other relationships between *A* and *B*). Therefore documents corresponding to parts (k) and (l) of the ideal IN *A* do not correspond to the emergent IN *B*. However, this case will be discussed later when considering pertinence. Recall from Chapter 2 that the actual IN *B* is a certain psychological condition of the user with boundaries that are not well defined (information need of type POIN). That is why in part (c) of Figure 5.5 we show the *perceived* IN represented by the area *C*. This is a kind of IN that the user really perceives. The areas *x*, *y*, and *z* are also rather interesting, but they will be considered later when we discuss

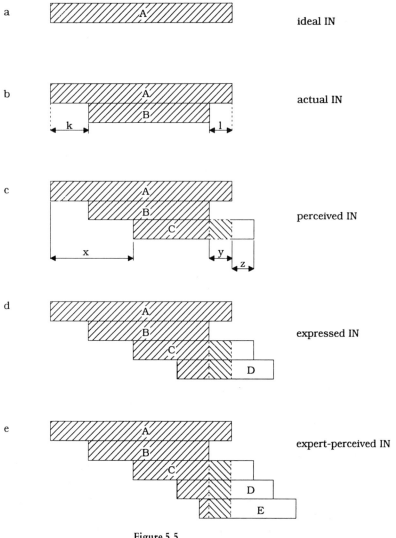

a   ideal IN

b   actual IN

c   perceived IN

d   expressed IN

e   expert-perceived IN

Figure 5.5
Various ways to consider IN.

pertinence. In part (d), the area *D* stands for the *expressed* IN, that is, the IN the user managed to express in the formulated search request. Finally, in part (e) the area *E* corresponds to the expert's understanding of the user's IN. This understanding appears after the expert has read the user's search request. It is this *expert-perceived* IN that serves for the evaluation of the relevance of retrieved documents. Naturally, this type of expert evaluation, as well as any other non-formalized expert evaluation in any other sphere, is of completely subjective nature. That is why many investigators consider the evaluation by a single expert insufficient and suggest that several experts should be engaged. For example, Lancaster noted that "it would certainly seem desirable to involve a group of judges and try to arrive at some group consensus as to which documents are relevant." (Lancaster, 1979). Apparently in this case each expert has his or her own imagined IN and performs the evaluation according to it. "Use of several judges," reasoned Lancaster.

> Working independently to make relevance decisions, would at least give us a ranking of documents in terms of "relevance consensus." We could then express the results of a particular search in the following form:
> 1. Thirty-five percent of the documents retrieved were judged relevant by all five judges.
> 2. Forty-three percent were judged relevant by at least four of the five judges.
> 3. Sixty-two percent were judged relevant by at least three of the judges, and so on. (Lancaster, 1979)

The third meaning of the term "relevance" (as noted earlier) coincides with that of the term "pertinence," because some investigators use the term "relevance" in situations where "pertinence" is meant. However, the majority of developers do differentiate between these two terms. Thus the term "pertinence" can be considered as universally accepted. In this connection, Lancaster noted that "pertinence refers to a relationship between a document and an information need, the decision in this case is being made exclusively by the person having the information need" (Lancaster, 1979). To illustrate several points concerning pertinence, let us return to Figure 5.5.

The user judges the pertinence of documents; that is, the user determines whether they contain the required information or not. But what kind of information does the user recognize as being interesting? The answer seems simple. The user should judge all documents corresponding to the perceived IN to be pertinent. However, as we can see from Figure 5.5, the perceived IN can be beyond the limits of not only actual IN, but also of the ideal IN. Hence, having read documents from the area z, the user may consider these documents as non-pertinent because they do not reduce the uncertainty of the user's behavior algorithm. What about areas x and y? Area y is a part of the perceived IN and a part of the ideal one, but it is not included in the actual IN. On the other hand, area x is a part of the ideal IN and the actual IN, but not the perceived IN. What is the importance of such a difference for the user? If documents containing information corresponding to these areas are presented to the user, they will reduce the user's uncertainty, thereby allowing the user to regard them as pertinent. Similar considerations are applicable to the areas k and l. Thus, any documents containing information corresponding to the ideal IN seem to be pertinent, because they can satisfy existing IN by eliminating the uncertainty. Nevertheless, this is not always the case. First, the information obtained by the user may be logically related to other information the user is not aware of. This means that, having read the information from a document D_1 before reading document D_2, the user can judge document D_1 as nonpertinent. Second, the level of presenting the subject as well as the material itself can cause certain difficulties in comprehension. For example, without knowledge of the probability theory, one cannot appreciate (and apply) a new probabilistic approach presented in a paper and would not be able to use it to solve one's problem. Third, the document may contain very little information useful for the reader and a considerable amount of information of no use to the reader. In this situation, although the user will use this small amount of information, he or she still can judge the document to be nonpertinent.

Clearly the situations described above can also cause difficulties in judging relevance. Besides, the list of similar situations can be expanded, for example, through situations described by Lancaster. However, these examples sufficiently show that the evaluation of pertinence is also not that precise. Because the user evaluates the pertinence according to the ideal IN and the expert judges relevance according to the expressed IN (and in both cases these evaluations are subjective), one can consider various interrelations between relevance and pertinence. For example, experts can judge a document relevant, while the user will regard it as nonpertinent. It is also conceivable that experts will judge a document as irrelevant, while the user marks it as pertinent. This phenomenon is quite familiar to investigators and was mentioned by a number of authors.

Pertinent documents are used for constructing query formulations as well as for correcting them based on the user's feedback. Relevant documents (as has been noted) are, as a rule, used in the evaluation (with the criteria defined by experts) of the quality of information retrieval itself. In essence, relevance is the basis for such popular IR system evaluation characteristics as recall and precision. Introduced in the mid-1950s, these characteristics are used in virtually all experiments conducted to evaluate the quality of retrieval in the system. The recall coefficient (the recall ratio) is defined as a ratio (often as a percent) of the number of relevant documents that are retrieved to the total number of relevant documents in the collection. The precision coefficient (precision ratio) is the (also often a percent) ratio of the number of retrieved relevant documents to the total number of retrieved documents. Analytically these coefficients can be written as follows:

$$R = \frac{n}{N}(\times 100\%) \qquad P = \frac{n}{M}(\times 100\%),$$

where

n = number of retrieved relevant documents;
N = number of relevant documents in the collection; and
M = number of documents retrieved.

In the following, when evaluating retrieval efficiency we will use these characteristics, namely recall and precision. When the user evaluates the results of the search (selected documents) it is necessary to modify the discussion by replacing the relevant documents with pertinent documents. However, this will not affect the computation of the evaluation characteristics.

5.8
Conclusion

In discussing the history of information retrieval, we showed that for thousands of years the process of search itself (more specifically, such operations as comparison and selection) was performed by humans, and natural language also served as the IRL. Because the participation of people in a search was always considered obligatory—and until the middle of the 20th century it was not even questioned—all the efforts toward creating and developing retrieval methods were oriented toward advancing the human search for information.

It should be pointed out that the development of retrieval methods traditionally proceeded in two directions. First, compression of the texts of documents allowed users to review the available collection much faster, and, second, compression of the collection itself served the same purpose. For thousands of years the work in this direction allowed people to avoid serious critical situations caused by the search for information. However, as Chapter 3 showed, the current information crisis exists because the traditional (manual) methods based on the ideas of compression are not able to cope with the existing flow of information. To overcome the existing crisis researchers, for the first time in history, took a close look at the human participation in a search process. Indeed, a person's speed in reviewing information is not only very low but is bounded by human physiology. As the result, a new, third direction, was developed whereby the human being does not participate in the search but is replaced by a computer. In other words, new direction was needed principally to develop search methods that were oriented toward a qualitatively new speed of reviewing (comparison and selection) documents in the collection. The absence of the human user during the search implied the impossibility of using natural language during the search. This was the reason for developing other IRLs that differed from natural languages. Such languages already exist and are called descriptor languages.

In describing these languages, this chapter not only examined different approaches to defining their lexical structures and the existing ideas of using different grammatical rules, but it also described different criteria of correspondence constructed on the basis of these languages. The analysis of these criteria revealed their strong and weak points and helped to explain the choice of these criteria in practice.

Thus this chapter considered the IRLs used in IR systems. Now, on the basis of one of the IRLs described earlier, it is possible to discuss how to realize every structural element of an IR system. As each of the following chapters concentrates on a specific element of the system, we will assume that the system uses the Boolean selection criterion and that all the processes are performed by a given system automatically. We will start our discussion with the process of translating documents from the natural language into IRL. This process is often called the indexing of documents.

References

Barry, C. L. (1994). User-defined relevance criteria: An exploratory study. *Journal of the American Society for Information Science, 45*(3).

Broadhurst, P. L. (1962). Coordinate indexing: A bibliography aid. *American Psychologist, 17*(3).

Chomsky, N. (1972). *Language and mind* (Enlarged ed.). New York: Harcourt, Brace, Jovanovich.

Francisco, R. L. (1956). Use of Uniterm coordinate indexing system in a large industrial concern. *Special Libraries, 47*(3).

Frants, V. I., & Shapiro, J. (1991). Control and feedback in a documentary information retrieval system. *Journal of the American Society for Information Science, 42*(9), 623–634, 1991

Hilf, J. W. (1963). Matching of descriptors in a selective dissemination system. In *Automation and Scientific Communication, Part 1.* Washington, DC: American Documentation Institute.

Howard, D. L. (1994). Pertinence as reflected in personal constructs. *Journal of the American Society for Information Science, 45*(3).

Jones, J. W. (1994). Other people's judgements: A comparison of users' and others' judgements of document relevance, topicality, and utility. *Journal of the American Society for Information Science, 45*(3).

Kraft, D. H. (1963). An operational selective dissemination of information (SDI) system for technical and nontechnical personnel using automatic indexing techniques. In *Automation and Scientific Communication, Part 1.* Washington, DC: American Documentation Institute.

Kucera, H. N., & Francis, W. N. (1968). *Computational analysis of present-day American English.* Providence, RI: Brown University Press.

Lancaster, F. W. (1979). *Information retrieval systems: Characteristics, testing, evaluation.* New York: John Wiley & Sons.

Mooers, C. N. (1948). New filing system developed for special collections. *Library Journal,* 73(10).

Mooers, C. N. (1955). Zatocoding applied to mathematical organization of knowledge. *American Documentation, 2*(1).

Ofer, K. D. (1964). Selective information dissemination and retrieval at Chemical and Phosphate Ltd. with an IBM-1401 DPS. In *Congresso Internazionale Sulla Documentazione e Informazione scientifico-tecnica,* vol. 1. Roma.

Park, T. K. (1994). Toward a theory of user-based relevance: A call for a new paradigm of inquiry. *Journal of the American Society for Information Science, 45*(3).

Salton, G. (1968). *Automatic information organization and retrieval.* New York: McGraw Hill.

Salton, G. (Ed.). (1971). *The SMART retrieval system—experiments in automatic document processing.* Englewood Cliffs, NJ: Prentice-Hall.

Salton, G., & McGill, M. J. (1983). *Introduction to modern information retrieval.* New York: McGraw Hill.

Taube, M., Gull, C. D., & Waschel, I. S. (1952). Unit terms in coordinate indexing. *American Documentation, 3*(4).

Tritschler, R. J. (1962). A computer-integrated system for centralized information dissemination, storage and retrieval. *Aslib Proceedings, 14*(12).

The Uniterm system of indexing: Operating manual. (1955). Washington, DC: Documentation Inc.

Voiskunskii, A. E. (1990). *I speak, we speak.* Moscow: Znanie.

Bibliographic Remarks

For further study we also recommend the following works.

Lancaster, F. W. (1979). *Information retrieval systems: Characteristics, testing, evaluation.* New York: John Wiley & Sons.

Saracevic, T. (1970). On the concept of relevance in information science, Ph.D. Dissertation. Cleveland, OH: Case Western University.

Soergel, D. (1970). *Indexing language and thesaurus: Construction and maintenance.* Los Angeles: Melville (Wiley).

6

Automatic Indexing of Documents

info. processing ≠ system construction

6.1

Introduction

In Chapter 4 we considered the goal, function, and structure of an IR system. However, the construction of a specific IR system—that is, the construction of each element that makes up an IR system's structure—can be quite different. First of all, as noted earlier, system construction depends on the IRL and the document selection criterion. The following discussion mainly concentrates on IR systems utilizing the descriptor IRL and the Boolean search criterion. Therefore, when describing various methods of information processing (i.e., the system construction), we will orient ourselves to the Boolean search. Such an orientation is justified because the Boolean search is used in the majority of existing IR systems, and one of the goals of this book is to help improve existing systems and, as a consequence, to enhance the quality of service to users.

The construction of every IR system element is based on the following global requirement: complete automation of all processes in the IR system. Thus, the construction of each system element should constitute an algorithm. Moreover, the IR system construction, described in this chapter and in a number of the chapters that follow, allows the creation of a Boolean system capable of adapting to the user and of performing the optimal search for each individual user. In other words, such a construction permits the implementation of the IR system function formulated in Chapter 4.

We begin the construction of the IR system with one of its basic elements, namely, the block of indexing of documents (BID) (see Chapter 4, Figure 4.8). In other words, this chapter is devoted to the consideration of various approaches to developing automatic document indexing algorithms, that is, algorithms to translate documents from natural language to IRL. We also give an example of such an algorithm. We would like to stress that we are interested only in the creation of completely automated IR systems. Therefore, we will not consider empirical (manual) methods and recommendations to indexers (people who perform indexing manually).

136

6.2 _____

On the Problem of Indexing

In previous chapters, in analyzing the process of information retrieval, the IRL, and the structure of IR systems, we showed that the problem of indexing arises because the natural language cannot be used in formal retrieval. Consequently, one needs to represent both retrieval objects (documents) and the search requirements (queries) by means of a certain retrieval language. In the framework of the Boolean criterion, the representations of documents and queries are different: documents are represented by unordered sets of descriptors, whereas queries are represented by disjunctive normal forms. Therefore, the processes of their translation are also different. That is why the indexing of documents and the indexing queries are commonly considered separately.

However, is it always necessary to perform indexing within the system; that is, is the indexing process necessary in all systems? This question may seem strange. Indeed, if queries and documents should be represented in IRL, then it seems reasonable that indexing processes should always be performed. However, this is not necessarily true. For instance, it is a well-known fact that a comparatively large number of existing systems do not receive user queries at all. Remember that by definition (see Chapter 3) a query is an expression of the user's IN (in our case POIN) in a natural language (only). Because these systems do not receive queries, query formulations are not constructed by the system. How then is the retrieval performed? When dealing with such systems, the user should provide query formulations instead of queries. In other words, users are required to express their INs not in natural language, but in IRL. Such systems are not something unusual, and therefore the absence of special query translation processes in them is not considered surprising.

The indexing of documents is a different matter. Until recently it has been assumed that indexing of documents in IR systems is necessary. However, an increasing number of practically implemented systems do not use any document indexing. From the retrieval point of view, document texts are not considered texts in a natural language, but rather document profiles that are directly entered into the system. Furthermore, from the point of view of the system, the author of the document does not write it (in the normal sense) but instead creates the document profile. Such a document profile (being for the system just an unordered set of descriptors) is input into the system as if it has been created by indexers. Attempts to eliminate indexing processes in IR systems started quite a while ago. For instance, some 20 years ago, many journals began to ask authors to send along with their manuscripts a set of key words characterizing the contents of the manuscript as precisely as possible. However, the very use of document texts as document profiles was the major step in this direction. As has been mentioned, such an approach is commonly called free text searching. It is clear that this approach cannot be used in systems incorporating weight coefficients in their document profiles. Intended mainly for the Boolean search, the free text search technique is increasingly popular among researchers and is becoming an important alternative in the creation and development of new systems, making them more attractive to the system workers. It essentially simplifies the formation of document profiles providing, at the same time, rather high levels of retrieval efficiency.

It is worth noting that for decades many researchers were convinced that free text search was unacceptable for practical applications. Their confidence was based on two factors. On one hand, until recently the level of technology (first, the level of hardware) did not allow any appropriate practical realization of such a search. In this sense the words of C. J. van Rijsbergen, a well-known researcher in the area of information retrieval, were rather characteristic. He was basing the necessity for indexing on the fact that "the computer is not likely to have stored the complete text of each document in natural language" (van Rijsbergen, 1979). On the other hand, it was believed that the quality of the free text search would be unsatisfactory. This point of view was well described by Salton and McGill, who indicated, "Many experts feel that an uncontrolled indexing vocabulary, which in principle can include the whole variety of natural language, introduces too many opportunities for ambiguity and error" (Salton & McGill, 1983). Indeed, numerous examples of language situations can be given to show the unsatisfactory quality of the free text search (although it is intuitively clear that the original document text has far more content possibilities than the set of its descriptors). However, today this line of development looks promising due, again, to progress in computer science.

In devoting this chapter to the automatic indexing of documents, we use the following considerations. First, this process (indexing) is already implemented in the majority of existing systems. Second, one can regard the free text search method as still being in the experimental phase (although the experiments are rather promising). Still this chapter is not only a nod to the tradition; it will be useful because even in free text search systems it is advantageous to use some traditional indexing procedures. We will consider this aspect after having examined the document indexing process.

To begin, we present the document indexing block (see Figure 4.8) in Figure 6.1 as a black box.

Figure 6.1
Block of indexing of documents.

The input of BID is made up of documents in natural language, whereas the output contains representations of these documents in IRL, that is, the document profiles. Recall that in the framework of the Boolean search criterion, document profiles consist of unordered sets of descriptors. Thus, the function of this subsystem is to translate the input documents from the natural language into IRL. It is clear that the translation result (the document profile) is not intended to be read by a human being (to understand its meaning) but is used for algorithmic (computer-based) information retrieval. Yet if the translation result is not intended for reading (reading gives one an opportunity to evaluate the text), how should one judge the translation quality? In other words, what objectives should the translation meet? We will try to answer this question.

The quality requirement of the input to output translation immediately follows from its function. One can easily see that the BID function is formulated according to the "minimal" quality; that is, in the framework of this function, the indexing subsystem is required only to translate the text from natural language to IRL. In this sense, one can consider the translation speed, stability, and cost as the main characteristics of its quality. However, one would hardly expect that any unordered set of descriptors (document profile), obtained after indexing of a concrete document, will lead to an equally successful (or unsuccessful) search when searching for this document based on the queries of users interested in this document. Clearly, the quality of the translation with respect to the search should be considered. But what does this mean if the translation result is just an unordered set of descriptors? This means that the quality requirements should be taken into account when including (or not including) a certain descriptor into the set. Consequently, when evaluating quality, one should consider the characteristics of individual descriptors (and not the whole set). But what are these characteristics and how can they be determined? Let us consider this problem in more detail.

It seems clear that when indexing documents, one should try to include the most important (in terms of meaning) descriptors in the document profiles. However, some researchers disagree and argue that document profiles should contain descriptors that allow the document to be retrieved successfully, rather than those that well represent a certain meaning. In other words, the document profile should allow the document to be found only by the users that are interested in it. This opinion is based on the assumption that a descriptor that is most appropriate for the purposes of retrieval and one that provides the best representation of meaning are different.

Our own experience, based on analysis of documents from dozens of queries (during an investigation of the efficiency of three different functioning systems, including an experiment that in essence repeated the famous Cranfield project), shows that such situations are not rare. This is partially due to the fact, well known to researchers, that sometimes the success of the document search by different queries is determined by different descriptors of the document profile. Moreover, in some cases the main content of the document is beyond the thematic orientation of the system (and, consequently, is beyond the spheres of interest of the users), and only side aspects of this document are of interest. That is true, but nevertheless many researchers reason that one should not use these situations as a base, not because such situations are not essential but because researchers do not have a choice. This is due mainly to the following reasons. First, when a document is being indexed, it is really not clear which descriptor will be most appropriate for the purposes of retrieval. Second, it is not clear whether a descriptor introduced into the document profile will be as good for future system users as for present ones. Third, it is not clear how the retrieval "usefulness" of a descriptor will depend on the query (that is, it is not clear which query, or set of queries, should be used to determine the usefulness of each descriptor included in the document profile). Certainly, this is only a partial list of reasons. But they are sufficient for researchers to reject the orientation of choosing and using descriptors that could be most appropriate for the purposes of a search. This does not mean that researchers are not interested in the quality of the search. In essence, researchers try to find the most promising search descriptors implicitly by choosing descriptors that are most important for the representation of the document's meaning. They assume that these descriptors will allow a good quality of search. Although its shortcomings are obvious, this approach is universally accepted, and at present no reasonable alternatives exist. It is quite evident that the practical implementation of this approach is characterized by its own complications. Indeed, it is not easy to find the most important descriptors in the document text. However, in this case one does not need to consider system users and their queries. In the framework of this approach, the attention is concentrated on the document.

We would like to emphasize here that, when speaking about the quality of indexing, researchers imply the quality of the actual search performed by the system. However, the obtained output and its quality do not entirely depend on the indexing of documents. The document indexing subsystem is only one element of the IR system. All other elements also influence the output. In this sense it is worth saying a few words about well-known experiments that were conducted to evaluate the quality of indexing methods. Although the indexing process itself is aimed at selecting the most important descriptors in the text (from a certain point of view), it is evaluated according not to the descriptor importance but to the quality of the retrieval performed by the entire system. By evaluating the output results, we can draw conclusions about advantages of one indexing method over another. Such conclusions should be treated with caution, however, because they only mean that given a certain composition of subsystems, the given indexing method appears to be better. They do no mean that if, for instance, the query formulation construction method is changed, the same document indexing method will again be the best. Thus, with the development of other elements of the system, many conclusions based on a number of well-known experiments would have to be reevaluated.

In summary, we note that indexing is the process of translating texts from natural language to IRL, and within the framework of the Boolean search criterion, the translation results consist of an unordered set of descriptors. As mentioned earlier, IR system developers, by aiming at quality information retrieval, are oriented toward introducing the most important descriptors (from a certain point of view) into the document profile during document indexing. But how can the importance of a descriptor meaning be determined automatically (algorithmically)? This is quite difficult to accomplish, even when attempted by a human intellect. However, we will consider this point next.

6.3
Main Directions in Automatic Indexing

When speaking about the importance of a descriptor, we mentioned that different points of view on the subject exist. We now discuss these points. Two approaches are used to determine the importance of a descriptor in terms of meaning. Those who adhere to the first approach assume that a descriptor in a document profile should most completely and accurately represent the very meaning of the document being indexed. Moreover, they frequently state that the descriptor should represent the main meaning, or the main theme, of this document. It is clear that the term "the main theme of the document" is rather subjective; for instance, the author and the user of the document may have different opinions on it. However, when developing automatic indexing methods, researchers do not use real opinions (sensible evaluations), but various formal criteria. This implies that any term contained in the document may be judged as reflecting its main meaning providing that it satisfies certain criteria (for instance, it reaches a certain threshold value present by the IR system developer). In other words, the vocabulary content in such systems is not fixed; it depends on the vocabulary content of the documents being indexed.

There is no universally accepted opinion about how well one can determine the importance of terms contained in the document using formal criteria. This is the subject of ongoing discussions that deal with a far broader scientific area than that covered by IR system development and even information science itself. Nevertheless, the absence of consensus on this question does not stop the efforts to use such formal procedures to develop automatic indexing methods. The majority of the literature about indexing is devoted to this particular investigative line.

It is worth noting that the entire investigative line, aimed at determining terms that most appropriately represent the meaning of documents being indexed, is of an experimental and theoretical nature rather than a matter of practice. Maybe that is why many works mainly focus on the problem of determining the importance of terms in a given document, while the information retrieval problem is somewhat of a second priority. In these works, indexing and creating abstracts are frequently considered similar tasks. However, there is a principal difference between indexing and abstracts: indexing is the process of translation from one language to another, whereas the creation of abstracts does not require translation. In addition, the result of indexing is not intended to be read, whereas that is the only objective of an abstract. The result of indexing is written in an artificial language, and it does not need the semantic components of natural language, whereas the abstract is always represented in natural language and, consequently, must operate with the semantic components of natural language. Thus, we would say that the specificity of indexing is closer to object classification than to creating abstracts.

The second direction proposes a completely different approach to determining the importance of terms contained in a document being indexed. In this case, when the document is analyzed by computer, the system determines how well a certain term represents the thematic area of the IR system is intended for, rather than the meaning of the document (its main meaning content). The term may be very important for the meaning of the document being indexed, but it will not be used as a descriptor (not included in the document profile). On the other hand, a certain term may concern second-priority issues that are not covered in detail in the document, but may be important for the thematic area covered by the system. Then the term will be regarded as a descriptor and will be included into the document profile.

In essence, the automatic indexing aimed at determining the importance of a term with respect to the thematic area of the system is significantly simplified. The point is that the selection of important terms (descriptors) is performed before indexing, during the selection of IRL lexical units (that is, during the creation of the system vocabulary). In other words, by definition (see Chapter 5) only the terms that most completely reflect the terminology used in the framework of the thematic area of the system are included in the descriptor dictionary. That is why the presence of fixed descriptor vocabularies is necessary for systems where indexing is performed according to the second approach. In essence, the document indexing procedure in these systems is confined to finding terms included in conditional equivalence classes of descriptors. These descriptors make up the document profile. This approach to the compilation of the document profile clearly provides "equality" (equal importance) to all descriptors with respect to the representation of the document meaning. This means that this approach is mainly intended for the Boolean search, because one can regard all descriptors as having no weights (or they all have equal weights). Indeed, this approach has practical implementations. It is worth noting that the developers of automatic indexing subsystems have found it attractive not only because the idea of its practical implementation is simple but because of other factors as well. The point is that methods based on this approach have demonstrated higher retrieval quality than those using the first approach. Although it is quite evident that the data on the comparative efficiency of indexing methods given in current

[handwritten: Vocabulary control ⟺ domain emphasis of indexing.]

publications are valid only for specific constructions of specific systems, these data have some general validity, at least for systems with similar construction.

The first realistic approaches to automatic indexing can be found in the late 1950s (Luhn, 1957; Luhn, 1958). H. P. Luhn, a well-known researcher at IBM, is probably the father of automatic indexing. It is noteworthy that he started both of the approaches mentioned earlier. For the first approach, he suggested that statistical characteristics of text should be used for indexing, that is, for determining descriptors that are most significant for representing meaning of the document being indexed. Additionally, he suggested a simplified but rather concrete method for this kind of indexing. With regard to the second approach, it was Luhn who adapted the idea of word-to-word translation with the aid of a dictionary for the purposes of indexing. Previously this idea was used in automatic translation of texts from one natural language to another. (In the late 1930s, the translation of texts from, say, English to French with the aid of an English-French dictionary was suggested.) Within the framework of the second approach, Luhn suggested the use of a precompiled descriptor dictionary for the automatic indexing of documents based on a vocabulary created for the IR system. The indexing procedure itself was merely a comparison of each word of the document with the words (descriptors) contained in the precompiled descriptor dictionary. Luhn reasoned that if the word from the text coincides with a word (descriptor) from the vocabulary, then this descriptor should be introduced into the document profile.

[handwritten margin note: mapping on simple co-occurrence of terms?]

As indicated previously, this particular idea has, in essence, served as a base for the majority of contemporary automatic indexing subsystems that are practically implemented and successfully operated. Because functioning IR systems are, as a rule, represented by the systems utilizing the Boolean search, such methods of automatic indexing are of particular interest to us here. Therefore, in the following discussion, we pay special attention to the indexing process using a dictionary and its practical implementation.

[handwritten margin note: really?]

6.4

Some Methods of Text Analysis for Automatic Indexing Using a Dictionary

It seems that the idea of automatic indexing using a dictionary could immediately allow us to describe some type of functioning algorithm. However, it will be useful to first describe the technical difficulties encountered in designing such an algorithm.

To begin with, note that people normally (for instance, when reading) comprehend the meaning of a text without analyzing the meaning of each word. In the majority of cases, we know all the words of the text very well and we recognize them easily, regardless of the grammatical forms (word forms) in which they are used. For example, if we know the word "system," we will not be surprised by the plural form of this word, "systems," or its form "system's." Moreover, having read the text (understood its meaning), we may not remember all the word forms used in it, although they correspond to familiar words. Recognizing words during the automatic indexing procedure is quite a different thing. Many problems arise here. Indeed, a computer does not know any natural language and consequently does not understand the text. It not only does not understand text (the meaning), but it also does not understand the meanings of words. For the computer, a word is not specifically a word, but a certain set of characters (to be precise, codes of characters). Therefore, the word "system" is one set of characters for the computer, "systems" is another, and "system's" is again another distinct set of characters. However, when indexing, we would like the computer to respond to these words in the same manner. Therefore, in automatically comparing words belonging to the text and to the descriptor dictionary, the computer encounters the problem of identifying various forms of the same word.

Traditionally, this problem has been solved in various languages by using the stem (main part) of the word. Researchers have assumed that the same stem corresponds to the same term. In reality this is not so. Words that have the same stem, such as KINDLE and KINDLY (we are not even speaking about homonyms), sometimes should be distinguished. Nevertheless, this idea has appeared to be rather viable. Its implementation normally requires all descriptors to have conditional equivalence classes consisting of lists of stems. These particular lists are then compared with stems separated from words of the text being indexed. If a stem of a word coincides with a stem contained in a certain conditional equivalence class, then this word is included in the document profile. Next we briefly consider the problem of automatic stem separation.

Today, one can find many stemming algorithms in scientific literature, and not only in the English language (Dawson, 1974; Frakes, 1992; Lovins, 1968; Paice, 1990; Porter, 1980; Salton, 1968). Functioning algorithms first appeared in the early 1960s. At that time the main aim of their developers was not automatic indexing, but automatic translation from one natural language to another. Later, the developers of stemming algorithms began to concentrate on automatic indexing, partially due to their modest successes in the automatic translation from natural languages to natural languages. Another cause was that the automatic indexing (translation to artificial languages) was becoming more and more popular.

The majority of the algorithms proposed are aimed mainly at separate affixes and endings of an analyzed word. Precompiled lists of suffixes, prefixes, and endings are used for this purpose. Suffix lists are frequently unified with lists of endings. These lists contain all known suffixes with all possible endings together with separate endings. Researchers frequently use these lists to determine stems of English words. Figure 6.2 gives a portion of such a list compiled by

e	en	ently	est
eable	ence	entum	et
eal	ency	eous	eta
ectual	eness	er	etion
ed	ening	ered	etic
edly	ent	erer	ette
edness	entia	eress	etum
ee	entiae	erial	ety
eer	ential	ery	eur
el	entialness	es	euse
ely	entiate	escent	
ement	entiation	ess	

Figure 6.2
Excerpt from a typical suffix list.

students in the Department of Computer and Information Science at Fordham University during an information retrieval system course.

The automatic stemming process consists of the character-to-character comparison of a given word with the list of suffixes. The comparison is performed from right to left. When a suffix or a group of possible suffixes is found in the word, the longest possible suffix is separated. It is clear that strict compliance with this rule will sometimes fail to provide stems (such as will occur when one separates the suffix ING from the word RING or the suffix ANCY from the word FANCY and so forth). Moreover, in some cases no part of the word will remain (for instance, when we try to separate the suffix ANTIC from the word ANTIC or the suffix ARISE from the word ARISE and so forth).

In this connection, van Rijsbergen wrote:

> Unfortunately, context free removal leads to a significant error rate. For example, we may well want UAL removed from FACTUAL but not from EQUAL. To avoid erroneously removing suffixes context rules are devised so that a suffix will be removed only if the context is right. "Right" may mean a number of things: (1) the length of the remaining stem exceeds a given number; the default is usually 2; (2) the stemending satisfies a certain condition, e.g. does not end with Q. (van Rijsbergen, 1979)

Obviously, the rules given by van Rijsbergen help to resolve the problem with the word EQUAL, but they do not solve many other linguistic problems. However, in our opinion, he was successful in indicating a certain general scheme used by many developers of stemming algorithms. This scheme was first represented completely and in full detail in the widely known algorithm constructed by J. B. Lovins, which was publicized in 1968 (Lovins, 1968). For instance, she divided all suffixes into three groups (A, B, C) and provided the list of all three groups. Lovins introduced the following rules: (1) any suffix from group A can be removed from the word without paying attention to the number of letters in the remaining part of the word (stem); (2) if a suffix from group B is removed, then the minimal remaining stem must be three letters long; (3) suffixes from group C can be removed only when the minimal remaining stem contains four letters. Lovins also introduced separate rules for several indexes. In particular, she specified that the suffix YL permits removal only after letters N or R, the suffix ING is removed in all cases unless the remaining word after deletion consists only of one letter or the letters TH, the suffix ALLIC specifies a minimum stem length of three (group B) and prevents suffix removal after MET and RYST; and so forth.

In addition, the so-called transformation rules are frequently used in the framework of stem separation. For example, the word ABSORB is transformed into ABSORPTION when the suffix TION is added. Special rules are introduced (they exist in the Lovins algorithm as well) to provide for the substitution of the letter P by the letter B when the suffix TION is removed. However, these rules, which are important for translation in natural languages, are not so essential for the purposes of indexing, because the main parts of words included in conditional equivalence classes should not necessarily be readable or grammatically correct. Moreover, the same word may have more than one stem.

Obviously, the variety of rules that Lovins proposed (we have described only some of them) do not cover all the linguistic situations that can arise in the recognition of words. Mainly this is due to a certain percentage of errors in the stem separation provided by her algorithm. It is worth noting that the literature in this area reveals that one of the main ways chosen by the developers of stemming algorithms to reduce errors is to detect cases that do not satisfy the existing rules and then to introduce new rules (frequently by expanding existing ones) that will account for such cases. Such new rules work until new situations that break these rules are found. Then developers must make new additions to the previous additions and so forth. At the same time, Meadow's opinion is that "A workable stemming program would probably require at least 10 – 20 rules (hundreds are possible), including large numbers of provisions for special cases and irregular words" (Meadows, 1992).

Other authors have also indicated that indexing does not necessarily require precise stemming algorithms. This seems to be so, because the introduction of any new rule makes the algorithm more awkward, degrading its performance and complicating its implementation. Moreover, a number of IR system properties compensate for errors occurring during the stemming procedure. Indeed, suppose a document contains five different word forms of a certain term and during stemming only one of them is correctly recognized and separated. This single recognition is sufficient for including the corresponding descriptor in the document profile. Even if the algorithm fails to recognize all five word forms and the corresponding descriptor is not included in the document profile, there is still a certain probability that the document will probably still be correctly retrieved owing to other descriptors in the document profile. In any case, many information retrieval experts do not see any problems with stemming. For instance, Salton and McGill reasoned, "It is not difficult to implement a suffix removal algorithm producing usable word stems for the vast majority of existing English word forms" (Salton & McGill, 1983).

We noted earlier that stemming algorithms in IR systems are used to alleviate the problem of recognizing words in the course of automatic indexing. However, using these algorithms is not a necessity. The fact that the very text of the document can be used as a document profile, eliminating any need for indexing procedures, is not the only reason for that. Even when automatic indexing is implemented, stems are not always identified. Another way to recognize different word forms exists. Since the 1960s, IR system developers understood that the simplest way to eliminate all the difficulties concerning the recognition of words was to include all possible word forms into the conditional equivalence classes containing these words. However, for the English language this would enlarge the descriptor dictionary 10- to 12-fold. Because at that time computer memory was rather restricted, this method was judged technically unacceptable. However, the technical capabilities of modern computers have allowed developers to implement this idea as an alternative to stem separation. Thus, the fact that the majority of modern systems use stemming algorithms is due more to inertia rather than to reasonable arguments. In any case, the alternative seems not only simpler and more convenient for its practical implementation but also more reliable and stable. Indeed, one can easily see that in this case automatic indexing constitutes merely a word-to-word comparison of words from the text being indexed with words from the descriptor dictionary.

Among other problems encountered in the development of automatic indexing algorithms, lexical homonyms (developers try to make the algorithm capable of recognizing the correct meaning of homonyms) and word combinations (an attempt to elucidate stable word combinations) are mentioned most frequently. It is commonly noted that solving these problems will reduce noise in the output. In principle, practically all researchers agree with that, although a number of experiments have indicated that in the vast majority of cases the effects of elucidating word forms and particularly of distinguishing homonyms are virtually negligible. Nevertheless, a brief description of these problems and the most typical methods solving them will be useful. Let us start with methods for distinguishing the meanings of homonyms.

In everyday speech, we recognize the meaning of a homonym through its surroundings, that is, in context. Therefore, when developing automatic methods for distinguishing these meanings, many researchers accept the quite reasonable assumption that there is a certain group of words that will explain the meaning of each homonym. Furthermore, they reason that when a homonym is encountered surrounded by one group of words, it adopts one meaning, and when the homonym is surrounded by another group of words, it has another meaning. This encourages the developers to try to isolate an explaining group of words for each homonym and to divide it into subgroups corresponding to the homonym's meanings (the number of subgroups is equal to the number of meanings the homonym can adopt). These explaining groups allow us to develop rather simple distinguishing algorithms. The essence of these algorithms is the following. First, a homonym that coincides with one from the descriptor dictionary is found in the text (such words are specially marked in the dictionary). Then the surrounding words are compared with the explaining words listed to determine the concrete meaning of the concrete homonym. Normally, the very first explaining word encountered determines the meaning of the given homonym. If the surrounding words do not include explaining words, the homonym is not distinguished. It is clear that when implementing this method one must determine the size of the surroundings (normally no more than several words) and the sequential order in which they should be examined. For instance, some researchers suggest that the following examination order is best: (1) the first word to the left, (2) the first word to the right, and (3) the second word to the right. In addition, in practice one must deal with rather large lists of explaining words. For example, in the description of one of the existing automatic indexing algorithms (the IR system in the electrical engineering area), a list of 631 explaining words has been compiled to recognize meanings of a single homonym. Of these, 411 words are used to help the IR system recognize one meaning and 220 words help it to recognize the other meaning. The experimental verification of distinguishing the meanings of this homonym has shown approximately 86% correct recognitions, 11 to 12% nondistinguishing responses, and 2 to 3% errors in the set of 1000 homonyms (Fedorow, 1973).

One can easily see that this method is sufficiently simple and effective. However, its effectiveness depends on the quality of the distinguishing word lists. These lists are compiled not on the basis of strict methods and scientific recommendations but on the basis of the developer's expertise. In addition, the need for hundreds of explaining words for each homonym makes the method rather awkward and reduces the performance of the entire indexing process. Given all the factors mentioned above and the small number of homonyms contained in the descriptor dictionary (this number, however, will depend on the natural language used), the lexical homonyms in many systems are not distinguished.

Methods for recognizing word combinations are used far more widely in practice. Normally, the word combination is understood as a rather stable sequence of two or more words (within the sentence) unified according to grammar and meaning. For instance, in computer science word combinations such as "artificial intelligence," "central processing unit," and "systems analysis" are universally accepted. When developing algorithms for recognition of these word combinations, researchers often divide them into two types. The first type includes word combinations that can be regarded as a single word: "binary system" is a good example. Word combinations of the second type are encountered in document texts similar to those of the first type, but they can also be encountered in a more separated form. For example, the document may contain the expression "primary and secondary memory," whereas the descriptor dictionary contains the word combinations "primary memory" and "secondary memory." (Obviously, in the course of automatic indexing only the word combinations included in the descriptor dictionary are recognized.)

The majority of the existing algorithms are based on the assumption that in sentences all words of the word combination can be encountered in an arbitrary order and are not separated by punctuation marks. Obviously, the same word can be contained in several word combinations with various words, for example, "binary system," "binary tree," "binary logic," and "binary code." Such a word (in this case "binary") is considered a main element (word) of the word combination. All such words from all word combinations contained in the dictionary are included in a "special" list. The following algorithm is a representative example.

An arbitrary current word from the sentence being analyzed is compared with main words. If the comparison result is negative, the system examines the next word of the sentence. Otherwise, it checks words to the right of the examined word (if that is possible) to see if one of them is not a main word. If successful, the system assumes that it has found a possible two-word word combination. It then compares this word combination with two-word word combinations included in the dictionary. If the same word combination exists in the dictionary, it is included in the document profile. Otherwise, the system then seeks the next, third word of the word combination among nonmain words. If it finds such a word, the system assumes that a possible three-word word combination is found, and so forth. Normally, systems use word combinations consisting of no more than four words. If the verification of words to the right of the word under examination (the main word) does not provide word combinations, then the system examines the group of words to the left. (A number of algorithms include some additional rules. For instance, it is supposed that words of a word combination should not be separated by more than three words.) If the word combination is not found after all the described operations, the system examines the next word of the text by the same procedures. As a rule, the verification of a word combination is continued until the end of the sentence or a comma. The remaining part of the sentence (after removal of the word combination found and commas, if present) is arranged into a sentence for further indexing.

As the preceding discussion shows, using the algorithm to help the IR system recognize word combinations is not too difficult to implement. In our opinion, such algorithms can be useful, particularly when the system dictionary contains a considerable number of word combinations. Although, as we have mentioned, several well-known experiments indicate the absence of significant improvements resulting from recognizing word combinations, it seems that this can be explained by the rather coarse methods of both implementation and evaluation of retrieval.

Another measure, probably the most frequently undertaken in automatic indexing, is to use lists of nonimportant terms. They are frequently called the lists of stop words (see Chapter 5). A portion of such a list is presented in Figure 6.3. This list was compiled at Fordham University by students in the information retrieval systems course.

Although the use of such lists in indexing with the aid of the descriptor dictionary is not necessary (their use does not influence the indexing result), it is very desirable, mainly for two reasons. First, the removal of stop words from the document being indexed (in the framework of the statistics of the given system) can enhance the performance of the entire automatic indexing process. Second, the use of stop word lists is important in a number of methods used for the automatic monitoring of the lexical vocabulary of the thematic area that the indexed document represents. Such monitoring is required to make a direct

a	ago	an	at
abound	all	and	be
about	allow	another	began
above	almost	any	became
across	alone	anyhow	because
admit	along	anyone	become
afere	already	anything	becomes
aforetime	also	anyway	becoming
after	although	anywhere	been
afterwards	always	are	before
again	among	around	beforehand
against	amongst	as	begin

Figure 6.3
Excerpt from a typical stop list.

change (correction) to the descriptor dictionary used for indexing. In other words, this makes the system speak the same language that is used by the authors of the documents being indexed. We next consider in detail each of the two reasons for using stop word lists.

We mentioned that the use of stop word lists can enhance indexing performance. To be more accurate, stop lists can help to improve (reduce) indexing time. Let us consider how they can help to achieve this. In essence, the list of stop words not only consists of common words (their number in the English language is estimated at about 250) but also often contains words that are considered unimportant in the framework of the given IR system (at least by the creators of the descriptor dictionary) but that are frequently encountered in the documents being indexed. Common words make up about 50% of all words in document texts. Therefore, if all stop words that have been included (fixed) in the stop list are removed from the document, the indexed text will be substantially reduced. Thus, the time required to create the document profile is also reduced. This is particularly important when the automatic indexing algorithm involves morphological analysis (for example, stem separation), semantic analysis (determining meanings of homonyms), or syntactical analysis (recognizing word combinations), and especially their combination. In other words, the more procedures of text analysis involved in automatic text indexing, the more essential the positive effect of the stop list becomes. Theoretically, no positive effect may occur if stop lists are too large (due to the vast number of comparisons for each word in the text). However, we do not know practical examples of this kind.

Another reason for the use of stop lists is the correction of the descriptor dictionary itself. In essence, the necessity of such a correction is dictated by the dynamic nature of natural language, by its constant change. Changes are most noticeable in scientific literature, because in the course of scientific activities new effects and laws, as well as new objects and phenomena, are discovered. Naturally, discoveries like these provide new terminology, often altering the former terminology by attributing new meanings to old terms and sometimes just rejecting terms that were previously used. It is evident that IR system descriptor vocabularies should reflect the current terminology in the area it is created to assist. This, in turn, should improve the quality both of indexing and of retrieval in general. Although the automatic correction of descriptor vocabularies has only an indirect relation to automatic indexing, it should nevertheless be performed in the course of indexing, at least partially. Mainly this is determined by the fact that automatic indexing includes the total examination of all words contained in each document text being indexed. During indexing assisted by a stop list, the appearance of a new, somewhat accepted term (i.e., a term that is encountered in documents of the collection but is not included either on the stop list or in the descriptor dictionary) cannot be missed. Such a control allows the IR system to correct not only the descriptor dictionary but the stop list as well. Here is one simple but sufficiently effective method to find new words that should be included in the descriptor dictionary (or the list of stop words). If a certain word is not included either in the stop list or in the descriptor dictionary, but is encountered in each M documents out of a total of N, then this word is regarded as a new term and is provided to IR system experts responsible for the maintenance (correction) of all vocabularies and lists of the system. These experts then decide on which dictionary list this word should be included. For example, if a certain word, W, is not included on any list or in vocabularies but is encountered in an average of 5 out of every 100 documents, then this word is given to the system experts. Implementing such a simple algorithm does not affect the performance of the automatic indexing and, at the same time, is useful for the overall operation of the system. Thus, the use of stop lists in the automatic indexing can be judged reasonable from various points of view.

We have considered the main methods of automatic text analysis used in the development of vocabulary-assisted automatic indexing algorithms. Now, we can consider one such algorithm.

6.5
Algorithm of the Automatic Indexing of Documents

Algorithms of automatic indexing, used in IR systems providing services to the users, appeared in the late 1960s. Some time later, several companies proposed various information retrieval software packages including automatic indexing procedures. The document program system (DPS) software package developed by IBM is one example. It is worth noting that during the past 20 years, no essential changes in the ideas of vocabulary-assisted automatic indexing algorithms, that is, algorithms for constructing document profiles from descriptors that are most characteristic for the given topic, have been made. Therefore, the algorithm described next can be regarded as rather typical for the entire family of algorithms utilizing the Boolean search (Frants & Voiskunskii, 1971).

This algorithm begins its work with the first sentence of the text that is input. Note that the title of the document is considered its opening sentence. The sentence separation is performed in the following manner. The algorithm considers any text standing before the first period or between two periods as a sentence. Additionally, all expressions standing in brackets within the sentence are also considered sentences. Words in quotations are rejected from consideration (from the sentence). At the next stage, all unimportant words contained in the stop list are removed from the sentence. In other words, each word of the separated sentence is compared with each word of the stop list. In case of coincidence (match), the word is removed from the sentence being analyzed. Then the algorithm begins to search for the sentence parts that can contain word combinations. These fragments are the group of words standing between two punctuation marks, between the beginning of the text and the punctuation mark, or between the punctuation mark and the end of the sentence. If no punctuation marks are contained within the sentence, all words of the sentence are considered to be fragments. In the framework of the algorithm under consideration, the following rules are used to recognize word combinations:

1. Three or four words of natural language make up a word combination and are always translated by the same descriptor if they are not separated by punctuation marks in the document text and if they are included in the word combination dictionary as a combination.
2. Two words of natural language make up a word combination and are always translated by the same descriptor if they are not separated by punctuation marks in the document text, if they are not separated by more than three words, and if they are included in the word combination dictionary as a combination.

First, the algorithm attempts to find a four-word word combination. It checks each fragment of the sentence to see whether its words contain a four-word combination; that is, each sequence of four words is compared with the vocabulary of four-word word combinations. If such a word combination is found, these words are removed from the fragment, and the corresponding descriptor is included in the document profile, providing that this descriptor has not been included earlier. The search is continued for the next four-word word combination until all four-word word combinations are recognized or until the algorithm finds that no four-word word combinations are included in the sentence. Then the algorithm begins to search for triple word combinations. The method of search is similar to that described for four-word combinations. In this case, word combinations also may or may not be found. If they are found, the algorithm removes such word combinations from the sentence, and the corresponding descriptors are included in the document profile, providing that these descriptors were not included earlier.

After the search for triple word combinations is completed, the algorithm begins to search for double word combinations. This procedure is implemented in two stages. At the first stage, the algorithm analyzes double word combinations in the same manner as it does for triple word and four-word word combinations; thus, all procedures performed with these word combinations are similar. But after the first stage is completed, the algorithm begins the second stage; that is, the search for double word combinations is continued in the following manner. The algorithm fixes the first word of the fragment and unifies it not with the word next to it on the right (this was done at the first stage) but with the following word to the right (of course, this is necessary only if there is such a word). (Note that the word to which other words are connected is called the base word.) The combination obtained is compared with word combinations from the dictionary of double word combinations. If the combination coincides, then the algorithm implements the procedures described earlier. If the combination does not coincide, the base word is unified with the next, more remote word (again, if there is such a word in the fragment) and the procedure is repeated. The most remote word connected to the base word is one separated from the base word by three words (see rule 2). If no words to the right of the base word form word combinations with it, the algorithm examines words to the left of the base word. If such words exist (which are, again, separated from the base word by three words at the most), they are connected to the base word from the proper side (i.e., the base word is always the first word of the word combination), and all procedures are repeated. Clearly, when the base word is the first word of the fragment, the left part of the fragment is absent. Having examined all the permitted words to the left of the base word, the algorithm selects the next word of the fragment (if there is one) as a base word and performs all the preceding procedures with it. Thus, the procedure is repeated until the last word of the last fragment is analyzed. Then the second stage of finding double sentence combinations is completed together with the whole process of finding sentence combinations in the sentence.

Then the algorithm removes all punctuation marks, stop words, and words in quotations from the sentence. It then compares the remaining part of the sentence with the descriptor dictionary to make certain decisions. The first word of the sentence is compared with all words (word forms) contained in the conditional equivalence classes of the descriptor dictionary. In case of coincidence, the corresponding descriptor is included in the document profile, providing that it was not included earlier, and the algorithm compares the next word of the sentence. If the analyzed word is not contained in the descriptor dictionary, it is included in the list of undefined words, providing that it was not introduced in this list earlier. Then the algorithm analyzes the next word of the sentence repeating the procedures described. This continues until the last word of the sentence is analyzed. Then the algorithm begins to analyze the next sentence of the document, and all the preceding procedures are repeated. After the last sentence has been analyzed, indexing of the given document is considered complete. The document profile constructed in the course of indexing is written into a special file. The "side product" of indexing, namely, the list of stop words, is used to update the special stop list of the system. Lists are arranged in a way that allows the IR system to account for the occurrence frequency of stop words in a given number of documents (e.g., in every hundred). If the list of the document contains a word that is not included in the system list, this word is added to the system list. Otherwise, its occurrence frequency is updated (enlarged by a unit). When the occurrence frequency of a certain word exceeds an established threshold, the system experts analyze it and decide whether this word should be included in either the descriptor dictionary or the stop list.

The general steps for constructing a document profile are given in Figure 6.4.

1. Separation of the sentence from the document text for further indexing.
2. Removal of stop words from the sentence.
3. Recognition and indexing of word combinations contained in the sentence.
4. Indexing of single words in the sentence and final creation of the document profile.

Figure 6.4
Steps for constructing a document profile.

The automatic indexing algorithm just presented is quite similar to that developed by the authors in 1970. The source code in the LISP programming language for this algorithm was developed and compiled by one of the authors. The main difference is that the algorithm of 1970 automatically separated stems. However, for a number of the reasons stated, we consider it more advantageous not to use stemming procedures.

Thus, we have considered the algorithm for selecting descriptors for document profile. Descriptors selected are those judged most important from the point of view of the topic of the collection. As mentioned previously, algorithms of this kind are most widely used in functioning IR systems. Nevertheless, let us briefly consider other methods used to select descriptors for the document profile that seek to select descriptors that more fully represent the meanings of the document being indexed. First, such indexing can be used in systems utilizing Boolean search and, second, we believe that familiarizing readers with the main ideas of this investigative line will be useful.

6.6 Statistical Indexing Methods

When considering the main directions in automatic indexing, we have already mentioned the problem of determining the most important (for the meaning) terms of documents. One would say that certain linguistic methods (algorithms) should be used for this purpose first. However, linguists lack any successful algorithms. That is why researchers use mainly statistical algorithms that calculate the measure of meaning in a term of the document. This seems very convenient for the methods incorporating descriptor weights, because the measure of meaning calculated can be considered as a weight.

In 1958 Luhn suggested that the frequency of word occurrence in an article could furnish a useful measurement of word significance in the article: "The justification of measuring word significance by use-frequency is based on

really meant measure of term significance in a given document.

the fact that a writer normally repeats certain words as he advances or varies his arguments and as he elaborates on an aspect of a subject" (Luhn, 1958). In the framework of this idea, Luhn proposed a method for measuring word significance for the purposes of search ("resolving power" of the index word). The essence of this method is the following. First the occurrence frequency of a word in the indexed text is calculated. Because in any "normal" text stop words, such as *the, of,* and *and* occur most frequently, it is suggested that the most frequently appearing words be regarded as insignificant in the given text and that they be excluded from the document profile. Luhn also proposed that the most seldom used words (e.g., words encountered only once) be considered insignificant and that they be excluded from the document profile. The largest resolving power value of the index words extracted from the document text should peak in the middle-frequency range. To illustrate the proposed approach, Luhn used the graph shown in Figure 6.5.

Thus he considered that after successful lower and upper cut-offs have been determined, all the words remaining between them can be regarded as descriptors making up a document profile of rather high quality. Although this particular approach turned out to be practically unacceptable, it was a starting point in the development of many statistical indexing methods. Since that time various researchers have proposed a considerable number of far more successful methods for measuring the significance of descriptors (see, for example, Damerau, 1965). For instance, some researchers have suggested that one should take into account not only the occurrence frequency of a word in the document text but also the frequency of its occurrence in the entire retrieval collection of documents. (Such a frequency has been obtained by totaling all of the occurrence frequencies of the word being calculated for all documents in the collection of documents.) They have suggested that if the occurrence frequency of the

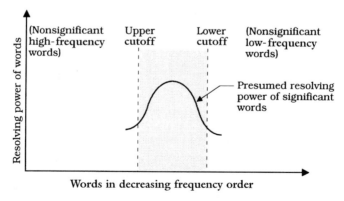

Figure 6.5
Resolving power of significant words.

word is rather high for the given document and relatively low for the entire collection, then the word is important for this particular document (i.e., it can be included in the document profile as a descriptor). Let us explain this idea with the following example.

Let us denote the frequency of occurrence of a term t in the document i as f_{ti}. Let F_t be the total occurrence frequency of the word in n documents. Then

$$F_t = \sum_{i=1}^{n} f_{ti}.$$

Let the significance of the term t for document i be denoted as IMP_{ti}. This value can be calculated as

$$\text{IMP}_{ti} = \frac{f_{ti}}{F_t}.$$

If the value of IMP_{ti} exceeds a certain preset threshold, then the term t is included in the document profile of document i as a descriptor.

According to another approach (Edmundson & Wyllys, 1961), one should take into account the frequency of occurrence of a given term in the document (f_{ti}) and the number of documents in the collection that contain this term (D_t). It is thought that if this term is rather frequently encountered in the document being indexed and the number of documents that contain it is rather small, then this term can be used as a descriptor. In this case, the simplest way to measure the significance of the term is

$$\text{IMP}_{ti} = \frac{f_{ti}}{D_t}.$$

Again, if the value of IMP_{ti} exceeds a certain preset threshold, then the term t is included in the document profile.

As was noted earlier, many approaches to measuring the importance of a term exist (see, for example, (Bookstein & Kraft, 1977; Bookstein & Swanson, 1974; Robertson & Sparck-Jones, 1976; Salton, 1975; and Sparck-Jones, 1972). We could mention one approach proposed by Sparck-Jones to calculate the so-called inverse document frequency weight (Sparck-Jones, 1972) or the approach proposed by Salton, in which the so-called discrimination values of a term are calculated in order to determine the degree to which the use of the term will help to distinguish the documents from each other (Salton, 1973, 1975). Because all these approaches are aimed mainly at the use of weights and are more of theoretical rather than practical interest, we refer interested readers to the book *Introduction to Modern Information Retrieval* by G. Salton and M. J. McGill (1983), in which many approaches of this kind are considered in detail.

It is worth noting that, because the very approach of measuring the word significance implies an uncontrolled vocabulary, stemming algorithms should be used before the occurrence frequencies are calculated.

6.7

Some Issues in Automatic Indexing

We have already mentioned that only automatic indexing with a dictionary has practical implementation in functioning IR systems. Such systems have been used successfully since the late 1960s. Why then have the statistical methods remained experimental for more than 30 years now (note that most scientific literature is devoted to these particular methods)? In answering this question we give several reasons that are, in our opinion, most essential.

First, note that indexing with a dictionary is a rather simple procedure (see, for example, the algorithm described earlier). This cannot be said about statistical methods. For instance, a large number of such methods are based either on term occurrence frequency calculated for the entire collection of documents or on the total number of documents that contain the analyzed term. Obviously, to obtain these data one needs to browse the whole collection of documents. This means that one must input all documents of the collection into the computer in order to begin indexing the first one. Furthermore, each document is indexed by analyzing all documents of the collection. We are not even discussing the technical aspects of such an indexing (such as the volume of computer memory and the time required for indexing one document). In addition, because functioning systems are, as a rule, Boolean ones, selection of descriptors for the document profile requires choosing appropriate thresholds in order to distinguish a significant word (descriptor) from an insignificant one, which is not a simple task. Another problem arises due to the necessity of recognizing word combinations (a necessity that is frequently indicated by researchers). The methods previously described cannot be used for this purpose. Problems of another type (e.g., ideological problems) arise due to insufficient knowledge about statistical laws of natural-language texts. Therefore, assumptions made in various approaches are often very rough approximations of reality. Nevertheless, the argument given by Salton and McGill (1983) seems the strongest.

Salton developed the experimental IR system called SMART, which included several automatic indexing subsystems. Not only were subsystems implementing various approaches to the problem of word significance measurement involved, but subsystems performing indexing with a dictionary also played a part. This situation (in essence, this has been a unique situation) allowed the researchers to conduct the comparative experiment to determine the most effective (clearly, for this particular system) method of automatic indexing. This experiment was unique in providing comparison performed by using the same queries, the same group of researchers, and the same (structural) system. The results obtained by the SMART system were compared to those obtained by the MEDLARS system, which was the most well-known functioning system. The results of this experiment are presented in Figure 6.6.

The analysis of the results presented in Figure 6.6 shows that the best re-

System Analysis method	Recall	Percent difference from MEDLARS	Precision	Percent difference from MEDLARS
MEDLARS (manual indexing)	0.3117		0.6110	
SMART (word stems with frequency weights)	0.2622	-16	0.4901	-19
SMART (word stems with discrimination value weghting)	0.2872	-8	0.5879	-4
SMART (thesaurus)	0.3223	+4	0.6106	0

Figure 6.6
A comparison of indexing methods. Source: Adapted from G. Salton and M. J. McGill, *Introduction to Modern Information Retrieval* (New York: McGraw Hill, 1983), 104.

→ refer to comments on p. 163

sults are achieved with the method of indexing using a descriptor dictionary (in this case Salton and McGill use the term *thesaurus* for what we call *descriptor dictionary*). Other authors who have conducted other experiments have reported the same result. Because now the majority of functioning systems now involve indexing (remember that this process is not necessary), on the basis of the existing literature one would guess that in many cases indexing is performed automatically. But that is not so. At the same time one would hardly find works supporting the advantages of manual indexing over the automatic indexing. What is the problem then? Why are those engaged in the operation and development of existing IR systems unwilling to automate the indexing process? In the majority of cases, the main reason they give is that the size of the document profile is sharply increased. In other words, the number of descriptors included in the document profile in the course of automatic indexing considerably exceeds the number of descriptors selected during manual indexing. This, they reason, reduces the retrieval quality. Let us consider the main argument starting from the increased size of the document profile.

In discussing the indexing of documents we have not mentioned what kind of documents are considered. This point was omitted on purpose, because only general principles of indexing implementation are important for comprehending the essence of this process. However, now we can admit that not all documents are indexed automatically, for the following reason. During automatic indexing all terms of the text that are contained in the descriptor dictio-

Books vs. paper: do differentiated, need to be differentiated, text

nary (to be accurate, the descriptors corresponding to the terms) are included in the document profile. Therefore, the automatic indexing of a book may result in a document profile containing almost all descriptors of the descriptor dictionary. This means that this document will be given as output to any query of any user of the system. Moreover, this means that books do not have to be indexed at all and should just be given to any user as output. The same situation may occur for certain forms of technical references and scientific reports. Clearly, this situation is not satisfactory for the users and, as a result, for the IR developers. This circumstance can also apply to the indexing of journal articles, which make up (according to some estimates) the main part of the document collection that interests users. Although document profiles of articles are not as large as those of books, they still often contain a considerable part of the descriptor dictionary. Therefore, the increase in the document profile due to automatic indexing is a fact. That is why functioning systems with automatic indexing are oriented to indexing abstracts. Nevertheless, some researchers think that even the automatic indexing of abstracts provides document profiles that are too large. But what is a *large* document profile and what size should be judged normal? On what does the evaluation depend? Let us answer these questions and clarify the reasons for the developers' dissatisfaction.

To begin with, automatic indexing is not isolated and independent from other processes in the system. It is only an element in the whole complex of interrelated elements called the IR system. This interrelation is very important. When creating an IR system, or a system of any other nature, developers are oriented (sometimes deliberately and sometimes just intuitively) to certain internal parameters of a specific process in the system. These parameters and their values are chosen according to the parameter values characteristic of other interrelated processes in the system rather than to the features of this particular process. In other words, parameters are selected according to the operation of the entire system as a whole. This is one of the main methodological aspects of system development. It is this proposition that requires matching each process of the system with other processes that are interrelated with it. This, in turn, implies a certain tuning of the system, which is closest to a certain harmony or a certain imaginary balance. Systems analysis includes the following recommendation for achieving such a balance. Because among numerous processes in the system there are those that can be easily tuned and those with rather restricted tuning capabilities, it is useful to adjust (tune) tunable processes to those that are difficult to tune. In other words, one should first implement the processes that are hard to change and then, using the knowledge about their properties, set the required parameter values for the related processes. To show how this can be applied to the creation of an indexing subsystem for the IR system, first we determine which subsystem is interrelated with it. Next we analyze which process should be tuned according to the properties of the other. Finally, we determine what parameter of the tunable process should be changed and what value of this parameter is preferable.

Remember that the quality of the document indexing process is evaluated not according to the document profile constructed, but according to the output generated by the entire system. However, the system output depends not only on the quality of the document indexing but on other issues as well. Another important factor is the quality of the indexing of queries. In the mid-1960s, having conducted an extended experiment with the MEDLARS system, Lancaster (1968) showed that the main cause of retrieval failures is not a poorly constructed document profile, but a poorly constructed query formulation. In other words, the retrieval quality is affected more by the quality of the query indexing than by the quality of the document indexing. Nevertheless, the influence of document indexing results on the system output is quite obvious as is the interaction between document and query indexing processes in the course of the creation of output. In essence, the interaction of document profiles with query formulations follows from the very idea of information retrieval (see Chapter 5). We are, however, interested in the interaction between the very processes of indexing rather than that between the results of these processes; that is, we are interested in whether these processes influence each other. For this purpose, let us consider factors that are commonly addressed in assessing the quality of document indexing. What shortcomings of document indexing are, by common opinion, influencing the quality of the system output?

The common position of developers was probably most successfully expressed by Lancaster. He indicated that "there are two distinct types or failures determined by shortcoming of the indexing process: (1) failures caused by the indexers' errors and (2) failures resulting from the average number of terms attributed to the document in the course of indexing" (Lancaster, 1968). The first arises in manual indexing methods (when the automatic indexing is used, the quality of the term selection depends on the quality of the system descriptor dictionary, as was shown in Chapter 5), whereas the second cause is directly related to all document indexing methods and approaches. Indicating the importance of this problem, Lancaster wrote, "The most difficult problem of indexing methodology for any system is the computation of the average number of terms attributed to the document" (Lancaster, 1968). But why did developers indicate this problem 30 years ago, at the very beginning of IR systems development? The point is that the very practice of IR systems operation showed that the best results of retrieval are determined by certain values of certain parameters characteristic of both the document profile and the query formulation. These parameters are the average sizes of a document profile and a set of descriptors combined by operand AND in the query formulation. Moreover, the values of these parameters are interrelated; that is, if the value (size) of the parameter is changed, for example, for the document profile, then some changes in the query formulation are also required to provide the best retrieval quality. (Note that the best retrieval quality in the new case may be worse than the quality achieved in the previous case.) This means that if we know the real value of the parameter (the average number of descriptors in the set) for one indexing process, then, in order to obtain the best output from the system, we need to enforce certain requirements (on the value of the parameter) on another indexing process. This means, in turn, that not only the indexing results but also the very processes of indexing documents and queries are interrelated. We also know the parameter responsible for this interrelation, namely, the average size of descriptor sets obtained as a result of the indexing processes. Consider now which process should be adjusted to another.

From general considerations, the result of the document indexing (an unordered set of descriptors) is simpler than that of the query indexing (a set of descriptor sets represented in the normal disjunctive form). We are, however, interested in the very processes of obtaining the mentioned results. Which process is simpler and which is more complex depends on the principles and implementation approaches that the developers of concrete systems have accepted. This means that in one system the query formulation construction could be more complex, whereas the document profile construction could be more complex in another system. Because in this case we consider Boolean IR systems using manual methods of the query formulation construction (the majority of real systems) and in many systems query formulations are constructed by users, the developers of such systems try to adjust the document indexing process to the real value of the previously mentioned parameter (the number of descriptors combined by operand AND) of the query formulation. The manual construction of the query formulation normally provides two or three descriptors unified by the logical AND, sometimes three or four descriptors, and very seldom five or more. This parameter is taken into account by the system developers (in most cases intuitively) and determines the accepted average number of terms in the document profile. Let us illustrate real values of this parameter by the examples of systems we have worked with. For instance, the average length of sets included in the query formulation of IR systems providing services for the users in the area of information science is 2.7 descriptors, whereas the average size of the document profile is 6.3 descriptors. The same values for the IR system intended for the computer science area are 3.4 descriptors for the query formulation and 7.4 descriptors for the document profile. Of course, we do not consider these values optimal, but they illustrate the order of values used in functioning IR systems. In any case, the parameter values used in practice are quite close to those given here, although they are chosen empirically. The authors are not aware of any strict methods for calculating these values, even for the size of the document profile.

Let us return to automatic indexing. It is worth noting that, according to some researchers, the average size of the document profile is about 30 descriptors, even when only abstracts are indexed. For instance, when we performed automatic indexing of 1276 abstracts (for the nitrogen industry) with an average of 184 words and using a descriptor dictionary with as many as 979 descriptors, the resulting document profiles contained, on average, 34.8 descriptors. Now

not in the general sense of "constructing representation of doc content in system data structure".

we can understand why many IR system developers consider document profiles obtained by means of automatic indexing too large. The point is that such document profiles do not match existing query formulations and introduce a certain imbalance into the system, breaking certain harmony that developers intuitively find. Moreover, even in trying to adapt to this type of document indexing, it is not so easy to change the existing manual methods of the query formulation construction. This is particularly true when we deal with users. It is unrealistic to ask them to provide query formulations consisting of, say, 11 descriptors combined by operand AND. This is the main reason that automatic document indexing has not found a wide application in functioning systems. However, if the query indexing is also performed automatically and if the query set sizes can be easily changed (i.e., if the system might be easily adjusted), then the automatic document indexing algorithm will be completely vindicated and will be attractive for all systems where documents are indexed. Such algorithms have been developed and we consider them in Chapter 7, which deals with the automatic indexing of queries.

When considering the very problem of indexing, we have noted that there are systems in which document texts are considered document profiles. Consequently, no indexing is performed in such systems. Note, however, that in such systems documents are represented by abstracts. In some cases stop words are removed from the texts of abstracts, which virtually constitutes a simplified form of indexing. Therefore, at present the automatic indexing of documents is still a rather important process (see, for example, Fidel, 1994; Milstead, 1994; and Soergel, 1994) that, together with the automatic indexing of queries, can substantially improve retrieval results.

6.8
Conclusion

descriptors

This chapter described the first steps in the construction of a fully automated IR system. The basis of any algorithms for the automatic translation of a document from a natural language into IRL, or the automatic indexing of documents, is the well-known idea of word-for-word translation that was borrowed from a branch of artificial intelligence called "machine translation." Despite the simplicity of the idea, its practical realization faces many obstacles connected with the properties of natural language. Different approaches to dealing with these obstacles, such as stemming algorithms and stop lists, are analyzed in this chapter and, as an example, one of the possible algorithms (which is used in the functioning system) is described.

The different methods for constructing document profiles described in this chapter give an idea of how to develop methods for automatic indexing in the future. One of the indexing approaches emphasized—free text search—was

(margin handwritten notes:) ? see. modeling power of ... ; referring to the nature of the descriptors ... is too in part in ...

shown to incorporate some of the traditional methods used in automatic indexing today.

The problem of indexing full texts, such as books, has not been solved.
This problem emphasizes not only the drawbacks of existing descriptor languages but the drawbacks of artificial languages in general. Of the several approaches to solving this problem that have been suggested, the most promising
are those based on statistical indexing. However, the automatic indexing of
documents is a reality today, and it is used in systems where the documents are
short or are abstracts.

References

Bookstein, A., & Swanson, D. R. (1974). Probabilistic models for automatic indexing. *Journal of the American Society for Information Science, 25*(5).

Bookstein, A., & Kraft, D. (1977). Operations research applied to document indexing and retrieval decisions. *Journal of the ACM, 24*(3).

Damerau, F. J. (1965). An experiment in automatic indexing. *American Documentation, 16*(4).

Dawson, J. (1974). Suffix removal and word conflation. *ALLC Bulletin,* Michelmas.

Edmundson, H. P., & Wyllys, R. E. (1961). Automatic abstracting and indexing—survey and recommendation. *Communication of the ACM, 4*(5).

Fedorow, E. B. (1973). Principles of automatic indexing in descriptor IR systems. *INFORM-
ELECTRO.*

Fidel, R. (1994). User-centered indexing. *Journal of the American Society for Information Science, 45*(8).

Frakes, W. B. (1992). Stemming algorithms. In W. B. Frakes & Baeza-Yates (Eds.), *Information
retrieval (data structures and algorithms).* Englewood Cliffs, NJ: Prentice Hall.

Frants, V. I., & Voiskunskii, V. G. (1971). Automatic indexing in IR system for nitrogen industry.
Nauchno-Technicheskaya Informatsiya (NTI), ser. 2, no. 4.

Lancaster, F. W. (1968). *Information retrieval systems, characteristics, testing, and evaluation.* New York:
John Wiley and Sons.

Lovins, J. B. (1968). Developing of a stemming algorithm. *Mechanical Translation and Computational
Linguistics, 11*(1).

Luhn, H. P. (1957). A statistical approach to mechanized encoding and searching of literary information. *IBM Journal of Research and Development, 1*(4).

Luhn, H. P. (1958). The automatic creation of literature abstracts. *IBM Journal of Research and Development, 2*(2).

Meadow, C. T. (1992). *Text information retrieval systems.* New York: Academic Press.

Milstead, J. L. (1994). Needs for research in indexing. *Journal of the American Society for Information
Science, 45*(8).

Paice, C. D. (1990). Another stemmer. *SIGIR Forum, 24*(3).

Porter, M. F. (1980). An algorithm for suffix stripping. *Program, 14*(3).

van Rijsbergen, C. J. (1979). *Information retrieval* (2nd ed.). London: Buttersworths.

Robertson, S. E., & Sparck-Jones, K. (1976). Relevance weighting of search terms. *Journal of the
American Society for Information Science, 27*(3).

Salton, G. (1968). *Automatic information organization and retrieval.* New York: McGraw Hill.

Salton, G. (1975). A theory of indexing. Regional Conference Series in Applied Mathematics,
No. 18, Society for industrial and Applied Mathematics, Philadelphia, Pennsylvania, 1975.

Salton, G., & McGill, M. J. (1983). *Introduction to modern information retrieval.* New York: McGraw
Hill.

Salton, G., & Yang, C. S. (1973). On the specification of term values in automatic indexing. *Journal of Documentation, 29*(4).

Soergel, D. (1994). Indexing and retrieval performance: The logical evidence. *Journal of the American Society for Information Science, 45*(8).

Sparck-Jones, K. (1972). A statistical interpretation of term specificity and its application in retrieval. *Journal of Documentation, 28*(1).

Bibliographic Remarks

Additional basic information on automatic indexing may be obtained from the following references.

Damerau, F. J. (1976). Automated language processing. In M. E. Williams (eds.), *Annual review of information science and technology,* vol. 11. Washington, DC: American Society for Information Science.

van Rijsbergen, C. J. (1979). *Information retrieval* (2nd ed.). London: Buttersworths.

Salton, G., & McGill, M. J. (1983). *Introduction to modern information retrieval.* New York: McGraw Hill.

Readers who are interested in experimental approaches to automatic indexing are referred to the following publications.

Bookstein, A., & Kraft, D. (1977). Operations research applied to document indexing and retrieval decisions. *Journal of the ACM, 24*(3).

Robertson, S. E., & Sparck-Jones, K. (1976). Relevance weighting of search terms. *Journal of the American Society for Information Science, 27*(3).

7

Automatic Indexing of Search Requests

7.1

Introduction

This chapter continues the discussion of how to construct fully automated IR systems. Again we are interested in the element of the system's structure that is used for indexing, but this time the element will be a block of indexing of search requests (see the structure of an IR system illustrated in Chapter 4, Figure 4.8). We consider the indexing of search requests for two reasons: first, we will seek to implement this process in the system itself and, second, the search request is the most convenient and common form of expressing the psychological human condition known as the information need (IN) (in our case, this IN is called problem oriented information need, or POIN). Recall that the search request is a text in a natural language, a product of the user's attempt to express his psychological condition (POIN). Thus, the search request can be regarded as the most popular representation of POIN in the IR system, and the process of search request indexing can be considered the process of constructing query formulations.

The necessity for indexing and some of its aspects were discussed at length in Chapter 6. Recall that retrieval is not feasible without a language (IRL in our case) and that this language is used to represent both the objects of retrieval (documents in our case) and search requests for them (queries). It follows from the nature of any retrieval process that indexing presents one of the central problems in the creation of IR systems. The algorithm of the automatic indexing of documents (the process of the automatic construction of document profiles) considered in Chapter 6 is one of the alternatives for constructing a structural element of the IR system as a block of indexing of documents (BID). In this chapter, the emphasis is again on creating alternatives, this time for the BIQ (block of indexing of queries, or search requests). Because we are interested in Boolean information retrieval systems, the result of search request indexing (a query formulation) in such systems should be in a disjunctive normal form (as explained in Chapter 5).

166

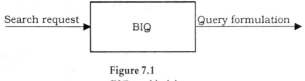

Figure 7.1
BIQ as a black box.

Therefore, we will consider later various approaches to designing algorithms for the creation of such query formulations and will give a specific example of BIQ construction; that is, we will give a detailed description of a successfully functioning algorithm. Moreover, the algorithm described in the following discussion will be designed to work together with an algorithm for the automatic indexing of documents. This means that the query formulation obtained by the algorithm we describe in this chapter will depend on the indexing of documents used in the system. In other words, query formulation obtained by the described algorithm of search request indexing in the system with the automatic indexing of documents and query formulation constructed by the same algorithm and in the same system but with the manual indexing of documents may substantially differ from each other. In addition, results of a search involving query formulations constructed with the automatic indexing of documents are far better as a rule. The importance of this aspect of the algorithm was emphasized in Chapter 6.

Figure 7.1 illustrates the problem under discussion. In the figure, BIQ is presented as a black box.

The input into the BIQ is a flow of information about the user's POIN (search request) and the output is a query formulation in Boolean form. The BIQ itself should be a mechanism (algorithm) that transforms the input information into the output. Because the input is in a natural language and the output is represented in an artificial language, the mechanism should be defined as the algorithm that translates search requests from a natural language into IRL. It is exactly this mechanism that we will now consider.

7.2
Some Aspects of Constructing Query Formulations

Today, in practically all functioning IR systems, query formulations are constructed manually. This is not due to any advantages of the known manual techniques for constructing disjunctive normal forms. On the contrary, the literature contains many complaints from both the IR system designers and those who construct query formulations about the labor-intensiveness and low quality of this process. Why is it that current practice has not changed? Why are the manual methods being used so widely? Clearly, researchers are not opposed in principle to automation. Moreover, the advantages of automatic methods are so evident today that there is practically no need to advocate them. So what is the problem? Perhaps, the main reason is as follows.

Even a cursory analysis is sufficient to show that the challenge encountered in constructing disjunctive normal forms or sets consisting of numerous unordered sets of descriptors is far greater than that of constructing only one unordered set of descriptors for each document (i.e., construction of the document profile). This challenge is also reflected in the existing approaches to automated indexing. Indeed, the idea of a word-for-word translation, which underlies the automatic indexing of documents, is not only simple but is also very intelligible to people with a different level of training.

On the other hand, the idea of the automatic construction of query formulations (i.e., the automatic indexing of queries) underlying the algorithm that will be described in this chapter is not always easy to comprehend (though we do not consider it complex), as we have often seen in practice. This conclusion is supported by the fact that the method used for the automatic indexing of documents, advanced for the first time by Luhn in the late 1950s (Luhn, 1957) was immediately accepted by researchers and was followed by a series of relevant publications in the early 1960s. But the method and the algorithm for the automatic indexing of queries for the Boolean search systems (i.e., the method of the automatic construction of query formulations in Boolean form) published for the first time in 1970 (see Frants, Voiskunski, & Frants, 1970) remained largely unnoticed for a quite a long time, despite the importance (stressed time and again by most researchers) of reducing labor intensiveness and raising the quality of the construction of query formulations (see, for example, Croft & Thompson, 1987; Lancaster, 1968; Meadow, 1967; and Spink, 1994).

Already in the 1960s, the construction of query formulations became one of the most important problems in designing IR systems. The importance of the problem was probably first emphasized by Lancaster (1968) who, while analyzing the reasons for an unsuccessful search in the IR system MEDLARS, concluded that the main reason for unsuccessful searches in IR systems is the low quality of query formulations. Despite this observation, far fewer publications deal with search request indexing than with document indexing. Though the situation has changed somewhat in the past few years (the researchers' interest has shifted toward the construction of query formulations), the automation of this process gets insufficient attention even on the part of researchers.

The point is that the automation of any intellectual activity—and it is precisely this kind of activity that we have to deal with when analyzing the existing practice of formulating disjunctive normal forms—is traditionally one of the most complex automation problems, and this complexity scares away many researchers. Some authors believe that without new important breakthroughs in the artificial intelligence area, it is pointless to try to automate the construction of query formulations. But the solution to the problem requires intellectual creativity only as long as there is no algorithm to solve it.

For example, the problem of finding the greatest common divider required a substantial intellectual effort before Euclid found an algorithm (Euclidean algorithm). Similarly, some problems can be intellectually challenging only because there are no algorithms for them. It should be noted, however, that the created algorithms do not necessarily have to copy intellectual processes. It is sufficient to make an algorithm as a working model of this activity; whether the model is close to the original is of secondary importance. These considerations underlie the available solutions.

To better understand the problems that occur in constructing query formulations, we will first discuss the most common features of the existing methods for obtaining query formulations. In most of the systems known to us, query formulations are obtained in one of the following two ways:

1. By the user, if the user expresses his or her POIN in the IRL.
2. By the system, if the user expresses his or her POIN in some language other than the IRL and the system translates his or her expression into the IRL.

The second method prevailed until the mid-1970s, as query formulations were being obtained primarily by the most qualified experts of the system (commonly known as intermediary searchers). With the emergence of on-line search, that is, when a dialogue was introduced into the information retrieval process, the construction of query formulations in an ever-increasing number of functioning systems was entrusted to the users themselves, and today this method appears to be more popular. (In this case, too, breakthroughs in computer science have had a marked impact on IR system progress).

Earlier we mentioned the wide use of the manual construction of query formulations in functioning IR systems. Clearly, when developers presuppose that a manual method will be used (incidentally it makes no difference who is going to implement it—the user or an intermediary searcher), they relieve themselves of the fairly labor-intensive and complex job of either implementing some existing algorithm of query indexing or developing a new algorithm. In this case, the developers usually limit themselves to providing some methodological recommendations. According to some experts even this is not necessary because in their opinion the offered recommendations are intended to clarify the problem facing an inexperienced searcher rather than to help in the construction of query formulations. In any case, we can say that an experienced intermediary searcher does not need a methodological manual to construct a query formulation. In a certain sense, the available methodologies are similar to those used when translating from one natural language into some other natural language, from English into Russian, for example. The regulatory part in such methodology may prove useful, such as the instruction to use (or not to use) abbreviations, to underline adjectives, and so on. If the translator does not know (or does not know well) the Russian language, for example, then any methodology will be useless. However, the translator who has a good command of both languages will manage, even without using any methodology. Returning now to the developers' selection of the method for manually constructing query formulations, we should note that such a simplified approach to the creation of an IR system undoubtedly makes life easier for the creators of such systems. But does the user benefit in any way from this state of affairs? What quality of the service does the user ultimately get? Let us discuss these questions in more detail.

First, it should be emphasized that most of the efforts toward constructing query formulations in such an approach are shifted to users or intermediaries. Also, in on-line systems these efforts are almost fully assigned to the user, despite the fact that one of the goals of creating the IR system is to reduce the time necessary for the user to retrieve information. As for additional efforts, note that in this case the user is forced to express his or her POIN in the IRL, which is more difficult than to use a natural language (it is much easier and faster to formulate a search request than to construct a query formulation).

It is noteworthy that the users themselves are not unanimous as to who should, in principle, construct a query formulation. Some think this should be done by an intermediary searcher whereas others insist on their own involvement. (The user often does not even suspect that alternative automatic methods exist.) Different positions originate primarily from the use of different evaluation criteria. In questioning users in the Aslib on-line information service (523 answers were received in all), researchers discovered the following: practically all users agreed that the work on the terminal should be handled by intermediary searchers, and only four of them favored the idea of entrusting the work to users. The main reason for this outcome is that although the user only needs the information from the IR system, he or she is initially presented with a fairly complex process requiring intellectual efforts and often a lot of time. Moreover, the quality of the search is frequently quite low, despite substantial efforts required of the user in constructing a query formulation. The other position is based on the users' perception of the quality of the search when the query formulation is constructed by an intermediary searcher. Users correctly assume that they know better than anybody else what they really want (i.e., they can feel their information need [POIN]), but they falsely conclude that nobody else can be as successful as they are in searching for information to satisfy their POIN. As a result, users often express dissatisfaction with the system's performance even when the search based on the user's query formulation was inferior to the search based on the query formulation constructed by the system (Lancaster, 1979).

We connected the quality of the output to the quality of the query formulation. But in Chapter 6 we noted that the system's output is also influenced by other factors. When using some other method of indexing documents, for example, the results of the search for the same query formulation may be different. Yet within the framework of the IRL available in the IR system and a collection of indexed documents, the results of the search (the system's output) may be used to evaluate the quality of the query formulation in a given IR system.

The problem with the quality of a query formulation obtained manually either by the user or by an intermediary searcher is well illustrated by the acuteness of the problem of constructing query formulations. Numerous experiments conducted in the 1960s to assess the quality of query formulations were focused primarily on one question: Who constructs them better (or worse), the user or an intermediary searcher? Most experiments, especially those conducted before the introduction of the on-line search, indicate that an intermediary searcher does it better. Why is it that some people do this better than others? Clearly, intermediary searchers do not conceal any secrets from the users. Moreover, when receiving requests from the users they are, as a rule, less aware of the users' real information needs (POIN). This is true not only because the requests often inaccurately reflect information about the user's POIN, but also because after receiving a request, the intermediary searcher tends to interpret it in his or her own way, that is, according to the request formulation and the searcher's knowledge of the subject matter; the searcher has his or her own notion (interpretation) of the user's POIN. This idea is illustrated in Figure 7.2, which presents just one of the possible scenarios.

Apart from the preceding situation when intermediary searchers have inaccurate knowledge of the POIN, it is also safe to assume that most of them are not as knowledgeable as users in the subject matter contained in the collection of documents in IR system. All this is true, and yet intermediary searchers have significant advantages. As a rule, they have a much better understanding of

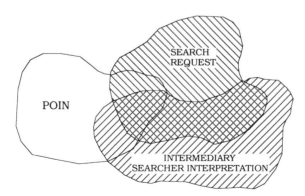

Figure 7.2
The interpretation of the user's POIN by the intermediary searcher.

the constructive features of the system's every element, of its possibilities, of the available documents in the collection, of the range of its statistical characteristics, and so on. Also, the experience searchers have in the construction of query formulations (query indexing)—which is their main activity—is much broader and diverse than that gained by the users. Probably, at a certain stage of the development of IR systems, the advantages enjoyed by intermediary searchers outweighed all of the mentioned disadvantages. At any rate, these advantages can be viewed as the main components of the best results achieved by an intermediary searcher. In many instances, these "best results" did not differ much from the results obtained by users. Also, the available experimental data were known mostly to researchers, whereas users, dealing with concrete results of a search done without their involvement, were often dissatisfied with its quality.

The emergence of on-line systems substantially decreased the number of users dissatisfied with the system's performance. This decrease was due, among other things, to an access to the system gained by a user who became actively involved in the search process. In other words, the user could construct his or her own query formulation. The quality of the query formulations constructed by users began to climb steadily and by the late 1970s researchers noticed that in a number of instances the results achieved by the users exceeded the results attained by intermediary searchers. This was something to be expected, because the introduction of a dialogue brought certain conveniences into the query formulation procedure. Moreover, the user obtained access to some internal information, such as the occurrence frequency of a specific term in the collection of documents and information on the number of documents retrieved at different stages of the search. Methods of using a thesaurus in the dialogue mode were developed in a number of systems; at the user's request some thesaurus fragments, which can be useful for creating query formulations, were put on the screen. Also, many years of research provided the user with helpful information that enabled him or her to adapt to a specific type of IR system. This largely accounts for the fact that at the present time in most of the functioning IR systems, query formulations are constructed by users. What is more, users today tend to give thoughtful considerations to methods for improving query formulations; that is, they assume the function of researchers in information retrieval. Publications written by users and mainly addressed to other users have also appeared; in them, users use their own experience to give useful advice (methodological recommendations) on how to construct query formulations that favorably compare to those formulated by experts in information science. In 1992, for instance, Goldman, an engineer and manager at Bell Northern Research, published a book with an indicative title *Online Information Hunting,* which gives an account of his search for his own information needs (Goldman, 1992). He is certain that "the retrieval of information by an intermediary searcher is, in principle, impossible unless the search is controlled by the subject expert himself." Goldman continued, "It looks like the classical information gathering intermediary . . . is going to be included in the list of endangered species in the very near future." Goldman's recommendations mainly replicated those contained in commonly known methodological manuals. He set forth a number of steps, such as how to organize a search strategy, input the first version, proceed with the initial on-line adaptation, and organize a final search version, citing examples of the query formulations he obtained. Yet Goldman did not go so far as to describe a concrete method of constructing a query formulation. As for the terms to be used in formulating disjunctive normal form, his major recommendation is to "think carefully" about which of the terms are likely to be more successful for the search. Incidentally, in each of the seven methodologies we examined, we found, in one way or another, the same recommendation.

Be that as it may, today many users can construct query formulations that are no worse than those constructed by intermediary searchers. However, the acuteness of the problem remains. Researchers think, like before, that it is one of the bottlenecks in the functioning of the IR system. Moreover, the widespread use of on-line IR systems prompted the developers of the systems to find methods of helping users to construct query formulations. This problem of interaction between IR systems and users is one of the most important in developing IR systems. It mainly consists of answering the following two questions:

1. What is the best way to help users construct better query formulations?
2. What is the best way to simplify the interaction between the user and the IR system in the process of constructing a query formulation (and in correcting it)?

It is important to observe that these two goals are at odds with each other. As mentioned earlier, to improve the quality of a query formulation the system typically has to provide the user with information about possible formulations, different statistics, descriptor relations, and so forth. This would force the user to spend a lot of time learning the system's internal characteristics and analyzing the information provided by the system on the screen. All this would clearly increase the complexity of the user's interaction with the IR system.

The problem of constructing a query formulation remains one of the most important problems in information retrieval, primarily because the process is performed by humans. Indeed, many papers dealing with this problem express this opinion. It is probably the reason for the growing interest in the automatic construction of query formulations. Next we focus our attention on this process.

7.3

Approaches to the Automatic Indexing of Search Requests

The creation of a method (algorithm) for the automatic indexing of queries is in some sense the creation of an automatic intermediary searcher. In other words, the creation of an algorithm is the creation of a model of the process

Not differentiating initial query indexing and relevance feedback,

performed by an intermediary searcher in translating a query from natural language into IRL. The automation of this intellectual process is difficult to carry out for several reasons. First, the information need (POIN) does not have clear boundaries and hence cannot be expressed precisely, even in natural language. Second, in terms of the search, the intermediary searcher has to guess the best combination of descriptors drawing on his or her own experience, intuition, and methodological recommendations instead of relying on formal rules. This process has traditionally been considered to be creative, and the efforts of the system developers are directed toward supplying the intermediary searcher with additional information about the system (such as the frequency of using descriptors), which, in their opinion, will improve the search quality. In creating automatic methods of query indexing, the researchers, understandably, do not even aspire to copy the intermediary searcher's intellectual activity. Typically, they proceed from what they think are pragmatic assumptions, which are often not formulated explicitly. Only a few algorithms for constructing disjunctive normal forms have been created so far. Next, we discuss the various approaches implemented in these algorithms.

In 1970, we suggested and published the first algorithm for the automatic construction of query formulations in Boolean form (Frants, et al.). Since 1969, the program implementing this algorithm (written in ALGOL) has been tested with encouraging results. In developing our algorithm, we used the following pragmatic assumptions.

Information about the user's POIN has to be presented to a system in a natural language (as mentioned previously, we refer to this representation as a search request). This assumption is based on the common notion that the natural language is the most convenient and simple form for the user to present his or her informational need. In other words, whenever the users express their POIN in the form most convenient to them, the system acquires the fullest and the most precise information about the POIN (see, for example, Barker, Veal, & Watt, 1972; and Schaffer, March, & Berndos, 1972). Yet different forms are possible in formulating search requests, which leads to the following assumption: the formulation of the search request has to be the most simple and convenient form for the user. How do we choose such a form? Search requests can be formulated either of two ways:

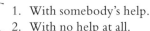

1. With somebody's help.
2. With no help at all.

In the first instance, users can be aided by both IR system experts (an intermediary searcher, for example) and/or outsiders (psychologists, for instance). Both methods (1 and 2) are used in practice, but the last one is more prevalent due to the fact that most experiments showed that this method is not only the simplest, but the most effective. Therefore, we consider it necessary to allow the user to formulate his or her own request.

Now, that's what is meant by "form"!

Even in cases where the users formulate their own requests, they can do it orally, in written form, or in the form of marked documents. We define a marked document as *a document that the user determines to pertain to an information need that the user wants to express in natural language.* The set of marked documents used to formulate a search request is called a *marked set.* We now elaborate on how a request is formulated using marked documents.

Back in the early 1960s, researchers noticed that in trying to explain his or her POIN to the intermediary, the user often presented certain documents that were intended to give an idea of what the user wanted. This situation is analogous to formulating a request with the aid of marked documents. We suppose that all documents in the collection are in a natural language and that all documents, which may be presented by the user as marked ones, are also written in a natural language. In other words, within the framework of the created method, we assume that whenever the user expresses his or her POIN by a set of marked documents (written in a natural language), we are dealing with a search request.

Several experiments have shown that a query formulation based on marked documents seems to be more effective than a query formulation constructed using other forms of search requests (see, for example, McCash & Carmichael, 1970; and Moody & Kays, 1972). Researchers also noticed that whenever the user had some marked documents and knew that he or she could formulate requests using these documents, the user was more willing to take this opportunity than other opportunities. For that reason, the created algorithm (called *M-algorithm* in the published work) was first and foremost designed for search requests formulated in the form of marked documents. We say "first and foremost" because not every user can (or wants) to make a request in such a form. Therefore, the users had the opportunity to formulate their requests in any form convenient to them. This option was taken into account in developing the M-algorithm, which means that in the system such a request was viewed as one marked document representing the user's POIN.

In creating the M-algorithm, we were mainly concerned with finding a way to allow the selection of useful (in terms of search) descriptors and combining them successfully (again in terms of search) into disjunctive normal form by the logical operators AND and OR. To determine a descriptor in a search request, which would be important in a search, we set forth an idea sometimes called an *inverse documents frequency.* This idea is based on the assumption that the importance of the descriptor is proportional to the frequency of its occurrence in the document profiles of the marked documents and inversely proportional to its occurrence frequency in the document profiles of the collection of documents. In other words, we talk of a "counter" probability when the maximum probability of descriptor occurrences is desired in the document profile of the marked documents and when the minimum probability of its occurrence is desired in the document profiles of the entire collection of documents.

To calculate the value of descriptor's importance for the search, the following formula was suggested:

$$\Psi_i = \frac{x_i \cdot X}{y \cdot Y_i},$$

where x_i is the number of documents on the marked set containing the i-th descriptor; X is the total number of documents in the search file; y is the total number of marked documents in the request; and Y_i is the number of documents in the search file containing the i-th descriptor.

This formula assigns a high degree of importance to terms (descriptors) occurring in only few documents of a collection. Within the framework of the M-algorithm, it was accepted that if Ψ_i was larger than a certain specified value α, then the i-th descriptor could be included in the query formulation as an independent set (consisting of one descriptor) and combined with other sets by the operator OR. Note that independent sets included in the query formulation and combined by the operator OR are referred to as *subrequests*. This can be illustrated by the following example. Let us assume that in a certain system the query formulation looks like this:

$$D \vee B \vee (E \wedge A) \vee (C \wedge A \wedge F \wedge G),$$

where A, B, C, D, E, F, and G are descriptors. The query formulation in this example consists of four sets connected by the logical operator OR: (1) D, (2) B, (3) (E $\wedge$ A), and (4) (C $\wedge$ A $\wedge$ F $\wedge$ G). These four sets are subrequests in the given query formulation.

After identifying subrequests consisting of one descriptor, the remaining descriptors are partitioned into zones so that the first zone includes descriptors with the occurrence frequency in the entire collection exceeding K_1, the second zone includes descriptors with a frequency higher than K_2 (but less than K_1), and so on. Figure 7.3 illustrates this breakdown.

Figure 7.3 shows that frequency zones were formulated as follows. A fixed step value (in this case 100) was chosen for a transition from one frequency zone to another. The first zone in the given example included descriptors with an occurrence frequency in the entire collection exceeding 500, in the second zone it ranged from 400 to 500, in the third zone it ranged from 300 to 400, and so on. Then subrequests consisting of two and more descriptors were constructed in the framework of the M-algorithm. From the last zone (zone 6 in the example), subrequests of two descriptors were constructed (i.e., the operator AND combined two descriptors); from the next zone (zone 5), subrequests of three descriptors, were constructed; and so forth. Such an approach evidently takes into account the fact that if a subrequest includes descriptors having a comparatively high frequency of occurrence in the collection of documents, then to avoid excessive noise the number of descriptors in the subrequest must be sufficiently large. At the final stage all the obtained subrequests (including those with

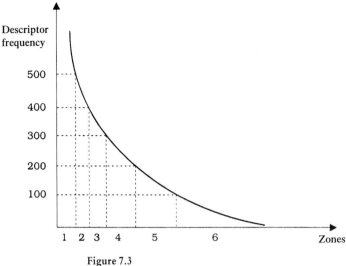

Figure 7.3
An example of the formulation of zones.

one descriptor) were combined by the operator OR into the query formulation finally constructed.

We have described the basic ideas used in the creation of the M–algorithm. Important as they are in the creation of the first automatic query indexing method for the Boolean IR system, they are even more important in the sense that, to a certain extent, they form a basis for almost all the automatic methods available today. Now let us take a closer look at these methods.

We start with the work published by J. Rickman (1972), who, generally speaking, considered some approaches to automating the process rather than focusing on a concrete path (to say nothing of an algorithm) of query indexing. The form of search request that he considered was also marked documents, although in his approach not only were the documents pertinent to the POIN taken into consideration, but so were any other documents assessed (positively or negatively) by the user (and included in the marked set). This choice was due primarily to the fact that Rickman did not seek the automatic construction of query formulations in response to a search request. He considered automation only as a feedback process, that is, to be used only when the user had already appraised the output—regardless of how it was retrieved—by either the manual or the automatic method of query indexing.

Rickman suggested a few methods of constructing query formulations. In one case for "refining a previous search," he suggested that all the descriptors from the document profile of the documents marked by the user as pertinent be

Relevance feedback

combined only by the operator AND, and he gave an example of such a query formulation:

$$+T_1 \wedge +T_2 \cdots \wedge +T_n. \tag{1}$$

(Note that $+T$ symbolizes descriptors from pertinent documents.) In another case, for "expanding the previous search" he suggested that all descriptors from the same documents be combined only by the operator OR when the query formulation appears as follows:

$$+T_1 \vee +T_2 \cdots \vee +T_n. \tag{2}$$

Checking his approach experimentally the author wrote, "Eight efforts to use query formulation (1), consisting of terms only from pertinent documents in a conjunctive search, ended in a failure. Whenever query formulation (1) was used anywhere in the iterative search process the next search usually retrieved zero documents." In another case he said, "In 7 attempts query formulation (2) retrieved a mean of 861% more documents than their previous queries."

Such results, understandably, do not suit even the author himself. In an attempt to improve them, Rickman therefore suggested using negatively assessed documents. In other words, for such descriptors use should be made of the BUTNOT ($\sim$) operator, "which will be equivalent to a set difference operator." To this end he set out to construct a query formulation in the following manner. To the query formulation for which the previous search was performed, Rickman added query formulation (1) either with the aid of the AND operator or query formulation (2) with the aid of the OR operator, and in both cases the BUTNOT operator helps "subtract" all the descriptors from the negatively assessed documents. Because this approach also failed, the author tried to use only nonpertinent documents by "subtracting" all their descriptors from the previous query formulation. Though this attempt was just as unsuccessful, the result nevertheless was not as negative as before. On this score Rickman wrote this conclusion:

> The refining query formulation was basically a negative feedback process and reduced recall more than desirable. A searcher could manually outperform the automatic technique since he would not be restricted by any fixed format for his reformulated query formulation. Having to choose any fixed format for an automatic technique appears to be a distinct disadvantage. The technique as implemented was relatively unstable as to the number of documents retrieved. (Rickman, 1972)

The work of Rickman is interesting, but not in terms of a practical method for the automatic construction of query formulations. What is important is that this is the first attempt to use only nonpertinent documents (nonrelevance feedback). It is also sufficiently illustrative of complexities encountered in the problem of automating query indexing.

In 1971, we published a somewhat improved version of the M-algorithm (Voiskunskii & Frants, 1971). It provided for the ranking of subrequests consisting of two and more descriptors. To this end, all subrequests that appeared in a given zone were assigned a weight corresponding to the number of the documents of the marked set having descriptors from the "weighed" subrequests in their document profiles. This helped us avoid including in query formulation those subrequests whose descriptors never appeared jointly in the marked documents (such subrequests weighed zero). This certainly enhanced the algorithm's performance (which was very important in the early 1970s) without practically affecting the search quality.

Even more substantial improvements were proposed in papers published later that decade (Voiskunskii & Frants, 1974a; 1974b). In suggesting an improved algorithm, we partitioned the descriptors into zones, based not on a descriptor's occurrence frequency in the document profiles of the collection of documents (as was done in the M-algorithm) but from its search significance (inverse documents frequency) calculated with the use of the formula presented earlier, which in the 1974 works looked as follows:

$$\Psi_i = \frac{r_i \cdot N}{n \cdot R_i}.$$

(3)

where

r_i = occurrence frequency of the i-th descriptor in document profiles of the marked set of documents;

n = number of documents in the marked set;

R_i = occurrence frequency of the i-th descriptor in the document profiles of the entire collection; and

N = number of documents in the collection.

We give this formula once again because it is in this form that it has been used in various publications for more than 20 years. In constructing an algorithm published in 1974, we tested several propositions discussed in the paper. For example, the following proposition looked rather attractive:

> A set of descriptors from the combined set of descriptors from the document profiles of marked documents may form a subrequest, provided the relative occurrence frequency of this set in the documents of the marked set exceeds several times an occurrence frequency of the same set in the documents of the entire collection.

Still the proposition was not used for constructing an algorithm, though the method for calculating the significance for a search of descriptor combinations (the method of calculating Ψ for descriptor combinations) seems very attractive. The point is that during the work of the algorithm, an extremely large number of search operations has to be completed to calculate the frequency of the joint occurrence of descriptors. We noted in this context that if proceeding from the frequency or relative frequency of the occurrence of descriptors in the collection one succeeds in determining the frequency or relative frequency of occurrence of any set of these descriptors in the same collection, then the algorithm constructed on the basis of the preceding proposition will be sufficiently effective. At any rate, the attempts made in the early 1970s to calculate the probability of the joint occurrence of descriptors in the collection did not yield satisfactory results; the attempts were based on the occurrence frequency of individual descriptors and the joint probability was computed using known formulas for calculating probabilities for independent events. (Linguists are well aware that the use of terms in the text is not independent.) Therefore, in constructing the algorithm we proceeded using the following assumption.

The set of descriptors may form a subrequest only if the value of Ψ_i for every descriptor of that set falls within a certain interval of values and if the set consists of the required number of descriptors. The required number of descriptors included in the set strictly depends on the lower bound of that interval of values within which the values of Ψ_i have fallen (the interval chosen is such that its lower bound is the maximum of what is possible for this set of descriptors), and the frequency of the occurrence of the set in the documents of the marked set is not less than a certain value.

The algorithm created on the basis of this proposition proved more effective than the M-algorithm. Dillon et al. used a very similar approach in two papers published in the early 1980s (Dillon & Desper, 1980; Dillon, Ulmsmeider, & Desper, 1983). They also made use of the marked set as information about the user's POIN, and the descriptor's significance for the search is calculated on the basis of its occurrence frequency in the marked set and in the entire collection. The descriptors for which the calculated value exceeds a certain established threshold are used as independent subrequests and those that did not reach the threshold are partitioned into zones and are used to form subrequests of two, three, and more descriptors, depending on the number of zones and the values chosen for these zones. Still, the algorithm proposed by Dillon and colleagues has a few substantial distinctions.

Like Rickman, Dillon and colleagues considered the automatic construction of query formulations only in the process of feedback, and in a marked set they utilized all user-assessed documents of the previous output (both pertinent and nonpertinent to the user's POIN). On the one hand, these nonpertinent documents are used for determining descriptors included in the query formulation with the NOT (AND NOT) operator; on the other hand (which is the most interesting point), they are used for calculating the descriptors' significance for the search. This is done as follows. First the descriptor's significance for the search (in our opinion, the authors aptly call it "prevalence") is calculated using only the pertinent documents (positive prevalence), and then the "insignificance" of the same descriptor is calculated using the nonpertinent documents (negative prevalence). Then the "genuine" significance (simply prevalence) is calculated for the given descriptor by subtracting negative prevalence from positive prevalence. This, naturally, is only a general idea for calculating the descriptor's prevalence in the search. We now show more explicitly how the authors practically calculate prevalence. For this we will use the notation we introduced previously and will introduce a few new notations for calculating negative prevalence, namely r_i^-—the occurrence frequency of the i-th descriptor in the document profile of nonpertinent documents—and n^-—the number of nonpertinent documents in the marked set. We will assume first that the i-th descriptor occurs only in pertinent documents. This means that negative prevalence will equal zero and then Ψ_i (prevalence) equals positive prevalence, that is, in this case Ψ_i is calculated only using pertinent documents. For this there is the following formula:

$$\Psi_i = \frac{r_i \cdot 1}{n \cdot R_i}.$$

In many ways this calculation is similar to that used in the M-algorithm, the only difference being that the authors disregard the size of the search collection. The authors, incidentally, use different symbols and a different form of writing. In addition, they normalize the result, but the essence of the result does not change. While preserving our notation, we will rewrite the formula as suggested by Dillon and colleagues:

$$\Psi_i = \frac{r_i/n}{\log R_i}.$$

Let us assume now that the output contains only nonpertinent documents (the marked set consists only of nonpertinent documents). In this case, positive prevalence for every descriptor will equal zero, while Ψ_i will equal negative prevalence:

$$-\Psi_i = \frac{r_i^-/n^-}{\log R_i}.$$

If the i-th descriptor occurs both in the pertinent and nonpertinent documents, Ψ_i is calculated this way:

$$(\pm)\Psi_i = [(r_i/n) - (r_i^-/n^-)]/\log R_i.$$

In our opinion, it is exactly such use of nonpertinent documents that presents certain interest, because it probably helps in a number of cases to more fully take into account the use of a descriptor in the search.

The next distinction lies in partitioning descriptors into zones. Dillon and colleagues suggested forming zones, not only for the descriptors whose value Ψ_i is positive, but also for the descriptors with negative values. Figure 7.4 illustrates this type of partitioning.

All zones range from 1 to -1, because the result of calculation of the descriptor search prevalence is normalized. With this type of partitioning, the

Figure 7.4
Example of partitioning into zones.

descriptors from the positive zones form one part of the final query formulation, and those from the negative zones form another part; furthermore, the descriptors from the negative zones may also form subrequests consisting of one or more descriptors. Then the second (negative) part is connected to the first one by means of the AND NOT operators. It is interesting to note that since the early 1960s, many researchers have been questioning this use of descriptors in a subject search. Having carried out a series of experiments, Dillon and colleagues formed this conclusion on this matter:

> Results using negative feedback in addition to positive feedback are disappointing and somewhat surprising. What was expected (or naively hoped for) was a means of increasing recall through lower thresholds in the positive scale and the achievement of reasonable precision through a judicious application of negative thresholds. Though our experimentation was by no means exhaustive, no negative thresholds were discovered that seemed to hold any promise of improving precision by NOTing documents that did not also diminish recall proportionally. (Dillon et al., 1983)

In general, however, if descriptors with the negative values of Ψ_i are not included in query formulation, that is, if the NOT operator is dismissed, the results of the experiments should be treated as positive.

Between 1983 and 1985, a number of publications appeared (Salton, Buckley, & Fox, 1983; Salton, Fox, & Voorhees, 1985; Salton, Fox, & Wu, 1983) that also dealt with the creation of a method for the automatic construction of query formulations. Their authors noted that within the framework of this method "user's initial natural language statement of information need could be taken as input to an automatic query formulation process. Alternatively, the texts of previously retrieved items judged to be relevant to a given query could be used." (Salton, Fox, & Voorhees, 1985). They especially emphasized that it is precisely the disjunctive normal form (the NOT operator was not used) that would be constructed automatically. The authors proposed that the search weight be calculated not only for individual descriptors in the marked set but also for pairs of descriptors, triples of descriptors, and so on. Moreover, the authors computed a joint occurrence frequency of descriptors (more precisely, the probability of their joint occurrence) for pairs, triples, and so forth based on the occurrence frequency of individual descriptors making up a pair, a triple and so on, by using commonly known formulas of multiplying probabilities for independent events. Thus, the probability of the occurrence of i and j descriptors jointly in the document profiles of some collection of documents, denoted by

$$P_i = \frac{R_i}{N}$$

P_{ij}, if one assumes that the occurrence of these descriptors in the document profile is independent (as is assumed by Salton et al.), can be calculated as

$$\frac{R_i \cdot R_j}{N^2}, \qquad \frac{R_i}{N} * \frac{R_j}{N}.$$

where R_i and R_j are occurrence frequencies of i-th and j-th descriptors in the document profile of the collection of N documents. In subsequent calculations, the authors use P_{ij} as R_{ij}, the frequency of joint occurrence of descriptors i and j. Therefore, in calculating the probability of the joint occurrence of three descriptors (three independent events), calculation is reduced to the previous one, namely, to the calculation of two independent events as before:

$$P_{ijt} = \frac{R_t \cdot R_{ij}}{N}.$$

As mentioned earlier, in 1974 (see Voiskunskii & Frants, 1974) we did not follow this path because we found the results of the experiment unsatisfactory, and we argued (in agreement with linguistics) that the occurrence of terms in a document should not be assumed independent. What is more, it is often assumed that in expressing certain meanings, words are used connected with these meanings. Yet Salton et al., making use of the given method of calculation, succeeded in creating an algorithm which, as is clear from the results of the experiment (we discuss this at length later on), leads in a number of cases to the construction of query formulations with better search performance as compared to that conducted by means of query formulations constructed manually.

In calculating the probability of the occurrence of pairs and triples in the document profiles of the collection, Salton et al. actually calculated the number of documents that can be retrieved by every pair or triple of descriptors. In the framework of the proposed method, of most importance for the search (i.e., having the highest weight) are those descriptors that help retrieve the least number of documents. The same holds true for determining the importance of descriptor pairs, triples, and so on. A certain threshold T, meaning a number of documents (wanted number) in the output, is used in constructing the disjunctive normal form. This is followed by the selection of M more significant (with higher weights) descriptors, and, continuing on the assumption that they do not occur jointly in the documents, calculation is made (by adding together the frequencies of joint occurrence of descriptors) of the number of documents in the output, which can be obtained by means of these M descriptors. If this number (Salton et al. call it estret) is far smaller than T, then the next (by weight) descriptor is added to the set M, and if it is far bigger, then the descriptor (from the set M) having the least weight is subtracted from the given set. Then another calculation is performed (both in the first and second cases) and the result is compared with T. Whenever in the next calculation estret is higher than T and the least valuable descriptor (from the remaining descriptors) is subtracted, then the descriptor earlier subtracted and the descriptor subtracted again make up a pair combined by the AND operator. For this pair, the number of documents that it can find (P_{ij}) is calculated, and this pair is added to the remaining single descriptors for a new calculation of estret. Calculation is performed by adding the occurrence frequencies' descriptors plus the number of documents that can be retrieved by the added pair. Then this is all repeated unless the calculated number of documents (estret) becomes equal to $T/2 \leq$ estret $\leq T$. In this case, all the remaining descriptors and all the added pairs are combined by the operator OR and the query formulation is finally considered constructed.

Note that whenever estret $> T$ and there are no more single descriptors to be subtracted, it is the pair with the least weight that is subtracted. If this process is repeated, then the pairs subtracted are used to form triples, which are added to the remaining pairs for a new calculation. In this case, with $T/2 \leq$ estret $\leq T,$ it is only the pairs (remaining) and triples that are combined by the OR operator into the final query formulation. This means that the query formulation consists only for pairs, triples, and so forth.

Experimentally, the algorithm was tested in the IR systems MEDLARS and INSPEC (Salton, Buckley, & Fox, 1983). During the experiment, results of the search performed on the basis of automatically constructed query formulations were compared with results obtained with query formulations constructed manually. In MEDLARS, 30 queries were used in a collection of 1033 documents in biomedicine. Five different versions of the search were tested; that is, five different values of T were used. In other words, in the first search (version), the 20 best documents were searched for all 30 queries; in the second search, 30 documents were searched, and then 50, 100, and 200 documents. In three versions out of five, the results of algorithm operation proved better as compared to the manual query formulation. In the INSPEC system (12,684 documents and 77 queries), four versions of search were used, that is, T was 20, 30, 50, and 100 documents, respectively. In all four cases, in this system the results of algorithm operation proved worse than those for manual operation.

We have considered the basic approaches to automatic query indexing. In so doing, we discussed, within the framework of each approach, the application of descriptors when using a more traditional form of search request as well as a marked set of documents. But where did descriptors originate? Practically all authors imply (if this is not explicitly discussed) that before the algorithm for the automatic construction of query formulations is used, the search request, formulated in any form, must be indexed with the aid of a document indexing algorithm. So the use of an automatic document indexing algorithm, for example, the one described in Chapter 6, in all cases must be a preliminary step before using an automatic query indexing algorithm—a step that makes it possible to determine the initial ("working") set of descriptors for each query. To put it differently, unordered sets of descriptors, obtained using an automatic document indexing algorithm, provide building blocks for constructing query formulations.

The main disadvantage of all proposed query indexing algorithms is the lack of any explanations for the use of thresholds; that is, apart from their selection not being automatic it is not even substantiated. This state of affairs exists despite the fact that the choice of thresholds substantially affects the final results of operation for both the algorithm and the system as a whole. The important thresholds include the number of zones and their ranges in the algorithms of the early 1970s (Frants, et al., 1970; Voiskunskii & Frants, 1971; 1974), as well as in the algorithm set forth by Dillon et al. (Dillon & Desper, 1980; Dillon, et al., 1983), the values of T, M, q-count, and excessive frequency in the algorithm set forth by Salton et al. (Salton, Buckley, et al., 1983; Salton, Fox, et al., 1983; Salton, et al., 1985). This is why when developing an algorithm we tried to concentrate on finding a way to eliminate this disadvantage. By the mid-1980s, we successfully found a simple and effective enough method to automatically choose thresholds that made it feasible to create an advanced algorithm for the automatic construction of query formulations in disjunctive normal forms. It was successfully tested in several experiments, and the algorithm was published in 1991 (Frants & Shapiro, 1991). We present it in the following section.

7.4
Algorithm for the Automatic Construction of Query Formulations in Boolean Form

It is easy to imagine a situation when in some functioning IR system the query formulation is constructed by the system experts from the user's search request given in the form of a marked set of documents. After reading these documents, the expert forms his or her interpretation of the user's information need (POIN) and constructs the query formulation using his or her own knowledge and experience. It is clear that if we could replace a human expert with an automatic expert (i.e., a computer program), which after "seeing" the marked documents would find all similar documents, our problem of creating an automatic expert would be solved. So our algorithm should allow the user to "show" the computer the pertinent documents and provide the user with an output consisting of similar documents. The suggested algorithm will construct the query formulation, which will be used to search for the appropriate documents.

We want to remind the reader that the query formulation constructed by the algorithm has to be in a Boolean form (specifically, disjunctive normal form). This means that we need to solve two problems. First, we must find the descriptors that will be used for the search, and, second, we must combine the descriptors using the logical operators AND or OR.

	A	B	C	D	E	F	G	H	I	J	K	L	M
1	x		x	x			x		x	x	x		x
2		x	x		x	x	x		x		x	x	
3	x	x	x	x		x			x	x	x		x
4	x		x				x	x			x	x	
5		x	x		x	x	x		x		x	x	x
6		x	x	x		x	x				x	x	x

Figure 7.5
Term–document matrix.

The first step in the algorithm is to translate the marked documents into the descriptor language using the same method of indexing that was used for the entire collection of documents in the IR system. Obviously, this is only needed when these documents are not already present in the system. Otherwise, we can use the existing document profiles. The next step is to create a term–document matrix (Lancaster, 1968). When creating such a matrix we use the marked documents. An example of a term matrix is given in Figure 7.5.

The column headings of this matrix come from the set that is the union of the sets of all descriptors appearing in the document profiles of the marked documents. Such a set will be called a *relevant neighborhood*. In our example, the set {A, B, C, . . . , M} is the relevant neighborhood for the search request represented by the documents 1, 2, . . . , 6. The relevant neighborhood is used to construct a query formulation. To decide which descriptors are going to be used and how to combine them will require formal criteria. The choice of these criteria is very important because they will determine the quality of the search.

First, we will determine the importance of each descriptor from the relevant neighborhood for the search of documents similar to the marked set. Actually, to determine the importance of a descriptor we use the same criterion that was introduced in 1970 in developing the M-algorithm. However, because we only mentioned it earlier without providing a detailed explanation, we would like to do so now.

When analyzing the term–document matrix in Figure 7.5, it is clear that the occurrence frequency of each descriptor from the relevant neighborhood varies from 1 to 6. For example, descriptors C and K appear in every pertinent document, whereas descriptor H appears only once. It would seem that we can conclude that descriptors C and K are more characteristic for the marked set under consideration (and hence for a search request) than is descriptor H. But that would be true only if all descriptors from a dictionary have the same frequency of occurrence in the entire collection of documents (more precisely, in the document profiles in the collection). But it is well known that such is not the case. Because we are interested in the importance of the term from the search point of view (and not its semantic importance in a search request), we use the following assumption: The most important (essential or characteristic) descriptors are the descriptors whose occurrence frequency in the marked set is maximal and in the entire collection is minimal.

The following formula (already known to us) realizes this assumption.

$$\Psi_i = \frac{r_i \cdot N}{n \cdot R_i}.$$

The value of Ψ_i determines the importance of the corresponding descriptor in the search process, and the descriptors that are more important have larger values for their Ψ_i. This is illustrated by the following example.

If in a collection of 1000 documents (this collection includes the marked set of six documents) the descriptor D (Figure 7.5) occurs 4 times and in our matrix the same descriptor occurs 3 times (in 3 pertinent documents out of 6), then it is reasonable to assume that the remaining document from the collection containing descriptor D is "similar" to our marked documents. In other words the system will consider it as likely to be relevant. The value Ψ_D for descriptor D is

$$\Psi_D = \frac{r_D \cdot N}{n \cdot R_D} = \frac{3 \cdot 1000}{6 \cdot 4} = 125.$$

On the other hand, if the descriptor C (which appears in every document in the marked set—i.e., it shows up six times) appears in 500 documents in the collection of 1000 documents, then is unlikely that the hundreds of documents that contain the descriptor C will be relevant. The value of Ψ_C for the descriptor C is 2.

The examples given show that when a descriptor weight (value Ψ) is greater than some predetermined value, then this descriptor can be used during search without combining it with other descriptors using the operator AND.

So the algorithm using the suggested criterion computes the "importance"—from the point of view of the search—of each descriptor in the relevant neighborhood. Now we are ready to discuss the process of query formulation construction in Boolean form. We mentioned earlier that a query formulation is convenient to represent in disjunctive normal form. The algorithm's goal is to select the best subrequests from the point of view of the search, regardless of how many descriptors are contained in each subrequest.

The construction of a query formulation begins with determining subrequests consisting of one descriptor. A descriptor from the relevant neighborhood will constitute a separate subrequest if the value Ψ_i for this descriptor (see the preceding definition of Ψ_i) is greater than a predetermined bound L, that is, $L < \Psi_i$. After these descriptors are determined by the algorithm, they become a part of the query formulation and are combined together by the logical operator OR. In further analysis, these descriptors are not considered, and they are removed from the term–document matrix and from the relevant neighborhood of the marked set. This is done because if we use such a descriptor as an element of a subrequest containing more than one descriptor, the result of the search will be a subset of the documents that were found by using a subrequest consisting of only this descriptor.

It is clear that not all query formulations will contain subrequests consisting of one descriptor. In some IR systems, query formulations containing subrequests consisting of one descriptor will be encountered often, in others they will be encountered very rarely. It depends on the lengths of document profiles in the system. For example, if in one IR system the average length of a document profile is 10 descriptors, and in the other the average length is 80, then it is clear that in the first case query formulations will often contain subrequests consisting of one descriptor, and in the second IR system it will be a rare occurrence. Moreover, the second system might contain subrequests, for example, consisting of more than 15 descriptors. Our algorithm should be able to construct subrequests consisting of any number of descriptors.

It would seem that to construct subrequests consisting of more than one descriptor we can again use the criterion Ψ_i to compute the importance, from the point of view of the search, of any combination of descriptors from the relevant neighborhood. In other words, we can compute the ratio of the occurrence frequency of any combination of descriptors in the relevant neighborhood of the marked set to the relative occurrence frequency of this combination in the document profiles of the entire collection of documents in the system. But it is easy to see that this approach requires an incredibly large number of computations and therefore is not acceptable in practice. If we could find a way to compute the relative occurrence frequency of any set of descriptors from the relative occurrence frequency of each descriptor in the set, then the number of required computations would be much smaller and practically feasible. Next we describe our idea of how to decide when a subrequest should be formed by more than one descriptor.

We use the assumption that if several descriptors have values of Ψ_i, which are smaller than some bound L but still are very close to L, then the search based on the subrequest consisting of two such descriptors (which are "almost very important") will give us good results.

In other words, the descriptors whose Ψ_i values are greater than some lower bound L_1 but not greater than L; that is,

$$L_1 < \Psi_i \leq L$$

can be used in creating subrequests consisting of two descriptors. Analogous considerations lead to the construction of subrequests consisting of three descriptors. These subrequests include descriptors whose Ψ_i values are close enough to

L_1 and are greater than some bound L_2; that is,

$$L_2 < \Psi_i \le L_1.$$

The same is true for subrequests consisting of four descriptors:

$$L_3 < \Psi_i \le L_2.$$

Hence, after removing from the matrix all the descriptors whose Ψ_i values are greater than L, the algorithm transforms the matrix by placing the descriptors from right to left in decreasing order of their Ψ_i values. Then the matrix is divided into several intervals with predetermined upper and lower bounds for each interval.

For example, assuming a bound $L = 100$, the matrix in Figure 7.5 after the removal of descriptor D (value $= 125$), descriptor I (value $= 108$), and descriptor J (value $= 102$) is transformed into the matrix shown in Figure 7.6.

In Figure 7.6 the numbers in parenthesis represent the intervals for the Ψ_i values of the descriptors. Beneath these numbers are the descriptor names, together with their corresponding values. We can see that the first interval

$$(L_1, L]$$

includes descriptors L and C with $\Psi_i = 87$ and $\Psi_C = 94$. The second interval (L_2, L_1) contains descriptors M, B, A, and G. The third interval does not contain any descriptors because none of the descriptors from the relevant neighborhood

	$L_5=30$	$L_6=20$		$L_3=50$	$L_4=40$	$L_2=60$				$L=100$ $L_1=80$	
	(7)	(6)	(5)	(4)	(3)	(2)				(1)	
	K	H	E	F		M	B	A	G	L	C
	$\Psi=24$	$\Psi=35$	$\Psi=38$	$\Psi=48$		$\Psi=66$	$\Psi=68$	$\Psi=72$	$\Psi=79$	$\Psi=87$	$\Psi=94$
1	x					x		x	x		x
2	x		x	x			x		x	x	x
3	x			x		x	x	x			x
4	x	x					x	x	x	x	x
5	x		x	x		x	x		x	x	x
6	x			x		x	x		x	x	x

Figure 7.6
Transformed matrix.

have a value Ψ_i in the interval:

$$(L_3, \ L_2].$$

As we mentioned earlier, the algorithm will use the descriptors from the first interval to construct subrequests consisting of two descriptors, it will use the descriptors from the second interval to construct subrequests consisting of three descriptors, and so forth. The number of intervals (in our case 7) will depend on the average length of the document profiles in the IR system and has to be determined in advance by the developers of the IR system. For example, in an IR system where the average length of a document profile is 10 descriptors it is sufficient to use not more than 7 intervals which means that subrequests will contain at most 8 descriptors. On the other hand, in an IR system where the average length of a document profile is 80 descriptors, we might use 20 intervals and subrequests will contain at most 21 descriptors.

Now we will consider additional conditions used in constructing subrequests consisting of more than one descriptor. It is known that not all descriptors can simultaneously appear in one document. Therefore, when constructing subrequests we have to consider the simultaneous occurrence frequency of descriptors in the marked set.

Clearly it is possible to have some intervals of values j that do not contain any descriptors from the relevant neighborhood (for example, intervals 3 and 7 in Figure 7.6), and therefore we will not construct subrequests consisting of the number of descriptors corresponding to these intervals. In our example, the algorithm will not construct subrequests consisting of four or eight descriptors. It is also clear that in some intervals (in our example, intervals 4, 5, and 6) we will not have enough descriptors to construct subrequests containing descriptors from these intervals. For example, descriptor F from interval

$$(L_4, \ L_3]$$

has to be included in the subrequest consisting of five descriptors. Our algorithm deals with such a situation as follows.

When the algorithm constructs a subrequest consisting of more than two descriptors, it may use descriptors from intervals to the right of the interval under consideration (that is, intervals with larger L values). Thus, when constructing subrequests consisting of three descriptors, we will consider not interval

$$(L_2, \ L_1]$$

but rather interval

$$(L_2, \ L]$$

and we will require that each subrequest consisting of three descriptors contains at least one descriptor from interval

$$(L_2, \ L_1].$$

For subrequests consisting of four descriptors, we use interval

$$(L_3, L]$$

and require the presence of at least one descriptor from interval

$$(L_3, L_2].$$

The pragmatism of this approach can be seen from the following example. Say, interval $(L_1, L]$ contains only one descriptor. Then we cannot construct a subrequest consisting of two descriptors. But the usefulness of a descriptor whose Ψ_i value is very close to L is quite clear. In a case like this, we include the descriptor from the first interval into subrequests consisting of more than two descriptors.

It is important to consider the case when a subrequest constructed for a specific interval contains descriptors which themselves form a subrequest for another interval (to the right of the interval under consideration); that is, one subrequest properly contains another subrequest. The search using the larger subrequest can only find a subset of a set of documents that could be found using a smaller subrequest. Therefore, a subrequest that properly contains another subrequest we will call *extraneous*, and we will not include extraneous subrequests in our query formulation.

The algorithm begins its analysis of the transformed matrix by looking at the interval $(L_1, L]$; that is, it tries to find subrequests consisting of two descriptors. If interval $(L_1, L]$ contains more than one descriptor, then the algorithm analyzes all combinations of two descriptors from this interval. The set of two *how?* descriptors will constitute a subrequest only if the occurrence frequency of this set in the document profiles of the marked set is greater than some required value. For example, if we consider the search request represented by the transformed matrix in Figure 7.6 and require that any set consisting of two or more descriptors from interval $(L_1, L]$ should appear in at least five document profiles in the marked set, then we will not find any subrequest consisting of two descriptors.

After analyzing all possible combinations of two descriptors, the algorithm looks at the descriptors whose values are in the interval $(L_2, L]$ and using those descriptors constructs subrequests consisting of three descriptors. The set consisting of three descriptors will be considered a subrequest if (1) at least one of the descriptors from this set has Ψ_i value in the interval $(L_2, L_1]$, and (2) the occurrence frequency of this set in the documents of the marked set is greater than some required value. In our example, if the required frequency is 3, the algorithm will construct 6 subrequests consisting of 3 descriptors:

(1) $G \wedge L \wedge C$ (2) $B \wedge L \wedge C$ (3) $M \wedge B \wedge C$
(4) $B \wedge G \wedge C$ (5) $B \wedge G \wedge L$ (6) $M \wedge G \wedge C$

Recall that our query formulation already contains subrequests consisting of descriptors D, I, and J. Hence, at this point the query formulation will be as follows:

$$D \lor I \lor J \lor (G \land L \land C) \lor (B \land L \land C) \lor (M \land B \land C)$$
$$\lor (B \land G \land C) \lor (B \land G \land L) \lor (M \land G \land C)$$

After analyzing all possible combinations of three descriptors and discarding extraneous subrequests, if they exist, the algorithm looks at the descriptors with Ψ_i values in the next interval on the left and constructs subrequests consisting of four descriptors going through the steps described previously. This process will continue for all existing intervals. All constructed subrequests will be added to the query formulation and after the last interval is analyzed the final version of the query formulation will be used for the search.

Notice that the algorithm described earlier allows the system to automatically translate a search request into the information retrieval language, even in a case where the user formulates a search request without using a marked set of documents, that is, in a traditional natural language form. Then the search request is considered by the algorithm as a marked set consisting of one document and the algorithm proceeds as noted earlier. In this case the matrix becomes a one-dimensional array and the choice of bound values is performed automatically as described next. It should be mentioned that the quality of the search based on the query formulation obtained from one document is typically inferior to the search based on the query formulation obtained from several documents. The steps for constructing a query formulation are given in Table 7.1.

Table 7.1
Steps in Constructing a Query Formulation

---

1. Construct the relevant neighborhood (by indexing the incoming search request).

2. Construct the term-document matrix.

3. Compute Ψ_i values for all descriptors in the relevant neighborhood.

4. Compute the bound values for the intervals where each interval determines how many descriptors will be combined in one subrequest.

5. Find all the descriptors whose Ψ_i values are greater than L. Each of these descriptors will constitute a separate subrequest in a final query formulation.

6. Remove all descriptors found in step 5 from the relevant neighborhood, transform the term-document matrix, and place all remaining descriptors in corresponding intervals.

7. Analyze every interval and construct subrequests corresponding to each interval (using the Boolean operator AND).

8. Remove extraneous subrequests.

9. Combine all remaining subrequests into final query formulation using the Boolean operator OR.

7.5
The Choice of Bound Values

From the description of the preceding algorithm, it is clear that the choice of the bound values

$$(L, L_1, L_2, \ldots, L_n)$$

determines the quality of the query formulation (given two query formulations Q1 and Q2, we say that Q1 is "better" than Q2 if the search based on Q1 gives better results than the search based on Q2, for example, using recall and precision levels for comparison). If we increase the bound values, the number of subrequests in our query formulation decreases, but at the same time we may increase the probability that the documents found during the search will correspond to the information need of the user. In other words, by making the bounds more strict, we increase the precision of the search but decrease the recall level. It is clear that the ranges of the bound values for the intervals, the maximum number of descriptors allowed in a subrequest, and the required occurrence frequency of the set of descriptors in the documents of the marked set either have to be defined in advance or a method has to be established that would allow the algorithm to compute these values automatically.

When the values are entered into the system in advance, the developers of the system could determine these values (as we did it earlier) on the basis of the required precision and recall levels, using the characteristics of the collection of documents (for example, the average length of the document profile), the requirements of individual users, and other factors. In Figure 7.6 the bound values were determined for a collection of documents consisting of 2504 abstracts from computer science with the average length of an abstract profile approximately equal to 12 descriptors. Obviously there is no reason to believe that the chosen bound values were optimal. But these values were used as the basis for subsequent experiments, and as a result of these experiments we found a method whereby the bound values are determined automatically by a new algorithm.

The algorithm computes the bound values for each individual user. We assume that a user provides the system with the information about the number of documents that should be contained in the output. For example, when the user begins a retrospective search from a collection containing 30,000 documents, he or she might indicate that the output should contain 50 documents; from a collection of 1000 documents, the user might request an output of 10 documents; and so on. In both cases the algorithm uses some initial bound values (see, for example, Figure 7.6) to obtain the query formulation that is going to be used for the initial search. But the results of the search are not given to the user and are used by the algorithm for further calculations. The algorithm compares the number of documents found during the initial search with the number of documents requested by the user. If the two numbers are equal, then the obtained documents are given to the user. If the first number is larger, then all bound values are increased by some predetermined value (our incremental value is equal to 20). The matrix is transformed with the new bound values and the algorithm constructs a new query formulation. This query formulation is used for a new search, and the number of obtained documents is compared with the number requested by the user. If the numbers are equal, the output is given to the user; if the number of documents found during search is greater than requested, then the bound values are incremented again (using the same incremental value); and if the obtained number of documents is smaller than requested, then the incremental value is divided by 2 and a new value is used to decrease the bound values. Again the matrix is transformed, a new query formulation is constructed, and another search is performed. If the number of obtained documents is different from the required number, then the incremental value is divided by 2 and the result is added to the bound values if the difference between the obtained and required number of documents is positive or subtracted from the bound values if the difference is negative. This procedure is repeated until the numbers are equal or the incremental value is less than 1. (System developers who do not need such precision can choose any desirable approximation.) In both cases the output is given to the user and in the second case the output contains the number of documents closest to the required number.

This method of automatically computing bound values can be used even when the user does not tell the system the number of documents required in the output. In this case, the algorithm chooses a default (provided by the system's developers), for example, 10 documents.

This approach can be used to determine the likely order of importance of the documents for the user. When we increase the bound values, the number of descriptors in the subrequests is increased and we expect to obtain a higher precision level in the search. Now given the user's query (a marked set of documents) we can set bound value to obtain an output consisting of, say, 10 documents, and then decrease the bound values to obtain an output consisting of 20 documents. Then from assumptions of our algorithm we can conclude that the first 10 documents will be a subset in the second output and they will be more important (relevant) than the rest of the documents in the second output.

7.6

Some Aspects of Algorithm Functioning in Information Retrieval Systems

In this chapter we described an algorithm that a system can use to automatically construct a query formulation thereby replacing a human expert. The algorithm is designed to make a user's interaction with the IR system as simple as possible. It frees the user from many complicated and time-consuming operations required in constructing query formulations. It is clear that very little preparation is required from a user to successfully perform a search in an information retrieval system where the suggested algorithm is implemented. Such a system also simplifies the correction of query formulation on the basis of the search output. The user only needs to indicate which documents in the output are pertinent. These documents will be added to the marked set, and the algorithm will construct a modified (more precise) query formulation. However, as was mentioned earlier, the problem of correcting a query formulation is quite complex and for this reason will be considered further in Chapter 9.

In discussing when a specific set of descriptors will be considered as a subrequest, we mentioned that one of the criteria is the occurrence frequency of this set in the marked set of documents. These occurrence frequencies will be chosen automatically by the algorithm and will depend on the number of documents in the marked set.

In the experiment described earlier we obtained the occurrence frequencies by analyzing requests where the number of documents in the marked set (m.s.) varied from 1 to 12. In each of these cases, we compared the results of the searches for all possible occurrence frequencies. For example, when m.s. = 5, we tried occurrence frequencies of 1, 2, 3, 4, and 5 and compared the results of the search. In this case we found that an occurrence frequency (o.f.) of 2 gave the best results. Similarly we found the best occurrence frequencies for all m.s. with values from 1 to 12.

Based on our experiments we concluded that the best occurrence frequency is equal to k where $3*(k-1) <$ m.s. $\leq 3*k$. Hence, if $1 <$ m.s. ≤ 3, then the occurrence frequency is equal to 1 (we write o.f. = 1); for $4 \leq$ m.s. $\leq$ 6, o.f. = 2; for $7 \leq$ m.s. ≤ 9, o.f. = 3; and for $10 \leq$ m.s. ≤ 12, o.f. = 4. So this formula seems to provide a simple decision rule for choosing occurrence frequencies for a set of descriptors that will determine if this set of descriptors will be considered as a separate subrequest. Yet clearly the system developers can choose some other, possibly more sophisticated method for determining the best values of occurrence frequencies.

It is important to mention that the ability to vary the bound values and the occurrence frequencies of different sets of descriptors in the marked set of documents provides a necessary flexibility of the algorithm, which makes it adaptable to the requirements of different information retrieval systems.

Now we are going to take a look at another important feature of our algorithm. As we mentioned earlier, in the construction of a query formulation the main problem is to decide which descriptors should be included and how they should be combined in a query formulation. The result of this decision process is quite different for the manual construction and the proposed algorithm. In selecting descriptors for subrequests, a human being uses reasoning and chooses the descriptors that are most personally meaningful. However, it is not at all clear that a desirable query formulation should be constructed only from the most meaningful descriptors. Moreover, the combination of descriptors does not necessarily have to be meaningful. While constructing a query formulation in the following example, our algorithm used a descriptor presumably void of any meaning. That query formulation gave a better search result than the one based on the expert's query formulation.

In one of the search requests on which the algorithm was tested, the user was interested in the design and functioning of computers used on moving objects, such as ships, airplanes, and rockets. The search was performed on the collection of 6323 documents selected from the journal of abstracts *Computer Science* (Moscow, VINITI, 1967). The search request was given by the user in the form of seven pertinent documents. The expert analyzing the given search request constructed the following query formulation:

(ship AND computer) OR (aircraft AND computer)
OR (sputnik AND computer) OR (rocket AND computer)
OR (flying machine AND computer) OR (submarine AND computer)

Each of the combinations (every subrequest) makes sense and was easily found using the system's thesaurus. But the output based on this query formulation contained a lot of noise (nonpertinent documents). For example, among the retrieved documents were many documents that dealt with processing data collected from moving objects, but the computers were located elsewhere.

The search based on the query formulation constructed by the algorithm gave much better results. This query formulation contained subrequests that did not seem too meaningful, and the subrequest that gave the best search result consisted of one descriptor "foundation." The analysis of the results showed that, in their discussion of the computer features they developed for moving objects, the documents' authors often referred to what they considered to be an important achievement—the elimination of the necessity for a special foundation. Further analysis showed that at the beginning of the 1960s, many articles discussed special foundations that were built for computer rooms, and therefore the descriptor "foundation" was included in the thesaurus in *Computer Science*. But in the collection of documents published in 1967, there were no articles discussing the building of foundations. Therefore, any document containing the descriptor "foundation" turned out to be pertinent. This descriptor was also very effective when a search was performed on the documents published in 1968. Later this word disappeared from articles in *Computer Science*. Thus, when constructing a query formulation the algorithm "discovered" a style of writing articles that was prevalent during a specific period of the development of *Computer Science*. Clearly, it is very difficult, if not impossible, for an expert to identify such a subrequest as a "foundation."

Another important aspect of the described algorithm is that in information retrieval systems using this algorithm it is possible to perform an automatic indexing of the documents by simply looking up the terms of the documents in the system's dictionary. This method of automatic indexing was tried in many systems but it was not generally accepted because this system of indexing produces document profiles consisting of a very large number of descriptors. For example, the document profile of a 200-word abstract will typically contain several dozen descriptors. But when a query formulation is constructed by a human being, our experience shows that most subrequests consist of one, two, or three descriptors, rarely four, and very seldom five or six. In fact, because of the difficulty of constructing subrequests consisting of, say seventeen descriptors, such an approach to automatic indexing was considered unacceptable in systems using Boolean search. The algorithm described in this chapter allows the successful use of automatic indexing of the documents, because it can construct subrequests of practically any length. Moreover, automatic indexing of the documents becomes a desirable feature because it introduces uniformity and stability, which in turn improves the occurrence frequencies used by the suggested algorithm.

In this chapter we considered several assumptions that might be used in developing algorithms for the automatic construction of effective query formulations. On the basis of several pragmatic assumptions, we developed an algorithm for the automatic construction of query formulations in Boolean form. The suggested algorithm not only substitutes a traditional intellectual process for IR systems by an algorithmic process, but it also substantially simplifies the end-user problem. The simplicity of the communication between a user and an information retrieval system was one of the main considerations in designing the algorithm. The user expresses his or her search request by a set of documents pertinent to the user's need. This does not require any specialized knowledge on the part of the user about the system's operation and design. The quality of the search depends only on the algorithm and how completely and precisely the user's POIN is represented in the user's search request.

This algorithm is, without a doubt, not the last in the series of algorithms that could be created for indexing of queries. In the future we will see others that may be more suitable, both for certain users and for certain IR systems. This is true for all algorithms used in the IR system—not only for those involved in query indexing. However, the analyzed algorithm is a successfully functioning version of the design of an IR system's element (such as BIQ), and its use in conjunction with the algorithm for the indexing of documents provides a solution to the problem of the complete automation of indexing (documents and queries) in the Boolean IR system.

7.7
Conclusion

In the framework of developing and operating IR systems, it is traditionally acknowledged that one of the most complex problems is the automatic indexing of queries. This problem is even more complicated in Boolean systems, where a query formulation is presented in disjunctive normal form. This chapter addressed a solution to this problem.

Before developing an algorithm that would result in an acceptable output quality, different methods of formulating POIN were discussed. One of the methods chosen is the most convenient for the user yet allows the user to express POIN more precisely. This method (which assumes the formulation of a search request in the form of a marked set) was the basis for the algorithm for constructing query formulations described in this chapter. The main benefits of this algorithm are that it not only improves the search quality (recall/precision), but it also fully releases the user or the intermediary from the complex and time-consuming process of "manually" constructing query formulations. In addition, an automatic construction of query formulations is the basis for automatic feedback, at least in those cases where the process of feedback assumes (to improve search results) a change in the query formulation.

Despite a number of important advantages, only in the last few years have some of the functioning systems begun to use the automatic indexing of search requests. A number of reasons could be given to explain this delay, but two of them stand out. One is the lack of knowledge about the existence of such algorithms and another is the reluctance of developers to study these methods at a level of detail necessary for their implementation. However, questions about the automatic construction of query formulations are popular among researchers. Although the number of new algorithms is very small, the importance of this problem is constantly stressed.

In this chapter and in Chapter 6, we discussed some approaches to the automatic construction of document profiles and query formulations. The result of indexing is the input information of the BSR element in the system's structure, that is, the last of the elements in the object of control in an IR system. The next chapter discusses the construction of this BSR element.

References

Barker, F. H., Veal, D. C., & Watt, B. K. (1972). Towards automatic profile construction. *Journal of American Documentation, 28.*

Croft, W. B., & Thompson, R. H. (1987). A new approach to the design of document retrieval systems. *Journal of the American Society for Information Science, 38.*

Dillon, M., & Desper, J. (1980). The use of automatic relevance in Boolean retrieval systems. *Journal of Documentation, 36*(3).

Dillon, M., Ulmscmeider, J., & Desper, J. (1983). A prevalence formula for automatic relevance feedback in Boolean systems. *Information Processing and Management, 19*(1).

Frants, V. I., & Shapiro, J. (1991). Algorithm for automatic construction of query formulations in Boolean form. *Journal of the American Society for Information Science, 42*(1).

Frants, V. I., Voiskunskii, V. G., & Frants, Y. I. (1970). Evaluation of indexing and one method for automatic construction of query formulations. *Nauchno-Technicheskaya Informatsiya (NTI)*, ser. 2, no. 4.

Goldman, N. (1992). *Online information hunting*. Blue Ridge Summit, PA: Tab/Windcrest/Mc-Graw Hill.

Lancaster, F. W. (1968). *Information retrieval systems: Characteristics, testing, evaluation*. New York: John Wiley & Sons.

Lancaster, F. W. (1979). Information retrieval systems: Characteristics, testing, evaluation. New York: John Wiley & Sons.

Luhn, H. P. (1957). A statistical approach to mechanized encoding and searching of literary information. *IBM Journal of Research and Development, 1*(4).

McCash, W. H., & Carmichael, J. J. (1970). UDC user profiles as developed for computer-based SDI service in iron industry. *Journal of American Documentation, 26.*

Meadow, C. T. (1967). *The analysis of information systems: A programmer's introduction to information retrieval*. New York: John Wiley & Sons.

Moody, D. W., & Kays, D. (1972). Development of the U.S. geological survey bibliographic system using GIPSY. *Journal of the American Society for Information Science, 23.*

Rickman, J. T. (1972). Design considerations for a Boolean feedback system with automatic relevance feedback processing, Proceedings of the ACM annual conference, New York, 1972.

Salton, G., Buckley, C., & Fox, E. A. (1983). Automatic query formulation in information retrieval. *Journal of the American Society for Information Science, 34.*

Salton, G., Fox, E. A., & Wu, H. (1983). An automatic environment for Boolean information retrieval. In R. E. A. Mason (ed.), *Information Processing, 83* (Proc. 1983 IFIP Paris Congress), North-Holland.

Salton, G., Fox, E. A., Voorhees, E. (1985). Advanced feedback methods in information retrieval. *Journal of the American Society for Information Science, 36.*

Schaffer, F., March, J., & Berndos, J. (1972). An experiment to study the use of Boolean not logic to improve the precision of selective dissemination of information. *Journal of American Documentation, 23.*

Spink, A. (1994). Term relevance feedback and query expansion: Relation to design. Proceedings of the Seventeenth Annual International ACM SIGIR Conference on Research and Development in Information Retrieval, Dublin, Ireland, 1994.

Voiskunskii, V. G., & Frants, V. I. (1971). Automatic feedback in a descriptor IR system. *Nauchno-Technicheskaya Informatsiya (NTI)*, ser. 2, no. 8.

Voiskunskii, V. G., & Frants, V. I. (1974a). Algorithmization of construction of query formulations and their correction in the process of using documentary IR systems. *Automatic Systems and Computer Science*, (5).

Voiskunskii, V. G., & Frants, V. I. (1974b). Algorithmization of the translation of a request from a natural language to a descriptor language in a documentary information retrieval system. *Nauchno-Technicheskaya Informatsiya (NTI)*, ser. 2, no. 11.

Bibliographic Remarks _____

For further study of different algorithms, we recommend the following publications.

Dillon, M., Ulmscmeider, J., & Desper, J. (1983). A prevalence formula for automatic relevance feedback in Boolean systems. *Information Processing and Management, 19*(1).

Frants, V. I., & Shapiro, J. (1991). Algorithm for automatic construction of query formulations in Boolean form. *Journal of the American Society for Information Science, 42*(1).

Salton, G., Fox, E. A., & Wu, H. (1983). An automatic environment for Boolean information retrieval. In R. E. A. Mason (Ed.), *Information Processing 83* (Proc. 1983 IFIP Paris Congress), North-Holland.

Voiskunskii, V. G., & Frants, V. I. (1974). Algorithmization of the translation of a request from a natural language to a descriptor language in a documentary information retrieval system. *Nauchno-Technicheskaya Informatsiya (NTI),* ser. 2, no. 11.

8

Storage and Access to Information

8.1

Introduction

In previous chapters, namely Chapters 6 and 7, we discussed the process of translating documents and queries into IRL. When dealing with the process of information retrieval, we noted, in particular, that obtained document profiles and query formulations (constructed through indexing) made feasible both the comparison and subsequent selection of the documents the user needs. We will now consider how it could be implemented in practice.

First, it should be noted that at present there are no unresolved theoretical or practical problems that could prevent realization of the given operations, and their implementation does not pose any serious challenge. It is precisely the processes of comparison and selection that were automated as early as the late 1950s. For a long time they remained the only automated processes, both in the functioning and experimental IR systems. Moreover, automation of a search process, that is, of the comparison and selection of the information, is what gave rise to the automated IR system (and the term itself!), or simply IR system. This is why this chapter deals with commonly known and practical technical methods and approaches used in information retrieval rather than with methods of resolving any problems confronting the information retrieval process. We mean those technical methods and approaches that are widely applied (available) within the framework of computer science. Notice that these methods and approaches were not created specially for the IR system (and, as a rule, not by creators of such systems). They were actually devised for solving a series of practical problems having to do with diverse areas of human activity; that is, they were devised for a whole class of different applications. In this sense it could be said that a number of computer science methods proved useful in developing IR systems in general and the information retrieval process (i.e., an IR system structure element such as BSR [block of storage and retrieval], see Figure 4.8) in particular. Because this chapter presents the main approaches to the realization of the system's element BSR, it will also give insight into the BSR design.

As a matter of fact, the search quality characteristics, such as recall and precision, should not be affected by the choice of known technical solutions used by creators of the IR system in realizing BSR. In other words, any implementation methods of comparison and selection are logically equivalent in the sense that a search will yield the same output. Therefore, in realizing the given processes, use is made of another indicator (for practical reasons this indicator is used only in realizing BSR), namely, the time spent by the computer to process them. Therefore, whatever choice of technical solutions is made, it is made primarily on the basis of this indicator. We say "primarily" because sometimes one has to take into account other considerations, for example, the availability of primary storage, in particular when the system is being created on a microcomputer basis. In any case, subsequently, when ranking different technical solutions, we will first consider the time needed for the search carried out in the BSR. We should emphasize that this chapter, although of interest to those directly involved in the creation of software implementing the BSR design, is intended mostly for those who take an interest in the creation of the IR system as a whole and who want to know the basic ideas underlying the creation of the BSR design.

8.2
Sequential File and Sequential Access

As is seen in Figure 4.8, a flow of documents is entered through the IR system's input (input 1). As the result of indexing, each newly input document has its presentation in the IRL (document profile). As described earlier, document profiles are necessary in a search process, and since document profiles are used in a search for all requests coming into the system, a need arises for their storage, a step realized in BSR. Yet any output of the systems is not just a set of retrieved (in response to a request, of course) document profiles; it is rather a collection of documents corresponding to these retrieved document profiles. This means that the input documents also have to be stored in the IR system.

There is a number of well known ways of storing information, which are referred to as methods of *file organization*. Each of the known methods has its own advantages and shortcomings having to do with the way of accessing the information stored in the file, or with an efficient usage of memory, or with the file's maintenance. Practically every file organization known in computer science provides a more successful solution to a certain class of tasks (applications): in our context a "more successful solution" means a more rapid solution, as we have noted. Now the question arises: Which file organization should be used in the IR system? There is no single answer to this question, and, for example, for the Boolean systems and SMART systems the answers are different. It should also be noted that the Boolean systems can use any file organization, including the one that is best for the SMART system, whereas the file organization that is the best for the Boolean systems is not usable in the SMART system. We will consider this distinction in more detail later on.

We start the analysis with the simplest file organization. Let us assume that 10,000 documents are to be used as the search collection of an IR system, which means that the system needs to store not only 10,000 original documents but also 10,000 document profiles. It is probably easiest to store the original document and its document profile together. In other words, for every document entered into the system, upon its indexing, a *record* can be formed (Figure 8.1) consisting of two fields, namely field 1 and field 2. Field 1 will contain the original document, and the document profile will be stored in field 2. For the 10,000 documents, naturally, there must be 10,000 such records; that is, a file consisting of 10,000 records will be set up. The next question arises: How are these records to be organized in the file and what kind of access method will be used, that is, what will the file structure look like? The two access methods are sequential access and random access. The former is simpler and its realization involves a sequential file (Grosshans, 1986). *A sequential file is a file in which a record is stored immediately following the previous record.* A sequential file is also known as a *serial sequential file*. Figure 8.2 illustrates a sequential file consisting of 10,000 records.

In sequential file organization, the records are inserted into the file in order of their arrival, that is, in chronological order. In other words, a sequential file is organized by adding or *appending* records only at the end of the file. Thus, the first record in the file is the oldest and the last record in the file is the one most recently added (the last addition). The only access method that is valid for a sequential file is sequential access. *Sequential access is access that takes records in order, looking at the first, then the next, and so on.* Therefore, a subject search in the sequential file (Figure 8.2) can be performed as follows. After reading the first record of the formed file, the search program compares the document profile (the content of field 2) with subrequests of the query formulation constructed from the search request entered into the system. Whenever any subrequest is

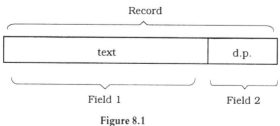

Figure 8.1
Document record.

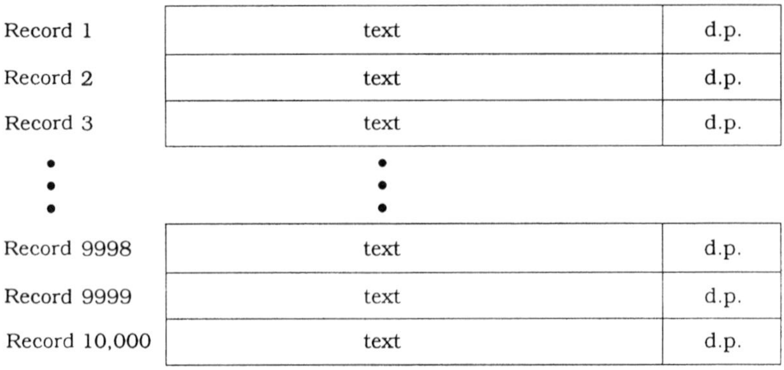

Record 1	text	d.p.
Record 2	text	d.p.
Record 3	text	d.p.
⋮	⋮	
Record 9998	text	d.p.
Record 9999	text	d.p.
Record 10,000	text	d.p.

Figure 8.2
Sequential file organization.

contained in a document profile, the document is considered found and its text (the content of field 1) is included in the output. Then the program reads the record next in order, performing operations similar to those carried out with the previous record, and this goes on until the end of the file when the last (10,000th) record is read. Then the search is considered over, and the output formed is presented to the user. Whenever the system receives another request, the whole procedure repeats itself in the same manner: again, like in the previous case, the 10,000 records will be read one following another and the query formulation will be compared with the document profile 10,000 times.

Realization of this idea, incidentally, is a simple task for any programmer. For this, the programmer does not need even a cursory acquaintance with the IR system: a basic knowledge of data structures and file organization will be quite sufficient. However, this idea is never implemented in such a simple way because in practice this kind of search would be very slow. Now, before we describe the main methods of speeding up the process of the search, it would be helpful to review the reasons why this search takes so much time.

8.3

Primary and Secondary Storage

The analysis starts with another look at the sequential access search pattern, this time presenting it as a sum of two highly generalized processes. The first process is getting a record from storage (reading a record) and the second one is comparison of the document profile, as it was entered into this record, with the query formulation. The question of storing information has been mentioned several times. What is the actual (physical) place of file storage? The file is kept in the system's memory or, more precisely, in the memory of a computer. The latter has two memories, however. One is *primary storage* and the other is *secondary storage*. Primary storage is part of the central processing unit (*CPU*), that is, part of the computer subsystem where an arithmetic or logical information-processing operation is carried out on program instructions. In our case (search), the comparison of document profile and query formulation (logical operation) is performed in the CPU. As a matter of fact, all program instructions are performed in that part of the CPU, which is called the arithmetic and logic unit (A&LU). The information processed according to the program comes into this part of the CPU from primary storage. In our case such information is a record consisting of the text (field 1) and the document profile (field 2). Although any record of any file arrives in the A&LU from primary storage, it is practically impossible to keep the files in the primary storage. In this case the storage of a file should be understood as a situation in which a large amount of "permanent" data needs to be saved for repeated use and updating. Also, the file must remain in memory even though the programs using it are idle, such as when the computer is shut down. We should stress here that a file cannot be kept in primary storage, not because it is difficult or expensive but because primary storage is intended for a different use. It has quite different functions, one of which is to keep ready the file records that are to be processed by the program next, that is, following the record being processed at a given moment. Primary storage is electronic memory consisting of special chip-based electronic circuits, and it is characterized by a high speed of operation and a high cost.

Now let us consider the following question. If a file is not kept in the primary storage, where is it kept? The files are stored in the secondary storage, a medium specifically created with the aim of storing files. Most commonly such storage is a magnetic disk or, simply, disk. The magnetic disk is the most important form of secondary storage today. Disks can take on many different forms, including floppy disks, cartridge disks, and fixed-head disks. The most common type used in mainframe computers is the hard, moving-head disk, and it is this type that we will concentrate on.

The special advantages of the magnetic disk include its ability to store files organized in any of the known methods. This means that when a sequential file is recorded, the information (records) from it will be read only sequentially, that is, from the first record to the last one in order. Whenever the files are organized in some other manner, it is possible to read only one record or a collection of records of that file in any order. In other words, the file organization methods that are different from the sequential method require random access. This is why the disk is often called the *random access device.*

Usually the file stored on the disk is processed as follows. In the program processing the records of this file (a search program in our case), there is a certain instruction (usually called READ) making it possible to read part of the file from the disk into primary storage. When saying "part of the file" we imply that the whole file may take up far greater space than that available in primary storage. It is a real situation in many cases (practically always so in the IR system). So let us note one more significant difference between primary and secondary storage: primary storage is significantly smaller than secondary storage.

Hence, some part of the file is read (copied) into primary storage. But which part of the file should be transferred? Should one ensure that the whole file, or a large part of it, is read from the disk into primary storage? Or is it more expedient to read just one record and then, upon its processing in CPU (in our case, upon comparison of the document profile held in the record with the available query formulation), read the next one and so on? To answer these questions we need to have some idea about the design of the disk.

Hard disks are made of sheets of metal cut into disks, usually between 3 and 18 inches in diameter. The disks are coated with a thin layer of magnetic material similar to that used on tape. Several disks are mounted on a common axis or hub to form a disk pack. Typically, a half-dozen to a dozen disks are mounted in one pack. All the surfaces of the pack except the top surface of the top disk and the bottom surface of the bottom disk are used for recording. The recording is done on each disk surface on a series of concentric tracks. The tracks are separate and do not form a spiral as do the grooves of a phonograph record. Each track is divided into a series of blocks. The blocks are separated by a gap. *A block is the unit of data that actually gets transferred (i.e., input or output [I/O] to or from the user's file that is located on a particular device.* A block is the smallest amount of data that can be transferred with a single I/O operation. A block may contain one or more records. In fact, a block may contain only a partial record, so that to access the entire record more than one block will need to be read.

The reading and writing of the track is performed by a *head,* like that in a record player. Because there are usually a few hundred tracks on each surface, but only one head, it is necessary to move the head from track to track to reach all the tracks. The piece of metal that moves the head in and out and keeps it at a constant height above the surface of the disk is called the *arm.* The total time required to transfer data to or from a disk has three components. First is the time required to reposition the arm, which is called *seek time.* This usually varies from a few milliseconds for a one-track move to scores of milliseconds or more for a move from one end of the disk to another. Most drives give a specification for an average, or random, move, which should be used in calculations.

The second component is the time from when the arm is positioned to when the first block of the transfer moves under a head. This time is called *latency* and depends on the speed of the disk's rotation. In the best case there would be no wait at all; in the worst case, such as when the beginning of the block had just been missed, the wait would be the time required for a full revolution. On the average, the latency is equal to the time required for the disk to turn one half of a revolution. The average latency is the time required for one half of a revolution, which is, in many real cases (disks), approximately 8.3 milliseconds.

The time needed for the read/write head to pass over a block is called the *block transfer time*. This is the third component. During the block transfer time, the data can be transferred from the disk to primary storage or from primary storage to the disk. Very often the manufacturer of the disk drive will provide figures for average seek time (in milliseconds), average rotational latency time (in milliseconds), and data transfer time (in bytes per milliseconds). The byte is a standard, fixed-length code representing some symbol (such as a letter or a digit) defined for the given computer. Usually the average seek time is longer than the average rotational latency time, whereas the average rotational latency time is longer, as a rule, than the average necessary to transfer one block of information, which usually consists of a few thousand bytes.

Now we can state the main point in comparing primary and secondary storage: the time needed for reading (and writing) data on disks is much larger than the time needed for moving information around once it has been transferred to primary storage. This is because mechanical movement (a disk is a mechanical device), rather than electronic movement (primary storage is an electronic circuit), is involved. In other words, relative to the other parts of a computer, disks are slow. But how slow are they? The time it takes to get information back from even relatively slow electronic primary storage is about 120 nanoseconds, or 120 billionths of a second. Getting the same information from a typical disk might take 30 milliseconds, or 30 thousandths of a second. To understand the size of this difference, we need an analogy. Assume that primary storage access is like finding something in the index of this book. Let us say that this local, book-in-hand access takes 20 seconds. Assume that disk access is like going to a library for the information you cannot find here in this book. Given that our "primary storage access" takes 20 seconds, how long does the "disk access" to the library take, keeping the ratio the same as that of a real primary storage access and disk access? The disk access is a quarter of a million times longer than the primary storage access. This means that getting information back from the library takes 5,000,000 seconds, or almost 58 days. Disks are very slow compared to primary storage, and this fact has a crucial effect on the performance of any programs (applications) using large quantities of information. How should this situation be handled? There is no way to avoid using a disk, because secondary storage is simply indispensable and the disk today is one of the best devices for secondary storage. So, what is to be done?

In computer science today the problem is successfully solved by different methods of enhancing performance. The use of blocks is one such method. Indeed, as was mentioned earlier, information on the disk is stored (written) in blocks and exchange of information between the disk and primary storage can be done only through a block, despite the fact that any program works only with records. So, why is "communication" with secondary storage maintained by blocks? Consider the following example. Let us assume that we have two files with one of the files containing only 1 record per block and another containing 10 records per block. If one file contains 1 million records, the second file would require 900,000 fewer operations in order to read all the records! It is not uncommon to have disks with an average access time of 30 milliseconds. If this were the case, for the first file it would take about 8 hours longer to read all the records in the file.

This example illustrates why information on the disks is stored in blocks. Moreover, it is clear that the more records in the block, the fewer accesses to the disk are necessary, which speeds up the operations with the file. It should be noted that the number of records that can fit into a block is called the *blocking factor*. The blocking factor depends on both the size of the record and the physical size of the block. Both of these vary within certain limits. Blocks are limited in size because the computer system must allocate primary storage space to store at least one block. This space is called a *buffer*. As primary storage is essential for computer system operation in general, there is usually a specification of the maximum size (different for various computers) allowed for buffers, and consequently for blocks. Now the procedure of reading a file can be specified.

The block with the maximum possible blocking factor is transferred from disk into the buffer organized in primary storage. Next, only one record is read from that buffer and brought to another (smaller) buffer called a *record buffer*, which is equal in size to the biggest record available in the file. From there the record goes to the A&LU where it is processed according to the program. Naturally, reading record after record from block buffer (i.e., reading in electronic primary storage) is thousands of times faster than reading from the disk. Therefore, it is important to remember that a blocking factor greater than 1 will always improve overall performance and the system throughout by cutting down on the amount of I/O that the system must perform.

So, the greater the blocking factor, the higher the performance. But we have already pointed out that the size of a block is limited. This prompts the following question: If the block's size is limited, then is it possible to reduce the size of the record, thereby increasing the blocking factor? At first thought, the idea seems somewhat strange, because the record contains information needed to form the output. In our file, for example, the record keeps only the document text and the document profile (Figure 8.1). Yet this idea is fruitful, as can be seen in our next example.

It is quite clear that a subject search requires only document profiles, and the document texts are not involved in this process. This being the case, is it not possible to remove the biggest part of the record, that is, the document text (field 1)? This will allow us to substantially increase the blocking factor and, consequently, the speed of the search. Of course, it is possible and this is exactly how it is done in practice. But what about the output, which must contain the texts of the found documents? The answer lies in forming two files (and this is done in practice): one for the subject search (a file consisting of document profiles) and the other to form the output (a file consisting of the original documents). The records in these files are organized as follows. The record for subject

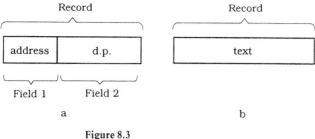

Figure 8.3
Records from newly formed files.

search also contains two fields: field 2, as before, contains a document profile, and field 1, instead of a full document (which is many times larger than the document profile), contains a short address of that document in the second file. Figure 8.3(a) gives an example of such a record.

In the second file, the record contains only the document text, and the whole record essentially consists of one field. An example of such a record is given in Figure 8.3(b). But from where is the address taken and what does it look like in practice? Perhaps the simplest way of explaining this is as follows. When each of the 10,000 documents are entered into the IR system (they are entered in order of their arrival), each document is assigned an ordinal number (from 0000 to 9999, for example). After indexing a document, records are formed (similar to those given in Figure 8.3), and the document's ordinal number is entered as an address into the document profile record (field 1). Then the records formed are put into the files, with the text record being put into that part of the text file that corresponds to the ordinal number. With this kind of file organization existing in the BSR, the process (in general) may look as follows.

There are two stages realized by the search program, which handles two files. The first stage has to do with the file of a document profile, and the second stage concerns the text file. In this case, the program essentially provides for two different searches (one following the other). The first is a subject search in the sequentially organized file of a document profile, and the other is an *address search,* that is, a search for specially selected addresses (a result of the first search) done in the text file providing for random access. It means that in the case of address search there is no need to read all the blocks from the text file sequentially, and only those containing needed records are read. Because it does not require reading the whole file, this approach understandably expedites the search and presupposes the imperative use of file organization, other than sequential organization. The kinds of file organization that can be used for random access is the subject of the next section of this chapter. Now we will give a more detailed description of the search carried out in the BSR.

At the start of the program operation, a block is read from the file containing document profiles into the block buffer organized in primary storage. Then the records are read in succession from the block buffer and every record is sent to the A&LU through the record buffer. In the A&LU, the record's field 2 (the document profile) is compared with the subrequests of the available query formulation. If all the descriptors in some subrequest are also contained in the document profile, the search is considered successful, and the address (of the document text required to form the output) contained in field 1 is temporarily recorded in primary storage. Then the next record is read from the block buffer and analogous operations are repeated with every record contained in the block buffer. When the last record from the block buffer has been processed, the next block on the disk is read and so on. When the last record (the 10,000th) from the last block is processed, the second part of the program comes into action; that is, an address search begins in the second file (text file) using the addresses found at the first stage. As we have not yet considered the random access file, for the time being we will not discuss the second part of the program.

Thus, we considered the methods of increasing search speed when using the sequential file, which, it should be noted, has a number of advantages over other file organizations (though it has some shortcomings too). The following list presents just a few of these advantages:

1. The sequential file is the most simple and convenient file organization to use.
2. The sequentially organized file takes less space in secondary storage than what would be needed by the same amount of information organized in another manner.
3. Any sorting, which is often needed and important in information retrieval, is feasible if the file being sorted has sequential organization.

Its most serious drawback is the fact that there is no random access in a sequential file in order to retrieve a particular record without reading all the records in the file that precedes it. This means that whenever we need access to only a few records in a sizable file (consisting of 10,000 records in our case), the whole system's performance drastically plummets and in some cases becomes unacceptable. Therefore, we will now consider the most simple file organization allowing for random access. Though being "the most simple," this file organization is sufficient enough to provide the main ideas about the basic techniques used in implementing the BSR structure.

8.4

Relative File and Random Access

In mentioning the shortcomings of sequential files we noted that it is impossible to randomly access individual records without reading all records pre-

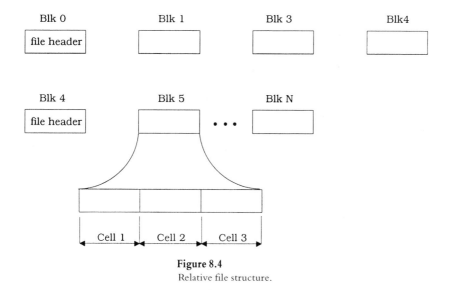

Figure 8.4
Relative file structure.

ceding it in the file. It is also true that records can be added only at the end of the file, which lengthens the access to the most recent records. We can design a file organization that has functionality of a sequential file but eliminates the problems that are inherent in sequential file design. This file type is known as the *relative file organization*. The relative file is one in which records can be accessed directly by using their record numbers as an external key (address). A relative file is made up of fixed-length blocks. Inside each block are fixed-length cells. Each cell can hold just one user data record and each cell must fit completely within a block. A relative file is illustrated in Figure 8.4. Indeed, cells are fixed-length containers within a block, much as an egg carton has a dozen fixed compartments each capable of holding only one egg. The cell size is based on the maximum-size user data record. Therefore, any cell can hold a valid data record of any size.

Each data record must have associated with it an integer key value (ordinal number) that will be used both to add the record into the file and to read the record out of the file. Later we will show how the access method converts the integer key (ordinal number) into a precise block and cell number within the entire file. Note, however, that the integer key is not physically part of the data record itself. Thus the responsibility falls on the first part of the search program (see our example) to make the correct association between data record and the record's ordinal number (key value).

The first block of the relative file is the *file header block*. It contains information that allows the relative file access method to process the data records correctly within the file. As mentioned earlier, the key to locating or addressing an individual record is the record's own record number, which is unique within

record ID may be considered as a key but a key doesn't need to be a record ID.

228

the file. This uniqueness is an explicit design decision, not because it is technically impossible to do otherwise. The records in a relative file are numbered from 1 to n, where n is defined as the highest possible record number in the file. The user data records must fit within a cell and cannot overlap between multiple cells. Therefore, the cells themselves are numbered from 1 to n. When the user defines a relative file, one of the parameters that can be set is n, known as the maximum record number. This number is of course the highest possible record number that the relative file access method can accept as being valid.

The formula for locating the cell with the target record is given below. Let x denote number of cells per block and r denote the target record number:

$$\text{block number} = \text{integer}\left(\frac{r - 1 + x}{x}\right);$$

$$\text{cell number in block} = 1 + \text{mod}\left(\frac{r - 1 + x}{x}\right).$$

Thus, to locate any record in a relative file, the access method must first convert the record number into a block and cell number within the file. Then, at the most, one I/O operation will have to be performed in order to read the target block into primary storage.

Now having considered the random access principle (taking a relative file as an example), let us make two substantial additions. The first addition concerns the performance of the IR system utilizing relative file organization. It is not accidental that the address of a record with the text from the text file (rather than the record number) is stored in field 1 of a corresponding record from the document profile file. Even at the stage of organizing a file document profile, it makes sense to immediately store the result of the above calculations, rather than the ordinal number of a document, into field 1. This result is an actual address made up of the block number and the cell number in the text file. In this case, during a search process (repeated for many search requests), there is no need to calculate the address, which improves the system's performance.

Another addition concerns the very calculation of the address. We have already seen that calculation makes possible the so-called one-disk-access method. In computer science such a calculation is called *hashing* (see, for example, Folk & Zoellick, 1992; Horbron, 1988; and Wartik, Fox, Heath, & Chen, 1992). A *hashing algorithm* or *hashing function* is a means of calculating the disk address of a block, and in our case also of a cell, containing a given record from the value of its key. Sometimes hashing is called key-to-address transformation. A hash function is like a black box that produces an address every time you drop a key. More formally, it is a function $h(K)$ that transforms a key K into an address. There are many hashing algorithms available that distribute the records within the file. In this sense the preceding formulas only illustrate implementation of one of the possible hashing algorithms. Hatching is commonly

Hashing here storage & retrieval side. What described here is only retrieval, not storage, which misses the main point.

considered to be an extraordinary discovery in computer science, one providing methods that yield truly amazing performance advantages. Indeed, this method has gained wide acceptance, though it is known to have certain drawbacks.

After discussing the random access principles, we may proceed to a more detailed examination of the second part of the search program, that is, the part responsible for the address search. Recall that as the result of the subject search, a collection of retrieved addresses is formed in primary storage and that every address consists of the block number and the cell number. It is precisely these addresses that underlie the search for addresses. This search begins with grouping the addresses selected during the subject search in primary storage. In other words, action is taken to determine if there are retrieved addresses giving the same block number. This type of grouping can enhance performance because to retrieve texts from such groups it is sufficient to read only the respective (one) block for a group of (searched) records contained in this block. Then blocks are retrieved from the file. The first blocks retrieved are those corresponding to the groups available, and from each block only those records (texts) are read that were found during the subject search. In primary storage an output begins to form of the read texts. The next blocks retrieved are those corresponding to the ungrouped addresses. The respective texts are also read out of these blocks, and after reading the last text from the last block, the output is considered formed and ready for the user.

Now, if this two-stage pattern of search is compared with the single-stage pattern given to clarify the principle of sequential access, then it can be considered sufficiently workable. At least the speed of formation of the output has increased significantly. Still, the relative file has a number of drawbacks, and in IR systems the most important one is poor disk space utilization. Indeed, the size of every cell must be equal to the size of the longest record in the file. In our example all cells must be equal to the longest of the 10,000 available texts. Even if the input texts are assumed to be only abstracts (which is quite realistic because only abstracts are utilized in many real systems) and among the 10,000 there is one that is ten times as large as the average abstract in the file, then 90% of the memory occupied by the file will be empty space. Nevertheless, when the subject search is supposed to use sequential file organization, then the described approach is quite promising.

We said, "when the subject search is supposed to use sequential file organization." But is it possible to do without sequential access if all available document profiles are supposed to be compared with the query formulation? For if it is necessary to read and then compare all the records, there is simply nothing better than sequential file organization. It turns out, however, that in the Boolean system one can do without sequential access; that is, in organizing a subject search in the Boolean system one can avoid comparing every document profile and query formulation. Moreover, none of the document profiles containing descriptors that correspond to a subrequest from the available query formulation will be lost. At first glance this looks somewhat improbable, but that lasts only until we encounter inverted files (see, Folk & Zoellick, 1992; and Horbron, 1988), which are the subject of the next section.

Inverted Files

The ideas underlying the creation of inverted files have been known since the 1960s. Even then this kind of file organization was successfully used in the Boolean IR system. Before analyzing inverted file organization, let us have another look at the illustration in Figure 8.3(a) of the record involved in a subject search. This record consists of the document's address (field 1) and a set of descriptors (field 2) obtained as a result of indexing this document. As was noted earlier, in a subject search such a record structure inevitably leads to a successive inspection of all records—something we would like to avoid. Thus, a need arose for some other kind of organization of data (record and file), and this other organization of data was supposed to secure not only a subject search but also to conduct it much faster; that is, it was to make direct access possible. But how can we do that in practice? What kind of file (record) must it be if it is to contain the same information? We will try to give a more detailed answer to these questions.

The record in Figure 8.3(a) contains an address and all the document descriptors. But what if we choose to do the opposite, placing a descriptor in the record together with all the addresses of documents containing this descriptor? In this case, the same information is represented in the file, but the new records are inversions of the old ones. This is actually the main idea of inversion in the IR system, and an inverted file consists exactly of such records. As we have not yet shown how a subject search can be organized in such a file, the positive effect of inversion is still unclear. For this reason we will consider in more detail the subject search process itself, looking first at a new "inverted" record. Figure 8.5 gives a general and simple description of such a record.

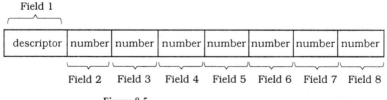

Figure 8.5
An example of a record in an inverted file.

It is clear from the figure that field 1 of this record contains a descriptor from the system's descriptor dictionary. All the other fields (from the second to the eighth) contain numbers of the documents where this descriptor appears. In other words, they are the documents containing at least one of the words included in the equivalence class of a given descriptor. The record, understandably, must have as many fields with numbers (addresses) as there are file documents indexed by the given descriptor. Our example contains seven such fields (from field 2 to field 8). Now it is clear that if you want to find documents indexed by the given descriptor it is enough to find only this record. The inverted file is composed of similar records. Earlier we gave an example of a certain IR system containing a search file with as many as 10,000 documents. Suppose that this same system has a descriptor dictionary containing as many as 800 descriptors (this size of a dictionary is realistic for many operating IR systems). Then the inverted file of this system might look as the one shown in Figure 8.6.

This example needs a detailed explanation. A1, A2, A3, . . . , I1, and I8 are descriptors from the system's descriptor dictionary. We see that every record corresponds to some descriptor written in the extreme left field. Only one record is organized for every descriptor in the file. Because we have assumed that the IR system contains a dictionary of 800 descriptors, it means that the file holds 800 records. The numbers written in all the other fields of the record are the numbers of the documents being introduced into the system upon their arrival (one after another). Because there are 10,000 documents in our example, the numbers, written in the other record fields, can only be within the range of 0 to 9999. It is clear from Figure 8.6 that the records could have different lengths

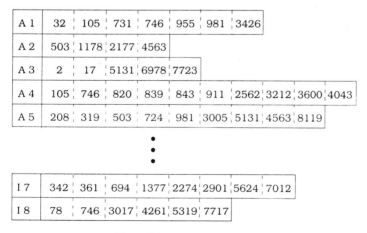

Figure 8.6
An example of an inverted file.

(these are known as *variable-length records*). The number of fields in the record minus one (the field 1 with the descriptor name) indicates the number of documents indexed by the descriptor in field 1. This number is the frequency of occurrence of the given descriptor in the file. Usually, this frequency is also stored in the file, yet in this case (to simplify things) it is not indicated. Also notice that the documents' numbers in the record are arranged in order of their arrival into the system, that is, in ascending order of numbers. Now that we have considered an inverted file, we will proceed to the main point and see how a subject search is carried out in file organization.

Let us assume that as a result of indexing a search request, the following query formulation has been constructed.

A2 OR (A34 AND B7) OR (D93 AND E16 AND F56)

The search procedure will be demonstrated using this query formulation consisting of three subrequests with one, two, and three descriptors, respectively. A search is performed for each of these subrequests, and it could be done in any order. The simplest search is for the first subrequest, that is, subrequest A2 consisting of one descriptor. In this case, the record containing descriptor A2 is retrieved from the 800 records. The retrieved record (with A2 in field 1) is one of the records presented in Figure 8.6. In it there are four fields with the numbers of the documents that have been indexed by descriptor A2. It means that at the stage of search for the first subrequest, four formally relevant documents have been found, and the numbers (addresses) corresponding to them are held in primary storage. This is followed by a search for the second subrequest consisting of two descriptors: A34 and B7. In this case two records are retrieved, corresponding to the given subrequest descriptors. Then the numbers, written in these records, are compared and those that are contained in every record (the same numbers) are again selected and put into the system's memory, since the documents corresponding to these numbers are considered formally relevant. Let us illustrate this process with the following example (Figure 8.7).

Let us suppose that descriptor A34 appears in 17 documents (more precisely, document profiles) and descriptor B7 appears in 46 documents. Then the record with descriptor A34 will have 17 numbers and the record with descriptor B7 will have 46 numbers. The comparison of every number from record A34

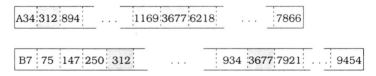

Figure 8.7
An example of a search for subrequests consisting of two descriptors.

with the numbers in record B7 revealed that only 2 numbers, namely 312 and 3677, are common to both records. Hence, the descriptors A34 and B7 are simultaneously contained in only 2 documents (numbered 312 and 3677). More formally, this process (the process of search for the second subrequest) can be presented as follows. Let S denote the set of the document numbers available in the system. In our example $|S| = 10,000$. Symbol A will denote the set of document numbers represented in record A34, and symbol B will denote the set of document numbers represented in record B7. It is quite evident that $A \subseteq S$ and $B \subseteq S$, with $|A| = 17$, and $|B| = 46$. The result of the search process (let it be N) is the intersection of sets A and B; that is, $N = A \cap B = \{312, 3677\}$.

Let us now consider a subject search for the subrequest consisting of descriptors D93, E16, and F56. In this case there are only 3 records, of the available 800, corresponding to the indicated descriptors. Then the numbers from the shortest record (of the 3 found records) are compared with the numbers of the next longest record. As a result of such a comparison, which incidentally is analogous to the comparison for the second subrequest, all numbers, which are contained in both compared records, are selected. Suppose we compared record D93 with record E16 and discovered 9 numbers contained in both records. Then the found numbers are compared with record F56. Let us also assume that 2 of the 9 are also contained in record F56. This means that a search for the third subrequest found 2 numbers (addresses) of formally relevant documents. Now, if the set of numbers from record D93 is denoted by D, the set of numbers from record E16 by E, and the set of numbers from record F56 by F, then $N = (D$ AND $E)$ AND F and $|N| = 2$. Because there were only three subrequests in the query formulation used as an example, after the search for the third subrequest a subject search for the input request is considered over. Then comes the next stage, that of an address search.

An address search begins by comparing all the numbers, found in the subject search with the aim of finding duplicates. After eliminating duplicates, the address of every document in the file of documents is calculated (for example, by using a hashing algorithm), and the output for the user is formed.

We have now considered the search process with the use of an inverted file and can now note its main advantage. The use of an inverted file allows us to substantially reduce (often, by orders of magnitude) search time and, consequently, to substantially improve the system's performance. Indeed, returning to our example we may now note that sequential access required comparison of query formulation with 10,000 document profiles written in 10,000 records. In the case of inverted file organization, however, the search will need only 6 of the 800 records available in the system (because the given query formulation contains only 6 descriptors). This leads to the conclusion that the use of inverted file organization cuts the number of comparisons (in our case 100 times less), reduces the number of I/O operations, and improves the time of search. This is why inverted files are used in most functioning IR systems.

In explaining inverted files, we concentrated on the idea of organizing such files and their usage. We might say that this is a logical presentation rather than a technical one. This presentation is probably quite sufficient to explain the approach in general. Yet because inverted files are used (in fact, probably by all functioning IR systems) and because it provides major resources for enhancing its performance, we consider it expedient to also describe the main techniques of realizing this approach. Actually, inverted files are described in most textbooks containing sections on file structures, but this is done without considering such an important application as the IR system. Here we will adapt well-known descriptions of inverted files to their application in IR systems.

At the beginning of this chapter we showed that document text and its document profile (see the record in Figure 8.1) are sufficient for conducting a search and forming the output. All the ideas considered subsequently only help to reduce the time spent on the given processes. This is true of the very idea of inverted files as well as the techniques used in implementing them. We started explaining the inverted file by describing the record in Figure 8.5. But technically it is inconvenient to create a file of such 800 records, primarily because some records will have only a few fields with numbers (addresses) of respective documents, whereas others will have thousands of such fields. Furthermore, it is impossible to know beforehand how long a particular record will be, and if new documents are added to the existing search file, it is not clear which records are likely to change and to what extent. Therefore, the idea presented earlier is realized in a somewhat different manner.

Recall that the first approaches to increase speed of a search were based on dividing the original record (Figure 8.1) into two parts (Figure 8.3). On the basis of these two types of records, two files were created: a file of document profiles and a file of documents. To realize an inverted file organization, the idea of creating several files is also used but in this case three files are created. The first file is the descriptor file. The record in this file consists of three fields. Field 1 contains a descriptor, field 2 contains the number of documents indexed by this descriptor (this number is the occurrence frequency of the descriptor in the collection of documents), field 3 contains the address of the block containing the addresses of documents whose document profiles include the descriptor from field 1. Returning to our example, it is easy to see that the first file consists of 800 short records (see Figure 8.8a). This is called an index file, and it has many advantages. An index file is quite small and could easily fit into primary storage where a fast search for a needed descriptor could be performed. Also the size of the file does not depend on the number of documents in the collection. The second file consists of a number of blocks where each block contains the addresses of those documents whose document profiles include a given descriptor.

In the simplest case, the second file will contain only 800 blocks (1 block for each descriptor if we assume that there are 800 different descriptors). However, it is possible (and quite likely) that some descriptors have very low occurrence frequencies while others have very high occurrence frequencies. In this case, some blocks might contain several lists of addresses corresponding to different descriptors (to save space), whereas some lists could span more than 1 block (corresponding to descriptors with very high occurrence frequencies). There is a well-known computer science technique to deal with such situations, and it uses linked lists and pointers. We will illustrate the idea of this method on the case where several blocks are used for addresses of documents whose document profiles contain the same descriptor, that is, the case of a descriptor with very high occurrence frequency. In Figure 8.8b every block is represented in the form of a record.

In our example, descriptor C71 has very high occurrence frequency and the addresses of all the documents whose document profiles contain C71 do not fit into one block. The address for the first block containing these addresses is 86, which is pointed to by the third element in the index record of descriptor C71. This element is called a pointer. The continuation of the list of addresses for documents whose document profiles include descriptor C71 is contained in block with address 911. This block is pointed to by a pointer at the end of block 86. The structure of block 911 is the same as that of block 86. The addresses of documents whose document profiles contain descriptor C71 are stored at the beginning of the block and at the end of the block—the pointer to block 1221. Block 1221 has the same structure, but because it is the last block containing addresses for descriptor C71, there is no need to point to another block with addresses. This is typically indicated by including a so-called null pointer, which identifies the end of the list. It is clear now why in the index file only one address is needed for each descriptor. This is the address of the first block containing the

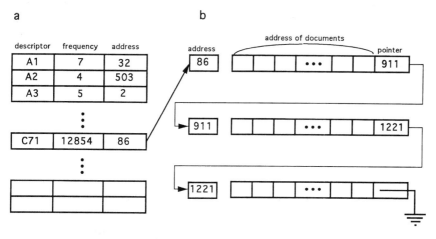

Figure 8.8
(a) Index file and (b) linked list.

addresses of documents indexed by the given descriptor. As we saw, in some cases this address is only the beginning of chain of blocks containing addresses of documents indexed by this descriptor.

As we mentioned earlier, an index file consists of 800 short (about a dozen bytes) records of fixed length. This file is used to search for descriptors contained in a query formulation. Because an index file is needed for a search based on any search request, it is read from disk into primary storage where it remains during the duration of search for all search requests. Any index file is always sorted, which substantially increases the speed of the search (compared to a sequential search). The methods that allow the speed of the search to increase (for example, a binary search or B^+ tree structure) are discussed in great detail in any textbook dealing with data structures (see, for example, Kruse, 1994). Therefore, we will not discuss them in this book. For now it is important (and sufficient) to know that such methods exist.

The occurrence frequency of a descriptor is needed for several purposes. First, it is used in the subsystem for indexing search requests. It also could be used to speech up searches for documents that match subrequests consisting of more than one descriptor. For example, to find an intersection of two sets of document numbers (or addresses) corresponding to two different descriptors and having cardinalities, say, 7 and 100, it is much faster to perform 7 searches on a set of 100 sorted numbers than 100 searches on a set of 7 sorted numbers. For other approaches to improving performance in inverted files see, for example, (Moffat & Bell, 1995).

So, the two files, illustrated in Figure 8.8, implement the idea of inverted file organization and are quite sufficient for a subject search. The third file, as noted previously, is a file of texts, which is indispensable in forming the output. The main ideas connected with its implementation were discussed earlier. It should be emphasized once again that inverted file organization is feasible for a Boolean search. It cannot be used, for example, for calculating the proximity between the search request vector and the document vector. This explains why in the beginning we pointed out that any known file organization can be used in the Boolean system.

8.6
Conclusion

This chapter is intended for those interested in the fundamental ideas of implementing the BSR (block of storage and retrieval) design rather than in the technical details. This is why we focused our attention on such ideas. It should be noted that developers of new IR systems are not always directly involved in the creation of BSR. Since the 1960s several companies (IBM, for example) proposed standard software packages for implementing BSR. With changing technology new ideas have emerged, and new packages as well. Currently, the inversion approach to providing multikey access is being used as the basis for physical database structures in commercially available database systems, including several relational systems (such as IBM's DB2, Relational Technology's Ingress, Oracle, Inc.'s Oracle, Intel's System-2000, and Software AG's Adabas). These systems were designed to provide rapid retrieval to data records via as many inversion keys (descriptors) as the designer cares to identify.

In concluding this chapter, we emphasize once again that any BSR design ultimately results in the same output. In the not-too-distant future the increasing speed of computer operations, particularly the advancement of parallel processing, will certain improve IR system performance, although even now users have no complaints about the speed of a search. It is probably for this reason that researchers emphasize improving the quality of the search by focusing on its recall and precision rather than on search speed in the IR system (as is clearly seen in periodic literature). Currently, one of the most active areas of research is the creation of effective feedback methods to improve the quality of a search. The feedback process and its implementation are the subjects of our next chapter.

References

Folk, M. J., & Zoellick, B. (1992). *File structure* (2nd ed.). New York: Addison Wesley.

Grosshans, D. (1986). *File systems: Design and implementation*. Englewood Cliffs, NJ: Prentice Hall.

Horbron, T. R. (1988). *File systems: structures and algorithms*. Englewood Cliffs, NJ: Prentice-Hall.

Kruse, R. L. (1994). *Data structures and program design*. Englewood Cliffs, NJ: Prentice Hall.

Moffat, A., & Bell, T. A. H. (1995). In Situ generation of compressed inverted files. *Journal of the American Society for Information Science, 46*(7).

Wartik, S., Fox, E. A., Heath, L., & Chen, Q. (1992). Hashing algorithms. In W. B. Frakes & R. Baeza-Yates (Eds.), *Information retrieval: Data structure and algorithms*. Englewood Cliffs, NJ: Prentice-Hall.

Bibliographic Remarks

The readers who are not familiar with the material typically taught in courses on data structures and file organization and who are interested in learning more about the subject are referred to the following books.

Grosshans, D. (1986). *File systems: Design and implementation*. Englewood Cliffs, NJ: Prentice Hall.

Kruse, R. L. (1994). *Data structures and program design*. Englewood Cliffs, NJ: Prentice Hall.

9

Control and Feedback in IR Systems

9.1

9.1

Introduction

As we discussed in Chapter 4, when developing an IR system it is necessary to think of it as a controllable system. This viewpoint follows from the definition of the function of an IR system and from its structure, which makes the system capable of fulfilling this function. The function of an IR system leads to its requirement for an optimal search, and optimization, as is well known, is one of the problems of control. In Chapter 4 we also showed that the properties of POIN (documentary IR systems are created to satisfy POIN) require the existence within the IR system of a mechanism that allows the system to adapt to existing POIN, and adaptation is also a problem of control.

In discussing the systems approach in Chapter 1, we mentioned that the study of the process of control is mainly concentrated in such scientific fields as cybernetics (Wiener, 1961). We remind the reader that cybernetics studies not all systems but only controllable systems, and the originality and strength of the cybernetic approach to control lies in its use of the general principle applicable to systems—the principle of feedback. Because any system with feedback is controllable and because feedback is necessary for realizing such processes as adaptation and optimization, we used the cybernetic approach in describing the structure of IR systems; that is, an IR system was considered a cybernetic system and, as explained in Chapter 1, any controllable system is by definition cybernetic. Therefore, the origins of feedback in IR systems, its character, and its properties were described in Chapter 4.

This chapter deals primarily with the construction of those elements of an IR system that assume the existence of feedback—that is, the construction of mechanisms of adaptation and optimization—and it presents algorithms realizing the mechanism of control (review the MC element in Figure 4.8). The chapter starts with an analysis of the mechanism of adaptation, even though, as we mentioned in describing the structure of an IR system, the mechanism of optimization is applied before adaptation. We begin with this analysis because the use of feedback in the mechanism of adaptation is at least 30 years old, and adaptation is commonly viewed as the primary function of feedback. Therefore, the existing literature on developing and using feedback in IR systems deals primarily with adaptation.

We begin the discussion by clarifying some of the details that explain the need for adaptation in IR systems and by stating some requirements for the creation of the mechanism of adaptation. Then we will be able to discuss the algorithms that effectively implement adaptation.

9.2

Some Questions for Constructing Adaptive IR Systems

Feedback in its general form is a mechanism that attempts to minimize the difference between the goal of the action and its result. We already mentioned that the goal of information retrieval (its goal of action) is satisfaction of POIN. But the quality of its satisfaction of POIN depends on how fully the IR system takes into account the properties of POIN, and one of the main properties of POIN is its constant change (the character of this change is not known) and the absence of clear boundaries (which, as a rule, prevents the clear expression of POIN). Therefore, the result of a search should be constantly corrected (adapting to the user's POIN) in the process of the user's interaction with the system. In other words, the system should have a mechanism that determines the difference between the actual user's POIN, which the system is trying to satisfy, and the representation of POIN that is currently available to the system. Such a mechanism is the mechanism of adaptation, which allows the system to adjust to the user's POIN. Because, in discussing the structure of IR systems (in Chapter 4) we gave a detailed analysis for the necessity of adaptation and also analyzed the nature and necessity of feedback in the IR system, we will not repeat it here. Remember, however, that the existence of the problem of adaptation in IR systems does not make these systems adaptive. It is necessary to create a mechanism of feedback that deals with the process of adaptation. The creation of such a mechanism requires the knowledge of *what to control* and *how to control*. To answer these questions, we need to look at the structure of the controllable system, which in our case is the IR system in Figure 4.8.

Now let us discuss how the object of control (OC) interacts with the mechanism of control (MC). Which elements of OC can be controlled? Clearly, we can control OC (i.e., change the system's output) by affecting every element of OC, which is indicated in Figure 4.8 by dotted lines. Let us look at how we can affect different elements of OC.

1. BID (block of indexing of documents)—The indexing of documents can be affected by one of the following changes:
   (a) A change in the method of indexing
   (b) A change in the dictionary
   (c) A change in both the method of indexing and the dictionary
2. BIQ (block of indexing of search requests)—The process of constructing query formulations can be affected by the following changes:
   (a) A change in the method of constructing query formulations
   (b) The use of different information about the user's POIN
   (c) A combination of (a) and (b)
3. BSR (block of storage and retrieval)—It is possible to control the actual search (the comparison of query formulations with document profiles) by changing output criteria.
4. It is also possible to use a combined approach to make changes simultaneously in two or more elements.

It should be pointed out that scientific literature covers all of the mentioned approaches (see, e.g., Belew, 1989; Dillon, 1980; Frants & Shapiro, 1991b; Gordon, 1988; Rickman, 1972; Salton, Voorhees, & Fox, 1984; and Voiskunskii & Frants, 1974). However, not all of these approaches are equally acceptable (for example, some are more time consuming). Therefore, we will consider which of the elements of OC is the most expedient to control.

Given that in this book we are primarily considering IR systems with the Boolean criterion of selection, we will not control the BSR element of OC. Another element that will not be controlled is BID. The process of indexing all documents in the collection (especially in the case of a retrospective search) is an extremely time-consuming operation. Because feedback will have to react to each user individually, the change in the process of indexing documents will have to be performed for each user (and, moreover, for each request) during each iteration. Although this is possible to do in principle, it seems to us to be impractical. Even if there are only a few dozen users, it may be necessary to store hundreds of different versions of the same collection obtained as the result of different indexing. It seems clear that the element of the IR system that could be controlled most effectively is its BIQ. The choice of this element is the most natural for a majority of developers, and in functioning systems today only query formulations are corrected.

Hence, the system's operation is controlled by changing the query formulation. The purpose of this control is to affect the output of the system to better satisfy the user's POIN, and this is only possible on the basis of some information. But what can we say about information during the realization of adaptation in an IR system? First, it is necessary to clarify *what* information (which object) the system needs for correcting query formulations. Second, it is

In all the preceding development, user has never been considered to be part of the loop!

important to know *who* will present this information and *how*. Third, there has to be a way of evaluating the result of control; that is, the system should be able to determine if its output is changing in the right direction. Any adaptation is performed on the basis of information characterizing the object to which one is adapting. This characterization is usually called a parameter. Hence, we first consider which parameter(s) is taken into consideration during adaptation.

We mentioned earlier that an IR system adapts to an actual user's POIN, and the goal of adaptation is satisfaction of POIN. All of the processes in the system (including adaptation) are created with this purpose. In the process of adaptation, the system should change into a state that satisfies POIN better than the old state. But what does "better" mean in connection with POIN? It means that the output of the system better corresponds to the thematical boundaries of POIN and that the output better corresponds to the user's level of perception. These conditions result in a decrease in the user's uncertainty. Hence, in providing information to the user, the system should try to take into account as precisely and fully as possible such characteristics of individual POIN as thematical boundaries and the level of perception. However, neither the first nor the second characteristic can be precisely discerned (and especially measured) because POIN does not have clear thematical boundaries and the level of perception, which depends on the existing patterns in the user's memory, can only be realized (and not always very clearly) by the user. Hence, the information necessary for adaptation could only come from the user.

This information from the user that the system utilizes for adaptation is often of low quality (see our discussion of the user's expression of POIN in Chapter 2) and, as a rule, does not provide any indication of the level of perception. In fact, the existing algorithms of adaptation do not actually consider the level of perception and only attempt to recognize the information related to the thematical boundaries of POIN (i.e., they try to adapt to these boundaries). It should be pointed out that the information about the POIN's boundaries has to be new, that is, information that was not available to the system before. If the system does not receive new (additional) information, then adaptation is not performed; this is because adaptation is only possible after the system has received new information. We say "additional" because the mechanism of adaptation is only activated after the initial search, that is, after the first output is formed. Clearly, to form the first output the system used some information about the user's POIN (for example, the search request), and any information characterizing POIN that was not entered into the system previously is considered additional information. This additional information should enter the system through the feedback line. Hence, in considering the mechanism of adaptation, we determined who provides necessary information, what this information describes, and the character of this information. But it is not yet clear in what form this information is presented to the system. We discuss this in some detail next.

Although the information used for adaptation is given by the user, the user represents it in the way that was required by the developers of the system. Already in developing the very first functioning IR systems, especially for the selective dissemination of information (SDI) in the early 1960s, the researchers were quite aware that during the first few iterations the system had to adapt to the user's POIN (see, e.g., Curtis & Rosenberg, 1965; and Meadow, 1967). The adaptation was done on the basis of previous outputs. This was typical adaptive feedback, although it was quite primitive in its implementation. At that time it was not called adaptation—since there were no on-line systems—and the user interacted with the system through an intermediary searcher. In the process of such feedback, the user's evaluation (or reaction) to the output after obtaining the pertinent documents was used as a signal to start adaptation, and the evaluated documents were used (analyzed) by intermediary searchers in the process of correcting query formulations.

The user's evaluation of the output was not always directly used for correcting query formulations. Often the developers of the system assumed that the user would reformulate the search request, and the developers therefore planned to use this new formulation, containing additional information, for correcting the old query formulation. But, as is clear from properties of POIN, it is possible that the user's new formulation may be worse than the original formulation (Frants & Brush, 1988). Also, constructing a new search request is often a problem for both the user and the developers of the system (for example, the user may be reluctant to change a previous request that he or she considers the best possible). These reasons probably led the developers to conclude that it is more expedient to obtain additional information about POIN directly from the user's evaluation of the previous output, that is, from marked (pertinent) documents. This approach clearly minimized the user's efforts in presenting additional information about his or her POIN, since the user evaluated the output regardless of the presence of feedback in the system.

It seems clear that the first (manual) attempts to realize feedback in IR systems were directed not toward developing a mechanism of adaptation but toward developing methods for collecting additional information about POIN. This gave some positive results; for example, researchers concluded that the marked documents provided the best way to represent the additional information about POIN as well as the easiest way for users to formulate search requests. After the first successful implementation of automatic feedback by Salton in the system SMART (which does not use the Boolean search criterion), the use of marked documents to provide additional information about POIN became predominant (Salton, 1968). Hence, that additional information about POIN entering the system through the line of feedback is now the user's reaction to the output. In the majority of systems, the user interacts with the system directly (on-line) and the user's reaction can be obtained very easily. It is sufficient to indicate for each document evaluated by the user if it is pertinent (for example, by pressing key "y") or not (by pressing "n").

Hence, we know now that the state of the system in changed (for the purpose of adapting to the user's POIN) by correcting query formulations on the basis of information contained in the user's reaction to the output. It seems that we are ready to proceed with the discussion of existing approaches to automate feedback process in IR systems. However, first it is necessary to look at the way the collection of documents is used during search because the mechanism of feedback depends on how we use this collection during search.

Two different cases affect the character of a system's adaptation to the user. The first occurs when the collection of documents does not change during each iteration (a *static collection*) and the control is performed, for example, during one session in the on-line system or in the case of a retrospective search. The second case occurs when the collection changes in different iterations (a *dynamic collection*), such as in the case of SDI.

In realizing feedback for a static collection of documents, the task of control consists of an attempt to find pertinent documents that were not found during the previous search without exceeding an acceptable noise level (for a given system) in the output. The feedback algorithm in this situation will construct a new query formulation, which will be used in an attempt to find new (presumably relevant) documents.

In realizing feedback for a dynamic collection of documents, the task of control is different from that in a static collection. In a static collection, we try to obtain a new query formulation (at every new iteration) that does not intersect with any of the previous query formulations. But in a dynamic collection, we only try to correct (improve) the previous query formulation. In other words, we try to remove all subrequests that led to the unsuccessful search and to add new (original) subrequests that will presumably give us pertinent documents. Hence, in the case of a dynamic collection our task is not to find relevant documents that were not found during a previous search but to have a more successful search in a new collection of documents; that is, we want to construct a new query formulation (by correcting the previous one) so that if we performed two searches in the same collection using the previous query formulation and the new one, the latter search would give us better results.

But what is the basic difference between two types of collections, that is, what kind of searches are performed in a static collection versus a dynamic collection? In both Chapter 2 and Chapter 4 we stressed that the design of an IR system depends on the properties of POIN, and in creating an IR system we are trying to take into account all of POIN's properties (and if a system contains some process or mechanism, it exists only because it is required by POIN). We know, for example, that SDI is based on attribute 3 of POIN and one time search (or search in one particular collection) is only a stage in a process of providing continuous service to the user. From the analysis of attributes of POIN, it is clear that the process of adaptive feedback in a static collection is directed primarily toward satisfying attribute 2 of POIN, whereas in a dynamic collection this process of feedback is connected, first of all, to attribute 4 of POIN.

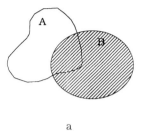
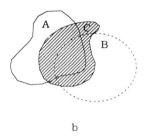

a   b

Figure 9.1
Adaptation in a static collection.

As an illustration, review Figure 9.1(a) and note that region A corresponds
to the actual POIN of some user. (By "actual" we mean a POIN that has to be
satisfied as the result of the search.) Because the request, as a rule, does not
represent POIN exactly—see attribute 2 of POIN—region B corresponds to
information about actual POIN that is received by the system. The query formulation is constructed by the system on the basis of region B rather than A,
and hence the search in the system is performed to satisfy region B. The part of
the POIN corresponding to A − B is not known to the system, and the information about this part of POIN (this "additional" information) is needed for
adaptation. When some part of this information (contained in the documents
corresponding to area A ∩ B) is received by the feedback mechanism and is used
to change the system into a different state, we may have a situation like that
represented in Figure 9.1(b). Area C corresponds to the new output and, as the
figure shows, this output covers a bigger part of area A. Also, the level of noise
corresponding to area C − A is lower than in the previous output. Hence, we
see the "direction" of adaptation (in the ideal case the system will eventually
produce an output that exactly corresponds to A). It is clear that at the next
iteration the additional information will be represented by some part of the area
(A ∩ C) − B and so on.

Note that the analysis of adaptation to region A is based on the assumption
that from one iteration to another the POIN does not change at all or changes
slightly. During retrospective search or in the case of one session in an on-line
system, this seems plausible. Because the search is performed in the same collection of documents, then it follows that in a static collection of documents the
character of adaptation is determined by attribute 2 of POIN. In other words,
the system is adapting to area A, which is, as a rule, stable, and the adaptation
consists of removing the inaccuracy in the POIN representation in the original
query formulation.

In the case of a dynamic collection (for example, in the case of SDI) the
situation is different. A search is performed in time intervals (for example, once
a month) in a new collection that was accumulated during this time period.

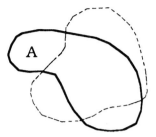

Figure 9.2
Adaptation in a dynamic collection.

Because the thematical limits of POIN may change in time (attribute 4 of POIN), which is quite common, the system has to adapt not to fixed area A but to constantly changing area A. Also, often the user does not realize that there is a change in his or her POIN.

Figure 9.2 illustrates this process. The area enclosed within the dotted line represents POIN at the time of the original request, and the area enclosed within the unbroken line corresponds to the current POIN, possibly after several iterations. The system has to satisfy the current POIN and, hence, the additional information to be supplied to the mechanism of feedback has to contain details about the POIN changed in time and try to adapt to this new POIN. Because thematical boundaries are constantly changing, the adaptation process will also be continuous. The IR system has to constantly monitor the POIN of every user (the user does not even have to be aware of this process) and change the query formulation to better reflect the new area A. Hence, it is clear that in the dynamic collection the character of adaptation is determined by attribute 4 of POIN. Now, after clarifying the importance of the type of the collection for the development of methods for adaptive feedback, we take a look at the approaches and ideas underlying the process of adaptation.

9.3

Some Approaches to the Realization of Adaptive Feedback

Automatic feedback for a system with Boolean search is traditionally one of the more complex processes to realize. This is also clear from the existing literature, which has very few publications containing constructive suggestions. Automatic feedback methods were introduced for Boolean systems more than 25 years ago (Voiskunskii & Frants, 1971). Almost simultaneously with the creation of the first method (algorithm) for automatic construction of query formulation, the M-algorithm developed in 1970 (see Chapter 7), the algorithm for automatic feedback was developed on the basis of the M–algorithm. As documented by a series of papers published from 1971 through 1974, this algorithm was substantially improved. The available experimental evidence indicates that substantial increases in effectiveness can be produced by the feedback procedures in Boolean systems.

It should be pointed out that researchers, in discussing the automatization of feedback, as a rule only refer to the automatization of the construction of query formulations. In some sense this is reasonable because, as was discussed earlier, from the earliest development of IR systems the developers knew that they could improve the expediency of control by correcting query formulations, and it is impossible to automatically correct query formulations without a method for automatically constructing query formulations. However, automatization of the construction of query formulations is not the same as automatization of all processes of feedback. Therefore, in this chapter we will not consider the methods of the automatic construction of query formulations (although the authors of these methods use them to automatize feedback in IR systems); however, these methods were described in Chapter 7 as they applied to the automatic indexing of search requests.

We start with a brief description of the method published in 1974 (Voiskunskii & Frants, 1974). This method is of interest not only because it was the first method of automatic feedback for IR systems with Boolean search but also because it was the first method to be used in the realization of automatic feedback for dynamic collections. The problem of automatization was solved by creating two separate algorithms: one algorithm for correcting query formulations in order to increase the precision level of the search and another algorithm for correcting query formulations in order to increase the recall level of the search. We describe both algorithms as follows.

The first algorithm is based on the following assumptions:

1. The decrease in the number of nonpertinent documents in the output formed by the corrected query formulation has to exceed (by a predefined factor) the decrease in the number of pertinent documents in the output formed by the corrected query formulation.

Within the framework of this assumption the following statement is true.

1.1. The predefined factor depends on both the number of pertinent documents in the output formed by the original query formulation (before correction) and the decrease in the number of pertinent documents.

We can formalize 1 and 1.1 as follows. Let N_1 and R_1 be, respectively, the number of nonpertinent and pertinent documents in the output formed by the original query formulation (before correction), and let N_2 and R_2 be, respectively, the same numbers for the corrected query formulation. Then the assumptions state that

$$(N_1 - N_2)/(R_1 - R_2) > f(R_1, R_2). \tag{1}$$

The predefined factor, denoted by $f(R_1, R_2)$ depends on the number of pertinent documents in both outputs (before and after the correction of the query formulation). This factor will be computed for each individual user, and the computation could be based on both the experimental results and the analytical investigations of this function.

The construction of the algorithm should take into account another consideration.

> 1.2. The satisfaction of inequality (1) on one collection of documents could be accidental and before making a decision about correcting a query formulation it is necessary to make sure that the satisfaction of inequality (1) was not accidental.

Now we describe an algorithm that is based on assumptions 1, 1.1, and 1.2.

After the system receives the user's evaluation of the output, the number of pertinent (R_1) and nonpertinent (N_1) documents is computed. Then every subrequest in the original query formulation is analyzed to see if it should be eliminated in the corrected query formulation to increase the quality of the search. This is done by performing the search among the documents in the output using the original query formulation, which has been modified by removal of the subrequest under consideration. In the new output, the numbers of pertinent (R_2) and nonpertinent (N_2) documents are computed (this could be done automatically using the user's evaluation of the original output). The inequality (1) is checked, and the information about the satisfaction (or the lack of satisfaction) of this inequality is recorded. This process is performed on a predefined number of collections of documents, which represents one evaluation cycle. The obtained information is used to accumulate statistical data that allow the algorithm to make a decision with respect to keeping the subrequest in the final version of the corrected query formulation. The evaluation cycle ends when enough statistical data are obtained.

The algorithm checks inequality (1) for every subrequest for each collection of documents in a corresponding evaluation cycle. If the query formulation is obtained again, then for each subrequest a new evaluation cycle begins immediately. If a query formulation is used after an evaluation cycle (and, naturally, after correction), then an evaluation cycle for a subrequest begins after inequality (1) is satisfied. If, as the result of the first evaluation cycle, more than one subrequest becomes a candidate for removal, then the subrequest removed first will be the one with the highest average value of $(N_1 - N_2)/(R_1 - R_2) -$

$f(R_1, R_2)$ computed for all collections of documents in one evaluation cycle. Then inequality (1) has to be checked again for other subrequests using the results of the evaluation cycle. The size of an evaluation cycle depends on the assumptions that the algorithm uses in deciding when to remove a subrequest. For example, if inequality (1) is satisfied at least four times in five collections of documents, then the subrequest could be removed and five could be taken as the number of collections of documents in one evaluation cycle.

In designing an algorithm to correct a query formulation with the intent of increasing the recall level of a search, the idea is to include additional subrequests in the query formulation, which would increase the recall level. This algorithm is based on the following assumptions:

2. Additional subrequests should be constructed automatically (using an algorithm for automatic indexing of search requests) on the basis of the additional information about POIN.
3. For some users not all new subrequests should be added but only those that result in substantially different output.
    3.1. Whether the difference in the outputs is sufficient for the inclusion of a new subrequest is determined for each user; the determination depends on the sizes of the outputs obtained from the original query formulation and from the new subrequest.

We introduce the following notation.

   C—the set of documents contained in the output from the original query formulation
   D—the set of documents contained in the output from the additional subrequest
$\alpha(x)$—the number of elements in set x

The following formula represents a possible way to use assumptions 3 and 3.1, that is, the higher ratio of $\alpha(D) - \alpha(C \cap D)$ to $\alpha(D)$ indicates more substantial difference in the outputs from the query formulation and from the new subrequest:

$$[\alpha(D) - \alpha(C \cap D)]/\alpha(D) > f(\alpha(C),\alpha(D)). \qquad (2)$$

Assumption 3.1 is indicated on the right-hand side because f depends on the cardinality of C and D. If $f(\alpha(C),\alpha(D)) = 0$ for some user, then all of the additional subrequests will be added in the new query formulation.

In constructing the algorithm, another assumption (analogous to assumption 1.2) is being used.

   3.2. The satisfaction of inequality (2) on one collection of documents could be accidental, and before making a decision about correcting a query formulation it is necessary to make sure that satisfaction of inequality (2) was not accidental.

Now we describe an algorithm that is based on assumptions 2, 3, 3.1, and 3.2.

On the basis of additional information received from the user the query formulation is constructed (by the algorithm for the automatic indexing of search requests). If this query formulation contains a new subrequest it is tested through an evaluation cycle. This is done as follows. The search is performed using the original query formulation and the new subrequest. Then the values of $\alpha(D)$ and $\alpha(C \cap D)$ are computed and inequality (2) is checked. The information about the satisfaction (or the lack of satisfaction) of this inequality is recorded in a corresponding cycle. This is done until enough statistical data are accumulated to allow the algorithm to make a decision with respect to including the subrequest in the final version of the corrected query formulation. If more than one subrequest is tested, then the subrequest to be added to the original query formulation is the one with the highest average value of

$$[\alpha(D) - \alpha(C \cap D)]/\alpha(D) - f(\alpha(C), \alpha(D))$$

computed for all collections of documents in one evaluation cycle. Then inequality (2) has to be checked again for other subrequests using the results of the same evaluation cycle. The query formulation used in this evaluation is a quasi-corrected (by other subrequest) query formulation. This is done for all remaining subrequests to be tested.

The size of an evaluation cycle depends on the assumptions that the algorithm uses in deciding when to add a subrequest. The computation is similar for the removal of subrequests. After adding new subrequests, the algorithm of "noise removal" (the first algorithm) is invoked to correct the obtained query formulation. After the first algorithm is finished, the final query formulation is considered constructed.

The described algorithm of adaptive feedback was tested in 1972 on the IR system Informatica. This system's collection of documents covered all areas of information science. The results clearly demonstrated an improvement in the precision and recall levels of search for every search request used in the experiments.

We mentioned earlier that in only a few papers were concrete methods proposed for automatic feedback in Boolean IR systems, and in describing automatic feedback some authors used only algorithms for the automatic indexing of search requests. Moreover, in the majority of these papers, the feedback process was only considered for static collection of documents, although it was not mentioned explicitly. As an example, we can mention the approach used by Salton and coauthors (Salton, Fox, & Voorhees, 1985) in realizing feedback in a static collection of documents. The authors proposed that researchers consider descriptors from the pertinent documents obtained from the first iteration (from the original query formulation) as well as from subsequent iterations (in the process of one session in an on-line search), but they assigned different weights to the descriptors depending on which iterations they obtained. They considered the descriptors used in the initial search more important. For this purpose they introduced "auxiliary query count (qcount) parameter designed to give extra weight to the original query terms." The use of qcount represents an artificial increase in the occurrence frequencies of the descriptors in the marked set of documents used for the automatic construction of query formulations.

The idea of qcount seems to be quite interesting although there are some questions as to the best way to use it. From our understanding of information need, in particular POIN, it seems more logical to use qcount for the descriptors appearing in the pertinent documents in the last output. This seems to follow from the changing boundaries of POIN attribute 4. The descriptors that were important for the search at the beginning may lose their significance, whereas new descriptors could better represent new boundaries of POIN. They will also be a part of the additional information necessary to construct a corrected query formulation. In any case, the use of qcount requires additional experimental support, and qcount could become a useful tool in better representing additional information about POIN. On the other hand, using qcount in static collections (as was done by the authors) does not seem to be as beneficial because there may be very little change in POIN.

In 1991 we published new, more complete algorithms of adaptive feedback both for static and dynamic collections of documents (Frants & Shapiro, 1991b). These algorithms formed the basis for the adaptive IR system developed at Fordham University. We describe these algorithms next, together with some experimental results. We start with the algorithm for the static collection of documents.

9.4

Feedback Algorithm for the Static Collection of Documents

We mentioned earlier that in realizing feedback for the static collection of documents, the task of control consists of an attempt to find pertinent documents, which were not found during the previous search, without an increase in the acceptable level of noise. A good illustration for better understanding this problem is presented in Figure 9.1. Here we discuss this figure with the goal of developing a feedback algorithm for the static collection of documents. The feedback algorithm in this situation will construct a new query formulation (area C), which will be used in an attempt to find new (presumably pertinent) documents. In other words, there is no reason to use in the new (corrected) query formulation any of the subrequests from the previous query formulation because such a subrequest can only find documents that form a subset of area B. Also, there is no reason to include in the output any documents found with the new query formulation that were contained in area B. In developing an algorithm, these cases are taken into account.

The algorithm is applied after the system receives the user's evaluation of the previous output. The algorithm selects all documents marked as pertinent by the user (we denote the set of these documents by OM). If there are no such documents—that is, if OM is empty—then the algorithm stops, because there is no additional information about POIN given to the system. If OM is not empty, then the algorithm proceeds by combining sets OM and PM, where PM is the set used to obtain the query formulation in the previous search. In the first feedback cycle this set PM is the user's initial request and may consist of either one document (if the user's request is given in a sentence form) or several documents (if the user's request is a set of pertinent documents). This construction is described in more detail in Chapter 7.

The next step in the algorithm is the construction of a new query formulation using CM, which denotes the union of OM and PM, as input (recall that the set of documents used as an input for the construction of a query formulation is called a "marked set"). This step is a complex problem in its own right. In our case it is only one part of a more general feedback algorithm, and the query formulation obtained in this step is only a preliminary version (we denote it by AQ), which could undergo substantial changes. In solving the problem of constructing a query formulation, it is possible to use one of the existing algorithms or methods that accept as an input a marked set of documents or, as an alternative, to develop a completely new algorithm. For several reasons we suggest using the algorithm described in Chapter 7. First, the experimental results showed this algorithm to be quite effective. Second (in our opinion, a very important consideration), the algorithm allows us to construct query formulations without any limitation on the number of descriptors appearing in each subrequest (i.e., a subrequest may consist of either one descriptor or two, three, four, or more descriptors joined by the Boolean operator AND). Third, the algorithm allows for a simple control of the number of documents in the output; that is, when the user is interested in obtaining a specific number of documents in the output the algorithm can easily meet this requirement. In addition, at the request of the user the documents in the output can be ranked.

After obtaining AQ, the algorithm compares it to the combined query formulation (we denote it by CQ), which is obtained by combining all query formulations used in the previous feedback iterations during a search process in the same collection of documents. In the case of the first iteration, CQ coincides with the query formulation constructed from the initial request. Then the algorithm obtains a new query formulation (NQ) by removing from AQ all subrequests that appear in CQ and also those subrequests that contain any of the subrequests appearing in CQ. For example, if a, b are descriptors from the system's dictionary, and $a \wedge b$ is a subrequest of AQ, it will not appear in NQ if $a \wedge b$ is a subrequest of CQ or if either a or b is a subrequest of CQ. This is done because all of the documents that can be found by these subrequests were already seen by the user in the process of obtaining CM (pertinent documents contained in the outputs from the previous searches).

If NQ is not empty (i.e., if it contains at least one subrequest), a new search is performed, and if a set of obtained documents contains any new documents not appearing in the previous outputs, these documents (new output) are given to the user from which he or she selects pertinent documents. The system keeps the entire output for the following iterations. The pertinent documents in this output as chosen by the user are added to all other pertinent documents from previous searches, a new query formulation is constructed, and a new search is performed. This iterative process continues until one of the following conditions is satisfied:

1. An auxiliary query formulation (AQ) does not contain new subrequests.
2. A set of documents obtained as the result of a new search does not contain any new documents.
3. An output does not contain any new pertinent documents.
4. The user does not provide any evaluation of the documents from the output (leaves the system).

Table 9.1 provides a summary of one iteration in the feedback algorithm for static collection.

This finishes our discussion of the feedback algorithm for a static collection of documents. Now we will consider the dynamic collection of documents, where each feedback iteration is performed on a new collection of documents.

Table 9.1
Summary of the Steps in One Iteration of the Feedback Algorithm for Static Collection

---

1. Pertinent documents from the previous output (using the user's evaluation) that were obtained as the result of the search based on the previous query formulation (PQ) are selected.

2. A new marked set is constructed by combining the pertinent documents obtained in Step 1 with the documents used for the construction of the previous query formulation.

3. The auxiliary query formulation (AQ) is constructed using as input the marked set from Step 2. This step uses an algorithm described in Chapter 7.

4. The new query formulation (NQ) is constructed by removing from AQ all subrequests appearing in PQ and all subrequests that contain subrequests from PQ.

5. The user is given the output obtained in two steps:
   (a) A search based on NQ
   (b) The removal from the obtained set of documents of all documents from the previous outputs

---

Feedback Algorithm for the Dynamic Collection of Documents

Recall that in realizing feedback for the dynamic collection of documents, the task of control is different from that in the static collection. In static collection, we try to obtain a new query formulation (at every new iteration) that does not intersect with any of the previous query formulations. But in dynamic collection, we only try to improve the previous query formulation. In other words, it is necessary to remove all subrequests that led to the unsuccessful search and to add new (original) subrequests that will presumably give us pertinent documents. Hence, in the case of dynamic collection the goal is not to find pertinent documents that were not found during a previous search but to have a more successful search of a new collection of documents; that is, in this case it is necessary to construct a new query formulation (by correcting the previous one) so that if we performed searches in the same collection using the previous query formulation and the new one, the latter search would give us better results.

The described feedback algorithm for the dynamic collection consists of two separate steps: (1) to increase the recall level (by adding new subrequests) and (2) to increase the precision (by removing "bad" subrequests). These steps will be called the "recall step" and the "precision step," respectively.

The input to the feedback algorithm consists of the user's evaluation of the system's output (a set of documents), which identifies pertinent (and hence nonpertinent) documents in this set. If there are no pertinent documents in the output, then the algorithm stops at this point (as is done with the static collection of documents), because there is no additional information about the user's actual POIN, and the search in the new collection is performed using the previous (unchanged) query formulation. If pertinent documents are found in the output, the recall step is executed. Then if the output does not contain nonpertinent documents, the feedback algorithm stops, and the search is performed using the query formulation obtained in this step. However, if nonpertinent documents are found in the output, then the precision step is executed. We now describe the recall and precision steps.

The recall step starts by adding to the set of pertinent documents all the documents used to construct the previous query formulation. This new marked set is used as an input to construct a new auxiliary query formulation (AQ) by applying the algorithm for the automatic construction of query formulations (described in Chapter 7). Then a new query formulation (denoted by NQ) is obtained by combining all subrequests from AQ and PQ (previous query formulation); that is, $NQ = AQ \cup PQ$. Notice that the application of the set union operator $\cup$ will prevent NQ from having any extraneous subrequests. Recall that a subrequest S is extraneous in query formulation Q if there exists a subrequest T in Q such that all descriptors in T also appear in S (i.e., S ∩ T = S). This NQ will become the final query formulation and will be used in the search of the new collection if there are no nonpertinent documents in the previous output. If, on the other hand, there are nonpertinent documents, then the feedback algorithm proceeds with the precision step.

The precision step starts by identifying all subrequests in PQ that were used to obtain nonpertinent documents. These subrequests are the candidates for removal from NQ. They will be removed from NQ if they did not appear in AQ, because they were used to retrieve noise and had low weight in the new marked set. However, they will be left as part of the final query formulation if they appear in AQ because their weight in the new marked set exceeded a certain threshold and possibly they will perform better in the new collection. After applying this procedure to all subrequests appearing in PQ and removing the appropriate subrequests from NQ, the final query formulation is obtained and it will be used for the search in the new collection of documents.

It is possible that the previous query formulation will be used for the search in the new collection of documents. This can occur in the following three cases:

1. There is no user's evaluation of the system's output.
2. The output from the previous collection does not contain any pertinent documents.
3. After the application of the feedback algorithm, the new query formulation coincides with the previous query formulation (i.e., no subrequests were removed from or added to the previous query formulation).

It is necessary to mention one more technical point about the feedback algorithm. From the previous discussion it is clear that when we construct a marked set at each iteration (for both static and dynamic collections) we combine pertinent documents from the last output with pertinent documents from previous outputs. This marked set may become very large and we may want to control its size by either reducing the number of iterations included (for example, to five or six iterations) or by putting a limit on the number of documents in the marked set and removing the documents from the earlier iterations. This consideration is more relevant for the dynamic collection of documents. Table 9.2 summarizes the steps involved in one iteration of the feedback algorithm for the dynamic collection of documents.

It is sometimes advantageous to combine two feedback algorithms (for static and dynamic collections). This would be appropriate, for example, if a user were interested in SDI using on-line systems. In this example, the user's interaction with the system during one session is similar to the case of the static collection, and the corresponding feedback algorithm can be applied. At the end of the session, the system stores the set of all pertinent documents used to con-

Table 9.2
Summary of the Steps in One Iteration of the Feedback Algorithm for Dynamic Collection

1. Pertinent documents from the previous output (using the user's evaluation) are selected. If there are no pertinent documents (or there is no user's evaluation), then the previous query formulation is used for the search in the new collection of documents (Step 7). If there are pertinent documents, then the system proceeds to Step 2.

2. A new marked set is constructed by combining the pertinent documents obtained in Step 1 and the pertinent documents used for the construction of the previous query formulation.

3. An auxiliary query formulation (AQ) is constructed using as input the marked set obtained in Step 2 and new descriptor frequencies from the new collection.

4. A modified query formulation (MQ) is constructed by adding new subrequests to AQ (using the recall step described earlier).

5. Nonpertinent documents are selected from the previous output. If there are no such documents, the modified query formulation from Step 4 becomes the final query formulation, and the search is performed (Step 7). If there are nonpertinent documents, then the system continues on to Step 6.

6. The subrequests from PQ that were used in finding nonpertinent documents are selected. These subrequests are removed from MQ if they did not appear in AQ (i.e., the precision step is applied). The resulting query formulation is the final query formulation for this iteration.

7. The final output is obtained as the result of the search in the new collection based on the final query formulation.

struct the final query formulation. A new session (with the new collection) begins with the construction of a new query formulation based on the marked set stored from the previous session and using the descriptor frequencies from the new collection (as in the feedback algorithm for the dynamic collection). After the search based on this query formulation has been completed and the user has evaluated the system's output, the feedback algorithm for the static collection is applied again. It should be pointed out that combining the two algorithms seems the most expedient because in this case the system takes into account two attributes (2 and 4) of POIN as it adapts to the user's need.

9.6

Evaluation

The feedback algorithms described in the chapter were tested experimentally on the IR system AIRS (adaptive IR system) developed at Fordham University. We will now describe the most important results of these experiments.

The collection consisted of 2504 documents in computer science, selected from the journal *Computer Abstracts,* and 28 queries with relevance judgments. The collection statistics are summarized in Table 9.3.

Table 9.3
Collection Statistics

Number of documents	2504
Size of the descriptor dictionary in AIRS	862
Average length of documents in the collection (in words)	94.6
Number of queries in the static collection	28
Number of queries in the dynamic collection	23
Average number of pertinent documents in the collection (per query)	15.4

The first experiment tested the feedback algorithm for a static collection of documents. The original search for each of the 28 queries was based on the query formulation constructed by the algorithm for the automatic construction of query formulations (see Chapter 7). The original user's requests consisted of marked sets of documents varying in size from four to six documents. Table 9.4 summarizes the results of this experiment.

The results in Table 9.4 were averaged for five different zones: queries with recall levels (1) less than 20%, (2) between 20% and 40%, (3) between 40% and 60%, (4) between 60% and 80%, (5) between 80% and 100%. The right side of Table 9.4 shows the averaged results for recall and precision levels after the feedback process. To demonstrate how the averaging was done for all zones, we chose one zone (20% to 40%) and tabulated all of the results in Table 9.5.

As the result of feedback all queries showed an improvement in recall levels, and 26 queries had an improvement in precision levels. The maximum number of iterations was seven (in two cases) and the minimum number was one (in four cases).

The second experiment was performed on the dynamic collection of documents. The collection was divided into three separate collections consisting of 850, 850, and 804 documents, respectively. There were 23 queries and the original search was performed on the first collection using query formulations constructed in the same way as done for the static collection. Table 9.6 gives the results of this experiment.

Table 9.4
The Results of the Experiment on the Static Collection

Original search		Final results after feedback	
Recall	Precision	Recall	Precision
20	57.8	69.5	64.7
40	50.0	78.6	55.2
60	46.2	76.8	58.4
80	30.5	90.5	50.4
100	9.4	96.2	36.2

Table 9.5
An Illustration of the Averaging for the Recall and Precision Levels

Number of relevant documents in a query	Initial search				Feedback iterations												Recall and precision levels at end of feedback process	
	Number of documents in the output		Recall (%)	Precision (%)	1		2		3		4		5		6		Rec.	Prec.
	Rel.	Nonrel.			Rel.	Nonrel.	Rel.	Nonrel.	Rel.	Nonrel.	Rel.	Nonrel.	Rel.	Nonrel.	Rel.	Nonrel.		
17	6	8	35.2	42.8	4	3	2	1	2	1	1	1	1	1	–	–	94.1	51.6
14	4	6	28.5	40.0	2	2	3	1	1	1	0	1	–	–	–	–	71.4	47.6
21	7	5	33.3	58.3	5	4	3	3	2	0	1	0	–	–	–	–	85.7	60.0
13	5	4	38.4	55.5	2	3	1	0	–	–	–	–	–	–	–	–	69.2	53.3
12	4	4	33.3	50.0	2	0	1	1	1	0	–	–	–	–	–	–	66.6	66.6
15	4	3	26.6	57.1	4	3	2	1	–	–	–	–	–	–	–	–	66.6	58.8
19	6	4	31.5	60.0	1	3	3	1	3	2	2	0	1	1	1	0	94.7	62.0
11	3	5	27.2	37.5	2	3	2	1	1	1	–	–	–	–	–	–	72.7	44.4

Table 9.6
The Results of the Experiment for the Dynamic Collection

Recall level (%)	Precision (%)		
	Original search	First iteration	Second iteration
20	61.4	72.3	76.2
40	53.8	58.1	63.1
60	49.3	55.7	59.0
80	26.5	32.2	38.4
100	5.6	14.8	17.3

The experiments just described showed that the suggested feedback algorithms increase both recall and precision levels of a search. In other words, as the result of the feedback process, the larger part of POIN (area A in Figures 9.1 and 9.2) is covered, with the reduction in noise represented by the area outside of area A.

The algorithms described allow the system to not only adapt to the user's POIN but also to completely automate this process. However, as was mentioned earlier, this type of feedback does not solve the problem of optimal search. For this it is necessary to develop a different mechanism, which we discuss next.

9.7

Feedback for Search Optimization

In describing the function of IR systems (see Chapter 7), we discussed the need for an optimal search to satisfy the user's POIN. In the same chapter we considered the structure of an IR system realizing this function and identified the element responsible for this function. In this section we consider the structure of such an element, which will allow us not only to realize the process of optimization but also to fully automate this process. In other words, we will describe the algorithms used to select the system's best state for the static and dynamic collection of documents (Frants, Shapiro, & Voiskunskii, 1993; 1996). But before describing the algorithms, we first discuss the problem of search optimization.

Success or failure in a fully automated search depends on the quality of search algorithms as well the quality of the IRL used. It is in these two directions that developers of IR systems concentrate their attention. They try to improve the quality of the search by, on the one hand, improving the grammar and vocabulary of the IRL and, on the other hand, developing and improving the search algorithms. It should be noted that the development of IRLs proceeds in the direction of bringing them closer to natural languages, and the development of search algorithms proceeds in the direction of establishing a more extensive consideration of the semantics of these languages. However, even when the information retrieval language is a natural language and there is an ideal search algorithm, failures in the search are possible. Here is why.

Because the goal of a search in an IR system is the information needed to satisfy the user's POIN, then it is quite obvious that the more precisely information about POIN is represented in the IRL (i.e., the more precisely the search request—and, in our case, the query formulation—represents the POIN), the more successful the search should be. However, obtaining a precise search request (query formulation) is difficult in principle. In fact, attribute 2 and, to a certain extent, attribute 3 of a POIN indicate that information about the POIN received by the system and the POIN itself generally differ from each other. Thus, even if we had an "ideal" method for constructing query formulations— i.e., even if we could absolutely precisely translate information about the POIN from natural language into the IRL—the query formulation obtained in this case would not ideally represent the POIN in the IRL. Moreover, the less the POIN and the search request correspond, the worse the search is, in spite of the "ideal" method of constructing query formulations. In creating IR systems, we cannot assume that in most cases users' requests will closely correspond to their POIN. Therefore, it is necessary to understand how the IR systems can function in this environment, what we can hope to achieve in satisfying users information needs, and how to realize these goals.

Today the efforts of the IR systems developers with respect to improving the quality of information service for users are concentrated in the direction of creating new, better methods and replacing the old methods with the new. In other words, the developers of the functioning IR systems use the best (from their point of view) methods (algorithms) for all processes existing in the system. However, as we showed earlier, even the creation of ideal methods does not solve the problem of a quality search. This by no means implies that better methods need not be created. On the contrary, their creation is necessary; but it is not sufficient. For the organization of a quality search, one must take into consideration attribute 2 of POIN.

Now we return to the function of an IR system. Recall that it was defined as follows: The function of a documentary information retrieval system is to fulfill an optimal (from the user's point of view) retrieval of information to satisfy this user's POIN with any information about the user's POIN given to the system. It should be pointed out that the requirement about *any information* about the POIN is a consideration of attribute 2 of POIN, which means that regardless of how well (or how badly) the request is stated, the user must obtain optimal output from the system. Recall that the concept "optimal" always means the best of all possibilities in the framework of a given system. Because "optimal" is the best of all possibilities, then consequently more than one possibility must be realized in the system. But this is not enough. The system must contain a mechanism permitting a choice of the best of possible alternatives. And what does more than one alternative or more than one possibility of realizing a search mean? We mentioned earlier that the developers of a system aim to use the best (from their point of view) available methods for realization of each process in the IR system. In other words, in functioning systems the developers use one method for indexing documents, one method for constructing query formulations, and one method of feedback. However, there does not exist (and in view of attribute 2 of POIN it is unlikely that it could be created) a method that on all collections (thematic, quantitative, linguistic, for any length of time), for all users (at any moment of their activity, for any request), for all IR systems would give in all respects better results than others. In other words, if in some system one algorithm gives better search results than another algorithm, for example, in 75% of the cases, then it means that we should use a different algorithm in the remaining 25% of the cases. Therefore the following conclusion suggests itself: each of the available methods (algorithms) under specific conditions can lead to lower results than any other. Thus an IR system with more than one possibility of realizing a search is a system that uses not one (best from some point of view) method that realizes some process, but some set of methods.

It should be pointed out that when we talk about multiplicity of methods we could also include a case of one algorithm containing a parameter(s) that when assign different values would result in different output. For example, in the algorithm for the automatic construction of query formulations described in Chapter 7, it is possible to assign different values of zones, which would result in different query formulations and, hence, different outputs. Clearly, for each search request it is possible to obtain many outputs for each iteration and, as mentioned earlier, this is one of the necessary conditions for performing an optimal search.

We recall that to perform information retrieval it is necessary to translate into the IRL the documents (first process) and information about the POIN, that is, the search requests (second process); next it is necessary to compare the document profiles and the query formulation according to some chosen criterion, that is, to perform a search (third process). However, as indicated previously, for optimal satisfaction of the POIN this is not sufficient because in the IR system realizing optimal search, at least one of the processes must contain more than one method. Therefore it is necessary to realize the choice of the best method (or combination of methods) for this process (or processes) or the best state of the system, which is essentially a fourth process. To make this choice it is necessary to have some values of search parameters for each of the alternatives and then to choose the best available among them, which assumes an evaluation of the output for each alternative; consequently, before beginning the work of the system, the choice of its optimal state is not possible. Only after obtaining this evaluation (preferably from the user) is it possible to use it for the choice, and this means the presence of feedback in the IR system.

Notice that in this case the character of feedback is quite different. Indeed, for the choice of the system's best state, that is, the state that will provide the best service for the individual user, there is no need to have additional information about POIN. The feedback process for optimization of the search is fundamentally different from the feedback process used for adaptation to the boundaries of POIN. For this reason, all the approaches and algorithms used in the adaptive feedback cannot be used in solving the problem of optimization. In this case it is necessary to create a principally different mechanism that will use different information from feedback, specifically information about the algorithm (or a set of algorithms) that resulted in the most successful search. The source of this information should be the user's evaluation of the output (for the same reasons as those given for adaptive feedback). In other words, the user's evaluation of the pertinence of the documents in the output is sufficient for choosing the best state of the system for a given user's search request.

Methods for a feedback of this type were not studied by the researchers, although the problem of an optimal search (and the questions it raises) was considered in great detail in our papers published from 1972 through 1974 (see, e.g., Voiskunskii & Frants, 1974). This is because for a long time researchers did not know how to automate the choice of the system's best state. The first algorithm realizing feedback for optimal search for IR systems with a static collection of documents was published in 1993 (Frants et al., 1993). (It will be described later.)

In discussing adaptation we pointed out that it seems most expedient (in creating adaptive IR systems) to control such an element as BIQ. But what should be controlled during the optimization of the search? We consider this question next.

As mentioned earlier, to choose the system's best state there has to be a set of different methods realizing, at a minimum, one process involved in forming an output in an IR system. Now we consider for which process (processes) it is the most expedient to consider several methods. Note that the following considerations are similar to those that provided the basis for control by correcting query formulations when adapting to the user's POIN.

Clearly, a set of different methods can be used in realizing any process in the system. A system that uses a set of different algorithms for at least one process affecting the output in the system is called *multiversion* (terminology originated in Frants et al., 1993). Because we restrict our discussion to the systems using the Boolean search criterion, we will only consider the expediency of multiple alternatives for the first and second processes, that is, for indexing documents and indexing search requests.

The indexing of documents by many methods, in spite of possible theoretical expediency, is not practically feasible. The problem is that indexing documents (particularly large collections of documents) is a time-consuming operation, and multiversion indexing would therefore require a substantial amount of time. In addition, space requirements for several versions of indexed documents might increase proportionally to the number of versions. Hence, we assume that only one version of document indexing is used, although the following discussion could be extended to multiversion indexing.

It is more practical to use the multiversion approach in constructing query formulations. There are several reasons why this is the case. First, as a rule, the collection of search requests in the system is many times smaller than the collection of documents. Second, the requests in many cases are shorter than the documents. Third, it is usually not necessary to keep the query formulations in the memory of the system.

Thus for creating an IR system capable of optimal search we will require the presence in this system of some set of algorithms for constructing query formulations. Clearly it must also contain a mechanism that permits a choice of the best available algorithm for each concrete request. To develop such a mechanism it is necessary to know how to evaluate the algorithms effectively (with a reasonable amount of effort) in order to determine which of them leads to the best search results for a given search request. Thus creation of a method of evaluating a search is a necessary condition for the creation of an IR system realizing optimal search. Next we describe a criterion for evaluating different alternatives.

9.8
Criterion for Selection of the Best System's State

In choosing the best among available system's states we will consider the outputs obtained by different query formulations. Let us assume that, on the basis of one search request, we construct a set of several query formulations (using different algorithms and/or parameters of these algorithms) and obtain a corresponding set of outputs as the result of the search in the same collection of documents. For each output, n will denote the number of documents in the output and r will denote the number of pertinent documents in the output. Then the best query formulation will be the one that provides the output with the highest value of r^2/n. Clearly, we need a justification for this criterion. The detailed description of this criterion and its justification was given in Voiskunskii (1982; 1987). Moreover, it will be discussed in great detail in Chapter 10. However, for the benefit of the reader we briefly discuss it now.

In comparing the quality of query formulations we will consider the quality of their corresponding outputs; that is, higher quality output indicates better query formulation. The question of designing and choosing characteristics to describe the quality of the output has been studied extensively (Bollmann, 1978; Cleverdon, 1970; Cooper, 1973; Kraft & Bookstein, 1978; Lancaster, 1979; Raghavan, Bollmann, & Jung, 1989; van Rijsbergen, 1979; Sparck-Jones, 1978). In these studies special attention was paid to characteristics that were the most convenient from a practical point of view. Such characteristics are typically based on standard measures of output quality: recall, denoted by R, and precision, denoted by P. For example, one of the commonly used characteristics is $R + P$. Larger values of $R + P$ indicate better output. This and other characteristics described in the literature require the computation of the number of pertinent documents in the entire collection of documents, denoted by c. For example, $R + P = r/c + r/n$.

The use in a search process of any characteristic that would require the user to determine all the pertinent documents in the entire collection of documents for every user's request is completely unacceptable because it is equivalent to the user conducting a manual search in the collection. Therefore, in developing an automatic method for determining the system's best state (on the basis of the best output) it is necessary to find a characteristic that would not require such a time-consuming operation as finding pertinent documents in a large collection of documents. Such characteristic, $\sqrt{R \cdot P}$, was proposed in 1982 (Voiskunskii, 1982). This characteristic allows one to compare the quality of outputs without computing c. The use of this characteristic seems to be justifiable because the function $\sqrt{R \cdot P}$ is monotonic in both R and P. However, it is possible to provide another argument that makes the use of $\sqrt{R \cdot P}$ even more desirable.

Let us assume that for a given search request it is known which documents in the collection are pertinent, and there is an output obtained as the result of the search using this request (more precisely, a corresponding query formulation). Let R and P be the recall and precision levels for this output. Now consider two vectors:

$$K = (k_1, k_2, \ldots, k_N) \text{ and } V = (v_1, v_2, \ldots, v_N),$$

where N is the number of documents in the collection; $k_i = 1$ if the i-th document in the collection is pertinent and $k_i = 0$ otherwise; and $v_i = 1$ if the i-th document is found during the search and $v_i = 0$ otherwise. Notice that these vectors represent the results of evaluating the collection of documents: K represents the user's evaluation of the documents' relevance to his or her information need, and V represents the system's evaluation of documents' relevance to the user's search request. Clearly, in the case of ideal output, vectors K and V would coincide. In most cases, however, the two vectors are going to be different and the quality of the output is determined by how "close" K and V are. The natural measure of "closeness" between two vectors, which is used in many fields (including information retrieval), is the cosine of the angle between the two vectors. We will use this measure to evaluate the quality of the output.

Let ϕ be the angle between vectors K and V defined in a standard way. We will now show that $\cos \phi = \sqrt{R \cdot P}$. The number of 1s in vector K is equal to c (number of pertinent documents), hence,

$$\sum_{i=1}^{N} (k_i)^2 = c.$$

The number of 1s in vector V is equal to n (number of documents in the output), hence,

$$\sum_{i=1}^{N} (v_i)^2 = n.$$

The number of positions where 1 is contained simultaneously in K and V is equal to r (number of pertinent documents in the output), hence,

$$\sum_{i=1}^{N} (k_i \cdot v_i) = r.$$

Then

$$\cos \phi = \frac{\sum_{i=1}^{N} (k_i \cdot v_i)}{\sqrt{\sum_{i=1}^{N} (k_i)^2} \cdot \sqrt{\sum_{i=1}^{N} (v_i)^2}} = \frac{r}{\sqrt{c} \cdot \sqrt{n}}$$

$$= \sqrt{\frac{r^2}{c \cdot n}} = \sqrt{\frac{r}{c} \cdot \frac{r}{n}} = \sqrt{R \cdot P}.$$

Hence, the use of characteristic $\sqrt{R \cdot P}$ to evaluate the quality of the output is, indeed, justified.

Now we want to show that the use of $\sqrt{R \cdot P}$ to compare different outputs will avoid the computation of c. Let q_1 and q_2 be two query formulations (constructed from the same search request) with two corresponding outputs with recall and precision levels R_1, P_1 and R_2, P_2. Because both query formulations are based on the same request, the number of pertinent documents in the entire collection c is the same for searches based on q_1 and q_2. Hence,

$$R_i = \frac{r_i}{c}, \ P_i = \frac{r_i}{n_i}, \ R_i \cdot P_i = \frac{r_i^2}{c \cdot n_i},$$

where r_i is the number of pertinent documents and n_i is the number of documents in the i-th output ($i = 1, 2$). To determine which of the two outputs (corresponding to q_1 and q_2) is better, we need to compare the values $\sqrt{R_1 \cdot P_1}$ and $\sqrt{R_2 \cdot P_2}$ (the output is better if its $\sqrt{R \cdot P}$ value is larger). Hence, we are interested in finding the order of $\sqrt{R_1 \cdot P_1}$ and $\sqrt{R_2 \cdot P_2}$, that is $\sqrt{R_1 \cdot P_1} < \sqrt{R_2 \cdot P_2}$ or $\sqrt{R_1 \cdot P_1} > \sqrt{R_2 \cdot P_2}$. But the order of $\sqrt{R_1 \cdot P_1}$ and $\sqrt{R_2 \cdot P_2}$ is the same as the order of $R_1 \cdot P_1$ and $R_2 \cdot P_2$ and, hence, the same as the order of r_1^2/n_1 and r_2^2/n_2 since c is a nonnegative constant. Therefore, we conclude that to determine the order of $R_1 \cdot P_1$ and $R_2 \cdot P_2$, it is sufficient to consider r_1^2/n_1 and r_2^2/n_2 and, hence, in comparing the quality of different outputs we just need to compare their corresponding values of r^2/n. The criterion for the comparison of outputs (r^2/n) described here avoids a time–consuming user's evaluation of the documents in the collection. The only task required from the user is determining the pertinent documents in the output (parameter r), which is a normal (and natural) task in the interaction between the user and the system. Clearly, it is preferable for the user (rather than some intermediary) to determine which documents are pertinent. The user's evaluation of the output will be used by a feedback mechanism of a multiversion IR system for determining the best query formulation (or a combination of query formulations). Therefore, it is important for IR systems performing optimal search to have a feedback mechanism that is capable of evaluating different versions of query formulations and determining the best one (or best ones) among the existing versions. In the 1993 paper such feedback was called *selective feedback* because it realized the process of selecting the most appropriate state of the system (Frants et al., 1993).

We have discussed the properties of feedback for optimal search. Note that the methods and the algorithms for selective feedback also depend on how the collection of documents is used: statically or dynamically. Therefore, the feedback algorithms, described next, which consider the choice of an optimal alternative for the search, are oriented toward a specific collection type. The developed selection criterion r^2/n permits evaluation not only of query formulations but also of every subrequest in each query formulation. This is especially important for a dynamic collection of documents.

In describing the algorithms for selective feedback, we will assume that in an IR system realizing an optimal search the Boolean search criterion is used, and this system includes some set of algorithms for constructing query formulations in Boolean form. This set could, for example, consist of the algorithms proposed by Voiskunskii and Frants (1971), Dillon, Ulmscmeider, and Desper (1983), Salton, Buckley, and Fox (1983), Frants and Shapiro (1991a), and others. In each of these algorithms it is possible to use a marked set of documents as a search request, and each of the algorithms constructs a query formulation in Boolean form. For these reasons, all further discussion is applicable to the algorithms for constructing query formulations in IR systems realizing optimal search.

Before the initial search for a given search request, the query formulations are constructed by each of the available algorithms. The initial search is then conducted by each of the constructed query formulations and all outputs are combined. In other words, combined output will be formed as a set union of all the outputs obtained by each query formulation.

9.9
Selective Algorithm for the Static Collection of Documents

As was indicated earlier, the initial search is performed for each of these query formulations, and all of the outputs are combined into one output (duplicates are removed), which is given to the user. The user evaluates this output—that is, the user indicates which documents are pertinent to his or her information need—and then returns the results to the system. The algorithm begins by checking if there are any pertinent documents in the output. If no pertinent documents are found in the output, then the algorithm stops (because there is no additional information for the selection of the best alternative). In general, this does not mean there is no more interaction between the user and the system. For example, the user can reformulate the request or change the search parameters (such as altering the acceptable number of documents in the output).

If pertinent documents exist in the combined output, the feedback algorithm computes the value r^2/n for each individual output (corresponding to a specific query formulation) containing at least one pertinent document. The output with the largest value r^2/n indicates that the algorithm that constructed the corresponding query formulation is the most appropriate (gives the best search results) for the given search request and a specific user. This algorithm is going to be used in the subsequent iterations of the feedback algorithm.

Denote by A the algorithm that constructed the query formulation (denoted by PQ) with the best output (largest r^2/n). The feedback algorithm constructs a new marked set by combining the marked set (used by A in constructing PQ) with the pertinent documents found by the user in the previous output. Then on the basis of this new marked set the A algorithm constructs a new query formulation, denoted by AQ (auxiliary query formulation). This query formulation is then compared to PQ, and the algorithm constructs a new query formulation, denoted by NQ, by removing from AQ all subrequests that appear in PQ and also those subrequests that contain any subrequests appearing in PQ.

It is possible for NQ to be empty (if all subrequests of AQ were removed). In this case, the algorithm stops because no new documents could be found. If NQ is not empty, then another search is performed and new documents not appearing in previous outputs (if such exist) are given to the user. This is the end of one feedback iteration.

In cases where several outputs have the same largest value $r^2/n,$ that is, there is more than one "best" algorithm, all of these algorithms are used to construct their AQs and then the logical operator OR ($\vee$) is used to join them into one query formulation (AQ). Notice that this AQ is also in a disjunctive normal form. Then NQ is constructed by removing from this AQ all the subrequests that either coincide with subrequests in the PQs constructed by the best algorithms or contain those subrequests as proper subsets (see the previous example). The NQ is used to perform the search and the new documents (not appearing in previous output) are given to the user.

Clearly it is possible to extend this process through several iterations. In this case, the pertinent documents found by the combined query formulation are added to the marked set used in the previous search and all the algorithms in the system are used to construct a new combined query formulation. This process is repeated for the new iteration, and if the evaluation of the alternatives gives the same result as the evaluation of alternatives from the previous iteration, then the system can be changed into a better state. Clearly, the number of iterations for which the results of evaluation coincide, as well as the level of this coincidence, has to be determined by the designers of the system and could vary substantially from system to system. After the system is changed into a better state it is expedient, for improving the quality of information service, to use adaptive feedback (a possible algorithm for adaptive feedback was described earlier). The expediency of such combined feedback was discussed in Chapter 4.

The algorithm for selective feedback stops in the following cases:

1. No evaluation of the output is provided by the user.
2. No pertinent documents are found (by the user) in the output.
3. No new subrequests are constructed, that is, NQ is empty.
4. No new documents are found by the system.

In Table 9.7 the main steps in the feedback algorithm for the IR system performing optimal search in a static collection of documents are described.

The preceding algorithms may be further developed and modified to satisfy special requirements of the developers as well as to satisfy users of the system. For example, when the collection of documents is very large (say, in a retrospective search) and the size of the output is too large for the user to consider, there are several ways to improve the feedback algorithm.

1. Using only part of the entire collection of documents at the first step. The selection of the sample is done randomly, and only this sample is used in the process of choosing the best algorithm and correcting query formulations. Then, at the user's request, the search with the corrected query formulation may be performed on the entire collection.

Table 9.7
Summary of the Steps in One Iteration of the Selective Feedback Algorithm for a Static Collection of Documents

1. Pertinent documents from the previous output (using the user's evaluation) are selected.
2. If the previous search was based on a combined query formulation, constructed by more than one algorithm, then these algorithms are compared using the criterion $\sqrt{R \cdot P}$ (or more precisely r^2/n) and the best algorithm is selected.
3. The best algorithm (algorithms if there are more than one) is used to construct an auxiliary query formulation (AQ) (combined from several query formulations in the case of more than one algorithm).
4. A new query formulation (NQ) is constructed by removing from AQ all subrequests that appear in PQ and subrequests that include subrequests of PQ.
5. If NQ is not empty, the search is performed and the preliminary output is obtained.
6. A new output is formed by removing from the preliminary output all the documents appearing in previous outputs. Then the new output (if not empty) is given to the user.

2. Restricting the output given to the user by finding the intersection of the outputs obtained during a search—by using different query formulations constructed by different algorithms—rather than by combining all these outputs. This not only reduces the size of the output but also increases the "pertinence" of every document in the output (because it was found by more than one algorithm). In this case, depending on the number of documents in the output and the number of algorithms, it is possible to vary the intersection from two to all of the obtained outputs.

3. Using algorithms for constructing query formulations (at least for the first step), which can restrict the output size and rank the documents in the output on the basis of their pertinence. Examples of such algorithms can be found in Chapter 7.

Notice that the first approach assumes the correction of the query formulation before the search is performed on the entire collection of documents. This correction is performed on the basis of the search characteristic $\sqrt{R \cdot P}$ described earlier. After the search is performed in a subcollection using combined query formulations, and the system obtains the user's evaluation of the pertinence of every document in the combined output, it is not only possible to select the best query formulation but also to compare all subrequests including subrequests from different query formulations. The correction may be done in several different ways. For example, we can select the best subrequests from all query formulations (obtained by different algorithms) used in the search and combine them into one query formulation, which will be used to search the entire collection. Another method would be to select the best algorithm, choose the best subrequests from the query formulation constructed by this algorithm, continue through several iteration steps on the same sample collection accumulating the best subrequests, and finally perform the search on the entire collection by using the combined query formulation.

The second and third approaches are suitable when the user explicitly bounds the number of documents in the output, for example, setting a limit of 20 documents. In this case, the third approach might be preferable because the ranking of documents provides a natural way to restrict the output. In the second approach the size of the output could still exceed the required bound.

9.10

Selective Feedback Algorithm for Dynamic Collection

The algorithm described next, which considers the choice of an optimal alternative for the search, is oriented toward a dynamic collection of documents. As in the case for a static collection, the user's evaluation of the output will be used as input to this algorithm. In other words, the algorithm can proceed only when the user's evaluation is given to the system.

Before the initial search for a given search request, the query formulations are constructed by each of the available algorithms. The initial search is then conducted by each of the constructed query formulations and all outputs are combined. In other words, a combined output will be formed as a set union of all the outputs obtained by each query formulation. Because it is possible that the size of the combined output will be too large, and the user either cannot or will not want to survey it all, the combined output is ranked. Those documents that are found by more than one query formulation are considered more impor-tant (having more "weight") in the ranking; that is, the larger the number of query formulations "matching" the document, the higher its rank. Then the ranked combined output is given to the user for evaluation, and the user marks the pertinent documents. It is obvious that when it is impossible to survey and evaluate all the output, the user will survey and mark only a part of it, and the survey will start with documents with the highest rank. In this case, only the documents analyzed by the user are considered as the system's output. In other words, in this situation the user determines the number of documents in the output. For example, if the system found 170 documents but the user only in-spects the 20 with the highest weight, then this situation is equivalent to the case in which the user requests the output of 20 documents and the system gives the user the 20 most important documents (see, for example, the method suggested by Salton, 1968).

At the first stage, the algorithm tests if there are any pertinent documents in the output. If there are none, the algorithm stops because there is no infor-mation for determining the choice of the system's best state. If pertinent docu-ments do exist, the algorithm determines by which query formulation(s) they are found, and then further analysis is applied to those query formulations by which at least one pertinent document is found. The best query formulation (or their combination), from the point of view of the criterion r^2/n, indicates also the best algorithm that was used in its construction.

After determination of the best algorithm(s), the best subrequests are se-lected from all query formulations that are not among the best. This is done for the following reasons. First, it is possible that the subrequests that do not appear in the best query formulations give good search results and can prove to be ef-fective for subsequent searches. Second, as was indicated earlier in the discussion of the character of feedback in a dynamic collection of documents, the best algorithm(s) will be used later for obtaining a new corrected query formulation, which means that there is no need to select the best subrequests from the best query formulations. Thus, for the evaluation of original subrequests in other than the best query formulations, the same criterion $\sqrt{R \cdot P}$ is used, and the best subrequests are considered to be those for which the value $\sqrt{R \cdot P}$ is *not lower* than value $\sqrt{R \cdot P}$ of the best query formulation.

Then the pertinent documents obtained from the user are added to those on the basis of which the best algorithm(s) constructed the best query formulation. After this, the best algorithm(s) constructs a new, *preliminary* query formulation, where occurrence frequencies of descriptors in document profiles of the new collection are used. Those original subrequests, which were selected before, are added to the obtained query formulation(s), and thus the final query formulation is constructed. Notice that all extraneous subrequests (a subrequest in a query formulation is considered extraneous if it contains another subrequest in the same query formulation) are removed from the final query formulation. Then a new search is performed using this new final query formulation and the new (obtained in the new collection of documents) output is given to the user. This is the end of first feedback iteration allowing us to change the system into better state. Beginning with the second output, the system realizes optimal service, because the best possible alternative was used for the search. Table 9.8 lists the basic steps of the feedback algorithm in an IR system performing optimal search in a dynamic collection of documents. We emphasize that an optimal search proceeds for an individual user and for a specific request regardless of how well the request was formulated, and this raises the quality of information service to the user.

Thus we have shown how an optimal search is realized in practice, that is, how an IR system is able to satisfy the function stated in Chapter 4.

Table 9.8
Basic Steps of the Algorithm for Selective Feedback for a Dynamic Collection of Documents

1. Pertinent documents from previous output are selected based on the user's evaluation of this output.

2. When a combined query formulation constructed by more than one algorithm was used in the previous search, an evaluation of available algorithms proceeds with the help of the criterion $\sqrt{R \cdot P}$. The highest value of this criterion determines the choice of best algorithm(s).

3. With the help of the same criterion $\sqrt{R \cdot P}$, the best original subrequests are determined among other than the best query formulations and those subrequests whose criterion values are not smaller than the highest value are selected for use in the search of the new collection of documents.

4. Pertinent documents found during the previous search are added to those on the basis of which the previous query formulation was constructed; that is, a more precise search request is obtained.

5. On the basis of the new marked set, a new preliminary query formulation is constructed by the best algorithm(s).

6. The final query formulation is constructed by adding the best original subrequests (see Step 3) to the preliminary query formulation.

7. A search is performed using the final query formulation, and a new output is given to the user.

Internal Control

Further improvement in the selective feedback algorithm in an IR system realizing optimal search can be achieved by *internal control,* which we describe next for both static and dynamic collections of documents. First, we look at a static case. After the initial search and the user's evaluation of the output, the best query formulation is determined and the values of r^2/n of all the outputs corresponding to query formulations used in the search are stored. After the first iteration, where the query formulation constructed by the best algorithm is used for the search, the value of r^2/n is computed to further compare the quality of the obtained output with other outputs. If the quality improved as compared to the previous output obtained by using the query formulation constructed by the best algorithm, then this indicates the pragmatism of using this algorithm further. However, if the quality decreased, then the obtained (lower) value is compared to the next highest value (corresponding to the second-best algorithm). If the obtained value in the new search is higher, then the next iteration uses the same algorithm as the previous iteration; otherwise, the next iteration uses the algorithm with the next highest value of r^2/n, and so on.

The additional control avoids a commitment to the algorithm, which was possibly not the best choice. Moreover, if the user's initial search request was not formulated well, then it is possible that at the initial step an algorithm gave better results precisely because the search request was not indicative of the user's information need (this was discussed previously). Then after obtaining additional information about POIN (the user's evaluation of the output), a different algorithm may give better search results. Hence, one of the main functions of internal control is to monitor the correctness of the selection algorithm.

There are other possible approaches to organizing internal control. For example, after selecting the best algorithm(s), other algorithms could still be used to construct query formulations for subsequent searches. The system gives the user only documents that were found using the query formulation constructed by the best algorithm. After receiving the user's evaluation of the output, the system could evaluate other query formulations to determine if they find the same pertinent documents with less noise. It is also possible for evaluating the documents found with other query formulations (and hence not given to the user) to introduce weights analogous to selective feedback for the dynamic collection of documents and to use these weights in selecting the best system's state. These and other approaches should be tested experimentally, but it is important to know that such approaches exist.

In the case of a dynamic collection of documents, the internal control could be implemented as follows. The initial output with the user's evaluation is the basis for the choice of the best algorithm for constructing query formulations. The values of r^2/n are computed for the outputs obtained from all subrequests of the best query formulation, and these values are stored for further analysis. After the search in the new collection of documents using the corrected query formulation (the first iteration) and the user's evaluation of the output, the values of r^2/n are computed for the outputs corresponding to the corrected query formulation and all its subrequests. Then the values of r^2/n for the corrected query formulation and for the previous query formulation are compared. If the quality of the search improved, then the query formulation is corrected and the next iteration is performed. If, on the other hand, the quality was lower, then all individual subrequests of the used query formulation are analyzed. Then the subrequests with a lower search quality than the previous query formulation are selected and divided into two sets. The first set contains all subrequests that were included in the previous query formulation, and the second set contains subrequests that were added after correction. If the first set is larger than the second, then this might indicate (especially, when the second set is empty) that the user's POIN changed and this change was correctly "observed" by the algorithm. Then the query formulation is corrected (for example, by removing the worst subrequests), a new search is performed, and so forth. However, if the second set is larger, then this could mean that the chosen algorithm was not the most appropriate. Hence, a new correction is performed for the previous algorithm and the algorithm with the next highest value of $\sqrt{R \cdot P}$. Then the search is conducted using two (corrected) query formulations, the comparison of the search quality is performed for both query formulations and their subrequests, and so on. If two algorithms have the same highest values of $\sqrt{R \cdot P}$, then the next iteration is performed on the basis of both algorithms. When eventually only one algorithm will give the best evaluation results, we will proceed with this algorithm as previously described.

It is clear that the proposed approach is only one way to realize internal control and, as before, it is important to realize the existence of different approaches to automatic internal control for both the static and the dynamic collection of documents. It is important to point out that the internal control, which becomes feasible with the introduction of the new characteristic $\sqrt{R \cdot P}$ of search quality, is an important part in the process of selective feedback.

9.12

Conclusion

It is difficult to overestimate the importance of feedback for the successful functioning of an IR system. Moreover, because the user is taking part in this process, an automatization of feedback becomes especially important. Such an automatization is a simple and convenient interface between the system and the user because there are no decisions (methodological or strategical) that the user has to make. The user's only responsibility is to evaluate the documents in the output for their pertinence and to provide this information to the system in a natural language (for example, by responding yes or no).

It should be emphasized again that it is possible to organize an optimal search for an individual user in any system, not only the ones that use Boolean search. In this connection, we will indicate some additional interesting possibilities. We mentioned earlier that for performing an optimal search it is more expedient to use a set of different methods for constructing query formulations. But today it is also realistic to use more than one method for indexing documents. In such a case it is not necessary to use a special method of indexing for each user in order to create a personalized collection of document profiles to be searched. The system may contain several versions of indexed documents, which will be used in a search process as follows.

Assume that in some IR system the documents are indexed using two different methods. This could be done in cases where there are two different descriptor dictionaries or when one descriptor dictionary is used together with free text search, for example. Then the system will contain two separate search collections representing the same collection of documents. In such a system the choice of the optimal system's state for an individual user means a choice of the search collection that gives better search results. Clearly, in some cases the best could be considered a search performed on both collections. To realize this approach, it is possible to use algorithms that are similar to the ones described earlier. In this case the initial search for each search request will be performed on both search collections and the combined output will be given to the user for evaluation. Then using the suggested criterion of selection (r^2/n) it is possible to obtain the best system's state.

In the preceding example, only two search collections were mentioned in order to keep our discussion simple. It is clearly possible to use many search collections corresponding to the same collection of documents and moreover to use them in combination with several methods for indexing search requests. This will increase the number of choices and this, in turn, will improve the quality of service provided to the users.

In this chapter we considered the construction (algorithms) of the last elements of an IR system (see Figure 4.8 in Chapter 4), that is, the elements realizing control in IR systems. These elements realize the type of control that leads to the optimal service for an individual user (thereby fulfilling the system's function described in Chapter 4) and also allow the system to adapt to the user's POIN, specifically, to take into account attributes 2, 3, and 4 of POIN. Therefore, now we have a complex of interconnected algorithms capable of realizing a fully automated IR system, thereby fulfilling the system's function to the maximum. Before creating such a system, however, another point has to be considered. Recall that one of the very important steps in creating any system is evaluating its functionality; hence, it is necessary to consider how this evaluation is performed in IR systems. This subject is discussed in the next chapter.

References

Belew, R. K. (1989). Adaptive information retrieval: Using a connectionist representation to retrieve and learn about documents. In Proceedings of the Twelfth Annual International ACMSIGIR Conference on Research and Development in Information Retrieval, Cambridge, MA.

Bollmann, P. (1978). A comparison of evaluation measures for document retrieval systems. *Journal of Informatics, (2)*.

Cleverdon, C. W. (1970). Evaluation of tests of information retrieval systems. *Journal of Documentation, 26.*

Cooper, W. S. (1973). On selecting a measure of retrieval effectiveness. *Journal of the American Society for Information Science, 24.*

Curtice, R. M., & Rosenberg, V. (1965). Optimizing retrieval results with man–machine interaction. Lehigh University, Center for the Information Science Report.

Dillon, M. (1980). Automatic relevance feedback in Boolean retrieval systems. *Journal of Documentation, 36.*

Dillon, M., Ulmscmeider, J., & Desper, J. (1983). A prevalence formula for automatic relevance feedback in Boolean systems. *Information Processing and Management, 19*(1).

Frants, V. I., & Brush, C. B. (1988). The need for information and some aspects of information retrieval systems construction. *Journal of the American Society for Information Science, 39,* 86–91.

Frants, V. I., & Shapiro, J. (1991a). Algorithm for automatic construction of query formulations in Boolean form. *Journal of the American Society for Information Science, 42*(1).

Frants, V. I., & Shapiro, J. (1991b). Control and feedback in a documentary information retrieval system. *JASIS, 42*(9), 623–634.

Frants, V. I., Shapiro, J., & Voiskunskii, V. G. (1993). Multiversion information retrieval systems and feedback with mechanism of selection. *Journal of the American Society for Information Science, 44*(1).

Frants, V. I., Shapiro, J., & Voiskunskii, V. G. (1996). Development of IR systems: New direction. *Information Processing and Management, 32*(3).

Gordon, M. (1988). An adaptive approach to document retrieval provides extremely effective distribution of various document descriptors. *Communications of ACM, 31.*

Kraft, D., & Bookstein, A. (1978). Evaluation of information retrieval systems: A decision theoretic approach. *Journal of the American Society for Information Science, 29.*

Lancaster, F. W. (1979). Information retrieval systems: Characteristics, testing, evaluation. New York: John Wiley & Sons.

Meadow, C. T. (1967). *The analysis of information systems.* New York: John Wiley and Sons.

Raghavan, V. V., Bollmann, P., & Jung, G. S. (1989). Retrieval system evaluation using recall and precision: Problems and answers (extended abstract). Proceedings of the Twelfth Annual International ACMSIGIR Conference on Research and Development in Information Retrieval, Cambridge, MA.

Rickman, J. T. (1972). Design considerations for a Boolean feedback system with automatic relevance feedback processing. Proceedings of the ACM Annual Conference, New York.

van Rijsbergen, C. J. (1979). *Information retrieval* (2nd ed.). London: Butterworths.

Salton, G. (1968). Automatic information organization and retrieval. New York: McGraw Hill.

Salton, G., Buckley, C., & Fox, E. A. (1983). Automatic query formulation in information retrieval. *Journal of the American Society for Information Science, 34.*

Salton, G., Fox, E. A., & Voorhees, E. (1985). Advanced feedback methods in information retrieval. *Journal of the American Society for Information Science, 36.*

Salton, G., Voorhees, E., & Fox, E. A. (1984). A comparison of two methods for Boolean query relevance feedback. *Information Processing and Management, 20.*

Sparck-Jones, K. (1978). Performance averaging for recall and precision. *Journal of Informatics, 2.*

Voiskunskii, V. G. (1982). Choosing an optimal version of search: Experimental investigation. *Nauchno-Teknicheskaya Informatsiya (NTI),* ser. 2, no. 9, 10–19.

Voiskunskii, V. G. (1987). Applicability of search characteristics. *Nauchno-Teknicheskaya Informatsiya (NTI), 21.*

Voiskunskii, V. G., & Frants, V. I. (1971). Automatic feedback in documentary information retrieval systems. *Nauchno-Teknicheskaya Informatsiya (NTI),* ser. 2, no. 2.

Voiskunskii, V. G., & Frants, V. I. (1974). Correction of query formulations in documentary information retrieval systems. *Nauchno-Teknicheskaya Informatsiya (NTI),* ser. 2, no. 2, 1–12.

Wiener, N. (1961). *Cybernetics or control and communication in the animal and the machine.* New York–London: The MIT Press and John Wiley & Sons.

Bibliographic Remarks ⎯⎯⎯⎯⎯⎯⎯⎯⎯⎯⎯⎯⎯⎯⎯⎯⎯

We also recommend the following publications.

Frants, V. I., & Shapiro, J. (1991). Control and feedback in a documentary information retrieval system. *JASIS, 42*(9), 623–634.

Frants, V. I., Shapiro, J., & Voiskunskii, V. G. (1993). Multiversion information retrieval systems and feedback with mechanism of selection. *Journal of the American Society for Information Science, 44*(1).

Salton, G., & Buckley, C. (1990). Improving retrieval performance for relevance feedback. *Journal of the American Society for Information Science, 41.*

10

Evaluation of Search Results

10.1
Introduction

As was shown in the previous chapter, an IR system construction is completed after development of adaptation and optimization mechanisms, that is, after creation of the last element of the IR system structure. It should be emphasized that the construction discussed in Chapters 6 to 9 implements the structure of the fully automated IR system performing the function defined for this system in Chapter 4. Now it would seem that the last stage is to implement the developed construction (in this case, algorithms), and this step is more technological than research oriented. However, implementation is not the last stage. When describing the system approach, we demonstrated that yet another stage exists that is very important for the creation of a system; that stage is evaluating what has been created. In other words, one must be able to evaluate how the construction of the developed system fulfills the defined function. This is important not only for better understanding the performance of the created system, but also for improving it in the future. Thus, it would be impossible to create and develop information retrieval systems and keep them in service unless evaluation is made both of the information search process itself and of the systems implementing this process.

This fact was recognized long ago in information science, as witnessed by the number of publications that concern these problems. These publications discuss a wide variety of topics related to evaluation, including the indexing languages used, the indexer's skill, indexing time, the mean number of terms assigned to documents and queries, query form, output form, file size, recall and precision of the search, query processing time, cost of the search, economic efficiency, functional efficiency, and the measurement precision of individual parameters. The variety of problems illustrates the complexity of the task as well as the lack of a uniform understanding of what must be evaluated and how the evaluation must be done. It is impractical, within the scope of this book, to discuss even briefly all facets of evaluation. Therefore, we must define our primary consideration in this intricate labyrinth of problems. To this end, let us look at what is to be evaluated; in other words, what will be our primary concentration when evaluating the results of information retrieval and the IR systems performing the search?

Aspects of Evaluating

We stated in Chapter 2, when considering the information need (IN), that any information process is generated by IN and is meaningful only in connection with its satisfaction. It is quite evident that information search is one of such processes, and an analysis of the present-day information crisis (see Chapter 3) shows that this process is of the utmost importance. Recall, that various types of IN exist and that they are characterized by a certain unique set of inherent properties (Frants & Brush, 1988). This is important in that, as stated earlier, to satisfy diverse types of IN, various types of systems must be created, respectively implementing different information search processes, that is, systems capable of taking into account sets of properties inherent to a particular IN type are needed. This is what determines both structural and design differences between IR systems to be created. However, is it necessary to use different means to evaluate searches carried out in various types of systems? In other words, do IN properties affect information search evaluation? As an example, let us consider IN types such as POIN and CIN, which we have singled out previously.

As discussed in Chapter 4, IR systems that have been developed to satisfy CIN are usually called factographic information retrieval systems, whereas IR systems created to satisfy POIN are called document retrieval systems (or sometimes text retrieval systems). As we also discussed earlier, in a case of a documentary IR system, for instance, such an important parameter as recall is used for search evaluation. However, it may be unused (superfluous) for evaluating factographic retrieval. Instead, we will use, for example, the "search success" concept: the search was successful if the required information was found; otherwise, the search was unsuccessful. (Generally, it is inessential in this case how many documents containing this information will be selected, whether one or a hundred documents. In our opinion, one document is even preferable.) This is apparent from attribute 3 for POIN and attribute 3 for CIN (see Figure 2.2). Thus, quite evidently, in information search evaluation one must take into account the type of IN to be satisfied by the search. Because in this book we consider only POIN satisfaction and only those IR systems that realize the information search for POIN satisfaction, we will discuss the evaluation of the information search for POIN satisfaction, that is, the document information search.

Regarding realization (organization) of the information search, it should be noted that it is also not quite singular. At present, there are two major approaches to realization of information search: document search with collection partitioning and document search with document ranking. Publications on document search deal mostly with these two approaches. Let us look at them in more detail.

Document search with collection partitioning is a process that results from dividing the search collection into two subcollections: (1) documents to be given to the user as an answer to the user's search request and (2) the rest of the documents in the collection. In this case, the output resulting from such a search is formally generated using a well-defined and explicit output criterion; that is, it is generated (automatically) without the user or anybody else browsing through the collection of documents. Generally, a large majority of systems do this kind of document search in practice, most of them being Boolean systems (discussed in previous chapters).

The other approach is a document search with document ranking. This search involves ranking search collection documents according to a decreasing degree of a certain formally calculated correspondence of documents to the search request and then generating output during browsing (usually by the user) of the ranked search collection. In other words, the document search with document ranking involves two stages: (1) ranking the collection of documents and (2) having the user browse through these documents (naturally, this is done after document ranking). It is understood that the user usually looks at only a negligible part of the collection, that is, those documents that have the highest correspondence values, and these documents form the output. This document search method has not been widely adapted in practice. Still, a great number of experiments associated with this approach have been conducted for more than 30 years. The most prominent system in this approach worth mentioning here is the well-known experimental system SMART, which was the first system capable of realizing this type of search (Salton & McGill, 1983).

To generate output (using the document ranking method) an "implicit" output criterion is used. "Implicitness" of the criterion means that it is the user who decides whether to include a document into the output (the user decides at his or her own discretion whether to browse through that particular document in the ranked collection); the output criterion, therefore, is not defined explicitly (and hence, not formally) in this situation.

As we have emphasized, we are seeking to create a fully automatic IR system. Naturally, use of the "implicit" output criterion makes this impossible, because the "central" subsystem of the IR system, which is the search subsystem, cannot operate automatically in this case, at least not fully. Therefore, only the first method of document search is of interest to us, and in discussing the problem of evaluation we will assume the type of search where the collection is divided into two subcollections: documents to be given to the user as an answer to his or her search request and documents not to be given to the user. In particular, as stated previously, we will use the Boolean output criterion.

As for document search evaluation, it is possible to consider both partial and complex search parameters. Partial parameters include parameters such as search time, recall level, and output form, among others. Complex parameters concern the economic efficiency and functional efficiency of the search. Usually economic efficiency is defined as a measure of expended money (or, in some instances, the time) needed for the system to perform its function (Salton, 1975). (In some cases, economic efficiency is evaluated by the profit from operating the system.)

Functional efficiency, it should be stressed, characterizes the quality of fulfillment of a function by the IR system. However, how should we understand the quality of function fulfillment? There are various opinions on this point. In some cases, consistency of fulfillment, which is usually called "performance," is considered to be the most important. However, of special interest for the researchers is *how* the goal of creating the system has been achieved by fulfilling its function. In other words, the functional efficiency of the search is usually defined as the extent to which it achieved the goal for which the search is carried out.

As stated earlier, the goal of a document search is to find information that will satisfy POIN. The higher the ability of the search output to satisfy POIN, the higher the search quality. Quite naturally, from the point of view of a particular user, an output will be of highest quality if it contains all those and only those documents from the search collection that satisfy his or her POIN. In this case, the system can be considered as having the highest value of functional efficiency. This is the goal that all developers, theoretically, are striving to reach. However, when discussing IR system operation, we pointed out that this value is very difficult to achieve (at least, at present). This is why function definitions do not contain such a quality requirement. However, because the closest approximation to the ideal means the highest functional efficiency of search, an evaluation of functional efficiency not only permits us to judge how far the created system is from the ideal, but it also makes it possible for us to compare it with other systems. Furthermore, such an evaluation permits us to make a judgment on how successful the technical solutions found during development of the system are.

All of the evaluations mentioned are important to the creation and development of IR systems. However, as stated earlier, it is impossible to consider the whole specter within the limits of this book. This is one of the reasons why we chose not to include the economic aspects of information search and related search parameters and to focus our attention on problems of evaluating the functional efficiency of a document search and those partial search parameters that are aspects of functional efficiency, such as the recall level of search.

Now that we have determined what aspects of information search evaluations will be discussed subsequently, we would like to point out that, in addition to document search and systems realizing it, there are a number of other objects that we are interested in evaluating in the context of this book. Document search consists of several distinct processes (see Chapter 4), such as translation of documents from natural language into IRL or translation of search requests from natural language into IRL. It is well known that such subprocesses are realized differently in different systems, even if the same IRL is used. Therefore, which realizations of a particular subprocess must be used in a particular situation? To answer this question it is necessary to be able to evaluate these subprocesses. This ability is crucial in designing and developing documentary IR systems, and the subprocesses in question must be included in the list of objects to be evaluated by developers of an IR system. As a matter of fact, we discussed this situation briefly in Chapter 6. Here we will examine the problem in greater detail.

Different approaches are available for evaluating subprocesses. For example, the evaluation may be based on the degree to which a process result corresponds with a standard result (for example, correspondence of the document profile, obtained by the corresponding subprocess, with the standard document profile). In this case, results will be regarded as standard if they have been obtained using the same initial data, while the subprocess has been performed by an expert. However, in this case there is no guarantee that a result (document profile) *close* to the standard one will perform better during the document search than a result that is more *remote* from the standard one. In other words, in this case the evaluation in question cannot predict how the evaluated process will affect document search results. Quite naturally, we are interested in an evaluation that is capable of making such prediction. Therefore we need an alternative approach in forming standard results or an alternative approach in carrying out evaluation.

As for the "correct" approach in forming required standards, to our knowledge it is not yet available in information science. Therefore, let us consider an alternative evaluation approach. This approach to evaluation of a corresponding subprocess is based on the results of searches conducted using this subprocess. Actually, in this case too there is the problem mentioned in Chapter 6, which has no satisfactory solution as yet. The point is that such subprocesses do not form search results alone; instead they form them jointly with other subprocesses available in the system. In such occurrences, there may be a situation in which the considered realization of a certain subprocess in combination with one set of realizations of the rest of the subprocesses will ensure, as a rule, a high-quality search, whereas when combined with another set of realizations of the same subprocesses the search quality, as a rule, will be low. Therefore, when one evaluates such a subprocess using available search results, one must know how other subprocesses have affected these results and take their effects into consideration. As noted, this problem has no satisfactory solution as yet, and regretfully we did not find any published information worth discussing in this book in connection with the problem in question.

It follows, therefore, that we also are not ready to discuss the general case of the evaluation in question. At the same time, in an important particular case we can present the general outline of the method of evaluation in question. We assume in this particular case that realizations of all subprocesses except the evaluated ones have already been selected and do not change during use of the evaluated realization. The importance of this case is in the fact that it is natural and occurs quite often in practice, for example, in automatic document indexing systems or in systems using "natural" language (i.e., using a document text as the document profile). All search subprocesses in these systems, except constructing query formulations, are realized according to certain algorithms that are unchanged during sufficiently long periods of time. In other words, in such systems during the period of time under consideration different realizations may only be used in the subprocess of constructing query formulations; that is, these very widely used systems belong to the special case that is of interest to us. For brevity we will refer to the subprocess for constructing query formulations as the QF subprocess.

It is clear that in the systems in question searches carried out on the same search request using different realizations of the QF subprocess may lead to different results, these differences resulting solely from the given realizations. Therefore, one may assume that the functional efficiency of a document search in these cases is determined by the used realization; that is, evaluation of functional efficiency of document search in such systems can be regarded as an indirect evaluation of the QF subprocess. If a functional efficiency evaluation is expressed numerically, it will be reasonable to use the determined values as values obtained as an evaluation result for the QF subprocess. For example, an evaluation based on such values will be quite justified if it is used to compare different realizations of the QF subprocess (in the event that the search is conducted on the same search request), because in the context of the discussed evaluation the best realization will ensure the highest functional efficiency of the document search. Note that tasks requiring such a comparative evaluation are of great practical value (see Chapters 6 and 7).

At the same time, the special case discussed earlier may require such an evaluation of the realization of a corresponding subprocess (i.e., a subprocess with a "nonprefixed" realization) that it will permit prediction of results of a search conducted using this realization on a search request that is being newly added to the system. For example, it may be necessary to form a set of the "best" realizations of the subprocess in order to use this set for choosing the most appropriate realization for each incoming search request; or, after forming such a set, it may be necessary to decide whether to include in it a newly proposed realization. There is no doubt that the required evaluation will be more difficult to conduct as compared with the preceding evaluation. However, approaches to make such an evaluation have been proposed in information science. These approaches are mostly based on averaging values of functional efficiency that were obtained in a specially organized series of searches. We will discuss this in detail in Chapter 11. We note here that objects that require averaging of the initial set of values for its evaluation will be called *macroevaluated objects*. Thus, the discussed subprocesses of document search can be regarded as macroevaluated objects in certain situations. Some objects, such as information retrieval systems and other objects to be discussed in Chapter 11, can also be regarded as macroevaluated.

Finally, in defining the framework for our consideration of the evaluation problem, we must discuss the following: a human's evaluation of the functional efficiency of a document search is determined by the concept-based views (i.e., views formed in one's mind) of the comparative merits of various outputs (Cherniavsky & Lakhuti, 1970). These concept-based views give a more accurate understanding of functional efficiency and are formed proceeding from a particular task for which the document search is conducted. In other words, it is this task that shapes concept-based views, which determine in the aggregate the position from which functional efficiency of document retrieval is evaluated. We will call these points of view content criteria of functional efficiency evaluation. It should be emphasized that the formation of concrete content criteria is affected to some extent by the scale of pertinence (relevance) that is employed by the user (expert) in analyzing a document. In this and subsequent chapters, we will assume that document analysis will be performed by the user; therefore, in the context of the analysis of a specific document, we will consider only pertinence evaluation. From our point of view, such an analysis is more correct, although it only affects the terminology: the contents of the discussion are not changed by substitution of the term "pertinent" for the term "relevant."

At present, almost always the binary scale is used, which involves two values of pertinence: pertinent and nonpertinent (they may also have numerical equivalents). In our opinion, this situation is due to the fact that it is essential to obtain, as a result of document search, all pertinent documents and nothing but pertinent documents available in the search collection. Generally speaking, the nonpertinence degree of nonpertinent documents (either included or not included in the output) is inessential, because such documents should not be included in the output. This point of view seems to conform to established practice. This is why, in practice, the binary scale of pertinence is sufficient for analyzing document search results. In these cases the documents are considered pertinent if the user judges that they should be included in the output; otherwise they are nonpertinent. It can be presumed that any user is able, in the end, to judge whether the analyzed document must be included in the output. Bearing the previous discussion in mind, we will assume that, unless specified otherwise, a binary scale of pertinence will be used by document users for analysis.

At the same time, during pertinence analysis of a document by a user, there may be situations when the user finds it so difficult to judge whether the analyzed document is pertinent that he or she will deem it helpful to take into account the nonpertinence degree of nonpertinent documents for the evaluation of the document search results. In this event, one of the judgments from a number of alternatives may be necessary: almost pertinent, possibly pertinent, almost nonpertinent, and so forth. Naturally, the binary scale of pertinence is out of the question here. Rather, a fuzzy scale is used, which includes, in addition to the pertinent and nonpertinent values, other values such as almost pertinent, almost nonpertinent, and so on. (All these values can also have numerical equivalents.) We will also consider the possibility of using a fuzzy scale of pertinence in the analysis of documents by the user.

10.3
Problems of Evaluating the Functional Effectiveness of a Document Search

An evaluation of the functional effectiveness of a document search includes the solution to different problems, for example, determining the achieved functional effectiveness level or finding the case of the highest effectiveness. It follows that in the course of the functional effectiveness evaluation one has to assess the quality of the produced output, to compare the outputs in search of the best, and to consider some other questions of a similar nature. As a rule, there are no simple ways to solve these problems. Moreover, in some cases such problems seem impossible to resolve. Suppose, for instance, that two searches (based on a single search request) in a collection of 10,000 documents result in two outputs, one with 9800 nonpertinent documents and 10 pertinent ones and the other with 9900 nonpertinent documents and 15 pertinent ones. It would be impossible to decide which of the two outputs is the best because neither of the two outputs can be considered useful and, in fact, should be rejected by the user irrespective of the number of pertinent documents in the search collection. In other words, there is no sensible way to say which of the two is better. Such outputs are, naturally, considered unacceptable. The outputs that can provide the basis for evaluation of the functional effectiveness we will call *admissible*. For example, the outputs containing only 15 pertinent documents or 20 pertinent and 10 nonpertinent materials can be considered admissible because such outputs allow for the solution of the questions considered in the evaluation process of the functional effectiveness. In the following discussion, unless it is explicitly stated, the outputs in question will be assumed admissible. Of course, our comment on the difficulties of document search evaluation is only relevant to admissible outputs, because with inadmissible outputs a functional effectiveness evaluation would generally seem unnecessary and impossible.

We should stress here that two methods of evaluation are available: formal and by content. With the by-content method, a person evaluates functional effectiveness on the basis of all information needed for this purpose (such as recall or precision level or information obtained in the course of analyzing the pro-

	Pertinent	Nonpertinent	
Retrieved	r	1	N = r + 1
Nonretrieved	b	d	M = b + d
	C = r + b	L = 1 + d	N₀= r + 1 + b + d

Figure 10.1
Conjugate table.

duced outputs and so on). The formal method also consists, in essence, of evaluating functional effectiveness on the basis of all required information, but this
evaluation method follows certain formal rules. Note that certain data, like the
number of pertinent documents in an output, are found by methods that are not
at all formal. However, in the course of evaluating functional effectiveness, such
data are given beforehand and for this reason the discussed method should be
considered a formal one.

The exhaustive information for the evaluation of functional effectiveness
is contained in the so-called conjugate table (Figure 10.1), which shows the state
of the collection after the search and evaluation of the pertinence of its
documents.

Researchers have found, however, that the conjugate table is not very convenient to use, either for the by-content evaluation of functional effectiveness
or for the development of formal rules for such an evaluation. Therefore, search
characteristics were suggested that are based on this table and are more convenient to use for the evaluation purposes. The most popular characteristics were
the recall and precision levels of search mentioned earlier. The way in which
these characteristics are described using the notation in the conjugate table is as
follows:

$$R = \frac{r}{r + b} = \frac{r}{C} \quad \text{is the recall level,}$$

$$P = \frac{r}{r + l} = \frac{r}{N} \quad \text{is the precision level.}$$

One more search characteristic and a parameter describing the search collection,
which are also often used, are noteworthy. We mean by this the characteristic
known as the search specificity:

$$S = \frac{d}{l + d} = \frac{d}{L},$$

and the parameter known as the coefficient of commonality:

$$P_0 = \frac{r + b}{r + l + b + d} = \frac{C}{N_0}.$$

It is interesting to note that these search characteristics and parameter P_0 are not independent of each other and their correspondence follows easily from the one described by Salton (1975). This ratio is written as follows:

$$P(1 - S)(1 - P_0) = R(1 - P)P_0.$$

Thus, in the evaluation of functional effectiveness, the search characteristics defined on the basis of the conjugate table are commonly used.

In the following discussion, we will mostly be concerned with the formal method of evaluation. First, note that outside of the development of content criteria for functional efficiency evaluation, there are practically no questions related to the purely by-content method (with a position to do an evaluation determined by content criteria, and having obtained the data required for the purpose, the evaluator generally acts as he or she sees fit). Second, the consideration of the formal method particularly meets the logic of our discussion; also, this is the only method enabling us to solve problems related to automation of the processes that are important for further progress in the field of document information retrieval (see Chapter 1). Therefore, development of the formal method of functional effectiveness evaluation has an important practical application.

The formal rules used for the discussed method are, naturally, based on search characteristics and usually the following is true:

1. Either, following the specified formal rules, a more complex search characteristic is made up from the search characteristics used in specifying these formal rules—such as $R + P$, which reflects the document search functional effectiveness as a whole and not some of its aspects, say, recall level (we will refer to such a characteristic as a *complex search characteristic* and often abbreviate it to CSC)—or such a CSC is specified as the initial one in the rules.
2. The rules under consideration include a formal criterion that enables one to evaluate the document search functional effectiveness on the basis of the obtained values of the respective CSC.

In Salton (1975), the complex search characteristics are also called single valued measures. We chose to call it a complex search characteristic based on the fact that these characteristics are intended for the evaluation of the complex search parameter. Clearly, use of the discussed formal method in informational practice requires that the CSCs within its framework allow pragmatically justified evaluation of the functional effectiveness; that is, that the obtained values of

the respective CSC would make it possible to draw conclusions similar to those
made by specialists in the course of by-content evaluation of this effectiveness.
Because by-content evaluation is based on a position determined by the totality
of the content criteria, one must use the same totality of the criteria in deciding
on the justifiable use of the specific CSC in a concrete case. Note that different
combinations of such criteria may lead to different solutions to this question
with the same CSC and in the same situations. We will follow the totality of
content criteria that has been formed in a search situation where the search is
related to obtaining some new result (a new method, a new approach, a new
solution, etc.) in the process of scientific activity. This is done primarily because
this situation is one of the most common. (A detailed analysis of search situations
can be found in Chapter 12.)

   It is not realistic to provide the preceding criteria for all possible cases of
evaluation, especially considering the fact that researchers are not always in
agreement about all the details of these criteria. However, for a relatively broad
range of cases determined by the preceding situation we will provide a number
of such criteria, particularly those that, in our view, fit the concept of the discussed criteria on which a majority of experts agree. In fact, many experts have
developed a pretty good idea (at least intuitively) of the content criteria evaluation, which is derived from the situation mentioned. These criteria are as
follows:

1. The closer the search output is to the "ideal" (containing all and only
    pertinent documents from the collection), the higher is the functional
    effectiveness of document search.
2. Recall and precision of the search are equally important (they mutu-
    ally complement each other), at least in cases of a search producing
    recall and precision levels of 0.5 and above.
3. When a document search produces recall and precision levels other
    than those stipulated by the previous criterion, such search character-
    istics may be found to be substantially unequal. For instance, when
    the search produces 0.5 or higher precision with a very low recall, the
    recall would be much more important.

   The formulated criteria, in our opinion, provide a full enough picture of
the position from which document search functional effectiveness is commonly
evaluated. It is on these criteria that a person usually bases his or her by-content
evaluation of functional effectiveness.

   Further, we will note an important fact: the content criteria, in a great
number of cases, leads to a negative resolution of the validity of using the CSC,
thus imposing certain limitations on using the formal method of the functional
effectiveness evaluation. To clarify this note, we will use the example of the most
common search characteristic, $I_1 = R + P$. We will assume that three different

searches for the same search request in a 10,000 document collection with 100 pertinent documents produced outputs that included the following:

1. 50 pertinent and 50 nonpertinent documents
2. 40 pertinent and 27 nonpertinent documents
3. One and only one pertinent document

Clearly, all three outputs are admissible. It seems reasonable to consider the functional effectiveness of the searches resulting in the first and second outputs as admissible while considering that leading to the third output as inadmissible. However, if in these cases the functional effectiveness is evaluated on the basis of achieved values of the complex search characteristic I_1, we find that the effectiveness in all three cases is close ($I_1^1 = 1$, $I_1^2 \approx 0.997$ and $I_1^3 = 1.01$), and, moreover, the highest functional effectiveness is reached in the third case. It means that whichever formal criterion (enabling a functional effectiveness evaluation based on the produced values of I_1) is used in this situation, in these cases it will not ensure a pragmatically justified evaluation of the functional effectiveness. For example, if one uses a "natural" criterion, which presupposes that the functional effectiveness is acceptable with I_1 values close to 1, then evaluating this effectiveness in cases of the searches producing the first and second outputs will be seen as pragmatically justified whereas in the case of the third output it will not be seen as such. (In the following we will assume that document search functional effectiveness is evaluated on the basis of "natural" formal criteria.)

The previous example illustrates the rather serious problem involved in the use of the formal method of functional effectiveness evaluation. The seriousness of the problem is clarified by the fact that the book's authors are not aware of complex search characteristics (probably because there are none and unlikely to appear) that can serve as the basis for a pragmatically justified evaluation of the functional effectiveness in every "admissible" situation, that is, when evaluation is being made of the functional effectiveness of a document search that resulted in admissible outputs.

10.4

Limits of Applicability of Complex Search Characteristics

It follows that to apply any complex search characteristics to an evaluation of the functional effectiveness of a document search, one must have an idea for which set of outputs it is justifiable to use this characteristic. We will call this set of outputs the *domain of objects* for which the complex search characteristic is applicable. Determining the limits of such a domain is one of the important questions discussed in this book.

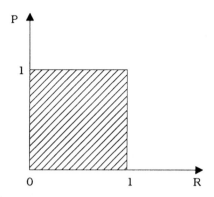

Figure 10.2
The square representing all possible pairs of R and P.

Different approaches may be used to determine the domains of objects for which a complex search characteristic is applicable. In our view a fruitful approach can be based on the following (relatively weak) assumption. Whether the obtained output belongs to the domain under consideration is a question that can be resolved correctly and in full by an analysis of the recall and precision levels achieved in obtaining this particular output.

It follows from this assumption that any two outputs with the same corresponding levels of recall and precision ($R^1 = R^2$ and $P^1 = P^2$) can be regarded as equivalent from the point of view of their membership in the domain of objects for which the complex search characteristic is applicable. This assumption also allows one to describe this domain in the following way. We introduce a coordinate system with recall marked up on the abscissa and precision on the ordinate axis. Then all the value pairs of recall and precision levels achievable in document search are represented by the points in the square delimited by straight lines: $R = 0$, $R = 1$, $P = 0$, and $P = 1$ (Figure 10.2).

This assumption implies that for every point of the square and any complex search characteristic F, the question can be resolved as to whether F will allow a pragmatically justified evaluation of the functional effectiveness of a document search that has resulted in the recall and precision levels corresponding to the coordinates of the given point. It means that a set of all points can be identified within the square where a positive resolution will be found for the question under discussion. We will denote this set by M_F. Then the domain of objects for which the complex search characteristic F is applicable is a set of all outputs whose recall and precision levels correspond to the coordinates of some point in M_F. This M_F set we will call the *domain of applicability of the complex search characteristic F*. Clearly, by defining the limits of M_F we will define the limits of the domain of objects for which characteristic F is applicable.

It would seem from the preceding discussion that one always has to determine the recall and precision levels of the search achieved in the particular situation in order to find out on the basis of the CSC applicability domain whether the formal method of functional effectiveness evaluation can be used in a given situation. Indeed, an overwhelming majority of the known CSCs presupposes such determination. In this, while the precision determination causes no difficulties, it is known that recall cannot be determined by the search results alone. This is a source of some inconvenience in deciding whether the formal method can be applied to evaluate functional effectiveness. To resolve the latter, however, one can use the recall value that is found with the help of information science methods (we will focus on this subject later). Besides, complex search characteristics exist today that make it possible to solve the question under consideration without defining the achieved recall level. Note that the use of such a CSC was demonstrated in Chapter 9. Later on we will describe this possibility in greater detail.

It should be noted that domains of applicability may turn out to be different for different CSCs. It seems that a CSC with very narrow domain of applicability should not be used for evaluating search functional effectiveness. Based on the notion of "domain of applicability," it will be helpful to attempt to formally separate the complex search characteristic that it seems expedient to use from the CSCs whose use is not expedient. Such an attempt, for example, may be based on the following assumption.

Use of a complex search characteristic to evaluate the functional effectiveness of a document search can be considered expedient if and only if the domain of applicability of this characteristic includes a square bounded by straight lines—$R = 0.5$, $R = 1$, $P = 0.5$, $P = 1$—which we will call the determining square (Figure 10.3).

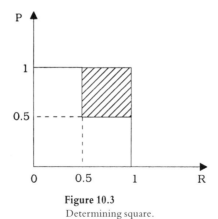

Figure 10.3
Determining square.

Note that it might be possible to determine more precisely the boundaries of the noted subdomain. However, within the framework of this book, we will assume that the subdomain has boundaries outlined in the formulated statement because they correspond to our intuition and allow us to build a workable criterion that enables separation of the CSCs that are expedient to use for evaluation of the functional effectiveness. In view of the previous discussion it is clear that the formulated statement is, in fact, the criterion with which we are concerned, namely, use of a complex search characteristic for evaluation of the functional effectiveness is expedient if the domain of applicability of this characteristic includes the determining square (Figure 10.3), and it is not expedient otherwise. In the following discussion, the complex search characteristics whose domains of applicability include the determining square will be called pragmatically justified.

As we take up the discussion of the determination of limits for the domains of applicability of specific CSCs, we must emphasize that this is important not only in using the formal method for evaluating functional effectiveness but also for information science in general. The authors, unfortunately, cannot offer a formalized method for solving this problem. The principal tools for the solution of this problem apparently are experience with using a specific complex search characteristic in the evaluation of functional effectiveness, a thorough analysis of specific situations involving the evaluation of functional effectiveness, and empirical verification of hypotheses arising during the evaluation process. Therefore, it is not surprising that the boundaries under discussion are quite fuzzy; for this reason any concrete definition of the boundaries of the domain of applicability is tentative, and particular care should be exercised when deciding which points near the assumed boundaries should be included in the domain of applicability of a complex search characteristic. Besides, any proposed boundaries of domain of applicability can be prone to criticism. In spite of this, for certain complex search characteristics, we will indicate boundaries of domain of applicability that we see as justified (with the reservations we make). Such domain boundaries are shown in Figure 10.4 for the complex search characteristic $I_1 = R + P$ (the lines restricting the considered domain of applicability are clear from the figure).

In determining the boundaries of a CSC domain of applicability, particular attention should be paid to those points that have values under 0.5 on the P-axis of coordinates. This is in connection to the somewhat negative view of search results with precision less than 0.5. In our opinion, this negative view has certain objective grounds, which we explain as follows. The number of documents that were not identified correctly during the search (using notation in the conjugate table in Figure 10.1) is equal to $b + l$ (b is the number of nonretrieved pertinent documents, and l is the number of retrieved nonpertinent documents). If $P < 0.5$, then $r/(r + l) < 0.5$, or $l > r$. It follows from this that with P below 0.5, $b + l > b + r = C$, meaning that the number of documents that were not identified correctly during search exceeds the number of pertinent documents

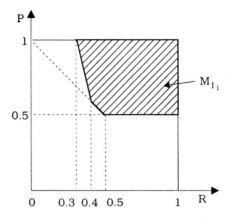

Figure 10.4
The domain of applicability of the complex search characteristic $I_1 = R + P$.

in the search collection. Possibly, this is an implicit cause of a somewhat negative view of the results of such a search.

Further, we will discuss the boundaries of the domain of applicability of the complex search characteristic $I_2 = \sqrt{R \cdot P}$. (This characteristic will be discussed in more detail later on in this book.) We think it is justified to assume that the boundaries of the domain of applicability of the characteristic I_2 are limited by lines: $R = 1$, $P = 0.5$, $P = 1$, and $R \cdot P = 0.01$ (Figure 10.5); maybe the last line could be better specified by the equation $R \cdot P = \beta$, where β is a constant of less than 0.01.

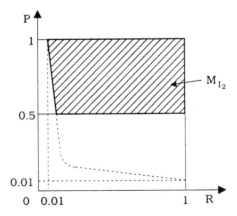

Figure 10.5
The domain of applicability of the complex search characteristic $I_2 = \sqrt{R \cdot P}$.

Two examples will illustrate the justification of the defined boundaries of domains of applicability of characteristics I_1 and I_2. We will assume that two searches are conducted using the same search request on a collection of 10,000 documents of which 100 are pertinent, and two outputs are created as the result of the search, which we will designate A and B. The points of the ROP plane, which correspond to the achieved "recall-precision" pairs (for outputs A and B), we will refer to as the points under analysis in the given example, whereas the values of the complex search characteristic I_1 (I_2) for outputs A and B we will denote, respectively, as $I_1^A(I_2^A)$ and $I_1^B(I_2^B)$. The two examples are as follows:

1. Output A contains 75 pertinent documents and 5 nonpertinent documents; output B contains 95 pertinent and 34 nonpertinent documents. It is evident that the document search functional effectiveness in these cases can be considered as reasonably close and adequately high. At the same time, $I_1^A \approx 1.688$, $I_1^B \approx 1.686$, $I_2^A \approx 0.839$, and $I_2^B \approx 0.836$. It follows from this that, from the point of view of chosen CSC, the functional effectiveness for these two cases is close to each other and quite high. Thus, the points under analysis in this example have been justifiably included into the domain of applicability of complex search characteristics I_1 and I_2.

2. Output A contains exactly 1 document, which is pertinent; output B contains 9 pertinent and 1 nonpertinent document. Evidently, the functional effectiveness of the document search resulting in output A should be considered low. The functional effectiveness of the search resulting in output B should be also considered as low, though this one is higher than that for the search resulting in output A. In these cases, $I_1^A = 1.01$ and $I_1^B = 0.99$. It is clear that the functional effectiveness should be considered acceptable and close in both cases in the sense of I_1. Therefore, the points under analysis in the second example have been justifiably not included in the domain of applicability of the search characteristic I_1. At the same time, $I_2^A = 0.1$ and $I_2^B \approx 0.284$. It follows then that the functional effectiveness of the search resulting in output A should be considered low in the I_2 sense, and that of the search resulting in output B also should be considered quite low though it is higher than that for the search resulting in output A. Therefore, the points under analysis in this second example are justifiably included in the domain of applicability of complex search characteristic I_2.

It is evident that two examples are not sufficient for a full justification in defining boundaries of domains of applicability of characteristics I_1 and I_2. However, it is unrealistic and beyond the scope of this book to consider all cases that would be adequate for such justification. Therefore, we have limited ourselves to the two examples that, in our opinion, provide a clear enough illustration of our approach to the justification for choosing boundaries of domains of applicability of these characteristics.

It follows from the analysis of the domains of applicability M_{I_1} and M_{I_2} that on attaining the recall and precision of the search that correspond to a point in the intersection of these domains (note that $M_{I_1} \subset M_{I_2}$) one can evaluate the functional effectiveness with the help of either complex search characteristic I_1 or complex search characteristic I_2. Such a situation makes possible a more flexible approach to an evaluation of functional effectiveness, although the choice of a specific CSC would need special justification.

Thus, we have considered the domains of applicability for two complex search characteristics, $I_1 = R + P$ and $I_2 = \sqrt{R \cdot P}$. These domains, in our opinion, also give an idea of possible boundaries for domains of applicability of other CSCs. It is clear as well that these domains define those limitations that take place in the application of the formal method of evaluation of functional effectiveness in cases when the method is based on complex search characteristic I_1 or complex search characteristic I_2.

Determining the boundaries of domain of applicability for a specific CSC is equivalent to solving the following problem: For which recall and precision levels it is pragmatically justified to evaluate the functional effectiveness of a search using a given CSC? Of interest also is another problem, namely, to determine what values should be reached by the specific complex search characteristic to serve as the basis for a pragmatically justified evaluation of the functional effectiveness of a document search, that is, for application of the formal method to evaluate functional effectiveness. The set of all values of the complex search characteristic that may be used to pragmatically justify an evaluation of the functional effectiveness of a document search we will call the *set of basic values of CSC*. The problem thus formulated is no less complex than the one discussed earlier, and we have no algorithm to solve it either. However, with complex search characteristics that are functions of R and P, a knowledge of their domains of applicability can substantially simplify the solution to the formulated problem. This is clarified in the following discussion. If a certain line is specified by equation $F(R, P) = \alpha$ (where α is a constant)—with a part of the line inside the square bounded by lines $R = 0$, $R = 1$, $P = 0$, and $P = 1$ (Figure 10.2)—each point of that part will correspond to the same value of the complex search characteristic $F(R, P)$ (which is equal to α). We will refer to this part of the line as the line of equal values of the complex search characteristic $F(R, P)$ and denote it by $Z_\alpha(F(R, P))$. Figure 10.6 illustrates the lines of equal values of complex search characteristics I_1 and I_2 with $\alpha = 1.5$ for I_1 and $\alpha = \sqrt{0.5}$ for I_2.

Clearly, if the equal values lines of the complex search characteristic $F(R, P)$, $Z_\alpha(F(R, P))$ is inside the domain of applicability for this characteristic, the constant α can be included into the set of basic values of this characteristic. Indeed, in the situation under discussion when the complex search characteristic $F(R, P)$ reaches a value equal to a, it can serve as the basis for pragmatically justified evaluation of the document search functional effectiveness. This conclusion follows from the fact that whatever the recall-precision pair produced in the search is, the point corresponding to this pair will be on the equal values line $Z_\alpha(F(R, P))$, which is within the domain of applicability of characteristic $F(R, P)$. In case the equal values line $Z_\alpha(F(R, P))$ is not totally inside the domain of applicability of the complex search characteristic $F(R, P)$,

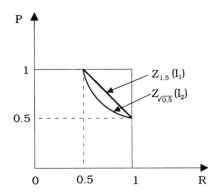

Figure 10.6
Lines of equal values of complex search characteristics I_1 and I_2.

the constant α cannot be included into the set of basic values of this characteristic. Indeed, during a search process the characteristic $F(R, P)$ may reach a
value equal to α, but the point corresponding to the recall–precision pair will
not belong to the domain of applicability of the complex search characteristic
$F(R, P)$; that is, this characteristic cannot serve as the basis for a pragmatically
justified evaluation of the document search functional effectiveness.

This allows us to determine the sets of basic values of complex search characteristics I_1 and I_2 in the cases of the boundaries of the domains of applicability
of these CSCs that we have defined. These sets are as follows: for I_1 interval
[1.5, 2], that is, $1.5 \leq \alpha \leq 2$; and for I_2 interval $[\sqrt{0.5}, 1]$, that is, $\sqrt{0.5} \leq \alpha \leq$
1. Thus, with complex search characteristic I_1 values within the interval [1.5, 2]
or with complex search characteristic I_2 values within the interval $[\sqrt{0.5}, 1]$,
one is justified in applying the formal method of evaluation of functional
effectiveness.

From a practical point of view it is also interesting to answer the following
modification of the preceding problem: What values should be reached by a
specific complex search characteristic to serve as the basis for a pragmatically
justified evaluation of the functional effectiveness of a search, provided its precision is not less than 0.5? In other words, we have to solve the previous problem
with the constraint that the precision is not below 0.5. For complex search characteristics I_1 and I_2, the discussed problem can be solved in the same way as the
preceding one, but keeping into account the fact that to solve this problem it
will be sufficient to consider inclusion of not the entire equal values lines of the
complex search characteristic but only that part of the equal values line that is a
set of points having a coordinate of 0.5 or above on the OP-axis. The resulting
set for complex search characteristic I_1 is interval [1.3, 2] (see Figure 10.4),
whereas for complex search characteristic I_2 it is interval [0.1, 1] (see Figure 10.5).

The results produced are indeed important for practical purposes because they justify the acceptance of the following assumption: if the precision is at least 0.5, then the formal method of evaluating functional effectiveness based on complex search characteristic $I_2 = \sqrt{R \cdot P}$ can be used with any value of this CSC. Recall that in discussing the boundaries of domain of applicability of characteristic I_2 (Figure 10.5), we considered it more precise to specify the limiting line by equation $R \cdot P = \beta$, where β is a constant under 0.01 (and not $R \cdot P = 0.01$). This assumption provides for a simpler solution to the question of whether it is justified to use the formal method of evaluating functional effectiveness based on characteristic I_2: it is sufficient to determine the precision, a procedure known for its simplicity. We will note also that the requirement of obtaining the precision level of at least 0.5 is common in the modern document IR systems. Therefore, one is justified in assuming that the functional effectiveness of the search performed in a modern IR system can, in almost every case, be evaluated by the formal method based on the complex search characteristic I_2.

It follows, therefore, that the limitations to the use of the formal method of evaluation of functional effectiveness, if it is based on characteristic I_2, are quite weak. However, in cases with other CSCs, such limitations may turn out to be more rigid. For example, it is true for the complex search characteristic $I_1 = R + P$, although a majority of searches in modern IR systems lead to recall-precision pairs that correspond to the points from the domain of applicability of the CSC I_1. By the way, it is not possible to decide if it is justified to use the formal method of evaluating functional effectiveness based on characteristic I_1 unless the achieved value of the recall is determined. To see this, it will suffice to analyze the domain of applicability of the complex search characteristic I_1 (this is also the case with many other CSCs). At the same time, important for information science, problems of evaluation that are based on the complex search characteristic I_2 can be solved (see Chapter 9) without determination of the recall level. It is this possibility that adds real practical substance to the results produced earlier, which are related to the determination of the justification of using the formal method of evaluating functional effectiveness. Still, it should be pointed out that in evaluating functional effectiveness there are many more situations when one must know the achieved values of the recall than there are cases where it is not needed. Therefore, as we promised earlier, we will discuss the methods of determining recall that are used in information science.

10.5

Determination of Recall

Determination of the accurate value of a recall involves, as is well known, identification of all documents in the collection that, in the opinion of the user, are pertinent to his or her need. In fact, it involves a parallel search by the user.

In cases of large retrospective collection, it is clearly unrealistic. Of course, a user can be "talked into" perusing a document collection of acceptable size. However, this can be done only in exceptional (experimental) situations. That is why development of methods to determine recall has long been underway within the information science framework with the aim of producing ways to attain adequately accurate values of this search characteristic with acceptable labor expense. Such methods have been suggested. We will discuss three varieties of these methods that, in our view, provide a full picture of the situation of recall determination in information science.

One method assumes that one can get an adequately accurate value of recall by determining the number of pertinent documents in a representative subcollection and by extrapolating this result to the entire search collection. Technically this can be done, for example, as follows. A random subcollection of, say, 3000 documents is given to the user for evaluation for pertinence. Let us assume that the user finds 20 pertinent documents. Then, if the entire collection contains 30,000 documents, it is assumed that the number of pertinent documents in the collection is 200.

Evidently, this method to determine recall employs the "selective approach" well known in mathematical statistics. Therefore, all the results needed to build the methods are borrowed from it, particularly the ways to specify the required size of the representative subcollection, ways of determining the precision of the results produced, and so forth. For this reason, we will not dwell on these problems, and we will note only that quite a large representative collection may be needed to obtain the required precision of recall. This, in its turn, may create problems resulting from the user's participation in this process.

Another method used to determine the recall is based on the assumption that if all document profiles in the collection are obtained by the same method, and the search is based on the same query formulation and uses same output criterion, the probability of getting a pertinent document in an output is equal for every pertinent document in the collection and has the same value as the recall. Some considerations on the justification of using such methods can be found in Frants, Voiskunskii, & Frants (1970). As an illustration of these methods, we will consider one method suggested in Frants, Voiskunskii, Frants.

Under this method, before the search based on some search request is conducted, the user requesting the search is asked to select and give to the system N_1 pertinent documents from, for example, the user's personal file. The document profiles for these documents are obtained by the method adopted in the IR system and are added to the collection, and then the search is performed in this expanded collection. Naturally, the pertinent documents given by the user are excluded from the produced output. Denote the number of excluded documents by n. Then the recall is determined (within the method under discussion) by the formula n/N_1.

It must be stressed that this application and similar methods for determining recall involve a number of problems, including theoretical ones that have yet to be solved. The most urgent of them, in our opinion, are those for evaluating the precision of the methods under discussion and the problem of finding such value of N_1, which would ensure determination of the recall with an acceptable precision.

Finally, the third variety of the methods to determine recall is based on the assumption that if the search is performed using several query formulations constructed for the same search request and the pertinent documents are combined from all outputs, then the number of documents in this set will be close to the number of actual pertinent documents in the collection. The technical aspects of these methods are self-evident; however, it must be recognized that the theoretical side of applicability of this variety of methods has the least foundation.

10.6
Construction of Complex Search Characteristics

We have just discussed certain problems involving use of a CSC in evaluating the functional effectiveness of a document search. Here we will consider their construction. First, we should note that quite a few complex search characteristics are described in the literature (see, for example, Bollmann, 1977; Bollmann, Raghavan, Jung, & Shu, 1992; Borko, 1967; Cleverdon, 1970; Cooper, 1973; Kraft & Bookstein, 1978; Lancaster, 1979; Raghavan, Bollmann, & Jung, 1989; Salton, 1975; Saracevic, 1995; Shaw, 1995; Sparck-Jones, 1980; and Voiskunskii, 1984), and at present two basic approaches have emerged in information science for the construction of complex search characteristics. One of the approaches can be called, with reservations, the empirical one, and the other can be called the theoretical one.

In the case of the empirical approach, a researcher proposes some new CSC, relying on accumulated experience and intuition. Naturally, a thorough experiment check of the proposed CSC is necessary. If testing reveals that the characteristic is pragmatically justified, it should be recommended for use in the information service. Such a CSC may find a broad acceptance at a later date, as is the case for complex search characteristic $I_1 = R + P$.

The theoretical approach to CSC construction is usually reduced to building a formal model for presentation and evaluation of the search results. In this, it is proposed that the complex search characteristics are based on the tools that are used for search results evaluation within these models. Clearly, not every model of this kind would lead to the construction of a pragmatically justified CSC. In our view, the best chances of getting such a CSC are with the models whose content justification is sufficiently evident, at least in cases of document search where the point corresponding to the achieved pair "recall-precision" belongs to the determining square (see Figure 10.3). We will discuss some of these models that, in our view, are best suited to the preceding consideration.

We will note also that these models allow for the construction of a large number of complex search characteristics.

The model we start with was suggested and described in detail in Voiskun-skii (1980, 1983, 1987, 1992) and led to the construction of a large specter of diverse CSCs. Now, let us assume that the search is performed in the collection containing N_0 documents. We will also assume that the documents retrieved in the search process are graded "1" and the other documents of the collection are graded"0." Finally, we will assume that the documents in the collection have been analyzed by the user and grade "1" was assigned to those that, in the user's opinion, should be included in the output (i.e., are pertinent); the remaining documents are graded "0." We will illustrate this as follows (Figure 10.7).

Thus, we can see that, in accordance with the assumptions, as the result of the search based on a user's search request and the user's analysis of the search collection, two sets of evaluations are produced, namely, a set of evaluations of "output/nonoutput" documents and a set of evaluations of "pertinent/non-pertinent" documents. It is clear that if we had an instrument to evaluate how close (that is, how much alike) the produced sets of evaluations are, that instrument could have been employed to evaluate the quality of the output resulting from the search. This leads to an idea that forms the foundation for constructing the CSCs based on the model under discussion: to assign the role of complex search characteristics to instruments that make it possible to evaluate the close-

a

Document	Document grade assigned as a result of the retrieval
D_1	1
D_2	0
D_3	0
D_4	1
.	.
.	.
.	.
.	.
.	.
D_{N_0-1}	0
D_{N_0}	1

b

Document	Document grade assigned by the user
D_1	1
D_2	0
D_3	1
D_4	0
.	.
.	.
.	.
.	.
.	.
D_{N_0-1}	1
D_{N_0}	1

Figure 10.7
Comparison of "states" of the document collection. (a) The state of document collection after retrieval; (b) The state of document collection after documents are analyzed by the user.

ness of the set of the grades "assigned" to collection documents after the search to the set of grades "assigned" to the collection documents by the user.

We present this now in a more formalized fashion. Let us assume that v_i is the correspondence coefficient of the i-th document of the search collection (D_i) to the query of a certain user, the coefficient calculated based on the search results, and k_i is the correspondence coefficient of the same document to the same query calculated outside the search, for instance, by the user. Also assume that k_i and v_i are determined by a binary scale; that is, $k_i = 1$ if the i-th document of the search collection is pertinent, and $k_i = 0$ if it is not, and $v_i = 1$ if the i-th document of the search collection was found during search, and $v_i = 0$ otherwise. If k_i and v_i are determined for each document of the collection of N_0 documents, they can be used in forming the following vectors:

$$K = (k_1, k_2, \ldots, k_{N_0}) \text{ and } V = (v_1, v_2, \ldots, v_{N_0}).$$

Then the complex search characteristics are introduced as functions that enable one to evaluate the closeness of these vectors.

It would be most natural, in our opinion, to use the following functions for this purpose (see, for instance Kolmogorov & Fomin, 1968):

$$1. \quad \cos \phi_{XY} = \frac{\sum_{i=1}^{N_0} x_i \cdot y_i}{\sqrt{\sum_{i=1}^{N_0} (x_i)^2} \cdot \sqrt{\sum_{i=1}^{N_0} (y_i)^2}},$$

$$2. \quad \rho(X, Y) = \sum_{i=1}^{N_0} |x_i - y_i|$$

$$3. \quad \rho_1(X, Y) = \sqrt{\sum_{i=1}^{N_0} (x_i - y_i)^2},$$

where X and Y are vectors such that $X = (x_1, x_2, \ldots, x_{N_0})$ and $Y = (y_1, y_2, \ldots, y_{N_0})$; $\cos \phi_{XY}$ is the cosine of the angle between vectors X and Y, $\rho(X, Y)$ and $\rho_1(X, Y)$ are the functions that specify the distance between the vectors. Before applying these functions to vectors K and V, we will note that the number of 1s in vector K is equal to the number of pertinent documents in the search collection, that is, to C. Consequently,

$$\sum_{i=1}^{N_0} (k_i)^2 = C.$$

The number of 1s in vector V is equal to the number of documents in the output, that is, to N. Consequently,

$$\sum_{i=1}^{N_0} (v_i)^2 = N.$$

retrieved pertinent ones.

The number of positions having 1 in both vector K and vector V is equal to the number of pertinent documents in the output, that is, to r. Consequently,

$$\sum_{i=1}^{N_0} k_i \cdot v_i = r.$$

Besides, $|k_i - v_i| = 1$ (and, consequently, $(k_i - v_i)^2 = 1$) in cases of $k_i = 1$ and $v_i = 0$, that is, in $(C - r)$ cases, and cases of $k_i = 0$ and $v_i = 1$, that is, in $(N - r)$ cases; in all other cases $|k_i - v_i| = 0$ (and, correspondingly, $(k_i - v_i)^2 = 0$). Then

$$\cos \phi_{KV} = \frac{\displaystyle\sum_{i=1}^{N_0} k_i \cdot v_i}{\sqrt{\displaystyle\sum_{i=1}^{N_0} (k_i)^2} \cdot \sqrt{\displaystyle\sum_{i=1}^{N_0} (v_i)^2}} = \frac{r}{\sqrt{C} \cdot \sqrt{N}}$$

$$= \sqrt{\frac{r^2}{C \cdot N}} = \sqrt{\frac{r}{C} \cdot \frac{r}{N}} = \sqrt{R \cdot P};$$

$$\rho(K, V) = \sum_{i=1}^{N_0} |k_i - v_i| = C - r + N - r = C + N - 2r;$$

$$\rho_1(K, V) = \sqrt{\sum_{i=1}^{N_0} (k_i - v_i)^2} = \sqrt{C + N - 2r}.$$

Thus the models discussed (as a matter of fact, three models we discussed differ from each other only by the instruments for the search results evaluations) led us to the complex search characteristic $I_2 = \sqrt{R \cdot P}$ (which was repeatedly mentioned earlier) and made it possible to obtain complex search characteristics $I_3 = C + N - 2r$ and $I_4 = \sqrt{C + N - 2r}$. We will note that characteristics I_3 and I_4 are equal from the point of view of their use for the evaluation of search results.

With characteristics I_3 and I_4 as the basis, one can construct a CSC of a more common representation. For example,

$$I_5 = 1 - \frac{I_3}{N_0} = 1 - \frac{C + N - 2r}{N_0} = \frac{N_0 - C - N + 2r}{N_0}$$

$$= \frac{L - l - r + 2r}{N_0} = \frac{d + r}{N_0} = \frac{d}{N_0} + \frac{r}{N_0} = \frac{d \cdot L}{L \cdot N_0} + \frac{r \cdot C}{C \cdot N_0}$$

$$= \frac{S(N_0 - C)}{N_0} + R \cdot P_0 = S(1 - P_0) + R \cdot P_0.$$

One can try to build up a "stock" of the CSCs by applying models similar to the ones used in the preceding. For this purpose one can, for example, use other functions for evaluating closeness of vectors K and V. Presently a number of functions for evaluation of vector closeness, which differ from those used earlier, are being considered by information science researchers although, in our opinion, they are less "natural" in this sense than the previous examples. Let us discuss one such function:

$$\gamma(X, Y) = \frac{\displaystyle\sum_{i=1}^{N_0} x_i \cdot y_i}{\displaystyle\sum_{i=1}^{N_0} (x_i)^2 + \sum_{i=1}^{N_0} (y_i)^2 - \sum_{i=1}^{N_0} x_i \cdot y_i}.$$

Applying this function to vectors K and V and replacing the corresponding expressions by C, N, and r, we get the following:

$$\gamma(K, V) = \frac{\displaystyle\sum_{i=1}^{N_0} k_i \cdot v_i}{\displaystyle\sum_{i=1}^{N_0} (k_i)^2 + \sum_{i=1}^{N_0} (v_i)^2 - \sum_{i=1}^{N_0} k_i \cdot v_i} = \frac{r}{C + N - r}.$$

By dividing the numerator and denominator of the produced expression by r (assuming $r \neq 0$) we get the following:

$$\gamma(K, V) = \frac{1}{\dfrac{C}{r} + \dfrac{N}{r} - 1} = \frac{1}{\dfrac{1}{R} + \dfrac{1}{P} - 1}.$$

Thus, application of $\gamma(X, Y)$ gives us the complex search characteristic

$$I_6 = \frac{1}{\dfrac{1}{R} + \dfrac{1}{P} - 1},$$

which is one more characteristic produced on the basis of the models under discussion. At the same time, we will note that similar CSCs constructed in other ways have already been reviewed by other authors (for instance, see van Rijsbergen, 1979). Nevertheless, the given example indicates that further use of the functions under discussion can provide a replenishment of the CSC "stock" with new characteristics.

    Now we will discuss a modification of the discussed models by using other scales to determine k_i and v_i. For this purpose we will use binary scales: $k_i = 1$ if the i-th document of the collection is pertinent, and $k_i = -1$ otherwise; $v_i = 1$ if the i-th document is found during search, and $v_i = -1$ otherwise. Would these scales lead us to the construction of complex search characteristics different from those produced earlier? To answer this question, we first note that $(k_i)^2 = 1$ and $(v_i)^2 = 1$ for all $1 \le i \le N_0$, whereas $k_i \cdot v_i$ is either 1 or -1 with $k_i \cdot v_i = 1$ when $k_i = 1$ and $v_i = 1$ (that is, in r cases) and when $k_i = -1$ and $v_i = -1$ (that is, in d cases), and $k_i \cdot v_i = -1$ when $k_i = 1$ and $v_i = -1$ (that is, in b cases) and when $k_i = -1$ and $v_i = 1$ (that is, in l cases). In addition, $|k_i - v_i| = 2$ and $(k_i - v_i)^2 = 4$, when $k_i = 1$, and $v_i = -1$ (that is, in b cases) and when $k_i = -1$, whereas $v_i = 1$ (that is, in l cases), and in the other cases $|k_i - v_i| = 0$ and $(k_i - v_i)^2 = 0$. With this in mind we get the following:

$$\cos \phi_{KV} = \frac{\sum_{i=1}^{N_0} k_i \cdot v_i}{\sqrt{\sum_{i=1}^{N_0} (k_i)^2} \cdot \sqrt{\sum_{i=1}^{N_0} (v_i)^2}} = \frac{r + d - b - l}{\sqrt{N_0} \cdot \sqrt{N_0}}$$

$$= \frac{r + d - (N_0 - r - d)}{N_0} = \frac{2(r + d)}{N_0} - 1 = 2\left(\frac{r}{N_0} + \frac{d}{N_0}\right) - 1$$

$$= 2\left(\frac{r \cdot C}{C \cdot N_0} + \frac{d \cdot L}{L \cdot N_0}\right) - 1 = 2\left(R \cdot P_0 + S \cdot \frac{N_0 - C}{N_0}\right) - 1$$

$$= 2[R \cdot P_0 + S(1 - P_0)] - 1;$$

$$\rho(K, V) = \sum_{i=1}^{N_0} |k_i - v_i| = 2(b + l) = 2(C + N - 2r);$$

$$\rho_1(K, V) = \sqrt{\sum_{i=1}^{N_0} (k_i - v_i)^2} = \sqrt{4(b + l)} = 2\sqrt{C + N - 2r};$$

$$\gamma(K, V) = \frac{\sum_{i=1}^{N_0} k_i \cdot v_i}{\sum_{i=1}^{N_0} (k_i)^2 + \sum_{i=1}^{N_0} (v_i)^2 - \sum_{i=1}^{N_0} k_i \cdot v_i} = \frac{r + d - b - l}{N_0 + N_0 - r - d + b + l}$$

$$= \frac{\frac{r + d - b - l}{N_0}}{2 - \frac{r + d - b - l}{N_0}} = \frac{2[R \cdot P_0 + S(1 - P_0)] - 1}{2 - 2[R \cdot P_0 + S(1 - P_0)] + 1}$$

$$= \frac{2[R \cdot P_0 + S(1 - P_0)] - 1}{3 - 2[R \cdot P_0 + S(1 - P_0)]}.$$

It follows from the obtained expressions of the complex search characteristics that, from the point of view of using these characteristics to evaluate search results, they are equivalent to some of the CSCs that were constructed with the help of binary scales employed earlier (for defining k_i and v_i). At the same time, the set of newly produced CSCs is substantially different from the set of characteristics previously produced. This means that it might be promising to consider other binary scales in defining k_i and v_i to produce new CSCs. However, we will not dwell on this problem here, though we will note that, generally speaking, larger-sized scales can be used instead of binary scales to construct complex search characteristics. This aspect of basic models modification deserves special discussion and will be considered in the subsequent section of this chapter.

One more source for CSC stock replenishment is the models that are similar to the ones discussed earlier but that are based on other vectors. For example, let us assume that vector $U = (R, P)$ is constructed from the achieved levels of recall and precision of search, and that vector $E = (1, 1)$ is introduced for discussion. The use of functions allowing evaluation of closeness of these vectors will lead, in particular, to the following complex search characteristics:

$$I_7 = \rho(E,\, U) = |1 - R| + |1 - P| = 2 - R - P,$$
$$I_8 = \rho_1(E,\, U) = \sqrt{(1 - R)^2 + (1 - P)^2}.$$

From the point of view of search result evaluation, characteristic I_7 is equivalent to characteristic $I_1 = R + P$, whereas characteristic I_8 should probably be included in the set of new CSCs.

To conclude the discussion of the proposed types of models, we will emphasize the accuracy of using functions allowing one to evaluate the closeness of vectors. For example, in the case of vectors E and U, one should not use the function $\cos \phi_{EU}$ to construct a complex search characteristic. Indeed,

$$\cos \phi_{EU} = \frac{\displaystyle\sum_{i=1}^{2} e_i \cdot u_i}{\sqrt{\displaystyle\sum_{i=1}^{2}(e_i)^2} \cdot \sqrt{\displaystyle\sum_{i=1}^{2}(u_i)^2}} = \frac{R + P}{\sqrt{2} \cdot \sqrt{R^2 + P^2}}.$$

It follows from this that with any $R = P \neq 0$, $\cos \phi_{EU} = 2R/(\sqrt{2} \cdot \sqrt{2R^2}) = 1$. In other words, if complex search characteristic $(R + P)/(\sqrt{2} \cdot \sqrt{R^2 + P^2})$ is employed to evaluate search results, it will be found that (for example, in the case of the search resulting in $R = 0.5$ and $P = 0.5$ and in the case of the search resulting in $R = 1$ and $P = 1$) the output quality would be seen as equal, which is clearly absurd. Similar examples can be provided for a situation with $R \neq P$.

Thus, in the case of vectors E and U, their closeness cannot be correctly determined by the angle between them. At the same time, it follows from the way vectors K and V are constructed that if the described binary scales are used to determine k_i and v_i, it seems justified that the closeness of vectors K and V

can be determined by the angle between them. This is also confirmed by the CSCs produced in the cases discussed.

Now let us consider one more model, which allows production of CSCs similar to characteristic I_6 (that is, we will demonstrate one other way to construct CSCs similar to I_6, as mentioned earlier). An interest in such models is explained by the rather large number of complex search characteristics, similar to characteristic I_6, proposed by other authors. Among these is the CSC

$$I_9 = 1 - \cfrac{1}{\cfrac{1}{R} + \cfrac{1}{P} - 1},$$

which was proposed by Heine (1973); the CSC

$$I_{10} = 1 - \cfrac{1}{\cfrac{2}{R} + \cfrac{2}{P} - 3},$$

which was proposed by Vickery and documented by Cleverdon, Mills, & Keen (1966); and the CSC

$$I_{11} = 1 - \cfrac{2}{\cfrac{1}{R} + \cfrac{1}{P}},$$

which was proposed by van Rijsbergen (1979). It is hardly expedient to consider all such models. Therefore, we will focus on the model developed by van Rijsbergen (1979), which is attractive because of its simplicity.

Now, by A let us denote the set of documents found during the search, and by B let us denote the set of pertinent documents in the search collection. The relationship between these sets represents the results of the search as illustrated in Figure 10.8

In this figure, the unshaded area represents the set of obtained pertinent documents during search, the shaded area A represents the set of obtained nonpertinent documents, and the shaded area B represents the set of pertinent documents not found during search. Clearly, the higher "degree of coincidence" of sets A and B, the better the search result. For example, in the case of a full coincidence of these sets, we get an "ideal" output. It is the tools used to determine the "degree of coincidence" of sets that are proposed for the evaluation of search results within the discussed model.

The following criterion seems to be a "natural" tool to determine the "degree of coincidence" of sets M and L:

$$\frac{|M \cap L|}{|M \cup L|},$$

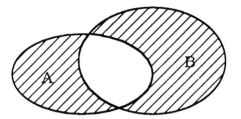

Figure 10.8
Relationship between sets A and B.

where M and L are finite sets, $|M \cap L|$ is the number of elements in the intersection of sets M and L, and $|M \cup L|$ is the number of elements in set union of M and L. Applying this criterion to sets A and B, keeping in mind that $|A \cap B| = r$ and $|A \cup B| = N + C - r$, and assuming that $r \neq 0$, we get the following:

$$\frac{|A \cap B|}{|A \cup B|} = \frac{r}{C + N - r} = \frac{1}{\dfrac{C}{r} + \dfrac{N}{r} - 1} = \frac{1}{\dfrac{1}{R} + \dfrac{1}{P} - 1}.$$

In other words, by application of the suggested criterion we arrive exactly at the complex search characteristic I_6. At the same time, van Rijsbergen used the following criterion as a tool to determine the "degree of coincidence," or rather the "degree of noncoincidence" of sets:

$$\frac{|M \cup L - M \cap L|}{|M| + |L|},$$

which, when applied to sets A and B, gives complex search characteristic I_{11}. This is shown as follows, assuming again that $r \neq 0$:

$$\frac{|A \cup B - A \cap B|}{|A| + |B|} = \frac{N + C - 2r}{N + C}$$

$$= 1 - \frac{2r}{C + N}$$

$$= 1 - \frac{2}{\dfrac{C}{r} + \dfrac{N}{r}} = 1 - \frac{2}{\dfrac{1}{R} + \dfrac{1}{P}}.$$

It should be kept in mind that it follows from the construction method of the described CSC that the higher the search results, the lower the values that are obtained by the characteristic. This completes our discussion of the model suggested in the work of van Rijsbergen (1979).

The last model that we consider in discussing the theoretical approach to CSC construction is the one proposed by D. O. Avetisyan (1975, 1977), which leads to a complex search characteristic we have not mentioned. Two random variables are used within Avetisyan's model: "to be an output document" and "to be a pertinent document." These variables will be denoted by X and Y, respectively, and could have the following values for a specific document: $X = 1$ if the document was found during search and $X = 0$ otherwise; $Y = 1$ if the document is pertinent and $Y = 0$ otherwise. It is clear that the "stronger" the connection between the two variables, the "closer" the produced output to the "ideal," that is, the better the outcome of the search. In other words, in an evaluation of the search results, one can attempt to use a tool that makes it possible to determine if there is a direct dependence between variables X and Y and what the "strength" of this dependence is.

The discussed model has one noteworthy feature: the model does not represent actual results of the search. At the same time it allows one to evaluate the search results, a feature quite adequate for the construction of complex search characteristics.

To determine if there exists a dependence between variables X and Y and what the "strength" of this dependence is, the model employs a coefficient of linear correlation

$$\frac{E(XY) - E(X) \cdot E(Y)}{\sqrt{D(X) \cdot D(Y)}},$$

where $E(XY)$, $E(X)$, and $E(Y)$ are expected values of random variables XY, X and Y, and $D(X)$, and $D(Y)$ are a dispersions of variables X and Y.

Using approaches common for such cases for determining the values of the components in the preceding expression, it was established within the framework of the model under consideration that

$$\frac{E(XY) - E(X) \cdot E(Y)}{\sqrt{D(X) \cdot D(Y)}} = \frac{rd - lb}{\sqrt{(r + l)(r + b)(b + d)(l + d)}}.$$

(Intermediate calculations are omitted because they are both clear and tedious.) Thus, the discussed model gives us a new complex search characteristic:

$$I_{12} = \frac{rd - lb}{\sqrt{(r + l)(r + b)(b + d)(l + d)}}.$$

The new CSC differs from the CSCs discussed earlier. However, under certain conditions the values of this new CSC will be close to those for CSC $I_2 = \sqrt{R \cdot P}$. This follows from the expression known from the folklore: $\lim_{d \to \infty} I_{12} = I_2$ (assuming that r, b, and l are bounded). We will demonstrate that this correlation does exist (regretfully, the authors failed to locate any publications of this correlation and its proof):

$$\lim_{d \to \infty} I_{12} = \lim_{d \to \infty} \frac{rd - lb}{\sqrt{(r + l)(r + b)(b + d)(l + d)}}$$

$$= \lim_{d \to \infty} \frac{r - \dfrac{lb}{d}}{\sqrt{(r + l)(r + b)\left(\dfrac{b}{d} + 1\right)\left(\dfrac{l}{d} + 1\right)}}$$

$$= \frac{r}{\sqrt{(r + l)(r + b)}} = \frac{r}{\sqrt{NC}} = \sqrt{R \cdot P} = I_2.$$

Thus, if d is much larger than $l \cdot b$, the values of characteristic I_{12} are indeed very close to characteristic I_2 values. Nevertheless, the complex search characteristics I_2 and I_{12} are substantially different, as will be seen from our further discussion (see Section 10.8, "Order Preservation Property").

Note that for complex search characteristic I_{12}, one can also derive the more common appearance (Avetisyan, 1975), shown here:

$$I_{12} = \frac{rd - lb}{\sqrt{(r + l)(r + b)(b + d)(l + d)}} = \frac{rd - lb}{\sqrt{N \cdot C \cdot (b + d) \cdot L}}$$

$$= \frac{\sqrt{r \cdot l} \cdot (rd - lb)}{\sqrt{N \cdot C \cdot L \cdot (r \cdot l \cdot b + r \cdot l \cdot d)}}$$

$$= \frac{\dfrac{\sqrt{r \cdot l} \cdot [rd - (L - d)(C - r)]}{N \cdot C \cdot L}}{\sqrt{\dfrac{r \cdot l \cdot b + r \cdot l \cdot d + r^2 \cdot d - r^2 \cdot d}{N \cdot C \cdot L}}}$$

$$= \frac{\sqrt{\dfrac{r \cdot l}{N^2}} \cdot \dfrac{rd - LC + dC + rL - rd}{C \cdot L}}{\sqrt{\dfrac{rd(l + r) - r(rd - lb)}{N \cdot C \cdot L}}} = \frac{\sqrt{\dfrac{r(N - r)}{N \cdot N}} \cdot \left(\dfrac{r}{C} + \dfrac{d}{L} - 1\right)}{\sqrt{\dfrac{r}{C} \cdot \dfrac{d}{L} \cdot \dfrac{N}{N} - \dfrac{r}{N} \cdot \dfrac{rd - lb}{C \cdot L}}}$$

$$= \frac{\sqrt{P(1 - P)} \cdot (R + S - 1)}{\sqrt{R \cdot S - P(R + S - 1)}}.$$

Finally, it is noteworthy that the linear correlation coefficient does not seem to be the only tool that will enable one to determine whether there is a direct dependence between random variables X and Y and what the "strength" of this dependence is. However, so far we have not encountered use of some other functions for this purpose in the context of constructing CSCs.

To summarize, we have discussed some formal models that make it possible to obtain complex search characteristics. Even though jointly they have brought a large enough set of CSCs, these models, naturally, do not exhaust a possible list of models of this kind. It seems that the discussed research line is promising and has quite a lot of potential, so there can be no reason to doubt the expediency of further work in this direction.

10.7

"Physical Meaning" of Complex Search Characteristics

When determining values of a complex search characteristic using a particular formula, the following question may arise: What does the obtained value of a CSC mean; that is, what is the "physical meaning" of the characteristic used? One cannot always find an answer. For example, with the empirical approach to CSC construction, it is very difficult to disclose the physical meaning of a proposed characteristic. Complex search characteristic $I_1 = R + P$ is a good illustration of this point.

At the same time, for CSCs obtained within a theoretical approach, their physical meaning is usually found easily. For example, complex search characteristic $I_7 = 2 - R - P$ has such a physical meaning. It is the distance between the points of the square shown in Figure 10.2, one point representing the "recall-precision" pair obtained by the search and the other point with coordinates (1, 1) representing the pair recall-precision obtained in the "ideal" output. (Naturally, the same physical meaning can be ascribed to complex search characteristic $I_1 = R + P$.) The physical meaning of complex search characteristic $I_2 = \sqrt{R \cdot P}$ is as follows: the cosine of the angle between vectors, one of the vectors representing the output resulting from the search and the other representing the ideal output. The physical meaning is also quite obvious for other CSCs discussed in the previous section. In this case, different CSCs may have the same physical meaning (for example, characteristics I_7 and I_8), or different physical meanings may be ascribed to the same CSCs (for example, to characteristic I_6). However, from our point of view, such situations do not in the least discredit the *interpretational* potential of formal models created in the framework of the theoretical approach to the construction of search characteristics.

It should be emphasized that difficulties in finding the physical meaning of a specific complex search characteristic may cause some to mistrust the CSC. This is another advantage to obtaining CSCs by the theoretical approach as opposed to obtaining them by the empirical approach; that is, the theoretical approach seems more reliable and it provides additional motivation for doing further research on developing new formal models.

10.8

Order Preservation Property

In this section we will deal with the property of complex search characteristics, which is important in practice and permits one to solve one of the most complex problems discussed in detail in Chapter 9, namely, creating a mechanism that will permit selection, for each search request, of the best search method (from a number of available methods). This property will be called the order preservation property. To define it, let us assume that we have two arbitrary search methods. Let us also assume that both methods have been used in a search on the same search request in the same search collection, and that values of a certain complex search characteristic F were determined from the results of this search. Let us denote the value of the given CSC obtained using the first search method as F^{i_1} and that obtained using the second search method as F^{i_2}. Then, if the sign of the difference $F^{i_1} - F^{i_2}$ does not depend on the value of C (i.e., the number of pertinent documents in the search collection), the complex search characteristic F possesses an *order preservation property*. Here we interpret independence of the sign of difference $F^{i_1} - F^{i_2}$ from the value of C as follows: either C is not included in the expression of the difference, or with any admissible value of C the sign of $F^{i_1} - F^{i_2}$ will be the same (naturally, provided that the values of the remaining quantities in this expression are not changed).

Let us explain why the defined property is called as it is. We will use as an example complex search characteristic $I_2 = \sqrt{R \cdot P}$ having the order preservation property (which will be shown later). Let us assume that there are several different search methods at our disposal, and we want to order them in decreasing order of values of I_2 obtained from the search using each corresponding method (in the same collection on the same search request). Let us demonstrate that the required ordering can be obtained using criterion r^2/N. To do this, we will note first that the sign of difference

$$I_2^{i_1} - I_2^{i_2}$$

coincides with the sign of difference

$$\frac{(r^{i_1})^2}{N^{i_1}} - \frac{(r^{i_2})^2}{N^{i_2}}.$$

In fact,

$$I_2^{i_1} - I_2^{i_2} = \sqrt{R^{i_1} \cdot P^{i_1}} - \sqrt{R^{i_2} \cdot P^{i_2}} = \sqrt{\frac{(r^{i_1})^2}{N^{i_1} \cdot C}} - \sqrt{\frac{(r^{i_2})^2}{N^{i_2} \cdot C}}.$$

From the existence of the order preservation property for characteristic I_2 it follows that the sign of difference $I_2^{i_1} - I_2^{i_2}$ coincides with the sign of this difference for $C = 1$. In other words, the sign of difference $I_2^{i_1} - I_2^{i_2}$ coincides with the sign of expression

$$\sqrt{\frac{(r^{i_1})^2}{N^{i_1} \cdot C}} - \sqrt{\frac{(r^{i_2})^2}{N^{i_2} \cdot C}}$$

for $C = 1$, that is, with the sign of difference

$$\sqrt{\frac{(r^{i_1})^2}{N^{i_1}}} - \sqrt{\frac{(r^{i_2})^2}{N^{i_2}}}.$$

Taking into consideration the identity

$$\frac{(r^{i_1})^2}{N^{i_1}} - \frac{(r^{i_2})^2}{N^{i_2}} = \left(\sqrt{\frac{(r^{i_1})^2}{N^{i_1}}} - \sqrt{\frac{(r^{i_2})^2}{N^{i_2}}}\right) \times \left(\sqrt{\frac{(r^{i_1})^2}{N^{i_1}}} + \sqrt{\frac{(r^{i_2})^2}{N^{i_2}}}\right)$$

we easily arrive at the following conclusion: the signs of differences

$$I_2^{i_1} - I_2^{i_2}$$

and

$$\frac{(r^{i_1})^2}{N^{i_1}} - \frac{(r^{i_2})^2}{N^{i_2}}$$

in fact coincide. We note further that the ordering of the values of a quantity (in decreasing order) in fact reduces to the determination and analysis of signs of differences in pairs of obtained values of the mentioned quantity. For example, if the sign of the difference of a pair of values is positive, then the first value of the given pair is greater than the second, and so on. Therefore, taking into account that for any two search methods (i_1 and i_2), the signs of differences

$$I_2^{i_1} - I_2^{i_2}$$

and

$$\frac{(r^{i_1})^2}{N^{i_1}} - \frac{(r^{i_2})^2}{N^{i_2}}$$

coincide, it is possible to assert that the ordering of available search methods in decreasing order of obtained values of characteristic I_2 and in decreasing order of obtained values of criterion r^2/N proves to be the same; that is, the necessary ordering in fact can be accomplished using the criterion r^2/N. In other words, the order established by means of criterion r^2/N is preserved also in the case of ordering by means of characteristic I_2. This was the reason why a property leading to this result was called the order preservation property.

Now we will show that some of the complex search characteristics I_1

through I_{12} discussed earlier, namely I_2, I_3, I_4, and I_5, possess the order preservation property. To show this, assuming that the condition of this property is fulfilled for each analyzed CSC, we will consider for any two search methods (i_1 and i_2) the following differences: $I_2^{i_1} - I_2^{i_2}$, $I_3^{i_1} - I_3^{i_2}$, $I_4^{i_1} - I_4^{i_2}$, and $I_5^{i_1} - I_5^{i_2}$. Thus,

1. $I_2^{i_1} - I_2^{i_2} = \sqrt{R^{i_1} \cdot P^{i_1}} - \sqrt{R^{i_2} \cdot P^{i_2}} = \sqrt{\dfrac{(r^{i_1})^2}{N^{i_1} \cdot C}} - \sqrt{\dfrac{(r^{i_2})^2}{N^{i_2} \cdot C}}$

$$= \frac{1}{\sqrt{C}}\left(\sqrt{\frac{(r^{i_1})^2}{N^{i_1}}} - \sqrt{\frac{(r^{i_2})^2}{N^{i_2}}}\right);$$

2. $I_3^{i_1} - I_3^{i_2} = C + N^{i_1} - 2r^{i_1} - C - N^{i_2} + 2r^{i_2}$

$$= N^{i_1} - 2r^{i_1} - N^{i_2} + 2r^{i_2};$$

3. $I_4^{i_1} - I_4^{i_2} = \sqrt{I_3^{i_1}} - \sqrt{I_3^{i_2}} = \dfrac{(\sqrt{I_3^{i_1}} - \sqrt{I_3^{i_2}})(\sqrt{I_3^{i_1}} + \sqrt{I_3^{i_2}})}{\sqrt{I_3^{i_1}} + \sqrt{I_3^{i_2}}}$

$$= \frac{I_3^{i_1} - I_3^{i_2}}{\sqrt{I_3^{i_1}} + \sqrt{I_3^{i_2}}};$$

4. $I_5^{i_1} - I_5^{i_2} = 1 - \dfrac{I_3^{i_1}}{N_0} - 1 + \dfrac{I_3^{i_2}}{N_0} = \dfrac{I_3^{i_2} - I_3^{i_1}}{N_0}.$

In Case 1, the sign of difference $I_2^{i_1} - I_2^{i_2}$ coincides with the sign of expression

$$\sqrt{\frac{(r^{i_1})^2}{N^{i_1}}} - \sqrt{\frac{(r^{i_2})^2}{N^{i_2}}}$$

for any permissible value of C, because for any of these values $\sqrt{C} > 0$. In other words, the sign of difference $I_2^{i_1} - I_2^{i_2}$ is determined by the sign of expression

$$\sqrt{\frac{(r^{i_1})^2}{N^{i_1}}} - \sqrt{\frac{(r^{i_2})^2}{N^{i_2}}}.$$

This expression does not contain quantity C; that is, the sign of this expression and, hence, the sign of the difference $I_2^{i_1} - I_2^{i_2}$ does not depend on value of C. It follows from this statement that complex search characteristic I_2 possesses order preservation property.

In Case 2, the expression for difference $I_3^{i_1} - I_3^{i_2}$ does not contain quantity C, from which it is obvious that complex search characteristic I_3 has the order preservation property.

In Case 3, quantity $\sqrt{I_3^{i_1}} + \sqrt{I_3^{i_2}}$ is nonnegative. Therefore, the sign of difference $I_4^{i_1} - I_4^{i_2}$ is determined by the sign of $I_3^{i_1} - I_3^{i_2}$, and it was established that the sign of the latter does not depend on the value of C. Hence, the sign of difference $I_{4}^{i_1} - I_{4}^{i_2}$ does not depend on the value of C, which means that complex search characteristic I_4 has the order preservation property.

Finally, in Case 4, which is similar to Case 2, the expression for difference $I_{5}^{i_1} - I_{5}^{i_2}$ does not contain C, as is evident from analysis of this expression. Therefore, complex search characteristic I_5, like the previously discussed CSC, has the order preservation property.

Next, let us show that the remainder of the previous complex search characteristics I_1 through I_{12}, namely, characteristics I_1, I_6, I_7, I_8, I_9, I_{10}, I_{11}, and I_{12}, do not have the order preservation property. First, let us show this for characteristics I_1, I_6, I_7, I_8, I_9, I_{10}, and I_{11}. Assume that we have two different search methods, each being used for the search on the same search request in a certain search collection. In addition, let us assume that in the case of the first search method an output is produced consisting of 20 documents, of which 8 documents are pertinent (i.e., $r^{i_1} = 8$ and $N^{i_1} = 20$), and, in the case of the second search method, the output consists of 12 documents of which 6 documents are pertinent (i.e., $r^{i_2} = 6$ and $N^{i_2} = 12$). Now, let us consider two possible situations.

1. The search collection contained 40 pertinent documents ($C = 40$). Note that in this situation,

$$R^{i_1} = \frac{r^{i_1}}{C} = \frac{8}{40}; \quad P^{i_1} = \frac{r^{i_1}}{N^{i_1}} = \frac{8}{20};$$

$$R^{i_2} = \frac{r^{i_2}}{C} = \frac{6}{40}; \quad P^{i_2} = \frac{r^{i_2}}{N^{i_2}} = \frac{6}{12}.$$

Then,

$$I_{1}^{i_1} - I_{1}^{i_2} = R^{i_1} + P^{i_1} - R^{i_2} - P^{i_2}$$

$$= \frac{8}{40} + \frac{8}{20} - \frac{6}{40} - \frac{6}{12} = -\frac{1}{20} < 0;$$

$$I_{6}^{i_1} - I_{6}^{i_2} = \frac{r^{i_1}}{C + N^{i_1} - r^{i_1}} - \frac{r^{i_2}}{C + N^{i_2} - r^{i_2}}$$

$$= \frac{8}{40 + 20 - 8} - \frac{6}{40 + 12 - 6}$$

$$= \frac{8}{52} - \frac{6}{46} = \frac{368 - 312}{52 \cdot 46} > 0;$$

$$I_{7}^{i_1} - I_{7}^{i_2} = 2 - I_{1}^{i_1} - 2 + I_{1}^{i_2} = -(I_{1}^{i_1} - I_{1}^{i_2}) > 0;$$

$$I_{8}^{i_1} - I_{8}^{i_2} = \sqrt{(1 - R^{i_1})^2 + (1 - P^{i_1})^2} - \sqrt{(1 - R^{i_2})^2 + (1 - P^{i_2})^2}$$

$$= \sqrt{\left(1 - \frac{8}{40}\right)^2 + \left(1 - \frac{8}{20}\right)^2} - \sqrt{\left(1 - \frac{6}{40}\right)^2 + \left(1 - \frac{6}{12}\right)^2}$$

$$= \sqrt{\left(\frac{4}{5}\right)^2 + \left(\frac{3}{5}\right)^2} - \sqrt{\left(\frac{17}{20}\right)^2 + \left(\frac{10}{20}\right)^2} = 1 - \sqrt{\frac{389}{400}} > 0;$$

$$I_{9'}^{i_1} - I_{9'}^{i_2} = 1 - I_6^{i_1} - 1 + I_6^{i_2} = -(I_6^{i_1} - I_6^{i_2}) < 0;$$

$$I_{10}^{i_1} - I_{10}^{i_2} = 1 - \cfrac{1}{\cfrac{2}{R^{i_1}} + \cfrac{2}{P^{i_1}} - 3} - 1 + \cfrac{1}{\cfrac{2}{R^{i_2}} + \cfrac{2}{P^{i_2}} - 3}$$

$$= \frac{r^{i_2}}{2C + 2N^{i_2} - 3r^{i_2}} - \frac{r^{i_1}}{2C + 2N^{i_1} - 3r^{i_1}}$$

$$= \frac{6}{80 + 24 - 18} - \frac{8}{80 + 40 - 24} = \frac{6}{86} - \frac{8}{96}$$

$$= \frac{576 - 688}{86 \cdot 96} < 0;$$

$$I_{11}^{i_1} - I_{11}^{i_2} = 1 - \cfrac{2}{\cfrac{1}{R^{i_1}} + \cfrac{1}{P^{i_1}}} - 1 + \cfrac{2}{\cfrac{1}{R^{i_2}} + \cfrac{1}{P^{i_2}}}$$

$$= \frac{2r^{i_2}}{C + N^{i_2}} - \frac{2r^{i_1}}{C + N^{i_1}} = \frac{12}{40 + 12} - \frac{16}{40 + 20}$$

$$= \frac{12}{52} - \frac{16}{60} = \frac{720 - 832}{52 \cdot 60} < 0.$$

2. The search collection contained 10 pertinent documents ($C = 10$). Note that in this situation,

$$R^{i_1} = \frac{r^{i_1}}{C} = \frac{8}{10}; \ P^{i_1} = \frac{r^{i_1}}{N^{i_1}} = \frac{8}{20};$$

$$R^{i_2} = \frac{r^{i_2}}{C} = \frac{6}{10}; \ P^{i_2} = \frac{r^{i_2}}{N^{i_2}} = \frac{6}{12}.$$

Then,

$$I_1^{i_1} - I_1^{i_2} = R^{i_1} + P^{i_1} - R^{i_2} - P^{i_2}$$

$$= \frac{8}{10} + \frac{8}{20} - \frac{6}{10} - \frac{6}{12} = \frac{1}{10} > 0;$$

$$I_6^{i_1} - I_6^{i_2} = \frac{r^{i_1}}{C + N^{i_1} - r^{i_1}} - \frac{r^{i_2}}{C + N^{i_2} - r^{i_2}}$$

$$= \frac{8}{10 + 20 - 8} - \frac{6}{10 + 12 - 6} = \frac{8}{22} - \frac{6}{16}$$

$$= \frac{128 - 132}{22 \cdot 16} < 0;$$

$$I_7^{i_1} - I_7^{i_2} = 2 - I_1^{i_1} - 2 + I_1^{i_2} = -(I_1^{i_1} - I_1^{i_2}) < 0;$$

$$I_8^{i_1} - I_8^{i_2} = \sqrt{(1 - R^{i_1})^2 + (1 - P^{i_1})^2} - \sqrt{(1 - R^{i_2})^2 + (1 - P^{i_2})^2}$$

$$= \sqrt{\left(1 - \frac{8}{10}\right)^2 + \left(1 - \frac{8}{20}\right)^2} - \sqrt{\left(1 - \frac{6}{10}\right)^2 + \left(1 - \frac{6}{12}\right)^2}$$

$$= \sqrt{\left(\frac{2}{10}\right)^2 + \left(\frac{6}{10}\right)^2} - \sqrt{\left(\frac{4}{10}\right)^2 + \left(\frac{5}{10}\right)^2}$$

$$= \sqrt{\frac{40}{100}} - \sqrt{\frac{41}{100}} < 0;$$

$$I_9^{i_1} - I_9^{i_2} = 1 - I_6^{i_1} - 1 + I_6^{i_2} = -(I_6^{i_1} - I_6^{i_2}) > 0;$$

$$I_{10}^{i_1} - I_{10}^{i_2} = \frac{r^{i_2}}{2C + 2N^{i_2} - 3r^{i_2}} - \frac{r^{i_1}}{2C + 2N^{i_1} - 3r^{i_1}}$$

$$= \frac{6}{20 + 24 - 18} - \frac{8}{20 + 40 - 24}$$

$$= \frac{6}{26} - \frac{8}{36} = \frac{216 - 208}{26 \cdot 36} > 0;$$

$$I_{11}^{i_1} - I_{11}^{i_2} = \frac{2r^{i_2}}{C + N^{i_2}} - \frac{2r^{i_1}}{C + N^{i_1}}$$

$$= \frac{12}{10 + 12} - \frac{16}{10 + 20}$$

$$= \frac{12}{22} - \frac{16}{30} = \frac{360 - 352}{22 \cdot 30} > 0.$$

Thus, we see that in situation 1 and situation 2 the corresponding differences have opposite signs, but the only parameter distinguishing two situations is the number of pertinent documents in the search collection, that is, only C. Hence, the signs of all the preceding differences depend on the value of C. This means that complex search characteristics I_1, I_6, I_7, I_8, I_9, I_{10}, and I_{11} do not possess the order preservation property.

Now, let us show that complex search characteristic I_{12} also does not have this property. We will do this with the same assumptions we used to demonstrate a similar statement of characteristics I_1, I_6, and so on with the only addition being that the search collection contains 1052 documents; that is, $N_0 = 1052$. Let us consider two possibilities, as we did previously.

1. The search collection contained 100 pertinent documents ($C = 100$). In this situation,

$$l^{i_1} = N^{i_1} - r^{i_1} = 12; \quad b^{i_1} = C - r^{i_1} = 92;$$
$$d^{i_1} = N_0 - C - l^{i_1} = 940;$$
$$l^{i_2} = N^{i_2} - r^{i_2} = 6; \quad b^{i_2} = C - r^{i_2} = 94;$$
$$d^{i_2} = N_0 - C - l^{i_2} = 946.$$

Then,

$$
\begin{aligned}
I^{i_1}_{1'2} - I^{i_2}_{1'2} &= \frac{r^{i_1} d^{i_1} - l^{i_1} b^{i_1}}{\sqrt{(r^{i_1} + l^{i_1})(r^{i_1} + b^{i_1})(b^{i_1} + d^{i_1})(l^{i_1} + d^{i_1})}} \\
&\quad - \frac{r^{i_2} \cdot d^{i_2} - l^{i_2} \cdot b^{i_2}}{\sqrt{(r^{i_2} + l^{i_2})(r^{i_2} + b^{i_2})(b^{i_2} + d^{i_2})(l^{i_2} + d^{i_2})}} \\
&= \frac{8 \cdot 940 - 12 \cdot 92}{\sqrt{20 \cdot 100 \cdot 1032 \cdot 952}} - \frac{6 \cdot 946 - 6 \cdot 94}{\sqrt{12 \cdot 100 \cdot 1040 \cdot 952}} \\
&= \frac{4}{\sqrt{100 \cdot 952}} \left(\frac{1880 - 276}{\sqrt{20 \cdot 1032}} - \frac{1419 - 141}{\sqrt{12 \cdot 1040}} \right) \\
&= \frac{4}{\sqrt{100 \cdot 952}} \left(\frac{1604}{\sqrt{20 \cdot 12 \cdot 2 \cdot 43}} - \frac{1278}{\sqrt{12 \cdot 20 \cdot 2 \cdot 26}} \right) \\
&= \frac{8}{\sqrt{100 \cdot 952 \cdot 480}} \left(\frac{802}{\sqrt{43}} - \frac{639}{\sqrt{26}} \right) \\
&= \frac{8}{\sqrt{100 \cdot 952 \cdot 480}} \\
&\quad \times \frac{\sqrt{802 \cdot 802 \cdot 26} - \sqrt{639 \cdot 639 \cdot 43}}{\sqrt{43} \cdot \sqrt{26}} \\
&= \frac{8}{\sqrt{100 \cdot 952 \cdot 480}} \cdot \frac{\sqrt{16723304} - \sqrt{17557803}}{\sqrt{43} \cdot \sqrt{26}} < 0
\end{aligned}
$$

2. The search collection contained 10 pertinent documents ($C = 10$). In this situation,

$$l^{i_1} = N^{i_1} - r^{i_1} = 12; \quad b^{i_1} = C - r^{i_1} = 2;$$
$$d^{i_1} = N_0 - C - l^{i_1} = 1030;$$
$$l^{i_2} = N^{i_2} - r^{i_2} = 6; \quad b^{i_2} = C - r^{i_2} = 4;$$
$$d^{i_2} = N_0 - C - l^{i_2} = 1036.$$

Then,

$$I_{12}^{i_1} - I_{12}^{i_2} = \frac{r^{i_1}d^{i_1} - l^{i_1}b^{i_1}}{\sqrt{(r^{i_1} + l^{i_1})(r^{i_1} + b^{i_1})(b^{i_1} + d^{i_1})(l^{i_1} + d^{i_1})}}$$

$$- \frac{r^{i_2} \cdot d^{i_2} - l^{i_2} \cdot b^{i_2}}{\sqrt{(r^{i_2} + l^{i_2})(r^{i_2} + b^{i_2})(b^{i_2} + d^{i_2})(l^{i_2} + d^{i_2})}}$$

$$= \frac{8 \cdot 1030 - 12 \cdot 2}{\sqrt{20 \cdot 10 \cdot 1032 \cdot 1042}} - \frac{6 \cdot 1036 - 6 \cdot 4}{\sqrt{12 \cdot 10 \cdot 1040 \cdot 1042}}$$

$$= \frac{8}{\sqrt{10 \cdot 1042}}\left(\frac{1030 - 3}{\sqrt{20 \cdot 1032}} - \frac{777 - 3}{\sqrt{12 \cdot 1040}}\right)$$

$$= \frac{8}{\sqrt{10 \cdot 1042 \cdot 480}}\left(\frac{1027}{\sqrt{43}} - \frac{774}{\sqrt{26}}\right)$$

$$= \frac{8}{\sqrt{10 \cdot 1042 \cdot 480}}$$

$$\times \frac{\sqrt{1027 \cdot 1027 \cdot 26} - \sqrt{774 \cdot 774 \cdot 43}}{\sqrt{43} \cdot \sqrt{26}}$$

$$= \frac{8}{\sqrt{10 \cdot 1042 \cdot 480}} \cdot \frac{\sqrt{27422954} - \sqrt{25760268}}{\sqrt{43} \cdot \sqrt{26}} > 0.$$

Thus, we see that in Situation 1 and in Situation 2 the difference $I_{12}^{i_1} - I_{12}^{i_2}$ has opposite signs, and the only parameter distinguishing two situations, as previously, is the number of pertinent documents in the search collection, that is, only in values of C. Hence, the sign of difference $I_{12}^{i_1} - I_{12}^{i_2}$ depends on the value of C. This means that complex search characteristic I_{12} does not have order preservation property.

Thus, we have determined whether certain CSCs have the order preservation property. In conclusion it should be pointed out that, as was stated before, characteristics I_2 and I_{12}, in spite of the proximity of the values under certain conditions, do differ significantly, as became evident during the consideration of the order preservation property as applied to these CSCs.

10.9

Fuzzy Scales of Pertinence

As we discussed in the first section of this chapter, during the pertinence analysis of a document by a user, situations may arise when a user would find it so difficult to judge whether the analyzed document is pertinent that he or she would consider it helpful for evaluation of document search results to take into account the nonpertinence degree of nonpertinent documents. In this case, some of the possible choices would be almost pertinent, possibly pertinent, almost nonpertinent, and so on. Naturally, the binary scale of pertinence is out of the question here. Rather, the fuzzy scale is used, which, in addition to the pertinent and nonpertinent values, includes "almost pertinent" and "almost nonpertinent," among other values. (All these values can also be expressed numerically.)

In discussing the possibility of using fuzzy scales of pertinence, it should be pointed out that taking into account the nonpertinence degree of nonpertinent documents in the process of evaluating the quality of a produced output is associated with a somewhat different understanding of the functional efficiency of document search, because in the previous discussion of the quality of the output and, hence, functional efficiency, we did not consider the nonpertinence degree of nonpertinent documents. It follows that it is necessary in this situation to specify the content criteria of a functional efficiency evaluation. (Recall that in the first section of this chapter we mentioned the scale of pertinence employed by the user in analyzing how a document affects the development of concrete content criteria.) Regretfully, neither informational practice nor an analysis of relevant publications help in establishing these criteria. What's more, in our opinion, researchers do not have a clear picture of these criteria, even on a intuitive level. (This is the result of the fact that, in practice, fuzzy scales of pertinence, as a rule, are not used.) We are also not prepared to define a set of content criteria of functional efficiency evaluation that would provide an adequate understanding of the position from which functional efficiency could be evaluated in the given situation. We note that to solve this problem, one must have a clear idea of what should be taken into consideration in an output quality evaluation: the nonpertinence degree of both found and not found nonpertinent documents or, say, only that of found nonpertinent documents, and so forth. We, too, have no clear understanding of how this should be taken into consideration. There is a point of view that one should not take into account the nonpertinence degree of not found nonpertinent documents when evaluating output quality. The attractiveness of this alternative is explained the following way. All nonpertinent documents not found during the search are not included in the output, in our opinion, with equal legitimacy, irrespective of their nonpertinence degree. However, other points of view could also have persuasive arguments. Because at present nobody has exhaustively analyzed this problem, let us choose the most convenient point of view; namely, let us assume that in output quality evaluations one must take into consideration the nonpertinence degree of both found and not found nonpertinent documents.

Keeping this point of view in mind, let us consider only one content criterion of the functional efficiency evaluation (we do not claim that this criterion could be used without any reservations). In the subsequent discussion, we will assume that in analyzing documents for their pertinence a fuzzy scale of pertinence is used with m possible choices: $f_1, f_2, \ldots, f_m$, where $f_1 = 1$ (a document is pertinent), $f_m = 0$ (a document is nonpertinent), and f_i—for $2 \le i \le m - 1$—

corresponds to intermediate values (results) of pertinence evaluations, where $f_1 > f_2 > \ldots > f_{m-1} > f_m$. Clearly, in this situation the coefficient of correspondence of the i-th document in the search collection to a user's query, determined by the user (i.e., coefficient k_i; see Section 10.6, "Construction of Complex Search Characteristics"), takes a value that coincides with one of the values in the fuzzy scale defined earlier. At the same time, the values of coefficient v_i (coefficient of correspondence of the i-th document in the search collection to a user's query, calculated from the search results) will be based, as before, on the binary scale, namely, $v_i = 1$ if the i-th document has been found during the search, and $v_i = 0$ otherwise. In the subsequent discussion, for clarity we will use symbol w_i instead of k_i, assuming that $w_i = f_p$, that is, is equal to one of the values of the fuzzy scale. If w_i and v_i are determined for each document of the search collection containing N_0 documents, then the following vectors can be formed from these values:

$$W = (w_1, w_2, \ldots, w_{N_0}) \quad \text{and} \quad V = (v_1, v_2, \ldots, v_{N_0}).$$

Then the content criterion of the functional efficiency evaluation will be defined as follows: the "closer" vectors W and V are, the higher the functional efficiencies of a document search.

The defined content criterion does not allow us to get sufficient clarity on the position of how to evaluate functional efficiency in the given situation (though, it gives some ideas for possible approaches). Yet, as was mentioned earlier, human beings use this position to evaluate functional efficiency. Hence, this leads to the conclusion that today we don't have any basis for successfully realizing any content-based method for evaluating functional effectiveness (in the discussed situation).

The situation is also not clear with a formal method of evaluating functional efficiency. We are unaware of any solutions regarding a realization of such a method. It is not even clear in this case on what principles formal rules must be based. We can only propose to base these rules on complex search characteristics, as is done in the case where a binary scale of pertinence is used in the context of the formal method. However, it is not likely that the use of CSCs discussed in this chapter will be expedient in this situation, and we will need other complex search characteristics. We propose to use several new CSCs which, we believe, may be useful, provided that one of the content criteria determining position from which functional efficiency evaluation is conducted will be the criterion defined in this section. These CSCs are introduced as functions that allow one to evaluate the closeness of vectors W and V. Previously (see Section 10.6, "Construction of Complex Search Characteristics"), for analogous purpose functions $\cos \phi_{XY}, \rho(X, Y)$ and $\rho_1(X, Y)$ were used. Recall that in that section we dealt with a special case of vector W, vector K. The use of function $\cos \phi_{XY}$ in this case, that is, its application to vectors K and V, led us to the complex search characteristic $I_2 = \sqrt{R \cdot P}$. At the same time, we showed that in the case of vectors E and U, the function $\cos \phi_{XY}$ should not be used for constructing complex search characteristics because the evaluation of the search results, based on the CSC constructed in such a way, could sometimes give absurd results. This illustrates why it is necessary to be very precise in using functions that would allow one to evaluate the closeness of vectors.

Analyzing the applicability of functions $\cos \phi_{XY}$, $\rho(X, Y)$, and $\rho_1(X, Y)$ for constructing complex search characteristics for the case of vectors W and V, we did not find any example that would compromise the use for this purpose of functions $\rho(X, Y)$ and $\rho_1(X, Y)$, but we found, in our opinion, such examples for the function $\cos \phi_{XY}$. We present one such example here.

Assume that in some search collection containing N_0 documents, two searches were performed using two different search requests and in the result of these searches the following vectors were formed:

$$V^1 = V^2 = (1;\ 1;\ 1;\ 1;\ 0;\ 0;\ \ldots\ 0).$$

Also assume that the search collection was analyzed for pertinence of the documents to each search request resulting in the following vectors of correspondence:

$$W^1 = (0.1;\ 0.1;\ 0.1;\ 0.1;\ 0;\ 0;\ \ldots\ ;\ 0)$$

and

$$W^2 = (0.1;\ 1;\ 1;\ 1;\ 0;\ 0;\ 0;\ \ldots\ ;\ 0).$$

Then,

$$\cos \phi_{W^1 V^1} = \frac{\displaystyle\sum_{i=1}^{N_0} w_i^1 v_i^1}{\sqrt{\displaystyle\sum_{i=1}^{N_0} (w_i^1)^2} \cdot \sqrt{\displaystyle\sum_{i=1}^{N_0} (v_i^1)^2}}$$

$$= \frac{4 \cdot 0.1}{\sqrt{4 \cdot 0.01} \cdot \sqrt{4}} = \frac{4 \cdot 0.1}{2 \cdot 0.1 \cdot 2} = 1;$$

$$\cos \phi_{W^2 V^2} = \frac{3.1}{\sqrt{3.01} \cdot \sqrt{4}} \approx 0.89.$$

It follows that if the results of the searches (using the assumptions just described) are evaluated on the basis of complex search characteristic

$$I_{13} = \cos \phi_{WV} = \frac{\displaystyle\sum_{i=1}^{N_0} w_i \cdot v_i}{\sqrt{\displaystyle\sum_{i=1}^{N_0} (w_i)^2} \cdot \sqrt{\displaystyle\sum_{i=1}^{N_0} (v_i)^2}},$$

then the result of the search based on the first search request is better than the result of the search for the second search request. However, in our opinion, the result of the first search (for the first request) is substantially worse than the result of the second search (for the second request).

Such examples led us to the conclusion that it is not expedient to use complex search characteristics I_{13} without providing additional arguments. Therefore, for constructing CSCs in the case of vectors W and V from the functions described earlier, only $\rho(X, Y)$ and $\rho_1(X, Y)$ could be used. Applying these functions to vectors W and V we obtain the following complex search characteristics:

$$I_{14} = \rho(W, V) = \sum_{i=1}^{N_0} |w_i - v_i|;$$

$$I_{15} = \rho_1(W, V) = \sqrt{\sum_{i=1}^{N_0} (w_i - v_i)^2}.$$

Note that these complex search characteristics could be paired with previous CSCs I_{14} and I_3, and also I_{15} and I_4, where both characteristics in each pair are based on the same function.

As stated earlier, from our point of view, it may be expedient to use complex search characteristics I_{14} and I_{15} for the functional efficiency evaluation in the discussed situation. In this respect it is only natural to ask this question: How well founded is this assumption? It is clear that the answer to this question will follow if we find an answer to the following question: Do complex search characteristics I_{14} and I_{15} permit the evaluation of functional efficiency (in the discussed situation) that is pragmatically justified, and if they do, then in what cases? It should be emphasized here that today we can only outline problems associated with the latter question, rather than propose their solution. Let us consider some of these problems.

1. In order to determine in which cases complex search characteristics I_{14} and I_{15} permit the pragmatically justified evaluation of functional efficiency and in which cases they do not, we first must have a clear understanding of the position from which functional efficiency is evaluated. However, at present we have no understanding of such a position and, as was stated before, are not ready to define a set of content criteria for functional efficiency evaluation that will give us the required understanding.

2. Obtaining an understanding of the position from which functional efficiency is evaluated is a necessary step, but it is not a sufficient one. In particular, it is not clear if we can find a method that will not require functional efficiency evaluation in order to find an answer to the question: Will the complex search characteristic I_{14} (I_{15}) permit

us in the discussed (arbitrary) case of document search to perform a pragmatically justified evaluation of functional efficiency? Note that to find an answer to a similar question regarding a number of CSCs considered before, such a method had been found (see Section 10.4, "Limits of Applicability of Complex Search Characteristics").

Naturally, the considered problems do not represent all problems associated with finding the answer to the following question: In what cases do complex search characteristics I_{14} and I_{15} permit (and when don't they permit) one to perform pragmatically justified functional efficiency evaluation? However, we will not consider any additional problems because we have not solved the previous problems. It follows from the preceding that we are not ready to make a decision as to expediency of using characteristics I_{14} and I_{15} for functional efficiency evaluation. By the way, it is conceivable that to make such a decision an additional conceptual apparatus will be needed (similar to what we have used in Section 10.4, "Limits of Applicability of Complex Search Characteristics").

Thus, for the present we cannot find a definite answer to the question of whether it is expedient to use characteristics I_{14} and I_{15} for functional efficiency evaluation (in the discussed situation); on the other hand, we can provide an answer to another question that is very important from the practical point of view: Do these CSCs have the order preservation property? Before answering this question, first note that in the discussed situation it is more convenient to use an essentially similar, but more pragmatically clear, formulation of the order preservation property. In order to state the required formulation, let us assume that we have a number of arbitrary search methods. Assuming that all these methods have been used in a search on the same query in the same search collection D and that this search resulted in outputs $h_1, h_2, \ldots, h_i, \ldots$, let us designate a union of the resulting outputs by h, that is, $h = \bigcup_i h_i$. (It is clear that h is a subset of D, and let us assume that set D contains N_0 documents and subset h contains p documents.) Further, note that values of search characteristics and parameters can be determined both from the results of search and analysis in collection D and from the results of search and analysis in subcollection h. To distinguish these situations, we will use the symbols $\wedge$ and $\sim$; namely, symbol $\wedge$ will be used for marking search characteristics and parameters in a situation where their values are determined from the results of search and analysis in collection D (for example, $\hat{F}$), and symbol $\sim$ will be used for marking the same search characteristics and parameters in a situation where their values are determined from the results of search and analysis in subcollection h (for example, $\tilde{F}$). Now, let us assume that as a result of using each of these search methods, values of a certain complex search characteristic F (both $\hat{F}$ and $\tilde{F}$) have been determined. Then the required formulation of the order preservation property will be as follows.

If in the case of any two used search methods, (i_1-th and i_2-th), the signs of differences $\hat{F}^{i_1} - \hat{F}^{i_2}$ and $\tilde{F}^{i_1} -_s \tilde{F}^{i_2}$ coincide, then complex search characteristic F has the order preservation property.

We will explain why this formulation of the order preservation property and the one used earlier are essentially similar. Let us assume that the search methods, mentioned in the new formulation of the order preservation property, are ordered, for instance, by the decreasing order of obtained values of $\tilde{F}$. If the complex search characteristic F has the stated property, then the order of the preceding search methods will be the same also in the case where these methods will be ordered in decreasing order of the obtained values of $\hat{F}$, which is clear from the discussed property and the similar reasoning in Section 10.8, "Order Preservation Property." In other words, if it is necessary to order applied search methods using the results of search and analysis in collection D in the sense of a certain CSC having the stated property, we can do this in the following way: we can order these methods using the results of search and analysis in subcollection h and use the obtained order as a desired result. On the other hand, a similar ordering of the same search methods, but in the sense of the CSC possessing the order preservation property according to the former formulation, can also be done using the results of search and analysis in subcollection h. This is what we meant when we stated that the latter and the former formulations of the property are essentially similar.

Now, we will show that complex search characteristics I_{14} and I_{15} have the property formulated in this section. For this purpose, assuming that the condition of the property is satisfied for each of the above CSCs, let us consider following pairs of differences for any two search methods (i_1-th and i_2-th), specified in the property condition, with the following pairs of differences:

1. $\hat{I}_{14}^{i_1} - \hat{I}_{14}^{i_2}$ and $\tilde{I}_{14}^{i_1} - \tilde{I}_{14}^{i_2}$;
2. $\hat{I}_{15}^{i_1} - \hat{I}_{15}^{i_2}$ and $\tilde{I}_{15}^{i_1} - \tilde{I}_{15}^{i_2}$.

Let us assume, for the purposes of convenience, that subcollection h is the first p documents in collection D (keeping in mind that the ordering of the collection does not affect the proof). Thus, the first difference of the first pair is

$$\hat{I}_{14}^{i_1} - \hat{I}_{14}^{i_2} = \sum_{k=1}^{N_0} \left| w_k - v_k^{i_1} \right| - \sum_{k=1}^{N_0} \left| w_k - v_k^{i_2} \right|$$

$$= \sum_{k=1}^{p} \left| w_k - v_k^{i_1} \right| + \sum_{k=p+1}^{N_0} \left| w_k - v_k^{i_1} \right|$$

$$- \sum_{k=1}^{p} \left| w_k - v_k^{i_2} \right| - \sum_{k=p+1}^{N_0} \left| w_k - v_k^{i_2} \right|.$$

Note that all $v_k^{i_1}$ and $v_k^{i_2}$, when $p + 1 \le k \le N_0$, are equal to zero, because they correspond to the documents not included in subcollection h. (Any document, corresponding to a nonzero value of $v_k^{i_1}$ or $v_k^{i_2}$ is included in subcollection h.) Therefore,

$$\sum_{k=p+1}^{N_0} |w_k - v_k^{i_1}| = \sum_{k=p+1}^{N_0} |w_k|$$

and

$$\sum_{k=p+1}^{N_0} |w_k - v_k^{i_2}| = \sum_{k=p+1}^{N_0} |w_k|.$$

Taking this into account, we have

$$\hat{I}_{14}^{i_1} - \hat{I}_{14}^{i_2} = \sum_{k=1}^{p} |w_k - v_k^{i_1}| + \sum_{k=p+1}^{N_0} |w_k| - \sum_{k=1}^{p} |w_k - v_k^{i_2}| - \sum_{k=p+1}^{N_0} |w_k|$$

$$= \sum_{k=1}^{p} |w_k - v_k^{i_1}| - \sum_{k=1}^{p} |w_k - v_k^{i_2}|.$$

Now let us look at the second difference:

$$\tilde{I}_{14}^{i_1} - \tilde{I}_{14}^{i_2} = \sum_{k=1}^{p} |w_k - v_k^{i_1}| - \sum_{k=1}^{p} |w_k - v_k^{i_2}|.$$

It follows that signs of differences $\hat{I}_{14}^{i_1} - \hat{I}_{14}^{i_2}$ and $\tilde{I}_{14}^{i_1} - \tilde{I}_{14}^{i_2}$ coincide. Hence, complex search characteristic I_{14} has the order preservation property. Now let us consider the first difference of the second pair:

$$\hat{I}_{15}^{i_1} - \hat{I}_{15}^{i_2} = \sqrt{\sum_{k=1}^{N_0} (w_k - v_k^{i_1})^2} - \sqrt{\sum_{k=1}^{N_0} (w_k - v_k^{i_2})^2}$$

$$= \left(\sqrt{\sum_{k=1}^{N_0} (w_k - v_k^{i_1})^2} - \sqrt{\sum_{k=1}^{N_0} (w_k - v_k^{i_2})^2} \right)$$

$$\times \frac{\sqrt{\sum_{k=1}^{N_0} (w_k - v_k^{i_1})^2} + \sqrt{\sum_{k=1}^{N_0} (w_k - v_k^{i_2})^2}}{\sqrt{\sum_{k=1}^{N_0} (w_k - v_k^{i_1})^2} + \sqrt{\sum_{k=1}^{N_0} (w_k - v_k^{i_2})^2}}$$

$$= \frac{\sum_{k=1}^{N_0} (w_k - v_k^{i_1})^2 - \sum_{k=1}^{N_0} (w_k - v_k^{i_2})^2}{\sqrt{\sum_{k=1}^{N_0} (w_k - v_k^{i_1})^2} + \sqrt{\sum_{k=1}^{N_0} (w_k - v_k^{i_2})^2}}.$$

This manipulation is impossible only in cases where

$$\sqrt{\sum_{k=1}^{N_0} (w_k - v_k^{i_1})^2} + \sqrt{\sum_{k=1}^{N_0} (w_k - v_k^{i_2})^2} = 0.$$

It is clear that this case takes place if and only if $v_k^{i_1} = v_k^{i_2} = w_k$, for any k in $1 \le k \le N_0$. This means that in this case the signs of differences $\hat{I}_{15}^{i_1} - \hat{I}_{15}^{i_2}$ and $\tilde{I}_{15}^{i_1} - \tilde{I}_{15}^{i_2}$ coincide. So we can assume that

$$\sqrt{\sum_{k=1}^{N_0} (w_k - v_k^{i_1})^2} + \sqrt{\sum_{k=1}^{N_0} (w_k - v_k^{i_2})^2} > 0.$$

Then,

$$\hat{I}_{15}^{i_1} - \hat{I}_{15}^{i_2} =$$

$$\frac{\sum_{k=1}^{p} (w_k - v_k^{i_1})^2 + \sum_{k=p+1}^{N_0} (w_k - v_k^{i_1})^2 - \sum_{k=1}^{p} (w_k - v_k^{i_2})^2 - \sum_{k=p+1}^{N_0} (w_k - v_k^{i_2})^2}{\sqrt{\sum_{k=1}^{N_0} (w_k - v_k^{i_1})^2} + \sqrt{\sum_{k=1}^{N_0} (w_k - v_k^{i_2})^2}}.$$

Similarly to the case of the first pair of differences, the following relationships can be obtained:

$$\sum_{k=p+1}^{N_0} (w_k - v_k^{i_1})^2 = \sum_{k=p+1}^{N_0} (w_k)^2$$

and

$$\sum_{k=p+1}^{N_0} (w_k - v_k^{i_2})^2 = \sum_{k=p+1}^{N_0} (w_k)^2.$$

Taking them into account, we will have

$$\hat{I}_{15}^{i_1} - \hat{I}_{15}^{i_2} = \frac{\sum_{k=1}^{p} (w_k - v_k^{i_1})^2 + \sum_{k=p+1}^{N_0} (w_k)^2 - \sum_{k=1}^{p} (w_k - v_k^{i_2})^2 - \sum_{k=p+1}^{N_0} (w_k)^2}{\sqrt{\sum_{k=1}^{N_0} (w_k - v_k^{i_1})^2} + \sqrt{\sum_{k=1}^{N_0} (w_k - v_k^{i_2})^2}}$$

$$= \frac{\sum_{k=1}^{p} (w_k - v_k^{i_1})^2 - \sum_{k=1}^{p} (w_k - v_k^{i_2})^2}{\sqrt{\sum_{k=1}^{N_0} (w_k - v_k^{i_1})^2} + \sqrt{\sum_{k=1}^{N_0} (w_k - v_k^{i_2})^2}}$$

$$= \left(\sqrt{\sum_{k=1}^{P} (w_k - v_k^{i_1})^2} - \sqrt{\sum_{k=1}^{P} (w_k - v_k^{i_2})^2} \right)$$

$$\times \frac{\left(\sqrt{\sum_{k=1}^{P} (w_k - v_k^{i_1})^2} + \sqrt{\sum_{k=1}^{P} (w_k - v_k^{i_2})^2} \right)}{\sqrt{\sum_{k=1}^{N_0} (w_k - v_k^{i_1})^2} + \sqrt{\sum_{k=1}^{N_0} (w_k - v_k^{i_2})^2}}.$$

Now let us look at the second difference:

$$\tilde{I}_{15}^{i_1} - \tilde{I}_{15}^{i_2} = \sqrt{\sum_{k=1}^{P} (w_k - v_k^{i_1})^2} - \sqrt{\sum_{k=1}^{P} (w_k - v_k^{i_2})^2}.$$

From the previous relationships, it follows that the signs of differences $\hat{I}_{15}^{i_1} - \hat{I}_{15}^{i_2}$ and $\tilde{I}_{15}^{i_1} - \tilde{I}_{15}^{i_2}$ coincide. Therefore, complex search characteristic I_{15} also has the order preservation property. Thus, we demonstrated that characteristics I_{14} and I_{15} do indeed have the order preservation property as formulated in this section.

In conclusion, we will give an example that could be used in the future to illustrate a difference in the understanding of the functional efficiency of a document search implied in this section from the understanding of functional efficiency implied earlier. We say "could be used in the future" meaning that to make a decision regarding the correctness of using such examples for the purpose described will only be possible when we learn to distinguish in which cases complex search characteristics of type I_{14} allow for a pragmatically justified evaluation of the functional effectiveness of a search. Thus, let us assume that two different search methods were used for a search based on the same query in a search collection containing N_0 documents and these searches resulted in the following vectors:

1. $V^1 = (1; 1; 1; 0; 0; 0; 0; \ldots ; 0)$
2. $V^2 = (1; 1; 1; 1; 1; 1; 0; \ldots ; 0)$

Let us assume also that the analysis of the search collection documents by the user resulted in the following vector:

$$W = (1; 1; 1; 1; 0.3; 0.3; 0; \ldots ; 0).$$

Next, let us determine values of complex search characteristic I_{14} based on the results of the described search:

$$I_{14}^1 = \sum_{i=1}^{N_0} |w_i - v_i^1| = 1.6;$$

$$I_{14}^2 = 1.4.$$

It is clear that if characteristic I_{14} allows for a pragmatically justified evaluation of the functional effectiveness in both cases of searches under discussion, we can conclude that the highest functional efficiency (according to this section) was achieved with the aid of the second search method.

Now let us turn our attention to the understanding of functional efficiency implied before this section. Recall that in this understanding of functional efficiency the nonpertinence degree of nonpertinent documents (both found and not found during search) was not taken into considerations. This means that if the user follows this approach in analyzing the pertinence of a document, then it is natural to assume that in the discussed example, vector K would be formed instead of vector W; that is,

$$K = (1;\ 1;\ 1;\ 1;\ 0;\ 0;\ 0;\ \ldots\ ;\ 0).$$

In this case, for the evaluation of functional effectiveness in both searches in our example (and resulting in forming vectors V^1 and V^2), it is expedient to use one of the CSCs described earlier, such as complex search characteristic I_2. We determine the values that would be achieved in the cases of searches mentioned earlier:

$$I_2^1 = \frac{\sum_{i=1}^{N_0} k_i v_i^1}{\sqrt{\sum_{i=1}^{N_0} (k_i)^2} \cdot \sqrt{\sum_{i=1}^{N_0} (v_i^1)^2}} = \frac{3}{\sqrt{4}\cdot\sqrt{3}} \approx 0.866;$$

$$I_2^2 = \frac{4}{\sqrt{4}\cdot\sqrt{6}} \approx 0.816.$$

Because characteristic I_2 allows for a pragmatically justified evaluation of the functional effectiveness of a search in both cases described earlier (indeed, $P^1 = 1$ and $P^2 = 4/6 \approx 0.667$), we can conclude that the first method of search leads to higher functional efficiency (based on the understanding implied before this section).

Thus, if the preceding example is correct, then it demonstrates that the choice of search method giving the highest functional efficiency may be different for the situation of the understanding of functional efficiency implied in this section and for the situation of the understanding of functional efficiency implied earlier. This means that there is a difference in the understanding of the functional efficiency of a document search in the described situations.

10.10

Another Formulation of the Goal of Document Search

In the final section of this chapter, we will illustrate the role of formulation of the goal for a document search in the context of the problem of evaluating the functional efficiency of such a search. Recall that in the first section of this chapter we pointed out that the functional efficiency of a search is determined by the extent to which the goal for which the search is carried out was fulfilled. We also pointed out that the goal of the document search (see also Chapter 4) is to find information satisfying POIN. The more complete and accurate the output given to the user, the higher the POIN satisfaction quality. In other words, we believe that functional efficiency is determined by output quality. It should be emphasized that all discussion in this chapter was based on the formulation of the goal of document search just given.

Next, it is important to recall that output quality is evaluated based on the task that is determined by the user's POIN. It is this task that forms concept-based views that jointly determine a position from which the functional efficiency of the document search is evaluated. These points of view were called content criteria of functional efficiency evaluation. It was pointed out in this respect that the formation of concrete content criteria was influenced to a certain degree by the scale of pertinence used by the user in analyzing a document. That is why not all the approaches and results proposed or obtained in this chapter were applicable when discussing problems associated with functional efficiency evaluation in the previous section. Even more influence on handling these problems may be expected from changing a task for which a document search is done and, naturally, from changing the formulation of the goal of the document search. In this section we will discuss only the influence determined by the change of the formulation of the goal of the document search.

In order to see that this influence exists, and also to have some idea of its limits, we propose to use a formulation of the document search goal that differs somewhat from the one used earlier (although it is sufficiently close to it). The goal of the document search is to obtain an exact identification of the documents in the search collection by retrieving as many pertinent documents as are available in the search collection and by not retrieving as many as possible nonpertinent documents available in the search collection (see, for example, Popov, 1981). In other words, in this case functional efficiency will be determined by how exact the identification (during the search) of the search collection documents is. At first glance one might think that this formulation of the document search goal is essentially identical to the one formulated previously. However, this is not so, and we will illustrate this by following examples.

1. Let us assume that a search in a collection containing 10,000 documents, 5 of which are pertinent, resulted in outputs consisting of
   - 5 pertinent and 3 nonpertinent documents;
   - 5 pertinent and 20 nonpertinent documents.

Naturally, these outputs differ significantly in their quality, although the correctness of the identification of documents in the search collection in these two cases appears (at least intuitively) to be very similar.

2. Let us assume that a search in a collection containing 10,020 documents, 20 of which are pertinent, resulted in outputs consisting of
- 18 pertinent documents and no nonpertinent documents;
- 20 pertinent and 1000 nonpertinent documents.

It is clear that quality of these two outputs is practically incomparable: the quality of the first is very high, whereas the second output most likely should be regarded as unacceptable (see Section 10.3, "Problems of Evaluating the Functional Effectiveness of a Document Search"). As to the correctness of the identification of the search collection in these cases, additional considerations are needed concerning concept-based views to determine the position from which identification correctness is evaluated. We have not found discussion of these points of view in literature. Nevertheless, our analysis of publications (see, for example, Popov, 1981; and Salton, 1975) leads us to conclude that some researchers believe (this belief is usually implicit) that a share of found pertinent documents, that is, recall (R), and a share of nonpertinent documents not found during the search, that is, specificity (S), are equally important (they mutually compensate each other) in evaluating the correctness of identification. (Note that in this context search recall and search specificity can be considered as coefficients of identification of pertinent and nonpertinent documents, respectively.) If one adopts this point of view (as it was stated, there are no other points of view!), then one can conclude that the correctness of document identification in a search collection (resulting in outputs discussed in the given example) is the same in both cases. Indeed, $R^1 = 0.9$, $S^1 = 1$, $R^2 = 1$, and $S^2 = 0.9$.

3. Let us assume that a search in a collection also containing 10,000 documents, 20 of which are pertinent, resulted in outputs, consisting of
- 14 pertinent documents and no nonpertinent documents;
- 20 pertinent and 9 nonpertinent documents.

The quality of these outputs are close, but the identification correctness of the search collection cannot be considered as close in these cases, keeping the previous example in mind.

Thus, the above examples confirm that, indeed, the new formulation of the goal of document search and the former formulation do have essential differences. This is confirmed both in the case of the intuitive evaluation of identification correctness and in the case of evaluation based on a certain point of view. Note in this connection that when a search is made in the same document collection, the high quality of the output implies a corresponding level of identification correctness of the search collection documents. The opposite implication is not true, which follows, in particular, from the second example.

Naturally, if we assume that the goal of document search is to ensure correct the identification of documents in a search collection, then we can say that there are also two methods of evaluating the functional efficiency of a search:

the by-content method and the formal method. (See Section 10.3 "Problems of Evaluating the Functional Effectiveness of a Document Search.") In that section we mentioned that if the functional efficiency of a document search is evaluated by a human (the by-content method) he or she uses appropriate concept-based views (determining a position from functional efficiency is evaluated). Here, once again, it should be pointed out that we have not seen any discussion of the concept-based views in a situation for which the correctness of the identification of the documents in a search collection must be evaluated. Recall that the concept-based views in question are formed taking into account the task for which the document search is carried out. However, we are also unaware of any tasks that would lead to a search whose goal is to correctly identify documents in a search collection. Tasks of this type are unlikely to be of practical interest, because, generally speaking, they assume that the user does not care about the precision of the search. Nevertheless, such tasks and, hence, formulation of the goal of the document search in this section are worth considering, even though at present we cannot expect successful realization of the by-content method for evaluating the functional efficiency of a document search (in the discussed case) because of the lack of both a theoretical and a practical basis.

The situation with the formal method of functional efficiency evaluation in the discussed case is even more complex. First, in this case there is no clear idea of what must be the basis for formal rules to be used in the evaluation method. Second, even if we assume that these rules are based on complex search characteristics, we do not know what kind of CSCs they can be. We should note here that in some publications (e.g., see Popov, 1981; and Salton, 1975) the search characteristic $R + S - 1$ is discussed, which, generally speaking, potentially could be used in formal rules. This assumption is based on the fact that the concept-based view cited earlier (namely, that in evaluating the correctness of the identification of the documents in a search collection, search recall and search specificity are equally important) does not exclude the possibility of using this characteristic as a basis for a pragmatically justified evaluation of functional efficiency in the discussed case. At the same time, we cannot give a strong argument for the expediency of using this characteristic in evaluating functional efficiency. The main reason is that at present there are no ideas about the position from which functional efficiency is evaluated (we are not even aware of tasks leading to a search whose goal is to identify, as correctly as possible, the documents in a search collection). Hence, before proposing required complex search characteristics or formal models for their construction, one must at least eliminate this reason. However, this is impossible at present. The preceding considerations cause the additional difficulties in realizing the formal method of evaluating functional efficiency in the discussed case.

The previous discussion, in our opinion, gives a clear idea of the role of formulation of the goal of a documentary search in the context of evaluating functional efficiency.

10.11

Conclusion

The problems that arise when evaluating information retrieval form a complex labyrinth, and in this chapter we analyzed our place in this labyrinth. As the result of this analysis, the following was determined:

- Only documentary search is being evaluated.
- The functional effectiveness of documentary search is being evaluated.
- As the result of this search, the search collection is divided into two subsets: the documents corresponding to the search request and the documents not corresponding to the search request.
- In analyzing documents, binary scale will be used (unless stated otherwise) describing whether the documents are pertinent or nonpertinent

The evaluation of the functional effectiveness of a documentary search assumes two methods: the formal method and the by-content method. Both methods were considered in the this chapter, but we stressed the first method. This method is based on using search characteristics of type $I_1 = R + P$, which were called complex search characteristics. For the complex search characteristic (CSC) I_1, we gave an example illustrating that this CSC would not allow a pragmatically justified evaluation of functional effectiveness in all situations. In extending this example, we formulated a more general result; the authors are not aware of any complex search characteristics that would allow for a pragmatically justified evaluation of the functional effectiveness in any "acceptable" situation, that is, that would allow one to evaluate the functional effectiveness of a documentary search, with any acceptable output (such search characteristics probably do not exist and are not likely to be developed).

That is why the problem of determining the boundaries of the applicability domain of complex search characteristics became one of our key concerns in this chapter. In this connection we presented special methods for solving this problem. Using these methods, domains of the applicability of complex search characteristics $I_1 = R + P$ and $I_2 = \sqrt{R \cdot P}$ were determined. Analysis of the domain of applicability of complex search characteristic I_2 led to a very important conclusion: evaluation of functional effectiveness based on this characteristic will be pragmatically justified in the case of any search whose precision is not less than 0.5, that is, in fact, in any search in contemporary information retrieval systems. At the same time, to determine in general if it is pragmatically justified to evaluate functional effectiveness in a given situation on the basis of some CSC, it is necessary to know recall level (in addition to precision level). Therefore, we also considered methods for determining recall level.

A large part of this chapter was devoted to constructing complex search characteristics. We considered several formal models that would allow one to construct such characteristics. One of these models led to a series of CSCs with the order preservation property. The existence of this property in some CSCs allows for a significant decrease in the required effort (to an acceptable level!) in comparison with a typical effort required for evaluating functional effectiveness. It was shown that, in particular, CSC $I_2 = \sqrt{R \cdot P}$ has an order preservation property. Taking this into account and using the analysis of the domain of applicability, it could be stated that the given CSC provides a pragmatically justified comparison of functional effectiveness with acceptable efforts required for this operation practically in any cases of search carried out in contemporary information retrieval systems. This conclusion has far-reaching consequences, in particular, the use of complex search characteristic I_2 allowed us (see Chapter 9) to solve one of the very important and complicated problems in information science—the problem of creating a selection mechanism that would allow the best search method to be selected for every search request (from a set of available methods).

The described results were obtained under the assumption that a binary scale of pertinence was used in evaluating documents. On the basis of these results, we also considered situations in which a "fuzzy" scale of pertinence is used. We constructed complex search characteristics for such cases. In addition, we adapted to this situation formulation of the order preservation property and showed that constructed CSCs have this property. Finally, we discussed some problems for which solutions are necessary in order to use these complex search characteristics. In concluding the chapter, we discussed the role of formulating the goal of documentary search in the context of the problem of evaluating the functional effectiveness of this search.

References

Avetisyan, D. O. (1975). *Statistical methods used in solving applied problems in information retrieval.* Ph.D. thesis, Nobvosibirsk.

Avetisyan, D. O. (1977). Evaluation of functional effectiveness of recognition systems. *Dokladi Academii Nauk of Armenian SSR, Applied Mathematics, 64,* (3).

Bollmann, P. (1977). A comparison of evaluation measures for document retrieval systems. *Journal of Informatics, 1,* 97–116.

Bollmann, P., Raghavan, V. V., Jung, G. S., & Shu, L. C. (1992). On probabilistic notions of precision as a function of recall. *Information Processing and Management, 28,* 291–315.

Borko, H. (1961). Research plan for evaluating effectiveness of various indexing systems. System Development Corporation, Report FN-5649. Santa Monica, CA: System Development Corporation, June 1961.

Cherniavsky, V. S., & Lakhuti, D. G. (1970). The problem of evaluating retrieval systems. *Nauchno-Teknicheskaya Informatsiya (NTI),* ser. 2, no. 1, 24–34.

Cleverdon, C. W. (1970). Evaluation of tests of information retrieval systems. *Journal of Documentation, 26,* 55–67.

Cleverdon, C. W., Mills, J., & Keen, M. (1966). Factors determining the performance of indexing systems, vol. 1–Design, vol. 2–Test results. ASLIB Cranfield Project, Cranfield.

Cooper, W. S. (1973). On selecting a measure of retrieval effectiveness. *Journal of the American Society for Information Science (JASIS), 24,* 87–100.

Frants, V. I., & Brush, C. B. (1988). The need for information and some aspects of information retrieval systems construction. *Journal of the American Society for Information Science, 39,* 86–91.

Frants, V. I., Voiskunskii, V. G., & Frants, Y. I. (1970). Evaluation of magnitude of possible losses of information during indexing. *Nauchno-Teknicheskaya Informatsiya (NTI),* ser. 2, no. 5, 14–15.

Heine, M. H. (1975). Distance between sets as an objective measure of retrieval effectiveness. *Information Storage and Retrieval, 9,* 181–198.

Kolmogorov, A. N., & Fomin S. B. (1968). *Elements of the theory of functions and functional analysis.* (2nd ed.). Moscow: Nauka.

Kraft, D., & Bookstein, A. (1978). Evaluation of information retrieval systems: A decision theoretic approach. *Journal of the American Society for Information Science (JASIS), 29,* 31–40.

Lancaster, F. W. (1979). *Information retrieval systems: Characteristics, testing, evaluation.* New York: John Wiley and Sons.

Popov, C. B. (1981). Characteristics of IR functioning and search situation. *Nauchno-Teknicheskaya Informatsiya (NTI),* ser. 2, no. 9, 9–13.

Raghavan, V. V., Bollmann, P., & Jung, G. S. (1989). Retrieval system evaluation using recall and precision: Problems and answers (extended abstract). Proceedings of the Twelfth Annual International ACM SIGIR Conference on research and development in information retrieval. Cambridge, MA, 59–68.

van Rijsbergen, C. J. (1979). Information retrieval (2nd ed.). London: Butterworths.

Salton, G. (1975). *Dynamic information and library processing.* Englewood Cliffs, NJ: Prentice Hall.

Salton, G., & McGill, M. J. (1983). *Introduction to modern information retrieval.* New York: McGraw Hill.

Saracevic, T. (1995). Evaluation of evaluation in information retrieval. Proceedings of the Eighteenth Annual International ACM SIGIR Conference on research and development in information retrieval. Seattle, WA, 138–146.

Shaw, W. M. (1995). Term-relevance computation and perfect retrieval performance. *Information Processing and Management, 31,* 491–498.

Sparck-Jones, K. (1980). Performance averaging for recall and precision. *Journal of Informatics, 2,* 95–105.

Voiskunskii, V. G. (1980). Search space and documentary search. *Nauchno-Teknicheskaya Informatsiya (NTI),* ser. 2, no. 9, 17–22.

Voiskunskii, V. G. (1983). One class of search characteristics. *Nauchno-Teknicheskaya Informatsiya (NTI),* ser. 2, no. 8, 12–15.

Voiskunskii, V. G. (1984). The distance in n-dimensional vector space and search characteristics. *Nauchno-Teknicheskaya Informatsiya (NTI),* ser. 2, no. 1, 18–20.

Voiskunskii, V. G. (1987). Applicability of search characteristics. *Nauchno-Teknicheskaya Informatsiya (NTI),* ser. 2, no. 12, 18–24.

Voiskunskii, V. G. (1992). Construction of search characteristics. *Nauchno-Teknicheskaya Informatsiya (NTI),* Ser. 2, No. 9, 6–9.

Bibliographic Remarks ⎯⎯⎯⎯⎯⎯⎯⎯⎯⎯⎯⎯⎯⎯⎯⎯

To get a deeper understanding of problems that arise when evaluating IR systems, we recommend the following publications.

van Rijsbergen, C. J. (1979). *Information retrieval* (2nd ed.). London: Butterworths.

Saracevic, T. (1995). Evaluation of evaluation in information retrieval. Proceedings of the Eighteenth Annual International ACM SIGIR Conference on research and development in information retrieval. Seattle, WA, 138–146.

Voiskunskii, V. G. (1980). Search space and documentary search. *Nauchno-Teknicheskaya Informatsiya (NTI)*, ser. 2, no. 9, 17–22.

Voiskunskii, V. G. (1992). Construction of search characteristics. *Nauchno-Teknicheskaya Informatsiya (NTI)*, ser. 2, no. 9, 6–9.

11

Evaluation of Macroevaluated Objects

11.1

Introduction

In the first section of Chapter 10 we emphasized that, along with the evaluation of the functional effectiveness of a search, we are also interested in the evaluation of objects with whose help or within the scope of which a search for documents proceeds. These objects include information retrieval systems as well as those subprocesses that involve document search (e.g., the translation of search requests from natural language to information retrieval language). In this chapter our concern will be such an evaluation of these objects, which could enable researchers to predict the search results for a newly entered search request when this search is performed with help or within the scope of the evaluated object. In Chapter 10 we described situations for which such an evaluation may be required. For example, when each subprocess of a document search, except for the subprocess under evaluation (for example, the translation of search requests from natural language to information retrieval language), proceeds using the same algorithm (for a corresponding subprocess) irrespective of the entered search request, then the formation of a set of "best" realizations of the subprocess under evaluation may be required for the purpose of using the set in selecting the most suitable realization for each search request entered; or, after forming such a set, it may be required to determine whether a newly proposed realization should be included in this set. In information science, as was pointed out earlier, different approaches for such an evaluation have been proposed. These approaches are based mainly on averaging functional effectiveness values obtained in a specially organized series of searches. By "functional effectiveness values" we mean the values of those search characteristics that are used in evaluating functional effectiveness. Note that the objects whose evaluation requires averaging of the original set of values we refer to as *macroevaluated*. This chapter deals with some of the problems related to evaluating macroevaluated objects.

11.2

Determination of Expediency for Evaluating Specific Macroevaluated Objects

Information science provides no clear picture as to which macroevaluated objects are expedient to evaluate and which are not. For example, in Cherniavsky & Lakhuti (1970) and Lakhuti (1971) the authors argue that it is expedient to evaluate not only retrieval services but also retrieval systems. In these references the notion of retrieval system is not defined formally but is introduced as a contraposition to the notion of retrieval service. In other words, on the one hand, any retrieval system is characterized by a language that includes the original alphabet or vocabulary and rules for constructing complex expressions, rules for indexing or translating texts from the natural language to a system language, and logic rules (which include comparison rules and possibly base relations between expressions of the system language). On the other hand, any functional retrieval system actually exists in the form of a particular collection of documents in a specific language derived from a specific source—personnel and hardware that realize search and indexing rules—and, finally, a particular circle of users serving as a source of search requests and in one way or another assessing search results. In the aggregate, all of these physical components are referred to as a retrieval service. The same retrieval system may be realized in different retrieval services and vice versa (the same retrieval service may use different retrieval systems).

In the view of Lakhuti (1971), basic considerations defining the expediency of evaluating retrieval systems are the need to study the behavior of a retrieval system for different classes of retrieval services realizing it to selecting a system optimal for a given service; the need to debug the system prior to its operation under the conditions of a specific retrieval service (pre-operation debugging); and the algorithmability of basic semantic processes of retrieval system operation (indexing and search), enabling one to consider the system as a model of human intellect.

From the standpoint of the authors of the mentioned articles, a retrieval service—in contrast to a retrieval system—includes or may include nonalgorithmized semantic processes such as search iteration based on a user's feedback; the preliminary screening of information noise by experts; and, especially, the content modification of queries and the formulation of subqueries or "search strategy." At the same time it is clear that the evaluation of retrieval services is at least as important as the evaluation of retrieval systems if for no other reason than the former should in general allow us to predict the functional effectiveness of a search based on user queries, whereas the existing evaluations of retrieval systems will permit such a prediction only in certain situations, if at all.

Hence, there are convincing arguments for the expediency of evaluating such objects as retrieval services, and not just retrieval systems. However, the expediency of evaluating other macroevaluated objects may also be arguable. An interesting example is a search strategy. By "a search strategy" we mean a set of rules (operations) governing the search process. In particular, these rules may provide for correcting a query formulation, selecting the best search method (from several different methods), and so forth. It is clear that the evaluation of a search strategy, much as the evaluation of a retrieval service, should allow for the prediction of the functional effectiveness of a search for specific queries. (In this context these objects may be considered similar.) At the same time, it is important to stress that a retrieval service represents a more "fuzzy" object from the perspective of evaluation than does a search strategy because, unlike the search strategy, the search process in a search service is not specified. For example, it is rather reasonable to assume that in a search for different search requests, a retrieval service may utilize different search strategies. Such a possibility should be pursued in further studies along with those addressed in Cherniavsky & Lakhuti (1970) and Lakhuti (1971) when dealing with the evaluation of retrieval services. Lakhuti also indicated this possibility when discussing the evaluation of retrieval services

> Evaluation of search with manual correction of queries, i.e., essentially the evaluation of a retrieval service, calls for a special study. It should be clearly realized that debugging and evaluation of (algorithmic) retrieval system and (non-algorithmic) retrieval service are very dissimilar. It is reasonable to debug and evaluate the algorithmic retrieval system in algorithmic mode without manual "query game," whereas the system should be used under specific conditions of a retrieval service using any procedures, including non-algorithmic ones, such as, for example, supplementary (test) "query game," and be evaluated in the same mode. (Lakhuti, 1971)

Lakhuti's remark also confirms our assumption that a retrieval service may provide for various search strategies; that is, it confirms the "fuzziness" of retrieval services from the point of their evaluation. Hence, for the purpose of a more accurate evaluation of a retrieval service, it is essential that in consideration of this object all search strategies used in it appear in an explicit form. Note that the prediction of the functional effectiveness of a search (for a specific search request) based on an evaluation of search strategy is more accurate than that based on the evaluation of retrieval service. The reasons for this assumption lie in the fact that the search strategy defines a more specific search process for any individual search request in comparison with a retrieval service (in general).

Furthermore, note that in connection with the realization of search strategies, a need arises to evaluate another macroevaluated object, namely, a scheme for the creation of a document search variant. Recall that in a number of papers by one of the authors (see, e.g., Voiskunskii, 1985), the *document search variant* was defined as a pair: ⟨query formulation, output criterion⟩. One of the methods for creating the document search variant follows from the definition involving the execution of two procedures: the construction of query formulations and the formulation of an output criterion. Note that each of these procedures may have different realizations, and by "realization" of a corresponding procedure we mean a certain algorithm or technique that enables the execution of a desired process. The set of specific realizations of the procedures mentioned earlier, whose execution allows the document search variant to be created, was named the *creation scheme of a document search variant.*

It is important to clarify the relationship of the notions discussed earlier. For this purpose consider a hypothetical retrieval service utilizing, for example, an interaction information retrieval system offering a retrospective retrieval function. Assume that a retrospective collection of document profiles in this system is formed automatically from some collection of documents. Also assume that several algorithms for constructing query formulations are available in the system and that each of these algorithms uses information obtained during a dialogue with a user. This information may be presented in the form of a search request in natural language, the user's evaluation of the documents obtained by the system, and so forth. Any of these algorithms is a corresponding (algorithmic!) realization of a procedure for constructing query formulations discussed earlier. As for the output criterion formulation procedure, it is not usually used in an explicit form because only one output criterion is generally used in retrieval systems. At the same time, the output criterion used in our information retrieval system may be thought of as a result of a certain realization of its formulation procedure. In general, such a realization, depending on particular conditions, may lead to different output criteria, but in our case the same output criterion will be always formulated. Such an assumption makes it possible to say that the information retrieval system under consideration has several creation schemes of document search variant, each consisting of a "conditional" realization of the output criterion formulation procedure and one of the available algorithms for constructing query formulations. It is clear that when created in this case document search variants for the same search request differ only in the query formulations. The possibility of creating different document search variants assumes that there is a mechanism for selecting the best variant (in a certain sense). We will assume that such a mechanism is available in our system, and it allows one to algorithmically select a document search variant that will attain the highest functional effectiveness among the available variants (this issue is described in more detail in Voiskunskii, 1985). Finally, we assume that the system considered has at its disposal an algorithm for ranking documents in descending order of pertinence.

Mechanisms available in our system allow for the creation of various search strategies. As an example, we will consider two such strategies. The first search strategy is oriented toward users who favor a high precision level in their search and who desire to obtain an output with no more than k documents (with rather small k values). The steps for this strategy follow:

Step 1. Obtain the user's search request in natural language.

Step 2. Construct a query formulation using the algorithm among those available that is most "concerned" with the attainment of high precision (maybe by reducing recall level).

Step 3. Conduct the search in the collection of documents.

Step 4. If more than k documents are found, rank them using the ranking algorithm; otherwise display these documents as an output.

Step 5. Display the first k documents from the ranked document list.

The second search strategy is oriented toward users who prefer an "optimal" search. Its steps are as follows:

Step 1. Obtain the user's search request in natural language.

Step 2. Construct a query formulation using the algorithm, as in the first strategy.

Step 3. Conduct search in the collection of documents.

Step 4. If fewer than five documents are found, display them (as a part of the output); otherwise rank these documents.

Step 5. Display the first five documents from the ranked document list (as a part of the output).

Step 6. Obtain from the user evaluations of the documents offered by the system.

Step 7. Construct query formulations using all available algorithms on the basis of the search request, documents viewed by the user, and their evaluations.

Step 8. Conduct the search in a representative subcollection of the collection of documents using all constructed query formulations.

Step 9. Display all documents found during Step 8 (as the next portion of output) without repeating any of the documents and without including the documents previously evaluated by the user.

Step 10. Obtain from the user the evaluations of the documents offered.

Step 11. On the basis of the obtained evaluations, select the "best" document search variant (query formulation) using a corresponding mechanism.

Step 12. Conduct the search in the remaining part of the collection of documents (without representative subcollections) using the selected query formulation.

Step 13. Display newly found documents (those not previously viewed by the user) as a final portion of output.

Note that the algorithms available in the information retrieval system are used as components of search strategies.

Which search strategy will be used is determined by the retrieval service interacting with the user. Perhaps this is the only "content" task of document search being solved by the retrieval service in our example. Its other tasks have a technological nature (e.g., retrospective database support).

From the preceding example it follows that in realization of a specific search strategy (for the purpose of executing a document search), one or several document search variants are used. These variants are governed by corresponding creation schemes, and practically only a limited number of such schemes may be used. Therefore, in realizing search strategies it is often necessary to choose one over the other. The main mechanism for solving this problem is the evaluation of the schemes, that is, the need for evaluating creation schemes of a document search variant actually arises in connection with the realization of search strategies.

Realizations of procedures involved in the creation scheme of a document search variant may be either algorithmic or nonalgorithmic. When a creation scheme of a document search variant is realized algorithmically, it constitutes an analogue of the retrieval system (as believed by Lakhuti) from the standpoint of approaches used to evaluate the given objects. It should be noted that many propositions underlying the algorithmic realizations of procedures are formulated with the help of various parameters, which clearly become the parameters of such realizations. Therefore, prior to applying given realizations in practice it is necessary to specify values for the parameters involved. It is important to stress that each new set of parameter values should be considered as the one defining a new creation scheme of a document search variant.

We next come to a case where a creation scheme of a document search variant is realized nonalgorithmically. In this situation, the approach used for the evaluation of the object under discussion differs from the approach used for the evaluation of the retrieval system and is rather similar to the approach used for the evaluation of the retrieval service. The evaluation for the case considered may be simplified by accepting the following assumption: If the techniques available in a particular creation scheme of a document search variant are realized for a certain set of search requests by the same person, then it may be considered that the same creation scheme was used for any of these search requests. In our opinion, such an assumption is not too strong.

Finally, completing the discussion of the "evaluation expediency" problem of macroevaluated objects, we turn our attention to another type of these objects, pointing out that their evaluation may be even more important than the evaluation of other objects. The objects we have in mind are realizations of the procedures used for creating document profiles, for example, procedures for normalizing words of natural language. The importance of evaluating these realizations is based on the following. It is well known that in performing a search through a set of documents, only one set of document profiles is constructed due to the difficulty of creating and supporting several similar sets simultaneously. It follows that only one realization of each procedure (participating in the creation of the document profiles) can be used; that is, if there are several realizations of a procedure, then the most preferred one should always be selected (unlike, say, a case in which there are several different creation schemes of a document search variant). Because fewer schemes are involved, they may all be used, thus eliminating the necessity for selection (for more detail, see, e.g., Voiskunskii, 1985). It is the necessity of selecting the preferred realization of a corresponding procedure that highlights the importance of its evaluation.

11.3

Averaging Values of Functional Effectiveness

At the beginning of the chapter, we stressed that our interest is in an evaluation of macroevaluated objects that could allow us to predict search results for a newly entered search request when such a search is executed with the help of or within the scope of the object under evaluation. Approaches to performing the required evaluation, as we also pointed out, are based primarily on averaging values of functional effectiveness attained in a specially organized search series. Different ways of averaging the mentioned values are known (see, e.g., Lakhuti, 1971; van Rijsbergen, 1979; and Salton, 1975). But we believe that in practice, within the scope of the evaluation concerned, it makes sense to apply only one of them, namely, the calculation of arithmetic means of existing values. This is dictated by three factors that favor the proposed approach: (1) the simplicity of processing found values (used in averaging), (2) the reliability of such a method, and (3) a well-known "predictive" value of arithmetic means. Considering these advantages, as well as the fact that other ways of averaging values of functional effectiveness have been discussed in sufficient detail in information science literature (see, e.g., van Rijsbergen, 1979; and Salton, 1979), we believe there is little reason to address them in this paper once more. Therefore throughout this paper, where we are dealing with averaging values of functional effectiveness, calculation of their arithmetic means is assumed.

Recall that technically this method is performed in the following manner. Let F^i be the values of arbitrary search characteristic F obtained during series of searches performed in a certain collection of documents for each search request from a given set, and let m represent the number of search requests in such a set. Then

$$F^{ave} = \frac{\sum_{i=1}^{m} F^i}{m}.$$

Regarding the averaging of values of functional effectiveness, it would be useful to discuss the problem of organizing a series of searches from which the values are obtained (we are interested in a series of searches that would allow reliable prediction based on the mentioned averaging of values). However, we will not consider this problem for the following reason: it has been discussed, as a rule, by any researcher dealing with issues of evaluating information retrieval systems (see, e.g., Cleverdon & Keen, 1966; Lakhuti, 1971; and Salton, 1968). As a result, there are established traditions in information science on how to organize such a series of searches. The researchers do not doubt that when following the established traditions the results obtained in performing evaluation can be safely trusted. Thus, instead of including a routine discussion of this problem (and obtaining the same conclusions once more!), it seems more appropriate in our opinion to simply present the established traditions in an explicit form.

These traditions assume that if the search whose results are predicted is executed in a retrospective monotopic search collection, then the series of searches should be performed in a random subcollection of this search collection containing 2000 to 4000 documents. As for the search request to be used in the series of searches, the search should be based on 20 to 50 search requests randomly chosen from a set of those search requests that arrived for performing the search in the mentioned search collection. Note that if a search whose results are predicted is performed in other search collections, then the established traditions are just a modification of the ones given here. For example, a "predictable" search is executed in the selective dissemination of information (SDI) mode in monotopic collections of current acquisitions. It is clear that each of these collections may be considered as a random sample from a retrospective search collection representing a set of collections of current acquisitions received over some period. Thus, the series of searches should be executed in a subcollection (of this retrospective collection), which is a union of current acquisitions collections (from the mentioned time period) that contains 2000 to 4000 documents. Further, in discussing problems related to the evaluation of macroevaluated objects, it will be assumed that the series of searches involved is organized in accordance with established traditions (which essentially have been presented here).

11.4
Requirements for Search Characteristics

Another problem related to performing an evaluation of macroevaluated objects is the lack of a clear view as to which search characteristics' averaged values should be used in the mentioned evaluation as well as when such an evaluation can be trusted and when it cannot. It is clear that we are dealing here only with those search characteristics that are used in evaluating the functional effectiveness of a document search and primarily with complex search characteristics. Recall from Chapter 10 that the functional effectiveness of a document search cannot always be justifiably evaluated using a given complex search characteristic. We will refer to those situations where it can be done as suitable for a complex search characteristic considered, and those situations where it is impossible we will refer to as nonsuitable. With this statement in mind, it is easy to imagine that in the evaluation of a certain macroevaluated object, the majority of values of a complex search characteristic used were obtained in nonsuitable situations.

It is clear that the evaluation based on a value derived from averaging such nonsuitable values is not very reliable. Here is a particular example. Suppose that we want to select the best search strategy from two strategies and for this purpose we have performed a search using the same search requests. Further, assume that the search using the first strategy essentially resulted in outputs that contain exactly 1 document and that it is pertinent, with 20 pertinent documents available in the collection of documents. (Then, the complex search characteristic I_1 has achieved values equal to 1.05.) Finally, assume that the search using the second strategy essentially resulted in outputs containing 10 pertinent and 10 nonpertinent documents, with 20 pertinent documents available in the collection of documents (the value of the complex search characteristic I_1 is 1). If two search strategies are evaluated on the basis of the values derived as the result of averaging values of characteristic I_1, then the first strategy is more likely to be preferred over the second strategy, whereas in a real situation for the vast majority of search requests, the search using the second strategy can provide higher functional effectiveness in comparison with the search using the first strategy. Thus, the evaluation based on a value derived by averaging values of a certain complex search characteristic cannot necessarily be trusted.

But in which cases can such an evaluation be trusted? Obviously, when all averaged values of a complex search characteristic used were obtained in suitable situations. However, from a practical point of view, such a requirement seems to be too strong. It would therefore be more appropriate to introduce into consideration a value representing a ratio (expressed as a percentage) between a number of those values of a complex search characteristic that was obtained under suitable situations and a number of all found values of this characteristic, and then to determine in test runs the threshold of this value upon attainment of which the evaluation discussed can be trusted. It should be pointed out that in this case the evaluation will involve averaging not all available values of a complex search characteristic but only those that were obtained in suitable situations. The threshold just mentioned will be called the "confidence threshold." It is clear that, in using a specific complex search characteristic, the wider the circle of suitable situations for this complex search characteristic, the more frequently the confidence threshold will be achieved. So not all complex search characteristics are equal from the point of view of their use in the evaluation process. Naturally, the wider the circle of suitable situations for a particular complex search characteristic, the more appropriate its use in an evaluation.

Analysis of the domains of applicability for complex search characteristics I_1 and I_2 (these domains were discussed in Chapter 10) shows that these domains are "wide" enough (and, correspondingly, a circle of suitable situations for complex search characteristics I_1 and I_2 is rather wide) and implies that it is appropriate to use these characteristics in the discussed evaluation. Also, the domain of applicability of characteristic I_2 turned out to be "wider" than that of the characteristic I_1. Furthermore, this domain was found to be so "wide" that the following statement important to information practice was considered in Chapter 10 as a rather moderate assumption: If the precision level of a search is not less than 0.5, its functional effectiveness may be justifiably evaluated on the basis of complex search characteristic I_2 practically at any attained value of the given characteristic; that is, virtually any situation would be suitable for this complex search characteristic.

The requirement of attaining a precision of no less than 0.5 appears reasonable in modern practice. Thus, taking into account the preceding statement, as well as the fact that the confidence threshold would more likely be lower than 100%, we can justifiably claim the following: If in the discussed evaluation complex search characteristic I_2 is used, then the result of such an evaluation can be practically always trusted. By the way, if nevertheless a need arises to confirm that the confidence threshold in evaluation has really been achieved, in the case of characteristic I_2 this should not cause any difficulties. Indeed, in this case making a decision on whether the situation considered is suitable can be justifiably based only on the analysis of an achieved precision level. To clarify, in this case whether or not the confidence threshold has been attained in the evaluation, there is no need to determine in the analyzed situations the recall level. On the other hand, to resolve the same problem in the case of complex search characteristic I_1, it is necessary to determine the recall level. (This statement follows from the results shown in Chapter 10.) Further, it would seem useful to consider the suitability of applying other complex search characteristics in the discussed evaluation, but we cannot give any recommendations about applications of these characteristics because we do not know of any studies where these characteristics were analyzed in the same manner as that presented in Chapter 10 regarding characteristics I_1 and I_2.

In summary, recall that the functional effectiveness of a document search may be evaluated on the basis of not only complex search characteristics but also on general search characteristics or, more precisely, their combination. In this connection there have been attempts to evaluate macroevaluated objects also using a set of averaged values of such characteristics. It should be acknowledged that the evaluation of macroevaluated objects based on a set of averaged recall values and averaged precision values is very popular in information science. Nevertheless, such an evaluation cannot be trusted in all cases. Consider the following example. Suppose that we evaluate a certain retrieval service within the scope of which a search using a number of search requests needed for performing the evaluation was performed. Assume further that during the search based on one half of the queries, outputs contained 1 pertinent document and only 1, whereas for the second half of the queries each output contained 500 documents with 20 pertinent ones. The collection of documents included a total of 20 pertinent documents. It is not difficult to determine that in this situation arithmetic means of recall and precision values achieved are equal to $R^{ave} = 0.525$ and $P^{ave} = 0.52$, respectively. Thus, having evaluated the search service on the basis of the set of values cited, we will conclude that it is of acceptable quality, whereas a user should hardly expect satisfactory search results from this service. This example shows that there are cases for which the evaluation based on a set of averaged values of general search characteristics cannot be trusted, at least in theory. Thus, it is necessary to have a clear idea of whether such cases occur in practice and, if they occur, to determine the conditions under which such an evaluation can be trusted. In other words, the question of when such an evaluation can be trusted and when it cannot remains open.

11.5
Comparative Evaluation of Macroevaluated Objects

The next issue that we will discuss in this chapter is the possibility of performing a comparative evaluation of macroevaluated objects without averaging the search characteristics values. Suppose that we want to select the best search strategy from two strategies, and to do so we have performed a search for the same search requests using both strategies. Assume further that for every search request the functional effectiveness of the search based on the first strategy was found to be higher than the functional effectiveness of the search based on the second strategy in terms of, say, a complex search characteristic I_2. Also assume that all I_2 values were obtained in suitable situations. It is clear that in this case we can legitimately select the first strategy as the best one (among the two compared). In other words, a comparative evaluation of macroevaluated objects can be done without averaging the values of a corresponding complex search characteristic. Note that a comparative evaluation based on averaging I_2 values will lead to the same conclusion.

Moreover, in our opinion, this can be done under less severe constraints than in the example cited. We have in mind the following. Suppose, as in the preceding, that for the purpose of performing a comparative evaluation of macroevaluated objects within the scope of each of them, a search is performed for the same search requests. Also suppose that all search requests were determined for which the functional effectiveness of the search performed within the scope of the first object was found to be higher (in terms of a certain complex search characteristic) than the functional effectiveness of the search performed within the scope of the second object, and the values of the complex search characteristic leading to these conclusions were attained in suitable situations. If the obtained search requests formed a "qualified majority" in relation to all search requests for which the search was performed, then, in our opinion, there is a basis to consider the first object superior to the second one. In other words, in this case it is also reasonable to evaluate (comparatively) macroevaluated objects without averaging values of a corresponding complex search characteristic. The use of the considered approach in information practice will require solving a number of theoretical and practical issues, in particular the problem of a "qualified majority." Besides, it should be noted that this approach has a specific constraint—namely, when comparing more than two objects, there is a good probability that not only a qualified majority of search requests, but also a simple majority, will not be "formed" for either of them. At the same time this approach has a useful advantage: in some cases it allows us to considerably reduce time-consuming operations in the comparative evaluation of macroevaluated objects in relation to the situation in which averaging is necessary. At this point we will not discuss when such a reduction can occur because all of these issues were discussed in detail in Chapter 10. We stress only that the given advantage of the considered approach to the comparative evaluation of macroevaluated objects justifies the need for further studies in this direction.

11.6
Some Experiments on the Evaluation of Macroevaluated Objects

We have considered the problems and approaches related to the evaluation of macroevaluated objects. Because many researchers have for some time fully appreciated the importance of such an evaluation, it is not surprising that at different times various experiments have been conducted within the scope of which these objects have been evaluated. The well-known Cranfield tests were perhaps the first of these experiments. Research started with experiments in indexing languages, such as the Cranfield I tests. The Cranfield II studies showed, for example, that the automatic indexing of documents was comparable to manual indexing, and this and the availability of computers created a major interest in the automatic indexing and searching of texts. In information science these experiments are justly considered as classic because they led to a number of fundamental results. Some of them are mentioned in Chapter 10.

Among macroevaluated experiments performed in recent years, the most prominent are those conducted within the scope of the Text Retrieval Conference (TREC). These experiments began in 1992 and continue up to the present time. The idea of these experiments is not to evaluate a specific system, its components, or various realizations of these components, but to allow a comparison of systems and any of their components or their various realizations on the basis of specially organized benchmark data. Conceptually, the benchmark data include collections of documents and collections of search requests, and the relevant documents available in the collection are known for each of these search requests. Hence, all systems participating in the experiment should use both documents and search requests from the benchmark data.

The collection of documents used in these experiments consists of approximately 1 million documents. The selection of such a large set is justified as follows: "Evaluation using the small collections currently available may not reflect performance of systems in large full-text searching" (Harman, 1995). In other words, it is assumed that in a smaller collection (say, of 100,000 documents), experiment results would be distorted. It should be noted that in the famous Cranfield experiments, the collection consisted of 1400 documents. Be that as it may, to participate in the experiment it is necessary first to index approximately 1 million documents and then to perform the search.

Another part of the benchmark was described as follows:

> retrieving lists of documents that could be considered relevant to each of the 50 topics in what was called "ad hoc" querying. A second information retrieval paradigm used was where 50 retrieval topics were known in advance and new documents were to be matched against the 50 standard queries simulating a "routing" operation. In both cases the queries were not really queries at all but carefully honed user need statements and were thus extensive descriptions of the topic of interest. (Report on TREC-2, 1993)

In other words the experiments are conducted not with real search requests and real users (output is evaluated by nonusers) but with specially matched topics and evaluations of the relevance of documents performed by experts.

Organizers of the experiment cite the following example of a topic and a document:

⟨top⟩
Attachment 1—Sample topic
⟨head⟩ Tipster Topic Description
⟨num⟩ Number: 028
⟨dom⟩ Domain: Science and Technology
⟨title⟩ Topic: AT&T Technical Efforts
⟨desc⟩ Description: Document must describe AT&T's technical efforts in computers and communications.
⟨nar⟩ Narrative: To be relevant, a document must contain information on the efforts of American Telephone and Telegraph (AT&T) in computers and communications. Examples of relevant subject matter would include product announcements, releases or cancellations, and a discussion of AT&T Bell Labs research. Documents focusing on either AT&T's efforts

to buy other computer companies, AT&T's legal battles with other organizations, or AT&T's Unix operating system are not relevant. For the purposes of this topic, the Regional Bell Operating Companies (RBOCs) or "Baby Bells" are not considered AT&T.

⟨con⟩ Concept(s):

1. AT&T, American Telephone and Telegraph
2. 3B-2 minicomputer, AT&T 386 PC
3. AT&T Starlan
4. PBX
5. Product announcements, product releases

⟨/top⟩

Attachment 2—Sample document (abridged)

⟨DOC⟩

⟨DOCNO⟩ WSJ880460-0090 ⟨/DOCNO⟩

⟨HL⟩ AT&T Unveils Services to Upgrade Phone Networks under Global Plan

⟨/HL⟩

⟨AUTHOR⟩ Janet Guyon (WSJ Staff) ⟨/AUTHOR⟩

⟨SO⟩ ⟨/SO⟩

⟨CO⟩ T ⟨/CO⟩

⟨IN⟩ TEL ⟨/IN⟩

⟨DATELINE⟩ NEW YORK ⟨/DATELINE⟩

⟨TEXT⟩ American Telegraph and Telephone Company introduced the first of a new generation of phone services with broad applications for computer and communications equipment makers.

AT&T said it is the first national long-distance carrier to announce prices for specific services under a worldwide plan to upgrade phone networks. By announcing commercial services under the plan, which the industry calls the Integrated Services Digital Network, AT&T will influence evolving communications standards to its advantage, consultants said, just as International Business Machines Corp. has created de facto computer standards favoring its products.

⟨/TEXT⟩

⟨/DOC⟩

It should be noted that the Cranfield experiment involved 225 real search requests (not topics) and a relevancy evaluation was performed by users. Con-

cerning the above, it should be remembered that in a real system there are cases
in which the same search request is specified by different users and the same
output is evaluated differently by these users. Discrepancies between user
evaluations and expert evaluations are not uncommon. Nevertheless, the approach selected by the experiment organizers makes it possible to avoid many
technical, methodical, and organizational difficulties in pursuing experiments.

There were 25 systems participating in TREC-1, using a wide range of
search techniques. They all received in advance the collection of documents and
topics. (We have learned from the experiment organizers that this collection,
which was recorded on two disks, cost $2500.) Upon conducting the searches,
results were directed to the experiment organizers for comparative analysis. A
second workshop (TREC-2) was held in September 1993; 31 systems participated. On the whole, the experiment scheme for conducting TREC-2 was not
changed.

In spite of the fact that one of the major objectives of the experiment was
comparison of the macroevaluated objects (systems, algorithms, methods, approaches, etc.), the organizers pointed out the following:

> There are so many variables in running the experiment and so many caveats about
> the evaluation methodologies used that it is very difficult to compare even two sys-
> tems directly and impossible to come up with a "ranking" of approaches . . . com-
> parisons across systems are very difficult to interpret. (Report on TREC-2, 1993)

Regarding evaluation the experimenters wrote:

> There is a real problem with using the standard measures for evaluation of search
> in something like TREC; looking at averages of averages is very superficial and
> hides most of what is actually going on with respect to performance. (Report on
> TREC-2, 1993)

These statements illustrate the importance of having the ability to evaluate
macroevaluated objects, that is, the importance of those approaches and methods discussed in this chapter.

As for the experiment itself, its organizers wrote the following:

> There are many different approaches to information retrieval represented among
> the TREC-II participants grouped roughly into probabilistic models and variants
> thereof, vector space approaches, NLP-based, bayesian networks, query expansion
> and dimensionality reduction, Boolean query construction, combination of results
> of different retrieval strategies, explorations into document structuring, . . . as well
> as some outliers like retrieval using n-grams, word pairs, hardware approaches, and
> some work on efficiency issues. Generalizing results across systems and across ap-
> proaches is difficult but some trends have already emerged. Simple systems with
> simple things are still doing really well and the more complex ones are catching up
> and in some cases surpassing the simple approaches. (Report on TREC-2, 1993)

It should be particularly emphasized that this result was obtained in both
TREC-1 and TREC-2 experiments. In this connection note the following: as

early as in late 1960s through the early 1970s (see Chapter 5) similar results were obtained. In Chapter 5 we said that as a rule a more thorough syntactical analysis of texts as well as attempts in using semantic analysis in retrieval only led to using more sophisticated programs, increased retrieval duration, and made it more expensive. Some researchers explained all this as insufficient progress in computer science (low speed, inadequate memory, etc.). Later, with progress in computer science, negative effects inherent in complex methods were attributed to the fact that the experiments were run on comparably small collections. Now the TREC experiments have produced results dispelling this reason as well. The existing algorithms of complex methods are seemingly so imperfect that it is too early to consider their positive effects.

The important result of the experiment is the fact that failed attempts of comparing macroevaluated objects are explained not by some deficiencies in the benchmark but by using imperfect methods of evaluating these objects. Thus, we have more support for the importance of selecting evaluation methods, and this should be done before running the experiment. In our opinion, any experiment, especially a comparative one, should be run on the basis of evaluation methods specified in advance and common to all experiment participants.

11.7
Conclusion

This chapter dealt with the problem of evaluating macroevaluated objects. We were interested in an evaluation that would allow for a given search request to predict the results of the search when the search was performed with or within the scope of evaluated object. There is no clear picture in information science as to what macroevaluated objects are expedient to evaluate and which are not. Therefore, we analyzed a number of different objects in an attempt to answer this question for a given object. The approaches used in evaluating these objects are based primarily on the averaging values of functional effectiveness attained in a specially organized series of searches. We showed that in practice, within the scope of the evaluation, it is expedient to apply only one of them, namely, calculation of the arithmetic means of existing values.

An important problem connected with evaluating macroevaluated objects is to determine which search characteristics should be recommended for this evaluation (and which should not be recommended) and in which cases this evaluation could be trusted (and in which cases it cannot be trusted). We showed that a useful instrument in solving this problem for complex search characteristics is the domain of applicability of these characteristics. In addition, for solving this problem we had to introduce the notion of a "confidence threshold," and the analysis for achieving this threshold allows us to solve the problem of "trust" for the performed evaluation. As a result, we determined that complex search characteristics I_1 and I_2 could be recommended for use when evaluating macroevaluated objects. Moreover, we concluded that if in this evaluation complex search characteristic I_2 is used, then the result of this evaluation could always be trusted. At the same time, we were unable to solve the problem of using general search characteristics in the evaluation or, more precisely, the combination of these characteristics (for example, the combination of recall and precision). We only showed an example illustrating the existence of cases for which the evaluation based on the combination of averaged values of general search characteristics cannot be trusted.

Finally, we discussed the possibility of performing a comparative evaluation of macroevaluated objects without averaging values of search characteristics. We suggested an approach to performing such an evaluation and showed that it allows us to substantially reduce time-consuming operations in the evaluation of macroevaluated objects when compared to the evaluation in which the averaging of values of the same search characteristic is used.

References

Cherniavsky, V. S., & Lakhuti, D. G. (1970). The problem of evaluating retrieval systems. *Nauchno-Teknicheskaya Informatsiya (NTI)*, ser. 2, no. 1, 24–34.

Cleverdon, C., & Keen, M. (1966). *Factors determining the performance of indexing systems* (Vol. 2). (Test Results), Cranfield, England: ASLIB Cranfield Res. Project.

Harman, D. (1995). Report on TREC-3. Proceedings of the Eighteenth Annual International ACM SIGIR Conference on Research and Development in Information Retrieval, Seattle, WA.

Lakhuti, D. G. (1971). *Evaluation of information retrieval systems*. Ph.D. thesis, Moscow, VINITI.

Report on TREC-2 (by the TREC-2 program committee). (1993). SIGIR Forum, vol. 27, no. 3.

van Rijsbergen, C. J. (1979). *Information retrieval* (2nd ed.). London: Butterworths.

Salton, G. (1968). *Automatic information organization and retrieval*. New York: McGraw-Hill.

Salton, G. (1979). *Dynamic information and library processing*. Englewood Cliffs, NJ: Prentice Hall.

Voiskunskii, V. G. (1985). Using filter and mechanism of automatic adjustment during information retrieval. *Nauchno-Teknicheskaya Informatsiya (NTI)*, ser. 2, no. 5, 1–10.

12

Some Directions in the Development of IR Systems

Introduction

If we take another look at the stages of creating an IR system (described in Chapter 1), we can see that the purpose for its creation, as well as its function and structure, has already been defined in the previous chapters of this book. In addition, several chapters describe the construction of each element of the system, which would allow one to fully automate all processes in the IR system. Furthermore, we have considered problems in connection with the evaluation of created systems. In other words, everything that directly precedes physical implementation of the system has been discussed. The book could conclude at this point, but we would like to move beyond just discussing stages of the systems approach in developing IR systems and to look at least briefly at the future of IR systems. This chapter has been written for that purpose.

Here we should make a reservation. We are not going to predict what kinds of systems will be at the user's disposal in the future; only the future will reveal this. Our task is rather modest: we will discuss the real benefits of some of the directions in IR systems development that today are commonly considered to be promising. Also, we will discuss one of the practical ways of improving IR systems.

Because many researchers associate the future development of IR systems with research in the field of artificial intelligence, it is with this point that we will begin.

IR Systems and Artificial Intelligence

Before discussing the role and potential of artificial intelligence (AI) for developing IR systems, let us clarify what we mean by AI. It may seem strange that we would feel the need to define artificial intelligence, since the field of AI has been in existence for more than 40 years. Why not accept the existing notion? The point is that there simply is no single universally recognized notion. What we have at our disposal was well described by Firebaugh (1988) in his book *Artificial Intelligence:*

> The field of artificial intelligence is gradually and painfully emerging as a science. The reasons for the birth pains are not difficult to understand: uncertainty as to what constitutes the subject matter, uncertainty on the goals of AI research, and uncertainty on the most effective approaches. Since each AI researcher's mental model of the mind helped shape his/her definition of the discipline, there were nearly as many schools of thought in the early days of AI as there were researchers. This has led to many sharp confrontations and controversies within this discipline.

Later, contemplating on the definition of AI, Firebaugh observed: "Each worker in the field of AI has his/her own definition of AI which seems to best express the goals and methods of his/her research." Perhaps, this is the only point where all AI researchers agree (see, for example Fisher & Firschein, 1987; Genesereth & Nilsson, 1992; Ginsberg, 1993; and McCorduck, 1979). Indeed, many definitions of AI exist. let us consider only some of them.

Charniak and McDermott (1985) held that "Artificial Intelligence is the study of mental faculties through the use of computational models." "Artificial Intelligence is the study of ideas that enable computers to be intelligent," wrote Winston (1984). Dean, Allen, and Aloimonos were of the opinion that "Artificial Intelligence is the design and study of computer programs that behave intelligently" (1995). The definition preferred by the authors and credited to Minsky of MIT is as follows: "Artificial Intelligence is the science of making machines do things that would require intelligence if done by human beings" (Boden, 1979).

In the context of this definition, as well as most other definitions known to us, automated information retrieval is one of the most striking examples of the success of AI. Indeed, as we showed in Chapters 3 and 5, the search process done by a human being, especially that of information retrieval, is an excellent illustration of typical human intellectual activity. The fact that a computer is now capable of performing a search without human participation is an example of the success of AI.

It should be noted that many researchers realize this. This is why for decades various periodicals and conferences dedicated to AI have been considering the problem of developing IR systems. However, only a part of the research on IR systems has anything to do with AI. For instance, papers on creating and developing any kind of manual information processing have nothing in common with AI. Papers related to AI are only those that deal with creating algorithms for the automatization of any informational process in an IR system. It is understood that a work will be considered successful only if it results in an algorithm making it possible to carry out a process at an acceptable level of quality. Typical examples of works related to AI are those on automatic abstracting, automatic indexing, and automatic feedback, although not all of these works can be considered successful.

It is clear that a number of papers in the field of information retrieval are not directly related to AI; however, this does not make them less significant. For instance, papers investigating information need or the creation of IRL are of utmost importance for the whole field both in practical and theoretical aspects. All we want to show is that the two fields of research, IR systems and AI, overlap to a certain degree. As a matter of fact, this overlap with AI is, to a large extent, the reason why the study of IR systems is one of the well-known fields in computer science.

Thus, we have discussed the relationship between the fields of information retrieval and AI. However, when discussing the importance of AI for future IR systems development, many IR systems researchers do not consider this well-known relationship. Therefore, we will now discuss what many researchers consider to be the application of AI to IR systems.

To begin with, research within the field of AI has branched out in a great number of very different directions, into areas such as game playing, expert systems, robotics, automated reasoning, machine learning, pattern recognition, natural language processing, and many others. To date, certain general ideas and approaches to AI have emerged that are applicable to all existing directions of research. However, each direction of research has its own specific approaches and ideas for solving problems that gave rise to a particular direction. Judging by available publications, these "foreign" ideas are most attractive to IR systems creators. In the very broad range of attempts to use specific ideas, the most popular directions of research stand out. Perhaps, the most frequently explored area of research addresses the study of natural language processing (NLP). Studies of the formal (computer) methods of using natural languages (for which the study of NLP has been developed) have been an important direction of AI research almost since the beginning of this field of learning. Two main goals motivate AI work on natural language. One is a theoretical goal that is close to the goal of the linguist, that is, to discover how we use language to communicate. The other is a technological goal, namely, to enable intelligent computer interfaces to be used in the future, thereby allowing natural language to become an important means of man–machine interaction.

So, what kinds of problems do IR system researchers contemplate solving using the approaches available (or anticipated) in NLP? Some of the researchers note that in the future foreign language documents could be dealt with automatically, which will make it possible, for example, to extend the automatic indexing techniques to include documents originally written in languages other than English (see, for example, Croft, 1995). This problem is undoubtedly of practical value and researchers have long been eager to solve it. For example, at the end of the 1960s there was an attempt to realize this idea for the IR system utilized in the field of electrical engineering and implemented (and utilized to this day) at the Moscow Institute INFORMelectro (Pevsner & Lachuti, 1973).

Documents in the Russian and English languages were entered into this system, and two similar programs of automatic document indexing were realized giving a common search collection. For the purpose of automatic indexing, two descriptor dictionaries were compiled for the English and Russian indexing versions, where descriptors denoting classes of conditional equivalence (see Chapter 5) were the same in both dictionaries and corresponded to the same notions, though in different languages. This bilingual system was successful in finding information and formulating outputs containing documents both in the Russian and English languages.

It is clear that this method of realization is also applicable to other languages, such as German, French, or Spanish. In their work the researchers used well-known approaches in the field of IR systems development. Then what has NLP got to do with the described problem? The system proved to be unusable because an overwhelming majority of users did not know English. In other words, the system's ability to accomplish document retrieval in different languages was only the first feasible phase in the creation of a multilingual IR system. The development of a mechanism capable of presenting retrieved information in a language understandable to the user is the next phase.

Such mechanisms are commonly called machine translation, and they are directly related to NLP. NLP was developed first for machine translation (Tanimoto, 1990). In this particular case, the IR system developers hoped that this line of work would provide the required mechanism or at least significant results that would make such a mechanism feasible. Next we discuss whether this hope was realistic.

During the 1950s, researchers hoped for machines that would be able to translate a text from one language into another. Projects were funded to develop systems that could translate Russian into English and vice versa. Years later the researchers found it very difficult to make machines do quality translation. The systems used during the 1960s usually employed dictionaries, as well as morphological and syntactic analyses. They were unable to use semantic analysis, however, because no real progress had been made in this area.

Here is a well-known example that revealed the limitations of automatic translation. Researchers wanted to use the system to translate the expression "The spirit is willing but the flesh is weak" from English into Russian. However, after it had been translated into Russian and then back into English, the sentence had become "The vodka is good but the meat is rotten."

In time, the initial optimism of machine translation researchers evaporated into thin air. It became evident that the problem of programming a system to recognize the meaning of the text written in a natural language, if at all solvable, was a task of utmost complexity. Seeing no practical results, the U.S. government lost interest in this work, and after many years of waiting ceased to finance it. In fact, the AI section of the Department of Defense manual for grants specifically states that no proposals on machine translation will be considered.

Thus, in practical terms machine translation was a flop. Nonetheless, almost two decades of intense work produced a number of interesting and useful achievements. We will mention only some of them.

First, the research showed once again that a *natural language should be considered as a whole,* and use and analysis of separate language components, such as its vocabulary or syntax, actually does not mean use and analysis of the natural language as such (Winograd, 1972).

Second, it became clear that it was impossible to analyze the meaning of what is expressed by means of natural language without a semantic analysis. Moreover, it became clear that to perform an analysis, a mechanism was needed that was not only based on formal rules for operating on meaning but that also contained knowledge (Tucker, 1984).

Third, information retrieval benefited from a number of practical results. For example, morphological analysis (the stemming algorithm) was developed initially for machine translation and later found practical application in IR systems. The same applies to the lexical analysis. All of these methods are widely used for automatic indexing (see Chapter 6). In general, some semantic analysis techniques, such as the analysis of paradigmatic and syntagmatic relations, already have long been used in NLP. However, all attempts to use them in IR systems after the 1960s yielded no positive results.

Another problem frequently mentioned is the problem of the automatic abstraction of documents. Some researchers believe that solving this problem will also help in solving the problem of indexing full document texts (such as book texts). It should be noted that problems associated with automatic abstracting (by abstract we mean a coherent text reflecting in a short form the meaning of the original document) are similar in many respects to those discussed here in connection with machine translation. Indeed, successful automatic abstracting requires both meaning recognition and the ability to operate on it. This is why automatic abstracting is virtually unfeasible at present.

Also questionable is the usefulness of automatic abstracting for indexing purposes, because if the machine can recognize the meaning of the document (which is indispensable for automatic abstracting), then it will be able to recognize the meaning of the search request as well. In this case, there will be no need for indexing because after comparing the two meanings the machine will be able to decide immediately whether to include the document in the output. In other words, in this case the search will be made in natural language. Rather, automatic abstracting could be reasonably utilized in forming outputs, for in some cases it may be useful to output abstracts rather than full document texts.

Naturally, it does not follow from the previous discussion that the problem of indexing the texts of full documents is nonexistent. Researchers are trying to solve this problem through different approaches to document reduction. In doing so, they are attempting in some cases to reduce the full text to an acceptable size, whereas in other cases their goal is to divide it into a number of independent parts of a size acceptable to the system. They are also pinning some hope on studies of coherent text structure as a direction of research in NLP. Within this direction researchers are trying to determine a comparative significance, which is statistically stable, of different parts of the text. Although some recommendations are now available, the reduction problem has not yet been solved.

Sometimes researchers argue that the indexing language should be natural language. By this they are usually referring to what is more frequently called a free text search (see Chapter 6). Recall that in this case the descriptors employed are words of natural language, and the lexical and morphological analyses certain bear a close relationship to NLP.

As shown earlier, many researchers associate IR development with successes in NLP. However, of ever-growing interest in recent years are attempts to use other directions in AI, such as a knowledge-based design, expert systems, and neural networks. First, let us take a closer look at the object of each of these directions, and after that we will show how researchers intend to use them for developing IR systems.

It would not be an exaggeration to say that to date the most popular (if not predominant) direction of AI research is a knowledge-based approach. Indeed, an overwhelming majority of approaches to the development of all kinds of systems assumes to take advantage of knowledge stored in the system itself. Because implemented AI systems use a computer, this means that knowledge must be introduced and stored in the computer; but it also means that there must be formal methods for using such knowledge. As a matter of fact, when speaking of a knowledge base we mean a certain organization in the computer of both knowledge and the means of using it. In AI we may think of knowledge as a collection of related facts, procedures, models, and heuristics that can be used in problem solving or inference systems. Knowledge may be regarded as information in context, as information organized so that it can be readily applied to solving problems, enhancing perception, and expanding learning. Knowledge varies in both content and appearance. It may, for example, be specific, general, exact, fuzzy, procedural, or declarative.

Today AI can already offer a number of implementation ideas for using knowledge that are not based on formal methods for the recognition of meaning expressed in natural language. One of these ideas, which is perhaps the most useful for information retrieval, is the idea of creating a knowledge base in the form of a semantic network (see, for example, Feigenbaum, Barr, & Cohen, 1982; and Quillan, 1968). Salton and McGill, for example, mention the applicability of a semantic network (though they do not provide any approaches to illustrate how it could be applied in information retrieval) and explain the idea of a semantic network in their book *Introduction to Modern Information Retrieval* (Salton & McGill, 1983). We will discuss semantic networks in more detail.

Semantic networks were first developed in order to represent the meanings of English sentences in terms of objects and relationships between them. This network was designed as a psychological model of human associative memory. The neural interconnections of the brain are clearly arranged in some type of network (apparently one with a highly complex structure), and the rough similarity between the artificial semantic nets and the natural brain helped to encourage the development of semantic nets. All semantic networks are constructed from two basic components:

- *Nodes,* representing objects, concepts, or situations, are indicated by boxes or circles.
- *Arcs,* representing relationships between nodes, are indicated by arrows connecting the nodes.

The following examples illustrate how knowledge may be represented and used in semantic networks. Let us assume that we wish to represent the fact that "Bob is a taxi driver." We can create two nodes—one to represent "Bob" and the other to represent "taxi driver"—and connect them with a very useful arc or link called an *isa* (Figure 12.1).

Clearly, this is very simple example. However, it illustrates how the method of writing (and storing) knowledge is used for creating the knowledge base. The idea of using semantic networks for information retrieval purposes may be described as follows.

Every node in the semantic net represents a text describing a concept, idea, situation, proof, and so on. Such text may be, for example, a segment of a book, an article, or a report. All meaningful relations are established between segments, not only between those of one document but also between the segments of any document entered into the system. Theoretically, such a semantic net may include existing ideas or situations that are contained in the documents entered into the system. The knowledge base built on such a net will become a very developed model of human knowledge and, theoretically, will be able to give an exhaustive answer to a query.

In principle, such knowledge may basically be created in the same fashion as is used to create an expert system. A group of experts is invited, and any document coming into the system is read by each expert. After completing this step, the experts jointly decide to enter into the knowledge base only text containing an original idea, situation, and so forth. In doing this, the experts establish in their own judgment all meaningful relationships between a newly created

Figure 12.1
Semantic network representation of the statement "Bob is a taxi driver."

node and those existing in the system. Each node contains not only a text itself, but also its representation in the form of a semantic network. One of the advantages of semantic networks is the simplicity with which logic can be performed to answer questions. A query to the system is written in terms of a network fragment, and the semantic network is then searched for a pattern matching the query fragment. If a matching pattern is found, the answer may be explored by following arcs away from the matching pattern. Note that a search that uses a semantic net avoids the type of ambiguities that had sometimes occurred (as illustrated by the well-known example "Venetian blind" versus "blind Venetian"). Obviously, these statements will have different representations. The proposed search method has many other principally new features. First, it is possible and perhaps expedient to output a set of found text segments (commonly called hypertext) instead of the documents themselves that contain the found ideas. Second, while reading the hypertext, the user may arrive at a new IN, and the search can be readily continued.

However, real implementation of such a knowledge base is still a long way off. Today, many theoretical and practical problems connected with both semantic networks and their implementation await solution. As a matter of fact, this direction of AI research is in its early phase, and it is not yet time to consider its practical utilization in IR systems.

From the standpoint of the AI researchers, a direction of development commonly called neural network looks much more interesting and promising. *Neural networks* are physical cellular systems that can acquire, store, and utilize experiential knowledge (Zurada, 1992). The knowledge is in the form of stable states or mappings embedded in networks that can be recalled in response to the presentation of cues.

A neural network's ability to perform computations is based on the hope that we can reproduce some of the flexibility and power of the human brain by artificial means. Network computation is performed by a dense mesh of computing nodes and connections. They operate collectively and simultaneously on most or all data and inputs. The basic processing elements of neural networks are called *artificial neurons* or nodes. Neurons perform as summing and nonlinear mapping junctions. In some cases, they can be considered as threshold units that fire when their total input exceeds certain bias levels. Neurons usually operate in parallel and are configured in regular architectures. They are often organized in layers, and feedback connections both within the layer and toward adjacent layers are allowed. Each connection strength is expressed by a numerical value called *weight,* which can be modified.

One of the most attractive aspects of the utilization of neural networks is their ability to self-organize and self-learn, which has been examined in a number of publications (see, for example, Zurada, 1992). Furthermore, the search process itself in such networks can be very rapid. It was these features that first interested the researchers developing IR systems. As an example, we will examine an interesting approach developed by Kwok (1989).

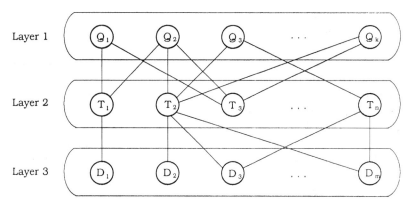

Figure 12.2
Three-layer network.

Kwok proposed utilizing, for information retrieval purposes, a three-layer network (Figure 12.2).

Nodes in Layer 1 are search requests, those in Layer 2 are descriptors, and those in Layer 3 are documents. The existence of connections is defined by the presence or absence of a descriptor in an item. Nodes of the search request and document layer serve both as input and output. In other words, in response to each search request relevant documents can be found, and for each document corresponding queries can be determined (for example, in systems performing SDI). This is precisely why query layer and document layer are bidirectionally connected with asymmetrical weights to the descriptor layer. To calculate weights, the author uses the probabilistic approach and expects to provide the users with a ranked output.

Basically, such a search arrangement is quite possible, and its drawbacks, which are mostly based on the probabilistic approach itself, are criticized in quite a number of well-known publications. In spite of this criticism, the first steps in the utilization of neural networks look quite promising.

In discussing the use of AI in developing IR systems, it is worthwhile to consider the attempts of applying to IR systems the typical methods and approaches of different AI fields, such as expert systems, machine learning, and automatic reasoning (see, for example, Daniels & Rissland, 1995; Kupiec, Pederson, & Chen, 1995; Yang, 1994; and Zahir & Chang, 1992). Most of the articles describing these attempts concentrate on the following two directions. One group of researchers is concerned with simplifying representation of the information found by the user (this was mentioned in Chapter 3), and the other group seeks to develop new automatic methods for conducting a search and to correct search during the process of feedback with the user.

The attempts to simplify the representation of information belong to the general direction of research that is often called the "intellectualization" of information retrieval. For example, researchers from this camp propose to automatically extract from the text some statements that do not appear explicitly in the text, that is, to create new text (and meaning) from semantically connected segments contained in different texts. Simplifying the representation of information also includes automatic abstracting, mentioned earlier, which is considered one of the directions for NLP research. Today, in a somewhat different form, this direction is called "text summarization," and it uses some methods that are not part of NLP. For example, in the research done by Kupiec and associates, the elements of learning are used for this purpose. Unfortunately, it is too early to talk about practical methods, and the main problem concerns the absence of reliable methods of semantical analysis.

The second direction of research, namely, the development of new methods for automatic information retrieval and feedback, includes many problems that are analogous to the ones discussed in Chapters 7 and 9. Indeed, in the construction of query formulations in learning systems it is assumed that the marked documents are used (in this case the pertinence is called the expert's evaluation). The created algorithms are the attempts of researchers to adapt for IR systems the existing algorithms for learning (for example, there is an attempt to use an algorithm developed for playing checkers, called Interactive Dichotomizer 3 [ID3]). As a rule, on the basis of "examples," different classifications are constructed and then used for a search. A good survey of the approaches in machine learning can be found in Chen (1992).

It should be pointed that the work in this direction also has very few practical applications. One of the main drawbacks is that it does not take into account many of the important properties and characteristics of information retrieval.

Thus, we have considered how some of the research directions in AI influence IR development. However, we strongly believe that resources of the information science itself are far from being exhausted. The future development of IR systems primarily lies in the utilization of such resources. Next we will consider one of the practical directions (Frants, Shapiro, & Voiskunskii, 1996) for utilizing these resources.

12.3

Satisfying IN: Additional Possibilities

As has been shown, any informational activity is connected directly or indirectly with satisfying IN. The activity includes a variety of methods and forms that actually exist and that, in the end, allow for the satisfaction of IN. These methods and forms supplement, rather than duplicate, each other in the sense that only together can they take into account (to a certain degree) IN properties and characteristics known to date.

Because IR systems (like any other form) are created only because IN exists and only in order to satisfy it, we will consider as evident the thesis that *the fuller the IN properties and characteristics are taken into account during the creation of IR systems, the more successful the satisfaction of IN will be*. In other words, if one succeeds in widening the range of IN properties that are taken into account during the creation of an IR system, one will arrive at a new qualitative level of servicing users.

It should be noted that this important thesis was mentioned in Chapter 4 during the discussion of IR system structure. However, of utmost significance is the fact that discovering new characteristics of IN with subsequent consideration of their influence, both on the nature of servicing users and on IR system construction, is an important and promising way of developing these systems (Frants & Brush, 1988). In fact, we already discussed IN in detail in Chapter 2. Now we will try to further develop the existing concept and discuss IN properties not previously mentioned.

It seems clear that a human being does not need information in general but instead needs rather specific information that pertains to his or her current situation. In other words, to choose the most successful line of behavior (in terms of survival) in a particular situation, a person should have the information about this situation, which is required for such behavior. But in order to have such information, a person should have a desire to have it; that is, the person should feel the need for such information. Hence, on the one hand a need may be considered a mechanism that pushes a person to seek necessary information, whereas on the other hand, it can be considered a tool that helps to determine the usefulness (significance) of signals among the multitude of signals perceived by a human being. Furthermore, a person's need is always the result of that person's present situation. It is the situation that gives rise to such a psychological state as IN. But how does this occur? How does IN originate?

A whole host of signals about both the status of the organism itself and its habitat are perceived by human beings through their receptors. These signals enter the brain where they are used for assessing the situation. If the assessed situation contains a problem—for example, if it is understood that the organism needs a supply of food or that a direct hazard exists in the habitat—then an instinct for solving the problem arises inside the human being. Since solving a problem is possible only via some line of behavior, and the behavior itself is dictated by a behavioral algorithm (which in turn is created on the basis of information), then in the event that the human being does not have a ready-made algorithm, the very realization of the existing problem itself creates a mental state that is perceived as a need for information required for creating a behavioral algorithm. Physically, such a state arises when receptors use signals to stimulate the brain, and it is determined by a section and a form of this stimulation in the brain. In summary, we underline once more that a mental state, such as an information need, precedes any activity and is its indispensable partner in satisfying any physiological need.

It is obvious that an IN is directed to some object or phenomenon of the world surrounding us; this is generally known as a thematic focus. Particular emphasis should be placed on the fact that each information user has a good idea about the thematic focus of his or her mental state, although, as pointed out earlier, in the event of POIN the thematic boundaries of this mental state are not always clearly defined. Because we are interested in satisfying IN by means of an IR system, the IR system should take into consideration the user's thematic focus of IN, which obviously enters the system directly from the user. However, because the user does not precisely sense the thematic boundaries of POIN, the user cannot present to the IR system adequate information about his or her actual mental state; that is, an IR system does not always have comprehensive enough information on POIN to satisfy POIN successfully. Consider next the way (how, in what form) the information on POIN enters the system. To begin with, for this purpose the user expresses his or her POIN. IN *expression* refers to a process that results in a representation of information on IN in some language. Recall that the formulation of information about this need in a natural language is commonly called a search request. Any search request includes a thematic focus of the user's IN. We note that in most cases the user expresses IN in the form of search requests, and the search requests frequently contain only a theme (a thematic focus of originated IN) or, as we will refer to it later, a thematic component of IN. For example, the search requests described in Chapter 2 that illustrated the existence of CIN and POIN contained only a thematic component. But which other components characterize a mental state such as POIN? This question will be considered next.

We will begin by stating that such an unpleasant state as IN comes up in a variety of life situations and these situations can determine different requirements for the information that a user needs. In other words, with the same thematic focus but in different situations, different information output may be more appropriate. Let us illustrate this condition with the following example.

Assume that a documentary IR system has received the following identical search request from Users A, B, and C: "Canning of vegetables." The thematic focus of this search request is clear and in many systems this is sufficient for constructing a query formulation (either automatically or via an intermediary) and subsequently performing a retrieval. As the result of the retrieval, each user who asked the search request gets the same output. Nevertheless, it is well known that in most cases the assessment of this output by users may be different. This fact is explained by the lack of clear thematic boundaries of the corresponding IN as noted earlier and by different knowledge levels inherent to each of the users. However, these are not the only causes of different assessments of information output.

In continuing our example, let us assume that User A is a researcher engaged in problems of long-term storage of vegetables and is interested in new ideas on canning of vegetables. Clearly, User A has little interest in popular literature, textbooks, and reviews of well-known works. Now let us suppose that User B wants to can several jars of cucumbers, tomatoes, and cabbage at home and his search request is related to this activity. In this case, User B will have little interest in recent theoretical works in this field and will be well satisfied by a popular article containing useful advice on canning procedures. Now suppose that User C has been offered several lines of research for selection (this search request is only one of such lines) and she wants to make a decision as to which one to use in the future. The most appropriate (and sufficient) for her would be, seemingly, a comprehensive review of scientific publications on canning vegetables.

As our example illustrates, in different life situations different mental states (INs) can arise; nevertheless, the thematic component of different mental states may be the same. Various states arising in different users assume distinctive output for different users. As the example makes clear, if a search request includes not only the IN thematic component but also other IN components, and if these complementary components could be taken into account in retrieval, then the user service could be improved. It is no coincidence that we call any other IN components complementary ones. The point is that the IN's thematic component should always be expressed (that is, actually done) and, as we have pointed out, it will be sufficient for retrieval. However, if any other component, but not a thematic component, is expressed, the retrieval becomes impossible. It is for this reason that we refer to any component that differs from the thematic component as *complementary*. This apparently explains why in most systems the users are required to express only the thematic component of IN. Nevertheless, as we have seen already, complementary components can provide a marked positive effect on user service.

To be fair, it should be noted that in a number of cases complementary IN components have essentially been used by those librarians who communicated directly with readers to help those readers carry out a retrieval. These were librarians who showed special care for a reader by personalizing the reader's need, that is, by taking into account some of the reader's wishes and features that were typical of him or her personally (i.e., the reader's situation) rather than simply following a search request (i.e., a thematic IN component). The librarians did this, of course, intuitively, as a result of their accumulated experience rather than from a serious scientific basis. Nevertheless, such personal care resulted in better service for the user. Unfortunately, in automated IR systems this aspect of retrieval does not draw much attention, although if these systems were built with the intent of providing special care to the user—typical of the approach taken by our featured librarians—then better effects could be expected from retrieval automation.

Returning to the previous example, note that the situations considered are related to the different goals facing the users. When we pointed out the usefulness of expressing complementary IN components in a search request, we proposed in essence complementing a thematic component through the description of a specific user's goal. However, the notion of "search requests" should perhaps retain a meaning customary for researchers and that is that a search request usually means the result of expressing an IN's thematic component in a natural language. Therefore, that "portion" of IN that is presented in a natural language and that is dedicated to the description of the goal at hand will be called its *task;* that is, a task is the result of expressing an IN's goal component in a natural language.

Thus, we have shown that it is reasonable to present the result of expressing IN in a natural language in the form of at least two independent retrieval directives: a search request and a task. We say "at least" because there are also other IN components, depending on the existing situation, whose consideration may improve retrieval results. These can be time restrictions on information retrieval and reading limitations related to a presentation level (the work is a purely philosophical one, whereas a more applied approach is desired), constraints pertaining to the language in which the document is written, and so on. In these cases we can talk about the time component, the level component, and the language component of IN. Clearly the result of expressing these components in a natural language assumes the availability of other retrieval directives.

12.4
The Effects of IN Components on the IR System

We will define a set of retrieval directives of different types, with at least one of them being a search request, as a retrieval situation. In this chapter we will discuss only the situations formed by a search request and a task, and in this case each new search request and each new task forms a new retrieval situation. Note that the same task can be combined with various search requests, and the same search request can be combined with various tasks. For example, a task of preparing a review can be combined with the following search requests: "Study of IN," "Drugs for a cold," and so forth; likewise the search request "Drugs for a cold" can be combined with the following tasks: "Making up a medicine chest for travel," "Developing recommendations for patients," and so on. Let us explain why the latter two tasks differ in essence from the standpoint of carrying out information retrieval. The first task suggests the retrieval of information on as little as two to three drugs that would be optimal in a certain sense for travelers, say, those that have compact, water-tight, nonbreakable packaging; those that are fast acting; and so forth. The second task, however, suggests finding information on all existing drugs for a cold in order to select the most suitable one for each patient.

Next, we will show some features of how a task affects both the retrieval process organization and the realization of its individual subprocesses. Let us consider two retrieval situations: one of them is stated by the search request "Waste-water treatment" and the task "Development of new or improved treatment methods," and the second is stated by the same search request and the task "Review preparation." Clearly the first retrieval situation assumes organizing the iterative retrieval process, but the second one can generally be restricted to a single retrospective retrieval. This example illustrates rather clearly how a task affects the organization of a retrieval process. Another illustrative example is given by two retrieval situations: one is formed by the search request "Development of extra-accurate watch mechanisms" and the task "Creation of new mechanisms," whereas the second is formed by the same search request and the task "Examining an idea for novelty." The first retrieval situation, as it is similar to that presented in the previous example, assumes the organization of an iterative retrieval process. For the second situation, however, it is sufficient, for example, to find a document for which the proposed idea has been already presented; that is, after finding such a document the retrieval process may be terminated.

We will next show how a task affects the realization of retrieval subprocesses as well. In this case, as can be seen from the following example, the differences involved in the realization of subprocesses are derived from the differences in the requirements of those or other tasks for retrieval results. Refer again to the retrieval situation that was stated by the search request "Drugs for a cold" and the task "Making up a medicine chest for a travel" and the second retrieval situation, which was formed by the same search request and the task "Developing recommendations for patients." As we mentioned earlier, the task of the first retrieval situation *necessitates* the finding of two to three drugs for a cold that will be optimal, in a certain sense, during travel, whereas the task of the second retrieval situation necessitates the finding of all existing drugs for a cold and perhaps even drugs of more general designation. To meet the requirements of the task "Making up a medicine chest for travel," it is first necessary to identify those indications of drugs for a cold that define usefulness of these drugs during travel, and second it is necessary to construct a query formulation so that it can be determined during the retrieval process whether or not the indications mentioned have the desired values. As the task "Developing recommendations for patients," consideration of its "requirements" leads to solving other problems, namely, constructing a query formulation so that it will be possible to determine during retrieval whether or not an illness such as a cold is found among the indications of the direct or prophylactic effect of the drug under consideration.

The example demonstrates clearly how a task affects the realization of such a subprocess of the retrieval process as a construction of query formulation. It should be noted that we are speaking of a subprocess of constructing a query formulation rather than a subprocess of translating a search request into IRL, because with the new understanding of IN, as well as of its representation in a natural language, the subprocess under consideration is not only a translation of a search request into IRL, but it is reduced to a presentation of the information about a user's information need in IRL that is contained in both a search request and a task. It is obvious that to employ such a subprocess a system's IRL should allow indexing of both a search request (this is always the case) and a task (this occurs seldom). Clearly it is possible that not all information about IN that is contained in a search request and a task will be represented in IRL. The information included depends on the quality of the system's IRL and on the methods of constructing query formulations. Note that it is natural to refer to the result of expressing a search request and a task in IRL as query formulation. This, by the way, agrees with the accepted understanding of query formulation, although the components other than the thematic component are rarely used. It is because of this fact that we call the subprocess under consideration a subprocess of constructing a query formulation.

It seems useful to consider a further example of a task influence on the realization of subprocesses of a retrieval process. With this aim we will refer again to the retrieval situations introduced earlier: one is formulated by the search request "Waste-water treatment" and by the task "Development of new or improved treatment methods," and the other is formulated by the same search request and by the task "Review preparation." It may be stated that usually in the selection of documents for review, thematic boundaries of search requests are essentially treated in a wider manner than they are in the selection of documents for developing new treatment methods. This can be taken into account in different ways. For example, in the construction of a query formulation within the scope of the second retrieval situation, we can additionally use a "broader" glossary than for the construction of a query formulation within the scope of the first retrieval situation. Alternatively, we can apply a tougher criterion on output within the scope of the first retrieval situation as compared to the second retrieval situation. It is obvious, however, that, regardless of the method selected, the realization of subprocesses of the retrieval process in given retrieval situations will be different. This confirms the existence of task influence on the realization of subprocesses of the retrieval process.

So, we have considered a number of examples showing that the task affects both the retrieval process organization and the realization of its individual subprocesses. Nevertheless, as noted earlier, in interaction with a user for the purpose of obtaining information on his or her IN, preference is usually given to expressing a thematic component of this need rather than some other (complementary) ones. In particular, special procedures allowing one to express a thematic component—such as formulating a list of key words "revealing" the user's IN (carried out by a user) or compiling a user-prepared list of document titles or abstracts conforming to the user's IN—are under development, which unfortunately is not done in order to express a goal component. We say "unfortunately" because we have already seen what an important role taking account of a goal IN component could play in forming required retrieval results.

It seems that the more accurately a goal component is expressed, the better one can expect the retrieval result to be. Hence, it is necessary to give due attention to the development of special procedures enabling one to express a goal component of IN in the most accurate way. We believe a good step in this direction is an approach to expressing IN that assumes the task formulation as an independent retrieval directive.

The very approach under consideration stimulates the user to recognize the goal component of his or her IN as clearly as possible. Furthermore, perhaps it would be simpler and more convenient for the user to submit separate formulations for the search request and the task than it would be to express both goal and thematic IN components in a single text. In this case, development of special procedures allowing the user to express a goal IN component becomes more purposeful. For example, in the case considered, a rather natural procedure would be for the user to examine the list of "typical" tasks. Then the user would easily "see" his or her task or, using this list, the user would be able to formulate the goal component clearly enough. We will focus on the concept of typical tasks in more detail.

We consider "typical" the tasks that are found rather frequently during information retrieval and that can form retrieval situations with a great number of various search requests. To the typical tasks may be rightfully attributed, say, the task "Developing new methods, devices, approaches, or machines" or the task "Review preparation." As for a task such as "Making up a medicine chest for travel," from our standpoint this task is not typical because of its too specific nature or, as we will say from here on, its not very high "generalization level." This level ranks below the generalization level of such tasks as "Developing new methods . . . " and "Review preparation."

It is clear that while identifying a specific task we can determine requirements of this task for organization of the retrieval process and its results. It is reasonable to include into the typical task list not only the task itself but also the requirements dictated by this typical task. This will help a user to understand what is concealed behind the formulation of a particular task and to obtain a more accurate notion of it. It should be noted that in the perception of some users a typical task may be related to requirements that differ from those in a typical task list. For example, initially the task "Development of new methods . . ." would have been related to the following natural requirement for retrieval results: output obtained should be as *close* as possible to an *ideal* one; that is, it should only contain all relevant documents available in the collection of documents. At the same time in the user's view the task mentioned may be related to the requirement of obtaining output containing no more than three documents, but only relevant ones. How should one respond in such a case? For a particular user the retrieval should be carried out on the basis of the user's understanding of a task, that is, using those requirements that the user designated in a typical task list or formulated as ones resulting from the given task, but only if realization of such requirements is feasible. For example, a requirement for obtaining output containing no fewer than 150 relevant documents may be impossible to meet, in principle, due to the lack of such a quantity of relevant documents even in a relatively large collection of documents.

It seems reasonable to include additional "feasible" requirements in the list of available typical tasks because they can provide other users with better insight into what is concealed behind the formulation of a corresponding task. In this case, some requirements may be mutually exclusive, as, for example, the requirements for retrieval results considered in the previous case when a collection of documents contained, say, 20 relevant documents. This, however, should not create problems because a user choosing a task from a typical task list should be able to select the most suitable task.

Note that practical experience shows that when considering if specific requirements follow from a given task some requirements are agreed on by the majority of users and some requirements are chosen only by a small number of users. Hence, in practice when using list of typical tasks it is possible for each task to determine (and isolate) a corresponding set (or sets) of requirements that are most often pointed out by users. The set (or sets) involved will be called a typical configuration (configurations) of requirements. From our standpoint it is reasonable to define, in connection with each task, two variations of typical configurations of requirements: a typical configuration of requirements for organization of the retrieval process and a typical configuration of requirements for its results. It is then possible to identify (for example, with a special mark) these configurations of requirements in a list of typical tasks, because such information may be helpful for a user.

Next we point out that the development of typical configurations of requirements assumes both the development of new methods and the updating of existing methods of information retrieval. For example, we recall from the requirements pertaining to the task "Review preparation" that for this task it may be advantageous to use a "broader" glossary in the query formulation than would be needed for the task "Development of new methods. . . ." This in turn may lead to the differences in methods of constructing query formulations within the limits of one system. This example illustrates, in essence, how requirements effect the IR system construction.

It is also a fact that the problem of defining typical configurations of requirements affects the problem of evaluating the functional efficiency of information retrieval. For example, if the task "Development of new methods . . ." is related to the requirement "obtained output should contain no more than three (but only relevant) documents," then the evaluation of the functional efficiency achieved is sufficiently transparent and requires the construction of a simple mathematical apparatus. But if this task is related to the requirement "obtained output should be as *close* as possible to the *ideal* one," then the evaluation of functional efficiency achieved requires the development of a rather sophisticated apparatus capable of determining a degree of "closeness" among different outputs.

So once more we call attention to the fact that with regard to the availability of tasks and requirements in the IR system we are, in essence, talking about a new element of a system structure—an element that provides a more comprehensive satisfaction of IN through consideration of its complementary components. The proposed method of incorporating this element—that is, the preparation of a list of tasks and requirements for them—can be easily realized and does not entail any considerable costs. It is also true that in various cases the quality of the realization may be different and eventually will be determined by the improvement in the user's service. For this reason, in the future it may be reasonable to create a type of procedure for the development of the proposed system element. However, the development of this system element constitutes only a part of the work. The following question arises: How can we practically interact this system element with other system elements and especially how can we automate this interaction? Of course, specific methods for the consideration of possible requirements will have to be developed. Nevertheless, we present as an example one of the methods developed that is suitable for the two tasks mentioned previously, namely, "Development of new methods . . ." and "Review preparation." As pointed out earlier, the first task provides for finding documents containing new ideas (approaches) contributing directly to the "development of new methods . . ." whereas the second task primarily requires the system to find those documents that contain descriptions of the most known and promising methods among existing ones. We will start from the fact that in the first case tougher requirements should be imposed upon the relevancy of found documents (based on the requirement for the first task), whereas in the second case such requirements could be much less stringent (based on the requirement for the second task).

Note that specific methods depend, to a large degree, on the approaches adopted in a system for organizing other system elements. In the given case, when solving a formulated task, we will consider the most typical existing IR systems—the systems that use Boolean search. Moreover, we will only consider automatic methods of taking the specified requirements into account. We believe it is reasonable to take into account the requirements given in the example at the stage of constructing a query formulation, that is, it is reasonable to form different (required) outputs from different query formulations. All of the previously listed conditions can be taken into account in those IR systems that use the algorithm for the automatic construction of query formulations described in Chapter 7 (Frants & Shapiro, 1991). The given algorithm provides a very important possibility for our situation, namely, this algorithm is suitable for constructing query formulations capable of finding a given number of documents, and the found documents will be the best (according to the chosen criteria) for the user. This feature is provided by the selection algorithm for query formulation, which is a part of the algorithm for constructing query formulations.

Returning to those requirements that we are going to take into account, we note that the requirement for the first task provides for a more "narrow" search; that is, in this case the output should be relatively small. As for the requirements for the second task, they provide for a "broader" search; that is, output resulting from such a search would be considerable. So, both requirements may contain either a user-specified desired number of documents in the output or, when this number is not specified by a user, some predetermined number specified by the system's developers as a standard parameter. Such a number for the requirement to the first task may be 10, whereas for the second task the number may be 100. The existing numbers are specified for the automatic zone selection algorithm following which the algorithm for the automatic construction of query formulations will generate two query formulations: one will form output consisting of the 10 best documents and the other will form output consisting of the best 100 documents. Note especially that the requirements in the described case are automatically taken into account.

12.5

Future Developments in Considering IN Components

The direction of research that focuses on improving the quality of the satisfaction of IN by means of the IR system represents a wide area for future studies. This section will briefly list only basic problems, whose solution will contribute to the development of improved IR systems. First we note that it will be necessary to continue the study of IN components—their properties and characteristics. This is clear because more profound insight into IN will not only introduce new elements into the IR system structure but will also change the meaning of some presently known approaches used in the systems.

Of interest are developments in the field of creating lists (tables) of tasks and requirements. To achieve better results, the creation of lists should be based on sufficiently effective procedures or algorithms. Undoubtedly, the development of these means will contribute to the success of the discussed approach.

Another important challenge is the development of methods (primarily, automatic) that take into account the effect of complementary IN components on the results of information retrieval. The optimal solution seems to be the development of an algorithm that takes into account each requirement on the list. Obviously, this is yet another direction in the development of the design of IR systems.

It should be noted that we have not explicitly dealt with a very promising direction—the development of user-friendly interfaces. However, both the orientation of this book toward helping the user to best express his or her IN and the cited methods that allow the system to take into account the complementary IN components are undoubtedly steps along this path. Moreover, the selection of methods mentioned could be an important element of future interfaces or at least could considerably stimulate their development. For this reason, future studies directed toward using complementary IN components in the process of user-system dialogue (the feedback process), in addition to their own value, are also important in the development of user-friendly interfaces.

In summarizing our discussion of the considered direction in developing IR systems, we should emphasize that the approach described is aimed at improving the quality of IN satisfaction. Moreover, this approach illustrates an important point, mentioned before, namely, satisfaction of IN is improved when its properties and characteristics are taken into account. Therefore, we took a closer look at the notion of IN. As a result, IN is presented as an object composed of different elements—not only of a thematic "plane" that the user is interested in (the thematic component) but also of other "planes," for example, the user's goal (the goal component). This observation led to the development of the IR system's structure, which included a list of tasks and requirements for them. Again we should point out that this approach can be used successfully with existing IR systems.

12.6

Conclusion

A future development of IR systems is of interest to everybody who works in the field. In this chapter we considered only some directions in this development, and the only reason we discussed AI as one of the directions is because it has attracted a lot of attention in recent years. In spite of a lack of any serious results in using AI in information retrieval (and we are not optimistic about any progress in the near future), attempts to use ideas from AI allow us to better understand the problems that arise in information retrieval, enhance our understanding of the language, and stimulate the creative activity of researchers.

The most common discussions of information retrieval in the AI literature papers dealing with free text search which, as was mentioned earlier, is directly related to NLP. In Chapter 6 we showed that in these papers the descriptor dictionary is constructed from all the terms appearing in the analyzed document. Such dictionaries are called uncontrollable. Although some authors assert that they use natural language, this is no more advanced or deep than using natural language when constructing a controllable descriptor dictionary. In these cases we are dealing with the effect of a more loud title without using natural language in a search process. It seems more promising to use approaches that stress a knowledge base. But even in this case we do not expect any substantial results in the near future. Hence, today AI has a minor role in developing IR systems.

The main new ideas used in information retrieval come from information science itself. These also include the ideas presented in this chapter. We believe that the composite view of IN will not only allow researchers to improve the quality of the satisfaction of IN, but it also will play an important role in organizing user-friendly interface in the future. In any case, the method described here for using a goal component of POIN shows one of the realistic directions for developing automated IR systems.

References

Boden, M. A. (1977). *Artificial intelligence and natural man.* New York: Basic Books.

Charniak, E., & McDermott, D. V. (1985). *Introduction to artificial intelligence.* Reading, MA: Addison-Wesley.

Chen, H. (1992). Machine learning for information retrieval: Neural networks, symbolic learning, and genetic algorithms. *Journal of the American Society for Information Science, 43*(5).

Croft, B. W. (1995). NSF center for intelligent information retrieval. *Communications of the ACM, 38*(4).

Daniels, J. J., & Rissland, E. L. (1995). A case-based approach to intelligent information retrieval. Proceedings of the Eighteenth Annual International ACM-SIGIR Conference on Research and Development in Information Retrieval, Seattle, WA.

Dean, T., Allen, J., & Aloimonos, Y. (1995). *Artificial intelligence: Theory and practice.* New York: Benjamin/Cummings.

Feigenbaum, E. A., Barr, A., & Cohen, P. R. (Eds.). (1982). *The handbook of artificial intelligence* (Vol. 1–3). Stanford, CA: Heuristech Press/William Kaufmann.

Firebaugh, M. W. (1988). *Artificial intelligence.* New York: Boyd and Fraser.

Fisher, M., & Firschein, O. (1987). *Intelligence: The eye, the brain, and the computer.* Reading, MA: Addison-Wesley.

Frants, V. I., & Brush, C. B. (1988). The need for information and some aspects of information retrieval systems construction. *Journal of the American Society for Information Science, 39,* 86–91.

Frants, V. I., & Shapiro, J. (1991). Algorithm for automatic construction of query formulations in Boolean form. *Journal of the American Society for Information Science, 42*(1).

Frants, V. I., Shapiro, J., & Voiskunskii, V. G. (1996). Development of IR systems: New direction. *Information Processing and Management, 32*(3).

Genesereth, M. R., & Nilsson, N. J. (1992). *Logical Foundations of Artificial Intelligence.* Los Altos, CA: Morgan Kaufmann.

Ginsberg, M. L. (1993). *Essentials of artificial intelligence.* San Mateo, CA: Morgan Kaufmann.

Kupiec, J., Pedersen, J., & Chen, F. (1995). A trainable document summarizer. Proceedings of the Eighteenth Annual International ACM-SIGIR Conference on Research and Development in Information Retrieval, Seattle, WA.

Kwok, K. L. (1989). A neural network for probabilistic information retrieval. Proceedings of the Twelfth Annual International ACM-SIGIR Conference on Research and Development in Information Retrieval.

McCorduck, P. (1979). *Machines who think*. New York: W. H. Freeman and Company.

Pevsner, B. R., & Lachuti, D. G. (1973). *Methodology of constructing foreign language IR systems*. Moscow: INFORMelectro.

Quillian, M. R. (1968). Semantic memory. In M. Minsky (Ed.), *Semantic Information Processing*. Cambridge, MA: MIT Press.

Salton, G., & McGill, M. J. (1983). *Introduction to modern information retrieval*. New York: McGraw Hill.

Tanimoto, S. L. (1990). *The elements of artificial intelligence*. New York: W. H. Freeman and Company.

Tucker, A. B., Jr. (1984). A perspective on machine translation: Theory and practice. *Communications of the ACM, 27*(4).

Winograd, T. (1972). *Understanding natural language*. New York: Academic Press.

Winston, P. H. (1984). *Artificial intelligence* (2nd ed.) Reading, MA: Addison-Wesley.

Yang, Y. (1994): Expert network: Effective and efficient learning from human decisions in text categorization and retrieval. Proceedings of the Seventeenth Annual International ACM-SIGIR Conference on Research and Development in Information Retrieval, Dublin.

Zahir, S., & Chang, C. L. (1992). Online Expert: An expert system for online database selection. *Journal of the American Society for Information Science, 43*(5).

Zurada, J. M. (1992). *Artificial neural systems*. Chicago: West Publishing.

Bibliographic Remarks

The following references are recommended for those who are interested in learning about alternative approaches for using NLP in IR systems.

Cooper, W. S. (1984). Bringing the gap between AI and IR. In *Research and Development in Information Retrieval*. Proceedings of the Third Joint BCS and ACM Symposium, ACM, Cambridge.

Doszkos, T. E. (1986). Natural language processing in information retrieval. *Journal of the American Society for Information Science, 37*(4).

Grisham, R. (1973). Natural language processing. *Journal of the American Society for Information Science, 35*(4).

Lewis, D. D., & Sparck-Jones, K. (1996). Natural language processing for information retrieval. *Communications of the ACM, 39*(1).

Sparck-Jones, K., & Kay, M. (1973). *Linguistics and information science*. New York: Academic Press.

For a deeper understanding of semantic networks and neural networks we recommend the following publications.

Firebaugh, M. W. (1988). *Artificial intelligence*. New York: Boyd and Fraser.

Zurada, J. M. (1992). *Artificial neural systems*. Chicago: West Publishing.

Index

Library and Information Science

(Continued from page ii)